Becoming Anorexic

Anorexia tends to be studied within health disciplines, such as medicine, psychoanalysis or psychology. When the condition is discussed in relation to society more broadly, focus is commonly restricted to considerations about the demise of the traditional family meal or the all-pervading obsession with thinness and media representations of 'size zero' models. But what can sociology tell us about anorexia and how a person becomes anorexic? This book draws on empirical research – both interviews and observation – conducted in and outside medical settings with anorexic girls, medical staff, teachers and other teenagers of the same age. As such, it offers the first fully sociological treatment of the condition, taking the reader closer to the actual experiences of people living with anorexia. It retraces the behaviours, practices and processes that create what is patterned as an anorexic 'career' and reveals the cultural and social characteristics of the people who engage on this path, taking them from a simple diet to hospitalization or recovery. Richly illustrated with qualitative research, *Becoming Anorexic* demonstrates that anorexia can be viewed as a very particular work of self-transformation, which requires specific – and social – 'dispositions'. As such, it will appeal to scholars of sociology and anthropology with an interest in health and illness, the body, social class and gender.

Muriel Darmon is a CNRS Senior Research Fellow at the CESSP (EHESS, Paris 1 Panthéon-Sorbonne), France.

Routledge Advances in Sociology

For a full list of titles in this series, please visit www.routledge.com/series/SE0511.

180 State Looteries
Historical continuity, rearticulations of racism, and American taxation
Kasey Henricks and David G. Embrick

181 Lesbian, Gay, Bisexual and Trans* Individuals Living with Dementia
Concepts, practice and rights
Edited by Sue Westwood and Elizabeth Price

182 Family, Culture, and Self in the Development of Eating Disorders
Susan Haworth-Hoeppner

183 Origins of Inequality in Human Societies
Bernd Baldus

184 Confronting the Challenges of Urbanization in China
Insights from social science perspectives
Edited by Zai Liang, Steven F. Messner, Youqin Huang and Cheng Chen

185 Social Policy and Planning for the 21st Century
In search of the next great social transformation
Donald G. Reid

186 Popular Music and Retro Culture in the Digital Era
Jean Hogarty

187 Muslim Americans
Debating the notions of American and un-American
Nahid Kabir

188 Human Sciences and Human Interests
Integrating the social, economic, and evolutionary sciences
Mikael Klintman

Becoming Anorexic

A sociological study

Muriel Darmon
Translated from the French by Lucy Garnier

Routledge
Taylor & Francis Group
LONDON AND NEW YORK

First published 2017
by Routledge

2 Park Square, Milton Park, Abingdon, Oxfordshire OX14 4RN
711 Third Avenue, New York, NY 10017

Routledge is an imprint of the Taylor & Francis Group, an informa business

First issued in paperback 2018

British Library Cataloguing in Publication Data
A catalogue record for this book is available from the British Library

Library of Congress Cataloging in Publication Data
Names: Darmon, Muriel, author.
Title: Becoming anorexic: a sociological study / Muriel Darmon; translated by Lucy Garnier.
Other titles: Devenir anorexique English.
Description: Milton Park, Abingdon, Oxon; New York, NY: Routledge, 2017.
Identifiers: LCCN 2016019184
Subjects: LCSH: Anorexia nervosa–Social aspects.
Classification: LCC RC552.A5 D3713 2017 | DDC 362.196/85262–dc23
LC record available at https://lccn.loc.gov/2016019184

ISBN: 978-1-4724-6650-1 (hbk)
ISBN: 978-1-138-35333-6 (pbk)

Typeset in Times New Roman
by Sunrise Setting Ltd, Brixham, UK

Contents

Acknowledgements

This book is based on my doctoral thesis in sociology. I would like to thank my supervisor François de Singly for his support throughout my research on such an unusual topic. I am also grateful to my PhD examiners Claudine Herzlich, Bernard Lahire, Eric Plaisance and Jean-Manuel de Queiroz for their comments, advice and constructive criticism.

I would also like to thank everyone who helped me as I wrote this book, by listening to me, encouraging me, asking questions, making suggestions or disagreeing with me. I am particularly grateful to the people who read the manuscript of either the thesis or the book: Anne-Marie Arborio, Isabelle Baszanger, Thomas Bénatouïl, Séverine Gojard, Hugues Jallon, Héloïse Kolebka, Bernard Lahire, Frédérique Matonti, Anne Paillet and Delphine Serre.

This monograph was first published in French in 2003. The English-language translation would not have been possible without the generous support of the TEPSIS LabEx project and the additional help of my research laboratory, the CESSP (European Centre for Sociology and Political Science). I am also very grateful to Neil Jordan at Routledge for having believed in this project enough to revive it when I was almost ready to turn the page. Finally, my deepest thanks go to Lucy Garnier for the extraordinary quality, subtlety and precision of her translation.

Last but not least, I would like to express my deep gratitude to all the people who agreed to become part of my fieldwork in one capacity or another. In order to protect their privacy, I cannot thank them by name, but suffice it to say that without them this book would not exist.

This book has been translated thanks to the generous support of the TEPSIS LabEx, ANR-11-LABX-0067, coordinated by the EHESS.

Introduction

Wallis Simpson is generally credited with having decreed 'a woman can never be too rich or too thin'. This book focuses on teenage girls who apply at least part of this saying to the letter and on a diagnosis that runs counter to its premise, by positing that young women *can* be too thin or have lost too much weight. 'Another book on anorexia?' you might ask and it's true that there have been quite a few. This book differs from the others, though, in one important way: it is grounded in sociology, a discipline that might seem to have a somewhat questionable remit for discussing anorexia. How can we 'do' a sociology of anorexia? Is it right, even just on an epistemological level, for sociology to study something that at first sight seems to fall only under the realm of the psychological and pathological?

How can we 'do' a sociology of anorexia?

In 1897, Emile Durkheim founded French sociology by applying his sociological method to suicide, 'an individual action affecting the individual only' which 'must seemingly depend exclusively on individual factors, thus belonging to psychology alone' (Durkheim 2005, xliv). This founding strategy has since been perpetuated through claims that it is legitimate to apply a sociological point of view to fields viewed as psychological. Sometimes a territorial metaphor is used to talk about this, showing that when attempts are made to apply sociology to psychological facts, the discipline is not on home ground but rather on ground to be gained. In his approach to psychoanalysis, for example, sociologist Peter Berger refers to a 'hunting ground' that should be 'trespassed' upon:

> The most important positive presupposition for such a sociological analysis is that it proceed within a frame of reference that is itself sociological. This means that sociological modes of analysis must be pushed to their own intrinsic limits and not be blocked by limits stipulated by another discipline. This procedure excludes the common practice of American sociologists of conceding extraterritorial preserves to the psychologists within the sociological universe of discourse (a courtesy, by the way, rarely reciprocated by the psychologists). Whatever may be the methodological merits of other disciplines, the sociologist cannot allow the scope of his work to be dictated by the

> latter. Thus, in different areas of investigation, the sociologist cannot allow the jurist or the theologian to put up 'no trespassing' signs on territory that, by the rules of his own game, is legitimate sociological hunting ground. In terms of the phenomenon that interests us here, the sociologist cannot concede to the psychologist exclusive rights to the vast area we commonly call psychological.
>
> (Berger 1965, 32)[1]

Putting forward a sociological approach to anorexia means offering an account of a 'foreign' object that, at first sight, seems not to fall under the remit of sociological analysis but rather to lie outside its disciplinary boundaries. This investigation therefore presupposes an epistemological stance that refuses the idea of disciplines having their own specific ground and that engages in a sort of 'epistemological Yalta'. Scientific disciplines are not defined by the objects they deal with, but rather by their approaches and their methods. Sociology therefore does not have its own specific objects any more than it has any forbidden ones; there are only objects which are socially foreign to the discipline. Anorexia may be a 'psychological' fact, in the sense that it lies in the psychological domain, but that does not mean it cannot be addressed by a non-psychological discipline.

However, the 'pathological' nature of anorexia does seem to present a second obstacle to applying a sociological point of view. How can sociology approach such an atypical and extreme phenomenon? Here again, there is an analytical tradition that has attempted to take on board this kind of foreign object. For the sociology of deviance, rather than being a limitation, the pathological actually invites a sociological point of view:

> It's generally a good sociological alternative to the null hypothesis of craziness to assume that the action to be studied makes perfect sense, only we don't know the sense it makes . . . . Analytically, that means discovering something that seems so bizarre and unintelligible that our only explanation is some form of 'They must be crazy' should alert us that we don't know enough about the behavior under study. It's better to assume that it makes some kind of sense and to look for the sense it makes.
>
> (Becker 1998, 25–8)

It is therefore possible to put forward a sociological approach to anorexia not *despite* its pathological dimension but *because* of it. In order to do so, it is important to set aside the distinction between the normal and the pathological as an essentialist division (it is not up to the sociologist to distinguish between what is normal and what is pathological in terms of the inherent characteristics of behaviour or people) and to *make this distinction into the object of study*, addressing it in terms of the labels ascribed to people. It is a question of identifying both the processes through which behaviour is labelled as deviant and the chronology in which this takes place.

At the intersection of different epistemological stances, a sociology of *anorexia* is therefore possible providing it does not claim to reveal a truth about 'anorexia per se' that other approaches have supposedly passed over in silence. However, as we will see, a *sociology* of anorexia is also possible, which does not necessarily have to be considered as interdisciplinary (a 'socio-psychology', a 'socio-biology' or a 'socio-psychoanalysis', for example).

Which sociological approach?

Which specific sociological approach is most appropriate, though? The most obvious, because it follows on from the perspective opened up by Emile Durkheim, consists in constructing anorexia as a 'social fact' and follows calls from the media to consider it in those terms. Anyone who reads a newspaper or a magazine today in France has heard about anorexia. These readers will also have had their attention drawn to an epidemic of eating disorders, as evidenced, for example, by excerpts taken from a single year in the French press (1998). An advert in *Le Monde des Livres* stated that 'Eating disorders are becoming a real public health issue today' (5 June 1998),[2] while an article in *Le Figaro* explained that 'In other words, by placing value on stereotypes, our society is making people ill!' (article entitled 'Bulimia, anorexia, everything hinges on the teenage years', Fourgnaud 1998). A piece published in Le Monde newspaper the same year explained:

> This is not a new pathology but it is estimated to be two or three times as frequent today as it was thirty years ago: it seems that one to two per cent of teenage girls present with more or less severe and complicated forms of anorexia.
>
> (Helfter 1998)

> And *Elle* magazine readers were presented with the information that 'Three to five per cent of teenage girls present with eating disorders around the age of thirteen or fourteen'.
>
> (Weissman 1998)

However, the epidemiological studies on which these media data are based are in fact more subtle and mention a number of methodological difficulties and types of bias inherent to collating this kind of data. The existence of an epidemic is subject to debate in the literature.[3] In epidemiological publications, and the analyses that draw upon them, certain authors refer to the 'myth' of an anorexia epidemic, whereas others conclude that it does in fact exist or that there has at least been an increase in the incidence of anorexia in Western countries since the 1970s. However, other data meet with more consensus: namely the predominance of females between fifteen and twenty-four years old from a middle- or upper-class social background among sufferers of anorexia. Through the recurring patterns and variations they describe, epidemiological statistics reveal the possibility of enrolling anorexia in the field of 'social facts' as defined since Durkheim: 'constancy when there are no changes in society (country, religion, social class, family); regulated and defined variation when several social factors vary simultaneously' (Baudelot and Establet 1990, 23). Certain works on anorexia have highlighted this, looking to establish a link between the epidemic and social changes, in other words a relationship between anorexia and society. Indeed, it is in the social sciences (sociology, anthropology, social history) and in feminist scholarship that the rise in incidence of anorexia is discussed with the most conviction. This is enhanced by the fact these approaches are used to prove the socially and historically situated nature of anorexia. According to these readings, the incidence of the condition increases as cultural and social factors become more favourable to its development.[4]

Does this mean, then, that the only way to consider anorexia sociologically consists in working at the level of these macro-sociological recurring patterns, considering that 'psychological' and 'pathological' approaches retain exclusive rights over all other levels of analysis? With anorexia seeming to fall under the remit of psychological, psychoanalytical, biological, genetic, psychiatric and medical approaches, the only reason for calling on sociological analysis appears to be highlighting socio-cultural elements (women's place in society, historical canons of female beauty, changes in eating habits, etc.) with a purely contextual effect. This frames sociology's role less as an approach in itself and more as a way of shedding light on the pathology by positioning it within a historically and socially constructed sphere, where it exists as a 'black box' that has been located but remains closed. It is this black box that I decided to open in my study, wagering that it was in fact possible to take a sociological approach to anorexia in practice and from the point of view of those engaged in it, rather than from the point of view of the social construction or perception of anorexia; an approach looking at what happens during anorexia rather than linking together a pathology and a social context considered as two separate entities; an approach focusing on what anorexics do and not what they represent. In many social science and humanities' studies, anorexics 'symbolize' something: modernity or, on the contrary, a medieval form of spirituality; masculine oppression or rebellion against that oppression; or even the 'philosophical bases of sociology (individual/society, nature/culture, mind/body)' and the 'antinomies of bourgeois thought' (Turner 1996, 179–81). Although these approaches do locate the meaning of anorexia in social processes, they remain tied to the ways in which other disciplines account for anorexia. As Gilles Deleuze underlines emphatically, making something symbolic is the exact opposite of analysing it:

> [Psychiatry and psychoanalysis] bring everything down to the level of a neuro-organic or symbolic code ('lack, lack . . .'). So the second question arises: why does the anorexic assemblage come so close to going off the rails, to becoming lethal? What are the dangers it constantly skirts and the dangers into which it falls? . . . we must try to find what dangers arise in the middle of a real experiment, and not the lack dominating a pre-established interpretation. People are always in the middle of some business, where nothing may be designated as its

> origin. Always things encountering each other, never things diminishing each other's contribution. A cartography and never a symbolics.
>
> (Deleuze and Parnet 1987, 111)

This book as a whole is informed by and organized according to this endeavour to establish a 'cartography'. However, if sociology can substitute cartography for symbolics, this is also because it is an empirical discipline. Analysing anorexia in practice from a sociological standpoint therefore required devising an appropriate investigative framework. I chose to emphasize interviews with anorexics as my main method. An initial corpus of interviews was collected at hospital H with female adolescent patients or ex-patients hospitalized for anorexia.[5] In parallel, to avoid being limited to the hospital field, interviews were also conducted through personal network sampling with 'former anorexics' who had been diagnosed with anorexia in the past but had never been admitted to hospital. Moreover, in order to position anorexic practices within the space of adolescent practices more broadly, a series of interviews presented as focusing on 'eating habits' was conducted with 'non-anorexic' secondary-school students (15–18 years old, mainly female) at school S. Following this fieldwork and initial analysis of the material, examining school practices emerged as a potentially relevant and fruitful avenue to explore, and the last part of my fieldwork was therefore conducted in a space that allowed me to take them into account directly. I collected my main interview corpus in a psychiatric clinic for teenagers, clinic C, which is defined as both a medical and an educational space. The clinic includes psychiatric care wards but also a proper secondary school. I carried out observations in two of the wards of this clinic (ward I for intensive care and ward E for educational care, where the patients were enrolled in the clinic's school). Interviews were also conducted with anorexic patients from ward E and with teachers who had taught them at the clinic's school.[6]

The findings in this book are presented in a way that reflects how my topic and approach were progressively devised and defined together. The first section retraces how I initially devised my object of study. It looks in particular at the effects of my choice to approach the issue through the medical sphere, that is to say through a medical diagnosis with its own history and through interviews conducted in a hospital setting. The first chapter discusses certain aspects of the historical and social configuration in which the medical diagnosis of anorexia appeared at the end of the nineteenth century and offers an initial form of 'objectivation' through history. The second chapter accounts for the medically based nature of the field, with its implications and its benefits, while also delineating the object of study and contextualizing the interview corpora collated. The second section of the book then uses these interviews to describe the process that constitutes anorexic activity in its concrete form and over time, answering the question: 'What do they do?' The interactionist notion of 'career' is put to productive use here as a tool for taking into account and objectivating the point of view of those engaged in anorexia. Four stages can be identified in the anorexic career: first, they begin taking themselves in hand; then they maintain this commitment; next, they carry on maintaining it despite alerts being given and monitoring being put in place; and finally, they are taken in hand by the medical institution. There are two key issues at stake here: first, showing how, in order to become anorexic, these girls have to do certain things; second, drawing attention to the existence of anorexic work aimed at self-transformation, some dimensions of which are patently obvious (the fact that the body is transformed) and others less obvious (the fact that this endeavour also has an academic and more generally cultural dimension). The third section of the book builds out from this work of self-transformation to show the extent to which it takes places in an oriented social space. I approach the anorexic activity described in the second section as a set of practices and representations and establish their social conditions of possibility, which draw on the social characteristics of the people involved (particularly gender, social background and age). In doing so, this final section of the book offers an answer to the question 'What do they have to be in order to do what they do?' The aim of my study is therefore not to provide an 'aetiology' – in the medical sense of the term – of anorexia, not even a social one. I do not talk about 'social causes' or even 'social factors', whether as primary or secondary issues. Rather, I try to offer a cartography that is inextricably spatial and temporal, linking together two approaches that have the reputation of being incompatible in sociology: an approach in terms of 'career' and an approach in terms of dispositions and social space.

How is this sociology of anorexia useful?

What is the possible value of this approach to anorexia?[7] Like any scientific study, its function is first and foremost to offer an empirically grounded analysis of a phenomenon or some of its aspects. In this particular case, my aim was to describe anorexic practices and their temporal and spatial dynamics as precisely as possible. But the scientific aim of such an investigation cannot only be defined in terms of its object. As I have already said, my project began with an epistemological wager about showing that the methods and concepts of sociology could be applied to fields that usually lie outside its remit, particularly the psychological and the pathological. Winning such a wager would therefore also show that sociology as a discipline has a wider remit for addressing reality than is often believed, sometimes even by sociologists themselves.

As for other potential uses, one might perhaps expect to hear about a possible therapeutic function, whether in the strict, almost medical, sense of the term or more broadly, in the sense that understanding social determinisms can offer a way of escaping them. However, the approach that I use here does not claim to contribute to treating anorexia and I do not take any particular stance on therapeutic issues. Equally, from a more strictly political point of view, my intention is not to 'free' anorexics from anything that might be construed as oppression by society or the medical sphere. The aim is therefore not critical in terms of the medical or psychological point of view, nor is it clinical – it is something quite different. One might ask whether this difference simply has scientific and epistemological stakes or whether it also has broader implications. I would hope that it might at least result in some distance being taken from dominant discourses (by which I mean discourses that have a monopoly over legitimate discussion of this object) or simply current discourses about a reality that they only describe partially. It is no mean feat, today, to suggest looking at the world in a way that differs from the perspectives taken by professionals of the psyche. My sociological approach suspends the need to decide what is normal and what is pathological; it looks at 'how' anorexia works rather than 'why' it exists; it breaks down this phenomenon – which is all too often reduced to a pre-existing nature – into stages and practices; and finally it highlights the institutions, interactions, norms and dispositions that structure such an extreme experience. In doing so, I would hope it offers a way of understanding this experience and of helping others understand it without any disgust or any fascination, as well as a way of making people aware of the social web that produces the most singular behaviours.

Notes

1 For other examples of the use of this territorial metaphor regarding the relationships between sociology and psychology, see for example Singly's refusal of 'reserved fields' (1997, 21) and Lahire's call against 'remain[ing] on the outskirts of the classical work done in psychology' (2003, 330 n. 1).
2 Translator's note: Unless otherwise indicated, all translations of quotations from French sources are mine.
3 For an overview of the epidemiological data, see, for example, Ledoux (1994), Flament (1995) and McClelland and Crisp (2001).
4 For a critical analysis of the use of epidemiological statistics on anorexia both in medicine and in the social sciences and humanities analysed in relation to the interests that various disciplines might have in asserting that there is an epidemic, see Hof and Nicolson (1996).
5 The names of the interviewees and the different institutions have been changed to respect the principle of anonymity in sociology: 'someone who does not know the place and people beforehand should not be able to discover them, to "find" them with the help of the text' ('La déontologie de l'enquête ethnographique' in Beaud and Weber 1997, 116–17).
6 The extracts from interviews and my field journal are quoted in inverted commas and indexed as follows: [FJ] for the field journal, [H] for the interviews conducted with patients in hospital H, [C] for the interviews in ward E at clinic C, [N] for the interviews through personal network sampling, [S] for the school S and [Mr or Mrs + initial] for the teachers interviewed.
7 For a presentation and discussion of the various possible functions of sociology, see Lahire (2002a).

Part I

Beginning with a diagnosis

1 A detour via the nineteenth century

Historical issues at stake

It seems logical that an object with a history should owe at least part of its existence to its social conditions. When it comes to addressing mental illness, the historical method has often seemed to be the social sciences' tool *par excellence*, to some extent a reflex reaction to the question 'What can social science say about mental illness?' While debates surrounding the notion of the 'historical and social construction of illnesses' do draw attention to the possible limitations, deviations and misconceptions of this issue,[1] they have nonetheless contributed to underscoring the value of historical contextualization: the benefits of looking at how, at a given place and time, it was *possible* for a diagnosis to be established (or invented, manufactured or discovered, depending on how provocative one wishes to be).

In this chapter, I draw on history's power to 'objectivate' things. It is especially useful in this case, because my investigation was based on a diagnosis and that diagnosis therefore has to be put in context, and particularly in historical context.[2] The history of the medical diagnosis of anorexia has been subject to much study, particularly in the United States. In addition to books solely devoted to retracing this history, almost all recent books on anorexia in the social sciences and humanities give substantial space to its history. On the basis of these studies – among which Joan Jacobs Brumberg's works deserve particular mention, as they are still the main reference in the field – it is possible to outline the historical and social configuration in which the first formulations of the diagnosis of anorexia emerged in France and in England, at the end of the nineteenth century.

Illness and diagnosis

The 'anorexic saints'

Even when these studies refer back to older attempts at establishing the diagnosis, they all agree on the fact that its modern formulations appeared at the end of the nineteenth century. They differ, however, in how they frame the links between the history of the diagnosis and the history of the illness itself. The question of historicizing anorexia is at the heart of lively debate in the social sciences and humanities (and not only in medicine): Did the diagnosis and the illness both appear relatively recently or did the diagnosis of a very old illness simply appear very late in the day? Discussion has centred on the question of the 'anorexic saints'.

This debate is not unrelated to internal debates taking place in the medical sphere, which also draw oppositions between different ways of calling on history.[3] But it has taken on a certain autonomy within the social sciences and humanities, where historians argue about the pathological labelling of certain medieval pious practices and ask how old 'anorexia' is as an illness. Were the medieval saints anorexic? In other words, did the *illness* exist before the *diagnosis* did?

> In medieval Europe, particularly in the years between 1200 and 1500, many women refused their food and prolonged fasting was considered a female miracle. The chronicles and hagiographies of this period tell numerous stories of women saints who ate almost nothing or claimed to be incapable of eating normal healthy fare . . . . Women who were reputed to live without eating – that is, without eating anything except the Eucharist – were particularly numerous in the thirteenth through fifteenth centuries . . . . By the seventeenth and eighteenth centuries, however, scientifically minded physicians began to pay close attention to food abstinence, so common among women of the High Middle Ages. They called it both inedia prodigiosa . . . and anorexia mirabilis (miraculously inspired loss of appetite). Some medical writers and historians claim that anorexia mirabilis and anorexia nervosa are really one and the same.
>
> (Brumberg 1989, 41–2)

Two authors stand out in this debate opposing those who believe that *anorexia mirabilis* and *anorexia nervosa* are two separate phenomena and those who believe in continuity between the two. In *Holy Anorexia,* historian Rudolph Bell retrospectively applies modern psychological theories to explain the case of medieval fasting and talks about an 'analogy' between the medieval and modern women who abstain from food: in his view, the medieval saints had 'anorexic behaviour patterns' (Bell 1985). Even though he does not claim that modern anorexics and medieval saints were the same – he describes them as 'anorexic saints' – he does present them as 'analogous', psychologically motivated by the same search for identity and autonomy in societies that oppress women: 'In this sense the anorexic response is timeless' (Bell 1985, 56). For medieval scholar Caroline Walker Bynum, however, renouncing food made sense within a much broader system of religious practices, which modern authors tend to forget when they give fasting such a predominant place (Bynum 1985). In her view, equivalence with anorexia is a historical misinterpretation and applying this diagnosis retrospectively is a mistake. She believes it is not even possible to talk about a single type of fasting behaviour that was simply viewed differently at different periods (as a pious act in the Middle Ages and an illness in the twentieth century): 'Medieval people did not see all refusal to eat as "fasting" (i.e. asceticism) or all extended abstinence as miraculous' (Bynum 1987, 195).

To take up Catherine Garrett's terms (1998, 112–16), this debate therefore opposes proponents of 'continuity'[4] (for whom there is a form of continuity between medieval religious anorexia and modern anorexia nervosa) and proponents of 'discontinuity' (for whom there is no sense in applying a modern diagnosis to medieval practices).[5] The discontinuity argument seems to be in the majority within the social sciences, whereas the continuity stance is much more visible in works in medicine or psychology. Discontinuity is mainly defended in the name of the principles of historical methodology, and in particular the problems inherent in applying a diagnosis retroactively, but also in order to avoid being too quick to assert the existence of an eternal feminine: 'The underlying assumption here [in Bell's text] is that the psychology of women is fixed in time and that past and present are the same' (Brumberg 1989, 43). For both these reasons, it is reasonable to follow the lead of the social historians advocating discontinuity and consider that the history of the illness and its diagnosis coincide.

From this perspective, anorexia can therefore appear as one of the 'transient mental illnesses' analysed by Ian Hacking: an illness 'that appears at a time, in a place, and later fades away' or 'reappear[s] from time to time' (Hacking 1998, 1). Using Hacking's terms, one might suggest that an initial 'niche', 'stable home' or 'habitat' for the medical diagnosis of anorexia emerged in France and in England at the end of the nineteenth century and that this niche then crumbled in the early twentieth century before being reconstructed, with some changes, from the 1960s onwards.[6] Showing how the diagnosis emerges requires looking in detail at its different constituents. I will give particular emphasis to three points: how the diagnosis slotted into medical taxonomies; what kinds of conditions of possibility were necessary to identify the practices covered by this diagnosis; and how representations of the female body were reconfigured when it was first formulated.

The diagnosis within medical taxonomies

Two distinct processes led to anorexia appearing in medical taxonomies: fasting practices were included in the sphere of medical competence, and fasting was recognized not as one of several symptoms of certain illnesses (particularly organic illnesses) but rather as a separate diagnostic entity in itself (in England) or an autonomous symptomatic group related to hysteria (in France).

Secularizing and medicalizing female fasting

After the miraculous fasting of the thirteenth to sixteenth century, cases arose that were more problematic for contemporary observers. Beginning in the seventeenth century, women who fasted became the subject of a classification quarrel between doctors and priests over who had the right to account for their practices. During the seventeenth and eighteenth centuries, prolonged abstinence from food was increasingly related to organic causes and considered the symptom of an illness rather than the sign of supernatural intervention. Losing appetite and fasting were progressively enrolled in the medical sphere, although not without some difficulty (Brumberg 1989, ch. 2). Finally, during the last third of the nineteenth century, this 'long transition from sainthood to patienthood' (60) once again created a very visible opposition between priests and doctors on the topic of the 'fasting girls' of the Victorian era. This term, used at the time by both the British and the Americans, served to designate cases of prolonged abstinence from food without specifying whether this fasting was of a religious or medical nature. In the case of one young woman, Sarah Jacob, she 'literally was killed by empirical design' (67) after medical observation was organized to verify her claims that she no longer ate: this surveillance was so efficient that the young woman died on the tenth day of observation.

Such events, largely publicized outside the medical sphere, gave medical science the chance to take the refusal to eat and change it from a religious act to a symptom of illness and thus to bring these women under their control. By the end of the nineteenth century, fasting behaviour was firmly enrolled in the sphere of medical competence. Behaviour was henceforth read through a secular lens and the medicalization of this behaviour contributed to professionalizing medicine – two processes that of course extended far beyond the question of female fasting.[7]

In parallel – and following the inclusion of fasting practices in the medical sphere – during the last two-thirds of the nineteenth century, fasting went from being the symptom of various illnesses, particularly organic ones, to being a diagnostic or symptomatic entity in itself (Brumberg 1989, 101–2). In 1873, a French doctor named Lasègue published an article entitled 'Of hysterical anorexia'. That same year, an English doctor named Gull presented a paper at a Clinical Society congress that was published shortly after under the title '*Anorexia Nervosa (Apepsia Hysterica, Anorexia Hysterica)*'. Both described cases of young women from good families who limited their food intake and lost weight, sometimes to the point of emaciation, while still maintaining or even increasing their physical movement and activities and without there seeming to be any physical causes for a state that therefore had to be considered, at least partly, 'nervous' or 'mental'. These two texts are traditionally defined as the first forms of medical diagnosis of anorexia and their authors as the founding fathers, discoverers or inventors of the diagnosis.[8] The early stages of the medical diagnosis of anorexia were therefore framed by the controversy opposing 'nervous' and 'hysterical' anorexia.

I shall not go into the details of these two diagnostic formulations as they have been very widely documented.[9] I will simply underline the fact that, as Ian Hacking has shown for 'transient mental illnesses', these diagnoses slotted into existing medical taxonomies without entailing any 'scientific revolution', in Kuhn's sense of the term, but that they also constituted topics of discussion or even controversy within the medical community (Hacking 1998, 38, 81). Lasègue's formulation took place within the search for the various manifestations of hysteria, while Gull's corresponded to efforts made by high-status consultants to make diagnostic acuity the hallmark of medical competence (Brumberg 1989, 111–12). The diagnosis gave rise to an interesting debate for doctors, given that it constituted a secondary battleground for the controversy surrounding hysteria.

This controversy did not oppose 'nervous' England and 'hysterical' France but rather took place within each country between proponents and opponents of the main national diagnosis. In France, Charcot himself, along with some of his students, questioned whether hysterical anorexia should be related to hysteria while, in England, Gull's opposition to theories of hysteria was strongly debated within English medicine, and some practitioners using Gull's term nonetheless still considered anorexia nervosa a variant of hysterical behaviour.[10] This debate is still in play today (although the stakes are not the same) in the importance given to each of the founding fathers of the diagnosis. Indeed, publications on anorexia differ in terms of which doctor they consider to have 'really' discovered the diagnosis and which doctor they credit with the most refined and 'modern' formulation. This choice to call on different traditions might initially seem to be mainly due to their national character (an English and then North American tradition, on the one hand, and a French one on the other); however, the question still needs to be repositioned within the current space of scholarly discourse about anorexia. Gull's medical approach focused on examining the symptoms of anorexia nervosa (extreme emaciation, loss of appetite, no menstrual cycles and substantial activity). Lasègue's was more psychological and gave substantial weight to the description and clinical study of the 'stages' or 'phases' through which the patient and her close family and friends went through. When researchers choose to call upon one founding father rather than the other, this therefore depends largely on their own theoretical approach.

Under the watchful eye of medicine and the family

These initial formulations of the medical diagnosis of anorexia share the common feature of defining a very specific clientele: young girls (between sixteen and twenty three for Gull, between fifteen and twenty for Lasègue) belonging to the middle and upper classes.[11] At the time, these were the classes where a whole apparatus observing the bodies and eating behaviour of women and adolescent girls was put in place – an apparatus that therefore constituted a second set of historical and social conditions of possibility for establishing the diagnosis. Indeed, in order to be able to label practices as deviant, they have to be *identifiable* first.[12]

In general, in the nineteenth century, the observation of bourgeois adolescent behaviour increased with changes in family structure and especially in the place ascribed to the child. In particular, a network observing female eating habits developed that placed young girls' restrictive eating habits under the watchful eye of both the medical institution and the family.

First of all, the medicalization of female conduct continued and grew stronger at the end of the century thanks to its potential to serve political interests, as Jan Goldstein has shown in the case of the medical diagnosis of hysteria:

> The popularization of the hysteria diagnosis and related 'nervous' conditions served the anticlerical cause .... It helped to sever the close traditional bond

> between women and priests, which nineteenth-century French anticlerical republicans had always found so odious, and to replace it with a dependency on the medical profession. 'Women must belong to science, or else they will belong to the church,' the republican politician Jules Ferry had warned in a speech of 1870. Ferry was arguing for the expansion of secular education for girls, which would purge their minds of dogma and superstition and insure that, as mothers, they would raise broods of little republican citizens. But another way to make women 'belong to science' was to habituate them to thinking of their bouts of emotional distress as medical conditions falling within the purview of the physician, rather than as moral failings or spiritual crises requiring the guidance of a priest.
>
> (Goldstein 1987, 373–4)

There was real political encouragement to place young girls under medical observation:

> The anticlerical republican politician Jules Simon even tried to help matters along by co-authoring a guidebook for mothers on the rearing of female children. He stressed the importance of regular medical attention (and the avoidance of 'charlatans') and the young girl's vulnerability to *malaises nerveux*.
>
> (Goldstein 1987, 375)

Placed under medical watch, 'nineteenth-century women were perpetual patients. . . . Along with pregnancy and childbirth, puberty and menopause had come to be seen as more or less dangerous ordeals' (Knibiehler 1998, 334). Young girls were very prone to consumption (which affected girls twice as much as boys) and to tuberculosis (335). They were also supposed to be prone to gastric disorders 'because of the superior sensitivity of the female digestive system' (Brumberg 1989, 174). Hysterical or nervous anorexia was therefore just one eating disorder among others, such as chlorosis and dyspepsia. Under medical guidance, adolescent female eating-illnesses led bourgeois parents to closely observe their daughters' food habits. Chlororis was even considered to be a normal stage in a young girl's development, requiring constant control of her diet (Brumberg 1982, 1471). And parents were all the more encouraged to exercise this surveillance because the stakes of deciphering eating habits were far from simply physical:

> Between 1850 and 1900 the most frequent warning issued to parents of girls had to do with forestalling the development of idiosyncracies, irregularities, or strange whims of appetite because these were precursors of disease as well as signs of questionable moral character.
>
> (Brumberg 1989, 174)

Parents were therefore educated in how they watched over their daughters and taught to focus on eating habits as a set of signs to be interpreted.

The practice of observing the body in medical and rational terms and evaluating it on the basis of precise figures also began to take hold, albeit slowly.[13] Nascent infant care at the end of the nineteenth century established – with some difficulty – the need to weigh children and maintain a weight curve as an 'indicator of a child's development'.[14] Housekeeping and home economics were introduced to programmes for female education from 1880 onwards (Boltanski 1984, 23–6) and this contributed to implementing a network of family observation of the child's body orchestrated by medicine and in which the mother was the main tool:

> Home economists and nutritionists of this period [the early twentieth century in the United States] told middle-class homemakers that both underweight and overweight were the result of failing to cook, feed, and eat correctly . . . . It did assign clear responsibility to the wife and mother for fat or thin family members . . . body size was becoming subject to rationality, control, and interventions.
>
> (Brumberg 1989, 236)

At the end of the nineteenth century, it became possible to observe the body and evaluate it in terms of figures and both these approaches were promoted by the new family norms that slowly became institutionalized.

Reconfiguring thinness

Along with this apparatus of observation came a reconfiguration of representations of the body, and particularly the female body. It would be reasonable to suggest that, from the mid nineteenth century onwards, the question of thinness was thoroughly overhauled in the social space of bodies. Fasting and thinness went from being the stigma of the poor to being attributes of female social excellence.

First of all, during this period, a Romantic apology of fasting and slenderness, and even of certain illnesses, can be identified:

> Among other things, [Romanticism translated into] an inordinate cult of pale, ghostly complexions, with a yellow, blue or green tinge, the painful but prestigious expression of inner fire, of vanquished destiny, of illness and imminent death. Consumption, tuberculosis and chlorosis were alive and well . . . The languid, stooping air of the tuberculosis patient, an 'interesting' air that was carefully cultivated, asserted a personal image, a personality; it expressed an individuality that was detached from outer realities . . . Presenting oneself as immaterial and dying, as celestial and translucent, required a whole daily regimen. The last 'bonny lasses' produced by the Empire, sprightly and stocky big-busted women, their words as strong as they themselves were stout, were quick to start suffering, drinking vinegar, eating lemons, fasting, staying up all night, and being consumed by tragic passions, until they finally took on the pallid aspect of a corpse . . . In the hey day of Romanticism . . . women

> cultivated this immaterial and vaporous air, became paler, lost weight, developed hollow, gaunt cheeks, chests and thighs, by adopting the gastrophobic rituals of the time, with vinegar and water, nibbling on rose petals and acid fruit . . . to become languid, bloodless and dying.
>
> (Perrot 1984, 143–4, 187)[15]

Both the dance and novels of the time contributed to showcasing this Romantic ideal of the body:

> The Romantics dreamed of an ethereal woman, and the opera's talented ballerinas aptly filled the bill. Dancing on 'points', a newly invented technique, thinned the silhouette and permitted flights of aerial weightlessness. Ballets such as *La Sylphide* (1932) and *Giselle* (1841) temporarily divested women of the burden of the flesh. The heroines of novels were slender and delicate. A languid pallor, if possible accentuated by black hair, dark circles around the eyes, and clouds of rice powder, symbolized the sufferings of the romantic self.
>
> (Knibiehler 1998, 327)

Although this model of the body waned in France from the 1850s onwards, it did not disappear completely or definitively. At the scale of the nineteenth century, the romantic body no doubt constituted a turning point rather than a temporary break: 'the changing standard of beauty among the upper strata can be seen around the time of the Romantic movement when, "for both women and men paleness, frailness, slenderness became the vogue"' (Mennell 1985, 37). However, this celebration of dietary restriction and the body type that went with it was not only a romantic fashion. It reveals how dietary control and slimness fit into a social topology that involved both class and gender.

Table manners and abundance of food had long been a touchstone of social status. However, during this period, moderation rather than abundance became the sign of distinction:

> The problem of self-control over appetite impinged first on the upper classes, who show clear signs of it by the eighteenth century. As food supplies became more abundant and more secure for more people, the upper classes could not distinguish themselves from those immediately below them simply through the quantity they ate, and they came to distance themselves more by the delicacy than the quantity of food. Nineteenth-century bourgeois gastronomes increasingly extolled the virtue of moderation.
>
> (Mennell 1996, 201–2)[16]

According to Joan Jacobs Brumberg, the practical and symbolic distance taken from food became a key issue for women and particularly for women from the wealthy middle classes whose social status could be uncertain: 'Advice books admonished [middle-class] women "not to be ashamed of the kitchen", but many still sought to separate themselves from both food and the working-class women they hired to do the preparation and cooking' (Brumberg 1989, 179).[17] Food therefore became potentially vulgar, both in its very nature and in its links with the working classes. This was particularly the case for women: 'a lady should never be seen eating' claimed an English saying of the time. Excessive eating in women was qualified as 'gluttony' and resulted in 'ugliness' that would compromise a young woman's chances on the marriage market. Meat in particular was seen as masculine food likely to give rise to uncontrollable passions and accelerate physical and sexual maturity. It was therefore something to remove from young women's diets, particularly given that, according to the medical lore of the time, they had delicate digestive systems that could not handle rich food anyway. The same food that was impossible for the working classes due to its price was forbidden to young women from bourgeois families who *did* have material access to it. More generally, a woman from high society was never hungry ('To be hungry, in any sense, was a social faux pas'; Brumberg 1989, 182) and a variety of strategies were deployed to avoid being seen eating. It is worth recalling here the scene in *Gone with the Wind,* where Scarlett's nurse forces her to eat before a garden party so that she does not then succumb to the temptation of food – something that would have been impossible anyway given the corset the woman was tightly lacing around Scarlett as she spoke. Controlling and restricting food intake therefore became the prerogative of women from wealthy backgrounds and derision or even social contempt awaited anyone who broke that rule.

The same combination of class and gender issues can be seen with regard to the body itself as well as the judgements made about it.[18] Female slenderness or even thinness became the sign of a social status that used to be indexed by the very opposite attributes. In this respect, Thorstein Veblen's 1899 study in *The Theory of the Leisure Class* is valuable in two ways as the author both observes this reconfiguration of thinness and theorizes the process that led to it. Veblen mentions the romantic model of the medieval maiden and claims that it had close links with the models of the female body in the European 'leisure class' at the end of the nineteenth century:

> It is more or less a rule that in communities which are at the stage of economic development at which women are valued by the upper class for their service, the ideal of female beauty is a robust, large-limbed woman . . . This ideal suffers a change in the succeeding development, when, in the conventional scheme, the office of the high-class wife comes to be a vicarious leisure simply. The ideal then includes the characteristics which are supposed to result from or to go with a life of leisure consistently enforced. . . . In the conventional scheme of those days ladies of high degree were conceived to be in perpetual tutelage, and to be scrupulously exempt from all useful work. The resulting chivalric or romantic ideal of beauty . . . dwells on . . . the delicacy of . . . the slender figure, and especially the slender waist. In the pictured representations of the women of that time [in the Middle Ages], and in modern romantic imitators of the chivalric thought and feeling, the waist is attenuated

> to a degree that implies extreme debility. The same ideal is still extant among a considerable portion of the population of modern industrial communities . . . . Survivals of this lackadaisical or romantic ideal occur freely in the tastes of the well-to-do classes of Continental countries . . . [:] the infirmly delicate, translucent, and hazardously slender.
>
> (Veblen 2007, 97–8)

If upper-class women had to be 'hazardously slender' it was because they had to publicly showcase the difference between the leisure class and the working class. These women were construed as objects, perhaps, but objects of distinction:

> It has already been noticed that at the stages of economic evolution at which conspicuous leisure is much regarded as a means of good repute, the ideal requires delicate and diminutive hands and feet and a slender waist. These features . . . go to show that the person so affected is incapable of useful effort and must therefore be supported in idleness by her owner. She is useless and expensive, and she is consequently valuable as evidence of pecuniary strength.
>
> (Veblen 2007, 99)

Men and women therefore interiorized the constraints of their social positions in the shape of new categories of judgements of taste. For women, this led to a desire for self-transformation in keeping with the tastes of the time, while men learned to see the seductive effects of a thin body:

> It results that at this cultural stage women take thought to alter their persons, so as to conform more nearly to the requirements of the instructed taste of the time; and under the guidance of the canon of pecuniary decency, the men find the resulting artificially induced pathological features attractive. So, for instance, the constricted waist which has had so wide and persistent a vogue in the communities of the Western culture, and so also the deformed foot of the Chinese.
>
> (Veblen 2007, 99)

Finally, the socially embedded nature of these categories of aesthetic judgement can be seen in the new oppositions they constructed. Just as imposing dietary restrictions made working-class gluttony into a counter model, the new legitimate body-type relegated plumpness and good health to the *dondons* – or hefty women – of the late eighteenth century in France: 'Being a *dondon* was the thing to avoid at all costs: as the Marquis de Caraccioli noted "it is only ever said of a common girl and it signifies a large fat person, of stocky build"' (Perrot 1984, 68). During the nineteenth century, there was recurrent discourse denouncing the heavy weight and large thighs of prostitutes, stigmata of their trade and the fact they belonged to the lowliest classes of society. Prostitutes were prone to 'excessive eating' and 'greed', and their 'plumpness of figure' (Corbin 1996, 7–9) was foregrounded as early as 1836 and then tirelessly taken up throughout the rest of the nineteenth century. At the end of the century, the 'portrait of the prostitute' included one main feature: 'a plumpness, the result of shorter stature and heavier weight than honest women (on average, prostitutes had thicker thighs than honest women)' (302). The celebration of dietary restriction and thinness therefore fit both into the space of food consumption and the space of bodies. The redistribution of attributes of female excellence and vulgarity that took place in the nineteenth century thus traced out a particular configuration, many aspects of which are still present today, as we will see later in chapter eight.

This rapid detour via the nineteenth century has highlighted several historical and social dimensions to anorexia. In particular, it raises the following productive questions: how the diagnosis is the locus for debates between different medical stances; how it is also a specific moment in the anorexic career; how tools of measurement, observability of conduct and labelling of deviance are linked together; and, finally, how anorexic practices are positioned in the social space of bodies and judgements about bodies. These questions will come up again and again throughout this book, although they will be expressed in different ways given the hundred years separating the period discussed here and my field study, which I will now go on to outline in some detail. As we change period and material, we will also move away from the mainly contextual approach I have taken so far and approach anorexia through practice instead, working as closely as possible to its content and the point of view of those engaged in it.

Notes

1 See, for example, Rosenberg and Golden (1992) and Hacking (1999).
2 It is true that by defining this research project as focusing on 'anorexia' and collecting empirical data on the basis of this category, I have gone against Durkheim's prohibition against taking 'as the subject of . . . research roughly assembled groups of facts corresponding to words of common usage' and his call to replace them with a definition elaborated in advance by the sociologist (Durkheim 2005, xxxix). In this research, I replaced this prior definition with my endeavour to contextualize the material, historicize the diagnosis and take into account the medically based nature of the field (ch 2).
3 There are many historical reminders in publications in medicine or psychology about anorexia. For an analysis of this 'use of history' (where history can paradoxically be used to dehistoricize and essentialize anorexia and to refute competing interpretations of the illness), see Darmon (2001, 121–7).
4 For example Bell (1985) and Banks (1992).
5 See Bynum (1987) and Brumberg (1989) for studies explicitly concerning the history of the diagnosis, but also, for example, Hepworth (1999) and MacSween (1993).
6 For a presentation and detailed application of Ian Hacking's theory to anorexia, see ch. 1 of Darmon (2001).
7 On the medicalization process, particularly in the case of female mental disorders, see for example Tomes (1990).
8 Different publications obviously disagree on this point too. Certain researchers (particular those who draw links between *anorexia mirabilis* and *anorexia nervosa*, or equate the two) consider that the diagnosis dates from a 1694 description by doctor Richard Morton. For a refutation of that position, see for example Brumberg (1989, 44) and ch. 1 of MacSween (1993).

9 See, for example, ch. 4 of Brumberg (1989), ch. 8 of Vandereycken and Van Deth (1994) and Shorter (1987).

10 On these different points, see Shorter (1987, 72), Vandereycken and Van Deth (1994, 166–9) and Brumberg (1989, 149).

11 See Brumberg (1989, 113 n. 33) and Shorter (1987, 69).

12 In the case of 'fugue' as a transient mental illness, Ian Hacking analyses how identifying the illness presupposed a 'system of surveillance and detection' of movements within and outside France (Hacking 1998, 82 and ch. 3). Similarly, the invention of 'illiteracy' is based on unemployment and its pedagogical treatment as conditions for the visibility of difficulties with reading and writing: 'In the 1970s, places for training and retraining, places devoted to social and professional integration, were therefore veritable *observatories* of the difficulties that the least educated parts of the population had with reading and writing' (Lahire 1999a, 85).

13 In the United States, between 1900 and 1920 doctors and insurance companies began to use tables of 'normal weight', personal weighing scales became widespread and standardized clothing sizes for off-the-peg ranges were introduced. See Brumberg (1989, 231–8).

14 See Rollet-Echalier (1990), particularly p. 196–7.

15 Joan Jacobs Brumberg also mentions, in England, a 'female fashion for sickness and debility' (1989, 171) and the recognized power of seduction wielded by chlorosis sufferers, seen as physically attractive (1982, 1472). Elaine Showalter also draws links between anorexia nervosa and the Victorian feminine ideal (1985, 128–9).

16 Bryan Turner also analyses the contribution of George Cheney's eighteenth-century restrictive dietary prescriptions, aimed at the middle and upper intellectual classes, to the 'government of bodies' (Turner 1982).

17 The rest of this paragraph is based on Brumberg (1989, 179–82).

18 According to Louis Chevalier, the physical embodiment of social judgement was already particularly strong in the first half of the nineteenth century: 'The judgments which each group passed on the other involved physical characteristics . . . . The violence of the social struggles in Paris during the period cannot be understood unless it is realized that it was based upon physical and, even more specifically, morphological, foundations. The groups considered each other, judged each other and confronted each other physically. . . . The physical characteristics of individuals and groups had never, perhaps, been so strongly emphasized as in these years of social upheaval; they were used as weapons both by the bourgeoisie and the common people' (Chevalier 1973, 409, 413).

2 A hospital-based approach

Methodological issues

The material collected for this investigation is firmly embedded in the medical sphere. This is due both to my decision to begin with the diagnosis and to the fact my corpora of interviews were collated in a hospital setting. There would be no sense in regretting the hospital-based nature of my fieldwork because it was also my main tool, both in defining my topic and in applying a sociological approach to a field that ostensibly lay outside its remit. In this chapter, I will look at the methodological issues inherent to this hospital-based fieldwork, taking the measure of its implications and discussing the role it played in defining my topic. In outlining my different field-settings, there are four particularly crucial issues to consider: how I selected and delimited my interviews on the basis of the diagnosis; the fact that the investigation and interviews took place in a hospital setting; how the content of the interviews I conducted was shaped by medical discourse; and, finally – although chronologically speaking this came first – how I was either granted or denied access to the medical field in my capacity as a sociologist.

Collating the interview corpora

Methodologically speaking, the medical diagnosis of anorexia served as a recruitment tool. I contacted and found volunteers to take part in the interviews on the basis of this diagnostic category. The hospital-based nature of my fieldwork was therefore the result of a dual form of medical selection. First, there was the selection inherent to the diagnosis itself, by which I mean who had been diagnosed as anorexic and in which medical department. Second, a further type of medical selection came into play within the group of patients diagnosed as anorexic, in terms of which patients I was allowed to interview. I did not have access to all the anorexic patients on the wards. In hospital H, I was directed towards patients who were not (or no longer) on a feeding tube. In clinic C, I was not allowed to ask for an interview with two specific patients who 'weren't very well at the moment'. Of course I never tried to circumvent these instructions aimed at protecting the patients. My own room for manoeuvre took place before my fieldwork, through the types of departments in which I chose to negotiate access. In this regard, I attempted to vary the field settings. My two main interview corpora were collated in departments with very different treatment orientations, and these differences proved extremely relevant for examining theoretical and therapeutic stances towards anorexia. Defined in broad – and voluntarily tautological – terms, hospital H could be described as falling under 'psychiatric psychiatry', whereas clinic C lay in the realm of psychoanalytically oriented psychiatry. This later enabled me to take into account the substantial variation between these two spaces in my analysis of the interviews.

The diagnosis in hospital H

Delimiting my corpus brought psychiatric diagnostic categories into play, in terms of which patients were considered anorexic in hospital H. It also highlighted how, by using a particular diagnostic classification tool and refusing another, the two departments classified themselves through their classification practices, to paraphrase Pierre Bourdieu (1996a). Their use of the American Psychiatric Association's *Diagnostic and Statistical Manual of Mental Disorders* (DSM) was a central criterion in this regard.

Throughout my investigation in hospital H, the importance of the DSM diagnosis of anorexia nervosa was self-evident. It was 'the' system used to classify and diagnose the anorexics I interviewed. When I arrived in the department in hospital H, the first informal interview I had with a psychiatrist focused on the question of classifying anorexia and the diagnostic criteria used in the department. The department's use of the DSM classification was explicitly linked to its position in the space of psychiatry: 'The department's main characteristic is that it is "biological", "psychiatric", and not psychoanalytical . . . . We use the DSM. There are lots of departments where they don't classify' [Psychiatrist, hospital H]. And indeed the DSM itself was physically on display in the office where we met. Patients' medical files systematically included the DSM code for anorexia and I progressively became familiar with the 307.10 diagnosis of anorexia nervosa as well as its different criteria designated by letters. The DSM-III-R – the edition in use in the department at the time and therefore my reference point as well – gives the following diagnostic criteria for anorexia nervosa:

Diagnostic Criteria for 307.10 Anorexia Nervosa

A Refusal to maintain body weight over a minimal normal weight for age and height, e.g., weight loss leading to maintenance of body weight 15% below that expected; or failure to make expected weight gain during period of growth, leading to body weight 15% below that expected.

B Intense fear of gaining weight or becoming fat, even though underweight.

C Disturbance in the way in which one's body weight, size or shape is experienced, e.g., the person claims to 'feel fat' even when emaciated, believes that one area of the body is 'too fat' even when obviously underweight.

D In females, absence of at least three consecutive menstrual cycles when otherwise expected to occur (primary or secondary amenorrhea). (A woman is considered to have amenorrhea if her periods occur only following hormone, e.g., oestrogen, administration.)

(American Psychiatric Association 1987, 67)

The patients in hospital H were therefore diagnosed on the basis of these criteria. The DSM is drawn up by the American Psychiatric Association for the purpose of diagnosing patients.[1] At the time of my study, five successive editions had been published: the DSM-I in 1952, the DSM-II in 1968, the DSM-III in 1980, the DSM-III-R (for 'revised') in 1987 and the DSMIV in 1994.[2] The introduction to the DSM-III, DSM-III-R and DSM-IV all emphasize its 'descriptive' dimension (the definitions of disorders are generally limited to describing clinical features) and 'atheoretical' dimension (the manual should be able to be used by clinicians of varying theoretical orientations and etiological criteria are no longer used to define disorders). The term 'neurosis' (with its psychoanalytical etiological connotations) was removed from the classification from the DSM-III onwards.[3] Between 1980 and 1993, this classification system – and the diagnosis of anorexia nervosa – evolved considerably. While it is not possible to go into all the details here, two aspects of these changes are worth underscoring. First, the fact that 'eating disorders' became a separate category, organized around anorexia nervosa and bulimia nervosa, and, second, the increasing importance given to physical criteria (particularly the question of 'weight') and biological criteria in the diagnosis of anorexia nervosa.[4]

The relationship between the medical diagnoses of anorexia and bulimia is an important and divisive component in diagnostic definitions of anorexia. It served as a second form of 'self-classification through classification' for the departments in my study. When I arrived in the field, I presented my work as a sociological approach to anorexia. In hospital H, this formulation did not pose a problem insofar as it corresponded to the clear distinction drawn in the department between the diagnoses of anorexia nervosa and bulimia nervosa: 'You want to just work on anorexia? Yes, that's possible. These days, medically, we differentiate the two [anorexia and bulimia] more and more' [Psychiatrist, hospital H]. This distinction between the two diagnoses reflects the current position of the DSM. The DSM-IV linked the two diagnoses to some extent by establishing the separate 'Eating Disorders' category focusing on both, but at the same time it also drew a clear diagnostic distinction between them based on the criterion of weight, unlike previous versions of the manual:

> In DSM-III-R, individuals would receive concurrent diagnoses of both Bulimia Nervosa and Anorexia Nervosa if their body image problems and loss of weight were also accompanied by purging behaviour. . . . [In DSM-IV] the diagnosis is either Anorexia Nervosa, Binge-Eating/Purging Type, if the patient is markedly underweight, or Bulimia Nervosa, if the patient is normal weight or overweight.
>
> (Frances and Ross 1996, 239–40)

The stance taken by hospital H towards the medical diagnosis of anorexia was therefore characterized by its use of the DSM and the clear distinction it drew between anorexia and bulimia. The situation was not the same in clinic C.

The diagnosis in clinic C

After observing the use of the DSM in hospital H and also seeing that, in several manuals, it was presented as the reference point for classifying 'mental disorders' (an expression established by the DSM itself in opposition with the term 'mental illness'), I had almost forgotten the words of the psychiatrist I had met at hospital H: that the department's use of the DSM was a 'characteristic' linked to its 'psychiatric' orientation. When I initially began my second field study at clinic C, in ward E, I therefore found myself looking perhaps not for the DSM itself but at least for comparable explanations and codes, which I did not find.

The different stances taken by these two departments towards diagnosis are easy to explain: clinic C fell into the category of psychoanalytically oriented psychiatry, which explicitly distances itself from the DSM.[5] The manual was therefore markedly absent from the departments I observed in clinic C, to the extent that I only heard it mentioned once. Nonetheless, this absence remained relative insofar as the DSM codes were still present in correspondence with other medical institutions (for example, letters between medical teams to introduce patients moving from one place to another), and there was also an abridged version of the DSM itself in the office of the head of ward E, albeit discreetly placed. The contrasting stances taken by hospital H and clinic C were therefore part of a wider opposition between 'psychiatry' and 'psychoanalysis', in which the DSM and its use represent a key point of contention.

More generally, refusing to use DSM codes could also be part of an explicit rejection of any classification. This question was implicitly present in the carefully chosen words used by the psychiatrist in hospital H:

> 'The problem with classification is that, on the one hand, it has an effect, it imprisons patients in the illness. But, on the other hand, it is sometimes necessary when introducing the hospital, whether it's for scientific purposes or to obtain funding.'
>
> [FJ]

Her emphasis on this 'problem with classification' may have been related to the fact she was talking to a student in sociology, a discipline renowned for its participation in the anti-psychiatry movement and its denunciation of the effects of labels. However, it was more likely to do with the internal opposition within adolescent psychiatry, which corresponds to some extent to the opposition between hospital H and clinic C. In the field, I had come to grasp the stakes surrounding the use of classification tools. However, I still continued to ask open questions about the discreet use of diagnostic classifications and tried to obtain explicit positions in this regard:

> I asked her [an intern on ward I] one last question about the diagnosis, saying that I had imagined that the diagnosis would be written in large letters on the cover of all files. She answered: 'Yes, but these are teenagers; well, some places do do that, but we don't, given that teenagers are evolving psychologically, it's difficult to put them in a box without making a mistake, it's difficult to label them'.
>
> [FJ]

In this example, the same caution expressed by the doctor in hospital H was clearly implemented and defended. Teenagers are 'evolving psychologically' and classification is therefore always a reductive 'box' or 'label'.

However, two elements blur the terms of this opposition to some extent. The first – which I can only mention in passing here as it would warrant an entire study in its own right – is the necessarily psychiatric dimension to psychoanalytically oriented psychiatry. In practice, the opposition I encountered was less between psychiatry and psychoanalysis than between what we could call 'psychiatric psychiatry' and 'psychoanalytical psychiatry'. A psychiatrist's role, whatever his or her orientation, includes establishing a diagnosis. Therefore, even in clinic C, the only people who were able to take a purely and radically critical stance towards any diagnostic category were not doctors. They included, for example, the teacher running the school within the clinic and a psychology student on placement who introduced herself as an 'analyst psychologist'. They were both somewhat distanced from the clinic's 'psychiatrists' (despite their analytical orientation). The latter were all 'doctors' and I was told I should observe their 'categories' in 'the medical files . . . of these young girls who have the [tone indicating distance] "diagnosis of anorexia"' [Director of the school, my emphasis]. According to the psychology student on placement, the doctors 'give diagnoses like "schizophrenia or whatever", whereas an analyst psychologist will try and understand and may refuse to give a diagnosis' [FJ].

The second element blurring the opposition between the two positions relates to the diagnosis itself. Even on the intensive care ward in clinic C, where it did not appear explicitly in the files and where this was an openly defended choice, I was still shown which patients were 'anorexic' when I arrived. I wasn't told, for example, that they could not fulfil my request due to their refusal to classify their adolescent patients. And they indicated the anorexic patients without any embarrassment or discomfort, with nothing to indicate that they were failing to respect a 'non-classification' norm. On my first day of fieldwork in the intensive care ward, for example, during the morning 'flash' meeting, the head of the ward reviewing the patients told me 'Hélène is young anorexic girl' and, shortly after, a nurse gave me a physical description of the two anorexic patients on the ward so that I would 'recognize them', adding 'although, you know, you can tell'. The same day, when a student nurse asked 'How many anorexics have there been on the ward this year?' another nurse answered his question and, similarly, another nurse suggested that they could 'focus their discussions more on anorexics' when I was there.

The ease with which the diagnosis of 'anorexia' circulates is partly due to its self-evident nature. Two days after I began my fieldwork, while I was with a nurse and the nursing manager in the nurses' station facing the ward through a big bay window, a young girl in pre-admissions, very tall and very thin, visited the ward with her parents. The nurse lent towards the nursing manager and asked in a low voice: 'She's anorexic, isn't she, the pre-admission?' He laughed out loud and answered in a gently ironic tone 'You're very observant!' The nurse then turned to me and said: 'There's a young anorexic'. The conversion with the intern in ward I, mentioned above, took place the evening of the same day. When she said 'It's difficult to label them', I answered spontaneously: 'Yes, except the anorexics?' and she replied: 'Yes, that's it, because there it's much more self-evident, we know it starts in adolescence etc., you know'. In this case, self-evidence won out over the desire to avoid classifying, meaning that staff members were able to point out and count anorexic patients. This self-evidence could, of course, be seen as the result of a diagnostic endeavour, based on pre-admission and clinical interviews and so on. But as we saw in the exchange where the nursing manager joked about the nurse being 'observant', it was actually mainly about what was visible at first glance – the body, its weight and more specifically its weight loss, combined with the fact that the young woman was a 'patient' and her presence on the ward was therefore defined by the fact there was a 'problem'.

As I stated earlier, changes in the DSM diagnostic criteria reveal the increasing importance given to weight and weight loss in diagnosing anorexia nervosa. These same criteria also played a practical role in the way a 'self-evident' diagnosis of anorexia came to circulate on the intensive care ward. On that ward, the desire to avoid classification paradoxically coincided with the DSM's classifying approach in the importance that was given to weight and weight loss in establishing a diagnosis, or at least in the way the latter circulated on the ward (I never actually observed a formal procedure diagnosing anorexia, as these had always taken place before my observations).

It is worth noting the very specific position of anorexia as a diagnosis in the opposing stances taken by the different departments towards classification – because of its 'self-evident' nature, this opposition seemed to arise less than for other pathologies. However, it did come into play at another level of classification, namely the relationship between anorexia and eating disorders and, more specifically, the link between the medical diagnoses of anorexia and bulimia.

The responses I received when I announced I was taking a sociological approach 'to anorexia' can be compared term for term between the two establishments. In clinic C, the reaction was immediately different than in hospital H: 'Well, on top of it, "anorexia" is a bit difficult . . . . It doesn't really make sense, you have to work on eating disorders' [Psychiatrist, unobserved ward, clinic C, FJ]; 'You shouldn't separate anorexia and bulimia' [Psychiatrist, unobserved ward, clinic C, FJ].[6] This position can be explained by the psychoanalytical stance taken in the clinic, which underlines the 'continuous spectrum' between pure restrictive anorexia and bulimia:

> For the majority [of authors], there seems to be a continuous spectrum ranging from forms of pure restrictive anorexia to bulimia. This evolution is interesting because it shows the limits of the desire to establish individual, clearly defined, entities that can then be contrasted with others on the basis of criteria that make them mutually exclusive.
>
> (Agman *et al.* 1994, 4)

Again, we can see the links between stances towards the DSM (which was the target of the quotation above) and conceptions of the relationship between anorexia and bulimia. The spectrum must be continuous because the aetiology – which the DSM does not call upon – is the same: 'Pure restrictive anorexia, anorexia-bulimia, vomiting bulimia with normal weight, bulimia with heavy weight, all relate to a central issue of dependency' (Corcos and Jeammet 1993, 315).

Using or refusing the DSM and conceptions of the relationship between anorexia and bulimia were therefore key criteria in the positions of the two fields where I conducted my study – at one end, a centre of 'psychiatric psychiatry' (hospital H) and at the other end, a centre of 'psychoanalytically oriented psychiatry' (clinic C). This strategy of working in different fields for my investigation allowed me to place this initial form of variation in diagnosis at the heart of my data collection.

Working on the research and interview situations

The effects of the hospital-based nature of my investigative fields were obviously not limited to the influence of the diagnosis and of medical diagnostic practices on the construction of my corpora. The medical institution also represents a specific context, which is particularly relevant in terms of how the interview situation is defined. It is worth looking at this situation in more detail, particularly the fact that my sociological interviews were conducted in an environment where clinical interviews are used as a treatment method. I will focus here on the fieldwork I conducted in clinic C, for two reasons. First, just like there are classification struggles within the medical world, there are also what we could call *treatment struggles*. They oppose different theoretical and therapeutic options and are characterized by more or less open conflicts between different orientations. Within the context of such struggles, the clinical interview was an openly favoured therapeutic tool in clinic C. Moreover, my longest observation periods took place in this clinic. It therefore affords the most detailed opportunity for examining my research situation, by which I mean the situation of investigator and interviewees, as well as the links between the two.

Quasi-professional mastery of discourse about the self

When I asked for 'an interview' with patients at clinic C, it is highly likely that, at first, the term had medical or clinical resonance for them. The medical or nursing interview was the main therapeutic tool used in ward E, in addition to interviews with the department's psychologist or with researchers from outside the clinic, as well as family interviews. For these patients, the interview that I negotiated as a sociology student was often their umpteenth interview of the day, week or month. All these patients were therefore used to talking about themselves and their anorexia. Some of them, having been hospitalized several times or for long periods, had developed quasi-professional mastery of discourse about the self.

Talking about 'professional' mastery is possible because of the way the clinical interview both *shapes* and *teaches* appropriate ways of talking about the self.[7] The most self-evident form of this socialization to a particular kind of discourse about the self can be seen when doctors explicitly suggest an interpretation, for example by putting forward a hypothesis. In such cases, we see what could be called an 'education in discourse' insofar as it is clear that the doctor is teaching, or perhaps even imposing, a particular way of seeing things. A good illustration of this process can be seen in the following excerpts taken from clinical interviews in ward I between an intern and an anorexic patient:

INTERN: 'So you were sort of the "punching bag", as it were?'

PATIENT: 'Yes.'

INTERN: 'But you know, maybe that comes from you a little bit too, there are people who wouldn't be told that, or who wouldn't take it that way.'

[. . .]

INTERN: 'You'd like your parents to get back together?'

PATIENT: 'No, no, I know it's impossible.'

INTERN: 'But, at the same time, even though you know it's impossible, you could still want that.'

PATIENT: 'Well, yes, of course. But I know it's not possible.'

INTERN: 'And you understand that your illness has brought your parents closer together?'

PATIENT: 'Well, yes.'

[During the follow-up discussion, the intern said to the nurse: 'It's little things, but it's important: she recognized that she wanted her parents to get back together, that she'd suffered from their separation'.]

[FJ]

The efficiency of this education in discourse can be seen when the patients then take up the doctors' interpretations, as illustrated in the following example taken from the family interview in ward E with Christine and her mother:

PSYCHIATRIST: 'But sometimes there are family positions that aren't as simple as that, things relating to parents, that are passed down from generation to generation. You can have the sense that everyone's place is self-evident, you [the patient's mother] aren't used to thinking in those terms. Christine is the second child.'

MOTHER: 'Yes, but on my side, and on her father's too, they were only children.'

CHRISTINE [TO HER MOTHER]: 'You're the second though aren't you?'

PSYCHIATRIST: 'Yes and, in a sense, being an only child means that the second child is absent.'

[. . .]

DOCTOR [TO CHRISTINE]: 'But isn't it a position that resembles your father's, holding out in face of everything, the way he doesn't come here [to the family interviews]? In terms of his alcoholism? A way of behaving that replaces words . . . Don't you think that you're calling on your father, to make him see the damage caused by such a stance, where things are expressed through behaviour?'

CHRISTINE: 'I don't know.'

MOTHER: 'I'd say that that's what you're doing, to show him that it doesn't work.'

CHRISTINE: 'But who am I to do something like that? I'm not capable of doing that.'

DOCTOR: 'Anyway there's someone else who is there to say that to your father, and that's your mother.'

[FJ]

Initially, Christine took up the medical interpretation in the face of her mother's critical stance but afterwards it was her mother who emphasized a different medical interpretation in reaction to her daughter's dubitative remarks. We can also note that, in both cases, the 'education in discourse' provided by the doctor took place through one final explicit remark in the dialogue, reinforcing the interpretation suggested previously.

However, socialization doesn't only operate during these explicit educational moments.[8] Sometimes only a gesture, a physical posture or a moment of silence are used to show the patient that the way she is talking about herself is inadequate or that what she has said has further implications than she is able or wants to recognize. This is most apparent when the patient, already socialized to this sort of discourse about the self, interprets the signals from the doctor and changes her discourse accordingly as shown in the following examples:

[The patient explains that she was criticized a lot at school]

INTERN: 'Criticized for what?'

PATIENT: 'Well, for being thin.'

INTERN, as if to say 'we're not quite there yet': 'Oh?'

[The patient then corrected herself and said that she had been thinking since the last time and that her problems went back further than she thought.]

[FJ]

DOCTOR: 'And what are the reasons for these [bulimic] crises?'

PATIENT: 'The crises, I see them as, it's not just psychological, it's my body catching up [from the previous fasting period].'

DOCTOR: 'Well, I don't know about that, because it's not as if you're a slave to your body, is it?'

PATIENT: 'No, but it's also that I set up constraints, it's not time to eat so I don't eat and then [she trails off].'

DOCTOR, in a dubitative tone: 'Hmmm [silence].'

PATIENT: 'And maybe it's also a way of punishing myself, of degrading myself.'

[FJ]

Talking as treatment implies talking in a certain way. For an interview to be perceived as positive, for it to show that the patient is making 'progress', the patient has to appear 'sincere' and 'authentic', there must be 'no facade' and 'suffering'[9] has to be expressed [FJ]. This interview also revealed that a particular way of talking about the self had been internalized, the kind most likely to have therapeutic effects according to the doctors: 'Talking is simultaneously a therapeutic modality and evidence of a patient's progress' (Young 1995, 185). 'Sincerity' is therefore the product of an 'endeavour' engaged in by and with the patient, providing the latter becomes willing to 'hear' what is being said or suggested. The verb 'to hear' was constantly used when patients were evaluated: patients who were 'ready to hear' or who 'really heard' what was being said were ready to accept the suggested point of view about themselves and demonstrated this in the way they talked about themselves or by adopting practices ('behaviour') that were appropriate for the institution. Treatment through talking is therefore about a circular link between 'hearing' and 'talking'; in other words it consists in being socialized to a particular kind of discourse about the self and in internalizing what that discourse should be. The clinical interview can also serve as a preliminary course preparing patients for further outpatient therapy; the issue is training the patient in a particular kind of discourse predicated on taking the effects of the past on the present into account (in particular, the family or parents' past and the present of the pathology):

> [Intern on ward E, during a discussion between interns in the canteen] 'I think the aim on the ward is that the patients go to therapy afterwards.'
>
> [FJ]

> [Doctor, head of ward E, commenting on the clinical interview cited above in a review meeting] 'There was something really unapologetic when she said she wanted to sleep with her father, it was quite exceptional, usually that's not something that you say. The patients are quite something today! She's caught up in what she's trying to do here, it's good, she can leave, she doesn't need the institutions, the walls, all that anymore. When they're caught up in it like that, we can let them go . . . She gave us the full works this morning, all the ways in which we can talk about bulimia and anorexia, repeating a degrading position, the relationship to femininity, to being stained, to blood, to giving birth. She can go on and do some quality therapy now.'
>
> [FJ]

Working to define a different interview situation

The interviewees' situation (with the structural nature of the clinical interview and the resulting quasi-professional mastery of discourse about the self) strongly contributed to defining my research situation, which took place in a sphere where the interview is a frequent clinical practice and a therapeutic tool in configuring the patients' experiences and discourse. While analysing the research situation is a necessary stage in the sociological approach,[10] it seemed necessary for me to also *work* on this situation to make sure that it would not follow on too naturally from the specific kinds of interviews described above. This therefore required me to devise investigative strategies that positioned my sociological interviews in a different context, on as structural a level as possible.

When I negotiated the interviews with the patients, I insisted each time that I was not part of the clinic, that I was neither a clinician nor a psychologist but a sociologist, and so the interviews would be very different from the interviews they were used to. Of course, the weight of these words might seem insignificant compared with the fact that, practically speaking, the interviews took place in the clinic. However, to give further credence to what I told them, I also tried to conduct all research activities that required me to be visible in the nurse's station for long periods of time (for example, the prolonged observation sequences or my consultations of the nurses' handover notes) after I had already carried out the majority of my interviews. I began my work observing ward I, where I familiarized myself with psychiatric categories and practices, but I did not conduct any interviews there. Conversely, I chose not to observe any clinical interviews with patients that I had interviewed or was going to interview in ward E, even when I was offered the opportunity to do so, choosing instead to observe clinical interviews with other patients on the ward.

I also tried to use the conditions of my interviews to distance them from the clinical interview situation. While my age (around 25 at the time) and the fact I was a woman defined the interview situation in important ways, it did not necessarily set it apart from clinical interviews, which were sometimes conducted by female interns roughly the same age as me. However, when I was offered the possibility of conducting my interviews in the offices used for clinical interviews, I declined and instead systematically asked the patients if we could do the interview in their rooms. They always agreed. After negotiating the interview, and before it began, I suggested that they use the informal '*tu*' form of address with me (as opposed to the formal '*vous*'), saying 'the age gap isn't that big, is it?' This set our interactions apart from the clinical interviews, where the use of *vous* is standard practice. I am obviously not claiming that using *tu* allowed more 'authentic' speech, but I would suggest that it positioned the interview as being somewhat different from the medical situations to which they were accustomed.

I was also able to play on two features specific to my particular interview context. First, I was alone, whereas clinical or family interviews involve a member of the medical team (senior doctor or intern) and a nurse, as well as sometimes a student psychologist, a social worker or a secretary from the department. Second, the clearest difference lay in the fact that it was obvious that the interview was a one-off event rather than a series of encounters – as an outsider to the clinic, I would leave as soon as I had collated my corpus. For this reason, there was some chance that the patients would take seriously my assurance that I would not tell anyone about the interview, whether other interviewees or members of staff.

Finally, when I negotiated interviews with patients, I insisted several times that they would help 'me, in my work', that it would be very useful 'for me', etc. This definition of the interview situation contrasted starkly with the clinical interview, defined by its usefulness for the patient ('Talking makes things change, move forward') [Psychiatrist, family interview, FJ]. Defining the interview as useful for me as an investigator was no doubt what created the biggest difference with the clinical interview, where speech is defined as therapeutic. In this sense, my sociological interviews, both as defined in practice and as analysed afterwards, were as distanced as possible from any ritual of confession, in Foucault's sense of the term, in which: 'the authority who requires the confession, prescribes and appreciates it, and intervenes in order to judge, punish, forgive, console and reconcile', where 'the truth is corroborated by the obstacles and resistances it has had to surmount in order to be formulated' and where 'the expression alone, independently of its external consequences, produces intrinsic modifications in the person who articulates it' (Foucault 1978, 61–2).

My work aimed at defining the research situation did not stop after I gave my initial instruction ('Can you tell me about your experience' 'with anorexia' or 'in relation to anorexia'?). As mentioned above, with the example of using the informal *tu* form of address, rather than the formal *vous*, the situation was continually defined throughout the whole process. Giving an opening instruction (whatever that instruction) was already a way of marking the difference between the sociological interview and the clinical interview in which the obviously therapeutic aim makes any instruction unnecessary. During my interviews, I would ask follow-up questions or questions on certain themes. The latter were not necessarily different from those that might be asked by a doctor or a psychologist (about eating habits, school, sport, etc.). However, I rarely brought up questions about the interviewees' families and asked even less about their parents.[11] Moreover, following Howard Becker's particularly relevant methodological advice, I used the question 'How?' as a follow-up much more than 'Why?' (Becker 1998, 105–9) in order to give as much space as possible to narratives about practices and points of view.

By outlining these various strategies, I am not trying to suggest that, compared with medical interviews, my interviews were more neutral or that I enabled speech that was freer, more sincere or 'more authentic' to take up the medical term. As with any social situation, the things that are said during an interview are constructed by the situation in question. My efforts simply allowed me to try to define an interview situation that was neither univocal nor exclusively defined by its medical setting. The material I collated drew on the variations inherent to an interview situation that enabled multiple roles and modes of discourse. The patients clearly addressed different 'figures' when they spoke to me. Sometimes, I was a 'student in psychology' who was not part of the clinic but who was necessarily attached to that discipline. Sometimes, I was someone conducting an investigation 'the way journalists do'. At other times, I was simply a young woman close to their age whose position outside the medical sphere allowed a model of friendly conversation or even, as we will see, the use of strategies of distinction. And there were also times when they saw me as a sociologist asking questions about things they did, about their school work or about their parents' social status, etc. Thanks to the specific interview situation constructed, the patients spoke from *within* the medical sphere, but also talked about it and sometimes stretched outside its usual bounds: '[with a surprised tone] I ended up telling you things I've never said before!' [Emilie, C]. My aim was not to uncover 'new', previously 'unsaid' things – these would be seen as positive in psychology, for example, but their relevance for sociology is much less immediately obvious. I simply wanted to obtain material allowing a sociological approach to anorexia that could extend beyond the medical diagnosis while still taking into account the effects of the medically based nature of the field.

Identifying how discourse is shaped

The medically based nature of my field also had a particularly significant impact on the content of the interviews I conducted with hospitalized patients. I emphasized the socializing effects of the clinical interview earlier not only because of its influence on defining the interview situations but also because of its influence on how patients talk about themselves. The narrative of experiences that I requested during my interviews led the patients to call upon 'institutional biographies' (that is, 'discourse about the self officially requested by a representative of an institution') (Memmi 2003, 59)[12] – biographies that they had worked on and repeated over and over again during their clinical interviews. The patients' speech in their interviews was shaped by their trajectories through the medical institution, revealing just how efficiently they had been socialized to a particular kind of discourse about the self, as mentioned above. It was also shaped very differently depending on the corpus in question – the differences between clinic C and hospital H provided both proof of how discourse is constructed by the medical institution and a way of analysing its effects. It is therefore necessary to identify this shaping of discourse so that it can be taken into account in analysing the interviews and examined as an object of study in its own right.

Explicit repetition

First, it was possible to identify the effects of medical discourse when the interviewees actually mentioned it explicitly, either to take the same perspective or to distance themselves from it. There were many forms of such explicit references in the interviews. They illustrated, for example, knowledge of general medical discourse about anorexia or anorexics, which the interviewees then linked to their own personal experience: 'when you're anorexic', 'like all anorexics', 'anorexia is', 'being anorexic means', etc. The girls often drew links between their own experience and medical discourse in ways that implied complicity with me – 'I did lots of sport, *obviously*' or '*of course,* it started with a diet' – based on our presupposed shared knowledge about 'the whole shebang' of anorexia (to take up the expression used by Sophie [C]).

The interviewees' explicit use of medical discourse can be placed on a continuum between two positions: at one end, discrediting a previous personal point of view on the basis of a newly discovered medical perspective and, at the other end, discrediting the medical perspective on the basis of their personal point of view. Medical discourse was also sometimes presented as revealing the truth, after the event, about behaviour that had previously been understood in different terms:

> It's afterwards, with the psychotherapy, that I was able to understand bit by bit what I'd been looking for, but at the time, it was really just 'I thought I was fat, I had to lose some weight', there were no other questions.
>
> [Christine, C]

The interviewees also sometimes explained medical discourse in order to differentiate it from their own personal experiences. This sometimes related to specific points that did not call the discourse itself into question (e.g. 'It's true that often people say that anorexics are waiting to see their bones. But for me, it wasn't that, I mean, yes, I weighed myself every day and it was seeing the number [on the scales] going down' [Julie, H]). In other cases, more radically, it related to the very principles of medical discourse (e.g. 'They called meetings with my parents, family things, they tried to see if there was a problem. They didn't manage to find it, you know' [Sidonie, H]). When the interviewees distanced themselves from medical discourse, they discussed it in explicit detail. Such references can help to identify the kinds of discourse these patients had heard from the institution:

> [Tone of someone reciting a lesson] Scared of growing up, scared of becoming a woman. I've heard that so many times, it did my head in. Yeah, ok, I don't like curves, I don't find a woman with curves pretty, but that's not because I don't want to grow up! Yeah, ok, I'm close to my parents, but straightaway they infer, a question I'll always remember, did my mum breastfeed me?!
>
> [Sidonie, H]

> Well, there's the, pfff, the easy stereotype that anorexia is linked to the mother. That everything is linked to the relationship you have with your mother. That bugs me a bit. The idea that, pfff [trails off]. For example, there, in the family interview, talking about my father's alcoholism, I really think it's a bit too easy.
>
> [Christine, C]

Finally, still more explicitly than implicitly, the interviewees sometimes used medical vocabulary to refer to their own practices. In these cases, medical discourse served as a tool for framing past practices in terms of medical categories, for example using the term 'hyperactivity' to refer to practices at school and in sports, talking about 'rituals' in reference to eating habits or saying they had a feeling of 'all-powerfulness' when discussing their relationship towards action and the world. This set of categories was present in the language used by the doctors and nurses I observed, as well as in the interviews I conducted.

Specific shaping of discourse

As well as taking up medical discourse in explicit fashions, the interviewees also called upon it in more internalized forms. This was clear, for example, in the topics they selected as being relevant for talking about anorexia (which I never brought up myself) and in how they explained anorexia. In this respect, the variations resulting from the different orientations of the departments in question became patently obvious. Certain topics were more present in the interviews in clinic C, for example the relationship to femininity or the question of family history (the relationship with the mother and, more rarely, the father, which reflects the more recent interest shown by psychoanalysis in the latter). My interviews were full of examples echoing the medical discourse and categories that I observed *in situ* in clinic C, which can all be related to the clinic's particular position in the space of discourse about anorexia (that is, the psychoanalytical end of the spectrum). Some of these same topics also appeared in the interviews I conducted in hospital H, particularly among patients who were also being treated by psychotherapists of psychoanalytical orientation. However, relatively speaking, other topics were more present in the corpus collated in hospital H, such as good and bad eating habits (treatment at hospital H used the cognitive–behavioural approach, which insists on this aspect). The interviews I conducted in each institution were therefore marked by this variation, as the patients' discourse had been shaped in different ways by the theoretical and therapeutic orientations of the institution.

Multiple shaping of discourse

However, in conclusion, it is also important to note that, while the interviews did have all the hallmarks of their specific medical context, none of them were shaped by one single point of view. The girls I interviewed as patients had all been in contact with different points of view during their medical trajectories, which had sometimes included hospitalizations in various departments, encounters with several points of view within the same department or treatment with therapists outside the hospital setting. It was therefore extremely rare to identify one single medical establishment that had shaped how they talked about themselves and their anorexia. Priscille's case offered a good example of this. I met her in clinic C, but she had previously been hospitalized in a department where the main approach was behavioural. Her discourse had therefore been medically shaped in different ways and included a mixture of analytical and behavioural points of view, along with genetic explanations. In her interview, she therefore pieced together all these different perspectives. While the interviewees' medically shaped discourse was more often internalized than explicitly discussed, this did not prevent them from taking a certain distance from medical perspectives, nor did it prevent them from being aware of, and sometimes explicitly commenting on, the fact that their way of taking about things had been shaped in this way.

Like anything said in an interview context, the discourse of the patients I interviewed was constructed by the situation in which the exchange took place. There is no sense in dreaming of a pure form of interview with no external influences afforded by some magical methodology. However, it makes no more sense to deplore the fact that this is impossible. The medically based nature of my research actually presented a substantial advantage – by conducting my investigation in this context, I was able to identify precisely, if not exhaustively, important agents involved in shaping what my interviewees had to say and how they said it. I not only obtained information about what shaped their discourse, my observations of clinical interviews allowed me to observe some of the processes through which this took place. In the following chapters, the effects of this medical shaping of discourse will therefore be taken into account and analysed when it proves relevant.

Opening the door to sociology

When it comes to taking into account the effects of the medically based nature of my research fields, it is also worth returning to what enabled this – namely the fact that both institutions agreed to my investigation. In my introduction, I emphasized the fact that applying a sociological point of view to a 'foreign object', lying outside the usual remit of sociology, was a wager. This assertion now requires qualifying to some extent. Within the medical perspective on anorexia, while sociology itself is perhaps excluded, social issues are given a certain place and this is best evidenced by the fact that the different departments accepted my presence as an interviewer or as both interviewer and observer in hospital H and clinic C. More specifically, the medical approach *ascribes a very particular place* to social issues. This can be seen in action, first, in the way I was granted or denied access to institutions as a sociology student and, second, in the different perceptions of the reasons behind my presence and of its relevance. By analysing my field access negotiations, I can draw up something that we could call a 'sociology of the place of sociology' within discourse on anorexia. Specifically, this entails asking and answering the following questions: What place is given to social issues in medical and psychological discourse? What was my place as an investigator in the medical sphere? And finally, how could I define the potential 'object' of a sociological approach to anorexia by looking outside these commonly prescribed parameters?

The weight of social issues

First it is important to note how 'social issues' seem to weigh upon discourse about anorexia. Indeed, for many reasons, discourse about anorexia is strongly encouraged to make room for this aspect, if only to refute it or take distance from it. In this context, two French psychiatrists published a book in 1995 that was entirely devoted to the 'weight of culture' in anorexia and bulimia, in the '*Medicine and Psychotherapy*' collection published by Masson (Guillemot and Laxenaire 1995). The 'weight' in question in the book was also the weight of 'culture' on medicine itself. Certain hypotheses could explain this prevailing pressure to include social issues. Of course, each stance within the range of discourses about anorexia has a (historically constructed) propensity to address social issues. Aside from this, though, it is also worth noting that the existence and development of epidemiology has encouraged psychological and medical publications to discuss the specific features they identify as being involved in the recruitment of the mental pathologies they examine.

Where anorexia is concerned, however, two more specific channels encouraging the inclusion of social issues can also be identified. First, in France, there is the effect of what we could call the 'imported weight' of American and British feminism. In the United States and in Great Britain, the feminist approach to anorexia is much more widespread than in France, to the extent that American medical-summary works about anorexia mention feminist texts, which is not the case in France.[13] French feminism has not played the same role by any stretch of the imagination, but the circulation of ideas between the United States and France has meant that the role played by feminism is mentioned in certain French publications providing overviews on the topic. This imported weight of American or British feminism also appears in the references made to these perspectives in French medical or psychological texts that approve, refute or discredit feminist approaches. While there are no specific institutions in France that support the feminist approach to anorexia, this does not mean that it does not weigh upon medical discourse on the subject through echoes of the situation in the United States, where its importance is much greater. One might also reasonably suggest that, in this respect, the French media plays an important role in importing the issue.

The second factor encouraging the inclusion of social issues is relatively specific to anorexia and consists in the existence of a veritable media aetiology. While the latter may well borrow from feminist arguments, it nonetheless exists almost completely autonomously. Like with other pathologies, the media plays its usual role in passing on medical discourse to the general public, particularly with a view to prevention. However, in the case of anorexia, the articles, special reports and programmes on the topic go far beyond this. Anorexia is specific in this respect not because of its presence in women's magazines and on television programmes, but rather because of the existence of a veritable media *theory* of anorexia. This theory is in itself the subject of internal debate within the media and raises the question of the fashion industry's responsibility in imposing a pathological model of thinness.[14] Certain women's fashion and society magazines with feminist leanings, such as the weekly *Elle* or monthly *Marie-Claire,* have taken up some aspects of these arguments – particularly, the objectification of women's bodies – by raising more specifically the question of the role of models in imposing an ideal body-type defined as dangerous. For example, in November 1996, the title on the front page of the French edition of *Elle* read: 'Warning! Danger! Stick-thin models: how skinny is too skinny?' The introduction to the report talked about:

> the rising controversy surrounding the catwalk and its excessively skinny super-models. Hollow hips, visible ribs and empty stares: are the canons of fashion turning away from curvy women and going for anorexics instead? Read our report including testimonials by designers and photographers who discuss the reasons behind this new fad as well as its dangers.
>
> (Werner and Dupuis 1996, 78)

This report was emblematic of many articles that are published on the topic in women's magazines. Two themes overlapped in the piece. On the one hand, the question of whether the models were anorexic or not (in some articles, modelling agencies were accused of having recruited models 'on the doorstep of a clinic for anorexics') and, on the other hand, the pathogenic nature of imposing such a model of femininity. The report began with a case study, taking the example of a certain Juliette whose 'role-model [wa]s Kate Moss' (the famous super-model known at the time for her extreme thinness) and who covered her bedroom walls with photos of models. It concluded on the following note: 'Juliette is a fashion victim who doesn't realize that she's sinking into anorexia'. What is most striking is the way these issues are broached within the fashion industry itself. The investigation in *Elle* was conducted with photographers (Jean-Loup Sieff) and major fashion designers (such as Corinne Cobson, Karl Lagerfeld and Azzedine Alaïa). The article was illustrated with excerpts from the interviews with these figures who came out for or against the trend of stick-thin models and the argument that this had an influence on anorexia. The medical side of things was also present, although much less visibly, in the shape of a brief quotation by Philippe Jeammet (which was actually used to say the exact opposite of its original meaning, as the journalist claimed Jeammet 'confirmed' something he was actually refuting):

> This [the fashion of stick-thin models] could perhaps explain the rise in eating disorders that doctors and psychologists have noticed over the past twenty years. 'The problem is very much in place', confirms Professor Jeammet, specialist in anorexia in France, on an alarmist note. 'The influence of fashion and the media in this situation should not be overestimated. Eating disorders have much deeper causes.'

The media theory of anorexia therefore brings social issues to bear upon medical discourse, leaving the latter forced to take a stance on a question that it may well find illegitimate. While it is more frequent to see the media fulfilling its more traditional role of passing on medical categories, this particular situation in which it imposes the issue itself is nonetheless significant enough to be noteworthy.

The weight of the media theory within the medical sphere can also be seen in the fact that my presence in the medical departments where I conducted my research was sometimes linked to this social aetiology. During one discussion

I observed between a psychologist and a nurse on ward I, the nurse referred to this kind of 'social factor':

> 'Yes anorexia doesn't really give rise to empathy, it's pretty unbelievable. And I think that there's also some jealousy because we're in a society [she looks at me] where a lot of value is placed on being slim and these girls, they manage it, you know' . . . . She goes on to talk about 'factors' like skinny models and what she calls the 'Spice Girls' Effect' ('little girls today don't have the time to grow up anymore and they worry about dieting very early').
>
> [FJ]

When I was negotiating field access, a range of different doctors asked me the same question, albeit formulated in different ways: 'What could possibly interest a sociologist in anorexia?' In my answers, I referred to the sociological tradition of studying certain themes, like eating practices, the relationship to the body, gender and the long-standing sociological interest in the question of the normal and the pathological. I never brought up the social question of fashion models or the current norm of thinness. From my point of view, it was a question of introducing myself in terms that drew a distinction between social issues and sociological issues; I could not content myself with just taking up the media theory. However, for some of the people I spoke to, this stance meant that I was not positioning my research in that particular vein and was therefore capable of understanding the 'deeper' issues of anorexia, perhaps even of taking on board their point of view. This may well have been an important factor in them accepting my presence and agreeing to my interviews with patients. Conversely, I never had to answer such a question when I negotiated the interviews with the patients and, for some of my respondents, my position as a sociologist implied that I necessarily agreed with the media theory. As we saw above, at certain moments of the interviews, the interviewees referred to our shared knowledge of medical discourse and they sometimes also mentioned the media theory in the same way:

> And of course it's [anorexia] also caused by the media. You see it in magazines, there's not a single magazine that doesn't talk about dieting now! It's becoming an obsession, all the women you see in magazines, they're all half anorexic.
>
> [Emilie, C]

The media theory was one of the rare explanations for anorexia that circulated in the interviews I conducted in school S. These interviews, as mentioned previously, focused broadly on 'eating habits', so spontaneous references to anorexia were in themselves proof of the circulation of the diagnosis: 'Also, there's the whole image of women you see in magazines they're super skinny and everything . . . the models who are anorexic and everything' [Juliette, S]. It is worth noting that the term 'anorexia' was much less recurrent than 'anorexic' which has become an almost everyday category.[15]

If anthropologist Tanya Marie Luhrmann is right in saying that 'Psychiatric knowledge seeps into popular culture like the dye from a red shirt in hot water' (2000, 20) then an important feature of the diagnosis of anorexia (and, more broadly, eating disorders) should be noted: the media (and, more specifically, women's magazines) do not only intervene by channelling information, they also aim to provide specific aetiological information on the subject. Social issues therefore weigh on medical discourse to some extent. This then raises the question of the concrete ways in which this happens.

Including social aspects

In very broad terms, social issues tend to be included in medical and psychological analyses in one of two ways. In the first, social aspects are included as a set of specific phenomena that have to be incorporated into the framework of a multifactorial approach. Social issues are seen as one factor among others that can explain, trigger or modify forms of anorexia. The DSM offers an interesting example in this regard. In the DSM-III-R, the text following the outline of diagnostic criteria for anorexia nervosa lists a certain number of themes: 'Associated features', 'Age of onset', 'Sex ratio', 'Prevalence', 'Course', 'Impairment', 'Complications', 'Familial pattern', etc. through to the 'differential diagnosis' (American Psychiatric Association 1987, 66). In the DSM-IV, another section was added entitled 'Specific culture, age, and gender features' that began with the following sentence: 'Anorexia Nervosa appears to be far more prevalent in industrialized societies, in which there is an abundance of food and in which, especially for females, being considered attractive is linked to being thin' (American Psychiatric Association 1994, 542). This official mention of 'cultural factors' was explained in the introduction to the manual:

> Evidence . . . suggests that the symptoms and course of a number of DSM-IV disorders are influenced by cultural and ethnic factors. To facilitate its application to individuals from diverse cultural and ethnic settings, the DSM-IV includes a new section in the text to cover culture-related features.
>
> (American Psychiatric Association 1994, xxiv)

The inclusion of these 'culture-related features' corresponds to a model in which socio-cultural issues act as one specific feature, and potentially one specific distinct factor, among a set of others that all interact together. In medical texts, social issues tend to be included on a similar mode: they are added into the analysis as a non-medical component, a factor that interacts with other kinds of factors (biological or psychological, for example).

This mode of inclusion of social issues was translated into practical terms when I was accepted in the field as an investigator. My request meant asking for 'space' to be given to social issues; it meant asking to be included in the medical sphere, in one form or another, as someone from outside that sphere. When I negotiated the principle of interviewing patients in hospital H, the doctor I met told me that she was interested in my potential work on the 'social aspects' of anorexia. When the head of ward E in clinic C advised me to introduce myself and my position in a department meeting, he also framed this in terms of 'complementary' approaches: 'You also have to specify [to the team] that the sociological approach does not claim to encroach on other approaches, but that it's a different point of view, that could be complementary and enriching' [FJ]. In practice, accepting my presence meant giving space to social issues, but a different space from that given to other approaches; it was potentially complementary but nonetheless dependent on pre-established medical divisions of fields of relevance.

There is also a second way in which social issues can be included in medical and psychological approaches to anorexia. Rather than being considered as a specific, separate kind of phenomenon, they are dealt with on the same scientific register used to describe the individual psychopathology. This occurs in certain psychoanalytical approaches for example. In this case, social aspects are no longer seen as one potential pathological factor, among others, that could lead to a mental disorder. Instead, they are directly pathologized within a single all-encompassing approach. One 'unifactorial' approach is applied to all phenomena and that includes elements that are defined as 'social'. An example of such an approach can be seen in the following text:

> Epidemiological variations can be explained in part by sociological data, which, while they are diverse, correspond to the increasing importance placed on narcissistic valorization to the detriment of relationships with others. The quality of the latter has changed considerably due to prevalent narcissistic involvement. The anticipated risk of relationships tends to generate controlling, or even domineering, behaviour, rather than acceptance of an exchange, of a possible source of loss. . . . C. Westhal has clearly denounced this evolution towards a 'civilisation of the self' . . . . The congruence between the evolution in women's place in society (more active, more aggressive, more masculine) and the ideal of thinness is fairly remarkable.
>
> (Corcos and Jeammet 1993, 323–4)

The 'social' elements in question – which are even designated as 'sociological' in this text – are therefore taken on board by the explanatory model in question, in this instance psychoanalysis, but as a subordinate question. Social issues are psychoanalysed, so to speak, insofar as the psychopathological register is applied to society the same way it would be applied to individual cases. We can see very clearly how the two approaches differ: on the one hand, social issues are viewed as external explanatory factors that are incorporated as they stand, on the other, they are seen as a set of phenomena that are actually incorporated into psychoanalysis.

The way my research situation and presence in the medical field were defined sometimes gave rise to the latter form of integration. In clinic C, my presence and choice of topic were sometimes reinterpreted from a psychological or even psychoanalytical standpoint. During my first meeting with the head of ward E, he suggested: 'You should think about what really interests you in the subject, about why you're interested in this. Maybe you've come close to anorexia yourself [trails off]' [FJ]. He brought this theme up again during our second meeting, also part of my negotiation of field access: 'You have to find out what you're looking for, you can't be neutral, because it affects you, anorexia, you're a woman. It would be good to write a chapter about that, but anyway, I'm not supervising your research' [FJ]. Considered from this perspective, my presence as a sociologist could not be justified solely by the reasons I gave (which were inherent to sociology as a discipline) – it necessarily had to be explained by elements relating to my personal trajectory and individual psychology. A psychologist from the clinic also asked me 'why' I had chosen to work on anorexia, immediately continuing with a set of questions that indicated the kind of answer she was looking for: 'Have you stopped eating since you've been working on anorexia? Because the patients reflect something very powerful within ourselves' [FJ]. In the same way that social issues can be psychoanalysed, as seen above, in this case my sociological investigation was written into the psychological space through the issue of my own psychology.

Keeping sociology firmly in its place

These two ways of including social aspects in medical approaches, as identified above, nonetheless share one common feature: while they both incorporate social issues, they also assign them a very specific place. In both cases, social questions are positioned outside a (medical or psychoanalytical) *core* that represents a form of 'no-entry' zone for sociology, keeping sociology firmly in its place.

In terms of approaches that include 'social factors', Robert Barrett's analysis of the 'bio-psycho-social' model is worth applying here. Barrett shows that this model reduces social aspects to nothing more than context, to a purely external effect compared with the precedence given to the biological point of view:

> At the same time that they encompass a range of perspectives, bio-psycho-social theories maintain medical dominance by giving precedence to biological knowledge . . . . When the model is represented diagrammatically as a set of concentric circles or squares . . . , biology occupies the innermost core, with successively peripheral zones designated psychological, interpersonal, social, and cultural . . . . The ideas that inform these representations are reflected in the language of bio-psycho-social psychiatry. The adjective 'biological' is usually associated with nouns such as 'roots', 'basis', 'substrate', or 'core', whereas 'cultural' usually refers to 'overlay' . . . . If [psychosocial factors] are attributed any influence at all, it is the weak influence of a secondary factor that does not cause the illness.
>
> (Barrett 1996, 244–5)

In this sense, social aspects are included through their exclusion not only from the biological core but also from the layers closest to that core (that is, the psychological and interpersonal).

This exclusion from the medical core can be seen at work in one case when I was refused field access. The negotiation took place with a professor in psychiatry, head of the hospital department and a firm proponent of including socio-cultural aspects in approaches to eating disorders. His refusal of my request for field access was fairly fierce, but this was less salient than the arguments he used to refute the legitimacy of my request:

> 'There are sociological studies on eating habits, so there are sociological studies on "anorexia". Sociology cannot focus on the pathology. . . . . It's as if a baker came to see me and said "I'd like to consider anorexia in terms of the bakery trade". Anorexia in terms of the bakery trade, it exists and it's easy: they don't eat bread. The bakery trade is a technique, I don't see the difference with sociology, where the methodology lacks rigour, but anyway, that's another problem . . . . It is absolutely out of the question for you to see any patients. What could you possibly say about their direct speech that you wouldn't have in indirect speech [of doctors about the patients]? . . . . Your topic is completely inappropriate, for sociology.'
>
> [FJ]

Aside from the more general question of the legitimacy of sociology as a discipline, the main problem was clearly that I wanted to place my research in a medical setting, that I intended to work on a 'pathology', that my aim was to conduct interviews to obtain 'direct' speech rather than 'indirect' (medical) speech and that I was not going to content myself with working on eating habits or bodies but was going to focus on 'anorexia' itself, which I had no more legitimacy to address than a 'baker' (a snipe that illustrated both contempt for a particular social class and for a particular discipline). This refusal of access to the field offers a practical illustration of Robert Barrett's analysis. Social aspects can be included provided they remain external and contextual; in their rightful place, in other words.

It should also be noted that this sort of refusal of field access cannot be linked to a specific 'medical' position as such. My investigation was accepted in hospital H, which also took a 'multifactorial' approach to the inclusion of social factors, but was refused by the head of one of the psychoanalytically oriented wards in clinic C for reasons very similar to those cited above:

> 'You have to know what you're doing, you're doing sociological work, not clinical work. And sociological work, I see it like [this], you have to work on discourse around anorexia, everything that's written about anorexia, the image of anorexia in the modern world. It seems difficult to me to bring you in [to the ward], these are very private moments and you aren't a clinician. . . . Sociology, anyway, isn't clinical. . . . I don't want any voyeurs on my ward, to put it bluntly. . . . And sociology can't do just anything, sociology studies social facts, it's not clinical, sociology has to stay in its place.'
>
> [FJ]

Again, it is striking that in the arguments used, sociology was assigned a specific 'place' that necessarily lay outside the 'clinical' object: sociology can work on 'discourse' and representations 'around' anorexia but as soon as it tries to come any closer, it necessarily becomes 'voyeurism'. The self-evident statement that 'sociology isn't clinical', taken up several times in this particular negotiation, has all the weight of tautology and its truth-value cannot be questioned. At the same time, it operates on a presupposition that *can* be questioned and that is based on assumptions which are taken for granted, namely that only a clinical point of view – that is to say, a point of view that is defined as therapeutic, both in terms of disciplinary affiliation and in practice – can be applied to a clinical object. Moreover, from this point of view, 'social facts', which are the only legitimate object for sociological study, exist in and of themselves, independently of the approach that constructs them: they consist in an order of phenomena with an a priori definition that does not include anorexia.

Of course, this active marginalization of the sociological point of view cannot be seen as the only reason I was refused field access: the desire to protect patients, not to 'throw them to the lions' with someone from outside the medical sphere ('You'll have to get the patients' agreement for the interviews, they're not cattle', said one doctor after having agreed to the interviews on principle) is of course a perfectly legitimate reason for refusing. However, the people I spoke to did not focus on these issues when they did refuse; instead, they emphasized definitions of the medical sphere and of sociology and its rightful place.

The desire of doctors to keep sociology firmly in its place is, of course, perfectly logical: sociologists themselves often do not appreciate psychological or genetic approaches to explaining social stratification or educational inequalities, for example. However, throughout my investigation and in the various reactions to my stated research topic (including on the part of sociologists), it was clear that the idea that a sociological approach could only be applied to the topics socially reserved for that discipline extended far beyond doctors. The following excerpt from an interview with one of the teachers in the school at clinic C offers a good illustration of this. Before I began recording, he had already stated that he didn't really understand what I wanted to do, that anorexia '[wa]sn't a sociological object'.

MD: 'Well, the construction of this [research] object, or all my work constructing it, aims to show that it is. I mean, generally speaking, I don't know if the object is sociological in itself but the idea is to see what applying a sociological point of view can do: Does it bring anything to knowledge about the object? Does it bring anything to sociology itself, confronting it with objects, which, at first sight, don't belong to it, which, socially speaking, don't belong to it. So, there's that ambition to some extent, i.e. 'Can the sociological point of view be applied to an object like that?'

TEACHER: 'And what's the object? In this case?'

MD: 'So, in this case, it's not constructed yet, its construction is in construction! But it would be anorexia, so, for example, seen as a set of practices. Eating practices, school practices, sports practices, bodily practices, etc. etc. So, I'm just at the start, you know, and it's [pauses] how can I put it? It's not going to be easy. . . . You're sceptical?'

T: 'Oh yes!'

MD: 'It's true that [trails off].'

T: 'Because, right [pauses], anorexia is a [pauses] psychopathological approach, I'd say it's something that brings a psychopathology into play. So, right, constructing an object might be [pauses], well, I don't see any other links than linking the psychopathological approach with social behaviour, but, so, [pauses] how is it a social practice? Yes [pauses] well, so [trails off].'

Once again, in this exchange, which was initially a refusal to give me an interview (which did take place in the end), the issue at stake was the fact that the sociological approach could only be external to an object that 'brought into play a psychopathology'. This appeared very clearly when my definition in terms of 'an approach' was not accepted and was immediately retranslated in terms of the object itself: 'Anorexia is a [pauses] psychopathological approach, I'd say, it's something that brings a psychopathology into play'. For this teacher, anorexia was not a social fact either and this object-based definition took precedence over any approach-based definition.

When social questions are considered as one factor among others, they can therefore be included – and yet at the same time excluded – from the medical core. But as some of the interview and field journal excerpts quoted above have already shown, the inclusion of social issues can produce similar effects when a psychopathologically oriented approach is adopted: in these cases, the psyche or individual psychopathology is taken as constituting the truth of social elements, which also results in social issues being excluded from the theoretical and practical core at hand.

Anne Guillemot and Michel Laxenaire's book entitled *Anorexie Mentale et Boulimie. Le Poids de la Culture* [*Anorexia Nervosa and Bulimia. The Weight of Culture*] offers a good example of this. The first chapters are devoted to analysing socio-cultural factors (with, in particular, a chapter on 'Narcissistic society', the kind of psychoanalysing of social issues mentioned above). Chapter nineteen then goes on to outline 'the main psychoanalytical hypotheses concerning eating disorders', and the final chapters and conclusion are devoted to summarizing socio-cultural and individual psychological factors as follows:

> How can the preceding psychopathological hypotheses be linked with socio-genetic approaches? First, by noting that a society like ours can only encourage narcissistic pathologies. Moreover, changes in society and family structures tend to encourage both the appearance and the expression of narcissistic vulnerability, in particular through parents' overinvestment in their children. The prevailing aesthetic ideal of thinness in our society should also be mentioned . . . . Sociocultural effects also play a role in issues of dependency, which is at the heart of the psychopathology of anorexia . . . . Indeed,

> our society encourages dependency on several levels. As many different consumer products are made available, individual happiness becomes dependent on the possibility of acquiring them . . . . Furthermore, the adolescent years now last longer and, with them, financial dependency on parents . . . Finally, the extension of social welfare does not contribute to promoting the autonomy of individuals, who are made dependent upon the State and society . . . . Our society that praises and encourages dependency may well, in the end, make things much harder for those who already have trouble being autonomous.
>
> (Guillemot and Laxenaire 1995, 115)

Setting aside the normative aspects to this argument (the blame ascribed to 'parents' overinvestment', the elitist denunciation of 'consumer society' or the accusation levied against social welfare as encouraging dependent behaviour), it is interesting to see that the reasoning at work is based on a process that necessarily places individual psychopathology at the heart of eating disorders, as their ultimate explanation ('those who already have trouble being autonomous'). According to this reading, society is just an external and contingent factor framing people's 'speech' and that speech must necessarily be must be drawn out and purified of everything that is nothing more than a social illusion:

> The role of sociological [= social] trends likely to influence the emergence of these disorders remains subject to much debate. They should not be artificially separated from other factors, in particular individual psychological factors . . . . Our society provides a narcissistic model, modifies eating habits, extends and aggravates dependency and gives women, the main 'candidates' for eating disorders, an uncomfortable place and role . . . . The fact remains that a symptom is always a way of communicating. Anorexics and bulimics use food-language as a way of addressing others. The form the message takes is linked to the sociocultural context in which it is delivered. Beyond this aspect, what matters is that the call is heard. It is up to the psychiatrist to discern, behind eating disorders which are so widespread, the specificities of a particular individual. It is then up to the psychotherapist to bring out the subject's true speech rather that the discourse promoted by society.
>
> (Guillemot and Laxenaire 1995, 128–9)

These final sentences of the book are very telling. Anorexia is presented as a language that is blurred by social elements, which give it a social form. Psychoanalysis therefore has to rid the 'subject's speech' of the residues of these social aspects.

In his 'sociohistoric psychoanalysis',[16] Jacques Maître (2000) is highly critical of Guillemot and Laxenaire's book, which he charges with not having sufficiently managed to rid itself of these residues:

> As a result, even doctors have begun insisting on the cultural dimension [footnote: see for example A. Guillemot and M. Laxenaire]. However, any discussion about anorexia nervosa limits its scope if it begins by defining the

> syndrome on the basis of the desire asserted by many modern anorectics to shape themselves to be thin.
>
> (Maître 2000, 24)

His conclusion reasserts the need to find a 'deeper meaning', beyond social issues:

> My approach remains directed by its initial channel: Catholic female affective mysticism from the twelfth century to today. It suggests sociocultural echoes, such as asceticism based on mind/body dualism, as well as very varied models in circulation and the emergence of an unconscious source that wells up until it becomes a highly ramified delta. . . . The possibilities for psychoanalysis to take on board the deep meanings of anorectic discourse, beyond socially accepted arguments, might also benefit from this.
>
> (Maître 2000, 189–90)

Once again, despite the desire to link together sociology and psychoanalysis, society only provides 'socially acceptable arguments'. And indeed, in this perspective, Maître returns several times in his book to the need not to 'define the syndrome on the basis of the desire asserted by many modern anorectics to shape themselves to be thin' (Maître 2000, 51) but on the basis of:

> the refusal to accept the female characteristic of the transmission of life [footnote: 'from as early as 1940, certain psychoanalysts identified the anxiety of becoming a mother one day as the *core* of anorexia'] and the ill-treatment of one's own body, analogous to the ill-treatment of a baby; the anorectic breaks the corporal chain of female lineage by denying the needs that originally characterized her total dependence on her mother's care.
>
> (Maître 2000, 8–9, emphasis added)

In this way, even though the psychoanalytical reference is supposed to avoid positing any 'chronological or anthropological universality, or a model transcending the ideological modulations brought to light in socio-history' (188), socio-history nonetheless only provides 'modulations' that must be surpassed. The 'core', already mentioned in the note on page 8, lies elsewhere:

> The common features [of mystics and patients] do not necessarily result from a pathology . . . . We can ask a broader question, taking into account the diverse historical realizations of anorectic ways of being in the world, the *core* of which is defined on the basis of psychoanalytical considerations.
>
> (8, emphasis added)

From this perspective, we ultimately return to a model that is the equivalent of the one mentioned previously with multifactorial approaches: social issues, sociologists and socio-historical concerns are defined as lying outside a central core that escapes them, to which they are necessarily subordinate and that keeps them firmly in their place.

'And couldn't we imagine that psychopathology might include sociology and anthropology?' asked a psychiatrist in clinic C during my fieldwork [FJ]. This is certainly possible and, as we have just seen, certain approaches do try to imagine this. In the present study, however, I try to 'imagine' something different and I do not draw on the different forms of psychopathology as a tool. This was not a point of principle or a stance taken against the relatively frequent practice in sociology of using psychoanalysis, for example, to study certain objects. Rather, it was an *ad hoc* attempt at giving the sociological approach a chance, without limiting it from the outset to a purely contextualizing approach and without keeping it 'in its place' by working on facts that are immediately defined by their 'social' nature. My aim was not to look at the 'place of social issues' – thereby considering social questions in addition to other factors – but rather to throw the door wide open to sociology, to make it inherent to my research in both its framework and application. And my fieldwork, with the methodological stakes outlined above, allowed me to do just that.

Notes

1 For a presentation of the DSM along with an analysis of how it is elaborated and the issues at stake in the changes from one version to the next, see, e.g.: Kirk and Hutchins (1992, 1997), Young (1995), Ehrenberg (1998) and Ehrenberg and Lovell (2001).
2 The DMS-V came out in 2013, but, given that it refers to diagnostic realities which post-date my field research, I will not discuss it here.
3 More precisely, it was initially only retained in its descriptive sense. On this subject, see Ehrenberg (1998, 170).
4 According to Allan Young, the DSM-IV as a whole became more 'biologized' by suggesting a more unified and biological conception of mental disorders (1995, 287–90).
5 For an example of psychoanalytical critiques of the DSM in cases of eating disorders, see Corcos and Jeammet (1993, 312–15). On the social science analysis of struggles between different segments of the American psychiatric community on the question of the DSM, see Young (1995, 99–101), Ehrenberg (1998, 162–72) and Ehrenberg and Lovell (2001, 9–39 and 101–26).
6 My investigative focus on anorexia therefore corresponded more to the point of view of hospital H than of clinic C. However, I had defined my project before having any contact with the psychiatry of anorexia. Above and beyond common knowledge of anorexia, my only source of information when I began my study was the media, in which, until recently, anorexia had been much more visible than bulimia. It is therefore probable that this media stance informed how I formulated my project. The relatively broad social dissemination and circulation of the diagnosis beyond the confines of psychiatry is, in fact, a specific feature of the subject in question (and I will come back to this).
7 In their analysis of psychiatric institutions, Anselm Strauss and his team mention the case of patients who begin speaking in a 'quasi-professional tongue' when presenting their mental illness as a psychological problem linked to their personal life story (Strauss *et al.* 1964, 264).
8 For an analysis of 'education courses' for schizophrenics (following the model of workshops or group therapy), see Barrett (1996, ch 9), who highlights the negotiation between patients and staff around the definition of schizophrenia, culminating in patients expressing 'acceptable descriptions' in keeping with medical categories (260).

9 On the importance of the expression of the patient's 'suffering' for hospital staff, see Barrett (1996, 262–5): 'Descriptions of suffering were elicited from patients and then amplified by the education programme. . . . Throughout the course, the staff directed their empathy towards such expressions of suffering and thereby encouraged and reinforced them. . . . The staff expected that patients should suffer from their schizophrenia because suffering established a proper channel for empathy. Whereas it was inappropriate for the staff to empathize with feelings of love towards Lucifer's mistress . . . they *could* direct their empathy onto the suffering patient'.

10 On the importance of analysing the research relationship and the interview situation, see Beaud and Weber (1997, 255–62).

11 The interviewees were therefore not specifically questioned about their parents' practices, and it should be noted that I did not include the parents themselves in my investigation. It is true that sociology often tries to show the influence of family practices and configurations on behaviour. In the case of anorexia, however, this influence is often mentioned in the discourse of both specialists and laymen. It therefore seemed to me that the sociological approach to this particular object could consist, at least at first, in setting this dimension aside and seeing what analysis was possible without involving it directly.

12 Dominique Memmi borrows this notion from Claude Pennetier and Bernard Pudal. Although in the end, in her view, the expression is not as adequate as it seems for the medical situations she analyses, it could be argued that it is extremely relevant in the present case.

13 In general, feminist approaches present anorexia as the result of societal patriarchy, with anorexics either its victims *par excellence* or representing a form of resistance. Often these perspectives combine feminist points of view and psychoanalytical approaches (particularly when they focus on the mother–daughter relationship). Kim Chernin (1985) argues that anorexia is a hidden struggle for autonomy within an unconscious conflict between mothers and daughters: in this paradigm, the obsession with food replaces the quest for freedom, both in the context of individual trajectories and in the wider context of the first generation of women with access to the public sphere; for Orbach (1986), anorexia is a form of protest against the oppression of women.

14 I am not contending that this argument originates in the media – it was effectively elaborated by feminist approaches – nor that it is only defended by the media. It would be more accurate to say that this 'media theory' is a feminist argument, offering a critique of the role played by the media (and in particular by women's magazines) in objectifying women's bodies, which is then taken up by the media itself.

15 Matra Robertson writes that the term anorexia nervosa 'has become a complex combination of folk term and medical category' (1992, 18–21).

16 'The original question of my work on mysticism was about the links between sociology and psychoanalysis . . . . The path I chose . . . involves taking into account individual "cases" where the discourse of a given person can be related to the ideological sphere as being socially positioned and invested with unconscious drives . . . . The socio-historical approach in itself can therefore take a clinical turn' (Maître 1996, 33, 35–6).

Part II

The anorexic career

3 'Turning people into activities'

As I have already demonstrated, scientific discourse about anorexia tends to ascribe a very specific place and function to sociological analysis. The latter is generally tasked with accounting for the 'recruitment' of anorexics in historical terms – why today? – and in social terms – particularly related to gender, social class and age. In other words, its role is to deal with the epidemiological dimensions and social context of the illness. The most obvious way of going about this 'sociologizing' consists in taking quantitative epidemiological data and then using interviews to try to explain the specific boundaries of this recruitment. This is the task that social historian Joan Jacobs Brumberg assigns to the social sciences, drawing a distinction between analysing recruitment – which requires sociological and historical approaches (what historical and social conditions mean that the disease appears at a given moment in time and in a specific part of the social space?) – and analysing individual careers, which should be left to biology and psychology:

> An individual may begin to restrict her food because of aesthetic and social reasons related to gender, class, age, and sense of style. This constitutes the initial 'recruitment' stage . . . . An individual's dieting moves across the spectrum from the normal to the obsessional because of other factors, namely emotional and personality issues, and personal physiology and body chemistry . . . . Anorexia nervosa can be conceptually divided into two stages. The first involves sociocultural context, or 'recruitment' to fasting behavior; the second incorporates the subsequent 'career' as an anorexic and includes physiological and psychological changes that condition the individual to exist in a starvation state. The second stage is obviously the concern of medicine and mental health professionals because it is relatively formulaic and historically invariant. Stage one involves the historian, whose task is to trace the forces and events that have led young women to this relatively stereotypical behavior pattern.
>
> (Brumberg 1989, 38–40)

This division both of the object itself and of scientific work about it is the direct result of the specific place ascribed to the social sciences, as mentioned above.

This is made obvious in a note by the same author about the opposition between recruitment and career: 'This distinction between recruitment and career evolved in conversations with Dr William Bennett, whose command of the medical literature (and sensitivity to historical concerns) improved my understanding of the relationship between etiology and symptoms' (Brumberg 1989, 293 n.72). It is no doubt the doctor's 'command of the medical literature' and 'sensitivity to historical concerns' (tellingly placed within parentheses) that led him to suggest this distinction between objects of study, which, in practice, meant a division of scientific work confining the social sciences to analysing the recruitment context. It is somewhat ironic that he chose the term 'career' to designate the space reserved for medical and mental health professionals. Indeed, the notion of career is very broadly called upon in sociology precisely because it offers such a good way of taking up and 'objectivating' objects that are 'foreign' to sociological analysis – as mentioned in the introduction –, objects that are 'outsiders' in the realm of obviously social facts.

Anorexia as an activity

Given that my intention was to work on anorexia *in practice*, I obviously could not accept the terms of this division of work. However, breaking with this trend meant first setting aside the question of 'who' ('who are anorexics?') and questioning their activity instead ('what do they do?'). Once posited, this approach then allowed for the possibility of describing what anorexics do in sociological terms, but also of expressing the question of their social characteristics in different ways (based on the processes identified).

By making anorexic activity the object of this initial stage in my analysis, and by waiving any immediate use of identity features as explanatory factors, my approach coincided with the practical epistemological stance proposed by Howard Becker in his analysis of 'tricks of the trade' in interactional sociology, namely 'turning people into activities'. This consists in no longer drawing up typologies of people wherein their actions are explained causally by their specific social or psychological features and instead analysing the kinds of behaviour in which people engage under certain conditions. The case of opiate addiction, studied by Alfred Lindesmith, or of marijuana use, examined by Howard Becker, are both emblematic of the stance adopted in this particular strategy for constructing a research object.

> [Lindesmith] didn't suppose there were types of people who became addicts; rather, he guessed there was an addictive kind of behavior that, under the right circumstances, people would engage in. He studied addictive behavior, not addicts. In the same way, in my own research I spoke of marijuana use as a kind of activity, not marijuana users as a kind of people. . . . . Typing people is a way of accounting for regularity in people's actions; typing situations and lines of activity is a different way. Focusing on activities rather than people

> nudges you into an interest in change rather than stability, in ideas of process rather than structure.
>
> (Becker 1998, 44–6)

The pragmatic wording of this postulate should not mislead us into underestimating its importance. What Becker was suggesting was a complete reversal of perspective; a 'conquering' or even hegemonic stance aimed at taking over new objects by making an important break with that 'major enemy of sociological thought' – 'social and scientific convention':

> Every subject we study has already been studied by lots of people with lots of ideas of their own, and is further the domain of the people who actually inhabit that world, who have ideas of their own about what it's about and what the objects and events in it mean. These experts by profession or group membership usually have an uninspected and unchallenged monopoly of ideas on 'their' subject. Newcomers to the study of the subject, whatever it is, can easily be seduced into adopting those conventional ideas as the uninspected premises of their research. . . . . So we need ways of expanding the reach of our thinking, of seeing what else we could be thinking and asking, of increasing the ability of our ideas to deal with the diversity of what goes on in the world.
>
> (Becker 1998, 7)

As we shall see, the notion of career is one method through which we can turn away from 'conventional ideas' and develop new analyses.

In her book *Anorexic Bodies: A Feminist and Sociological Perspective on Anorexia Nervosa*, Morag MacSween seems to be calling for the same shift in focus, moving away from explanatory identity characteristics and looking to activity instead. She describes this as an analysis in which 'a sociological perspective of anorexia will be taken to its fullest extent', unlike approaches which simply 'add on' a sociological dimension to analysis that is mainly psychological and in which 'it is a deficiency in the "pre-anorexic" girl's psychology which explains anorexia' (MacSween 1993, 1–2). Her aim is to undertake a detailed study of 'what anorexic women actually do', showing that 'the meanings of anorexia are expressed in, rather than "under", the symptom itself' (5). However, the results she draws from her study (interviews with eight anorexics and one bulimic, as well as a postal survey) are somewhat disappointing compared with this initial project. She ends up concluding that what anorexics 'do' is search for a 'solution' to the 'irreconcilability of individuality and feminity' (255): 'In the anorexic symptom women try to synthesize contradictory elements in their social position through the creation of an "anorexic body"'; 'owned, inviolate and needless' (248). 'The deconstruction of feminine appetite, then, is the central anorexic process: it is both aim and method' (5). Her analysis of actions therefore ultimately results in a certain symbolism that betrays her analytical aim and that should be eschewed by any study of activity.

This focus on activity is probably a paradoxical way of applying a sociological point of view given that epidemiology and its results do seem to call for a sociological analysis of recruitment. However, it is necessary to begin with activity in order to break with the division of work that restricts the sociologist to looking at the common features of a group of individuals or at contextual elements, and in order to then take a stance focusing, on the contrary, on the very core of the process and its variations. Instead of considering anorexia as a state or a personality, my focus is on showing how, in order to 'be' anorexic, it is necessary to 'do' certain things.

It is only after analysing 'what they do' that I will be able to ask 'who they are' (in the third section of this book) or, more specifically, 'Who do they have to be in order to do what they do?' At that stage, I will consider to what extent what they do is inextricably linked to who they are, in terms of the social conditions of possibility for their activity. Before addressing these questions, though, this second section of the book will focus on a particular activity, looking at anorexia as a work of self-transformation. Only afterwards will I be able to move on and place this activity in the social space, looking at anorexia as a process that is socially situated through the positions of those engaged in it. Without the third section, the second section would be blind, but without the second section, the third section would quite simply be empty.

In addition to the central principle in this second section – looking at anorexic activity – other related principles also have to be taken into account. First, my approach means building out from the field itself, and more specifically from my interview material, in order to identify and describe this activity. Choosing activity as an analytical focus is a methodological stance as much as it is a theoretical one: it entails building out from the narratives and categories that emerge in the field, rather than taking them as illustrative examples. This does not mean, of course, that sociologists simply pass on the words of others naively, or 'know' nothing more than the information they collate; it just means that, initially, their knowledge consists in building up a field by combining and analysing different points of view:

> Sociologists do know some things the people they study don't know. But that's true in a way that makes the claim neither unwarranted nor disrespectful . . . . They study the experiences of a great many people, people whose experiences overlap but aren't exactly the same. Hughes used to say, 'I don't know anything that someone in that group doesn't know but, since I know what they all know, I know more than any one of them'.
>
> (Becker 1998, 99)

My approach is therefore about studying what the interviewees do, or have done, from their own point of view. But at the same time, it is also a question of taking the measure of the interactions in which this activity takes place and taking into account what others do, around them, with them, against them or even to them.

An anorexic career

The notion of career – as introduced by Everett Hughes then reformulated and applied by Howard Becker and Erving Goffman – offers a way of turning people into activities while at the same time taking into account the point of view of the interviewees *and* making the necessary break with the conceptions of 'experts by profession' and 'experts by group membership' (in this case, the interviewees). Indeed, one of the main benefits of this notion is that it can be used both as a tool ensuring the analysis is empirically grounded and as a tool for objectivation.

Hughes is credited with having first applied the notion of career outside the professional sphere.[1] The texts he devoted to this notion provide a general definition of the term 'career' that is not only qualified in terms of its relationship to 'occupations':

> Career, the word, has itself a career. Once a race-course career came to mean figuratively a short gallop at full speed, even a charge of cavalry, the swift flight of a bird in hawking and the course of the sun and stars across the sky hence also full speed or impetus. Those meanings, all obsolete, have given place to this: 'A person's course or progress through life (or a distinct portion of life)'.
>
> (Hughes 1997, 389)

When it comes to studying occupations, Hughes' use of the notion of career results in 'introducing duration where, previously, occupations were understood synchronically and all complete' (Queiroz and Ziolkowski 1994, 68). More generally, though, it is about considering the phenomena being analysed as *processes*. The temporal dimension is taken into account through what could be called the 'sequencing' of a career – identifying a temporal thread that distinguishes 'moments', 'stages' or 'phases' of a career,[2] within phenomena that are not, or not necessarily, presented chronologically.[3] In this sense, one could even say that the sequencing of a career is in itself a result based on field analysis, which in each case both establishes and uses this temporal dimension. This is especially the case in the sequential model of deviance suggested by Howard Becker, which he contrasts with a 'multivariate analysis' where all causes operate simultaneously (Becker 1963, 22). The question of possibility ('how something was or became possible') takes priority over the question of necessity ('why something was or became necessary'), just like history replaces cause, epistemologically speaking: 'Assume that whatever you want to study has, not causes, but a history' (Becker 1998, 60–1). In this book, I will retrace this history by constructing four phases in the career of anorexics: first, when they begin taking themselves in hand; second, when they maintain this endeavour; third, when they carry on maintaining their commitment despite alerts being given and monitoring being put in place; and finally, when they are taken in hand by the medical institution.

Three dialectical avenues

Far from being a reductive schemata, the notion of career offers a way of combining seemingly contradictory analytical elements. I will draw on three of the possible dialectical avenues enabled by this framework, looking at (1) what the interviewees do and how they 'are done' by others, (2) the repetitions and variations that can be seen between their experiences, and (3) the things they do and the reactions generated by these acts.

The notion of career makes it possible to take into account the temporal aspect to processes while at the same time analysing the 'official position' of the individual and his or her 'internal matters' to quote Erving Goffman (1961, 127). Or, in Howard Becker's terms, combining the 'objective facts of social structure and changes in the perspectives . . . of the individual' (Becker 1963, 24).[4] Adopting a perspective in terms of career means:

> forcing oneself to examine the effects of the combination of two distinct processes over time and on an individual: the process of creating and imposing norms, and the process of socialization and identity construction. Goffman's description of the 'moral career' of inmates is the conceptual equivalent. He also showed the intersection between two structures – the institution and personal biography – in asylum interactions. If, as Hughes writes, 'society is interaction,' the concept of 'career' further specifies this general definition: it exhibits the concrete product of what actors do while being done.
>
> (Queiroz and Ziolkowski 1994, 69)

Learning is at the heart of this dialectic between 'doing' and 'being done' and it is no surprise that it holds such an important place in the analysis of the careers of marijuana users or, as we shall see, anorexics. In order to do something, you have to have learnt how to do it; in other words you have to have 'been done' by others. Learning draws a link between socialization and how norms and identities are imposed, on the one hand, and activities, on the other hand, with practices therefore the main locus for observing this combination.

The second dialectical avenue I will explore here concerns the relationship between repetition and variation. From this point of view, a career-based perspective has two objectives: first, showing the common elements shared by various individuals engaged in the same career, by bringing to light and constructing common phases within individual experience; second, identifying the variations that exist within these common phases from one person to another. The first of these two aims makes it possible to objectivize diverse experiences by showing that a temporal and social order does exist: 'There is a certain order in the lives of men in a society. Some of the ordering is open, intentional, and institutionalized; some of it happens without people quite knowing it until it is turned up by investigation' (Hughes 1984, 124). These words by Hughes have almost Durkheimian overtones: the 'order' in question is almost a sui generis reality, to take up one of Durkheim's key terms, existing in part outside the individual conscience and only made visible by the methodological operation that consists in aggregating and combining individual experiences, just like statistical aggregation. However, the second objective – taking variation into account – distances itself somewhat from this model. Variations are not analysed as classes of variation to be explained, as with Durkheim, but rather as the manifestation of the unique, albeit always social, character of individual experiences: 'In the study of careers we deal with the dialectic between the regular and repeated, on the one hand, and the unique on the other' (Hughes 1997, 390). Because of this, career analyses take a very specific form that can be a little disconcerting at first. Studies taking this approach may well present variations within common phases in and of themselves, without necessarily explaining them. For example, in Richard Ekins's analyses of cross-dressers and sex-changers, the first phase is identified as the 'beginning' of these practices and the commonly shared process lies in how a norm is transgressed and how the ensuing secrets, stigma and information are managed. But Richard Ekins also identifies how varied these beginnings can be, without explaining them; they can occur by chance or by design, in childhood, adolescence or adulthood, alone or with others, the clothes can belong to other people or have been bought, etc. More generally, this dialectic between repetition and variation can be seen in the way he introduces his object of study and the results of his research:

> [Male femaling] emerged as the single major social process being researched. It was pervasive and fundamental. It was patterned. It occurred over time and went on irrespective of the conditional variation of place. From then on, I found it increasingly illuminating to conceptualise male cross-dressers and sex-changers as male who 'female' in various ways, in various contexts, at various times, with various stagings and with various consequences. The emphasis could be on typing behaviours, not people.
>
> (Ekins 1997, 2)

There are therefore two results, which correspond to two aims: bringing to light a single social process while, at the same time, insisting on the various ways, contexts, moments, stagings and consequences of this process, with the latter considered not as data to be explained but as the result of a study of variation. In this sense, while the analysis of careers could seem to some extent like the qualitative version of the Durkheimian approach – bringing to light a social fact through methodological aggregation – this second dimension sets it apart from that: all variations do not have to be explained causally.

In addition to the analysis of these two dialectics between 'doing' and 'being done', between repetition and variation, the notion of career also allows a third dialectic to be taken into consideration, this time between 'the commission of a given act', to use Becker's terms, and the reactions it generates. As we will see later, when we look at the question of deviance, the notion of career gives substantial weight not just to what 'actors do while being done' but also to what other actors (who are also 'done') do in relation to what is done and how they therefore contribute to defining it. This phenomenon is therefore a 'process that warrants analysing in and of itself' (Queiroz and Ziolkowski 1994, 103). Any analysis in terms of career is of course developed from the point of view of the individuals engaged in that career and centred on that perspective. However, the main focus is the imprint left on the individual by all the interactions in which he or she is involved; for Howard Becker, with the deviant group and 'moral entrepreneurs'; for Erving Goffman, with family and the circuit of agents involved in the career – e.g. medical, psychiatric and social work professionals – as well as other patients. In this sense, any process is a set of overlapping and interweaving interactions, even when considered from a situated point of view.

The three avenues identified above will therefore guide my analysis of the anorexic career. The notion of career is also a useful tool for presenting data and describing the phenomena being studied. In this present case, I will provide the reader with a substantial portion of the material collated during my interviews, while at the same time pursuing my analysis of the interview situation. However, using the term 'career' does not necessarily mean espousing all its theoretical underpinnings. More specifically, one particular and important presupposition inherent to analyses in terms of career, or deviant career, is that every individual could potentially enter into a particular career or at least that analysis should not focus on personal and social characteristics as causes of engagement in that career. I will not work on this particular premise: the third section of this book is devoted precisely to establishing the social conditions of possibility for engaging in the anorexic career. However, I will give particular importance to the processes through which people can leave a career. This is an important corollary to the previous presupposition, asserting that the internal dynamic of a career – the driving force for those engaged in it – goes hand in hand with a set of possibilities for 'leaving' that career. Insofar as it is not a type of personality but a type of activity that defines a career, there is no reason to presuppose that once engaged in a given career, individuals have no choice but to remain in it. The different stages at which individuals leave the career and the interviews I conducted with 'non-anorexic' secondary-school students will be used in this regard as both a comparative measure and a way of demonstrating empirically what some of the girls interviewed as anorexics did that others also do or do not do.

Career and trajectory

I could also have used the notion of 'trajectory' as theorized, albeit differently, by Anselm Strauss and Pierre Bourdieu to account for anorexic activity as a practical and temporal process. However, as I pursued my analysis it became clear that the notion of career was much better suited to the kind of dynamic at work. In her article 'The Work Sites of an American Interactionist: Anselm L. Strauss, 1917–1996', Isabelle Baszanger retraces Anselm Strauss's different definitions and uses of the notion of trajectory. Applied to chronic illnesses,

> one of the first merits of the concept of trajectory is to remove the study of chronic illnesses from biological, medical, and psychological frames of thought and instead equip the researcher with a reflective stance based on the work involved – clearly and distinctively social phenomena.
>
> (Baszanger 1998a, 363)

This shift can also be compared with Becker's 'reframing of deviance, since the task for Strauss was to formulate a viewpoint on chronic illness autonomous and unique to the social sciences' (Baszanger 1998a, 363). Baszanger cites Strauss:

> [*Trajectory* refers] not only to the physiological unfolding of a patient's disease but to the total *organization of work* done over that course . . . . For different illnesses, the trajectory will involve different medical and nursing actions, different kinds of skills and other resources, a different parceling out of tasks among the workers (including perhaps, kin and the patient).
>
> (362–3)

More generally, the notion of trajectory refers to the course of a phenomenon and the things done to shape and manage it over time. For illnesses, the notion of trajectory allows analysis of 'work conjugated as action' (354), to which the patient contributes. Such an approach, outlined in its barest form here, could well have been applied to the analysis of hospital treatment of anorexia. However, it seems less directly relevant in the context of my sociological approach to anorexia. First, my investigative framework was not devised with a view to observing or reconstructing the different points of view and different actions engaged in around anorexia. The central perspective was the point of view of the patients interviewed. While 'work conjugated as action' did exist, this tended to work *against* the patient rather than following on from the patient's own work. Or at least this was the case before the hospital phase. During the latter, patients sometimes did start working alongside the team and, at this stage, but at this stage only, the situation could lend itself more to an analysis in terms of trajectory. Jumping ahead slightly to results that I will outline in detail further on, anorexia could be said to be less about teamwork than about a solitary endeavour, thus limiting the value of the notion of trajectory. Moreover, applying this notion to chronic illnesses brings out the patient's participation in the 'conjugated' work done to deal with the physiological illness. The notion of career, on the other hand, directly raises the question of what could be called – somewhat provocatively, at this stage – the anorexics' own work *producing* what is labelled as anorexia. Anorexia is not a case of an 'illness' that arises and is then managed, like the chronic illnesses studied by Anselm Strauss. My focus here is on the anorexic career from the point of view of the patient rather than on the hospital treatment of anorexics. From this point of view, the notion of career therefore offers more resources than the notion of trajectory as defined by Strauss.

The notion of trajectory is characterized very differently by Pierre Bourdieu, who insists in particular on the spatial dimension to this kind of dynamic temporal process. He defines the notion of trajectory as breaking with the 'artefact' that is 'life history' and the 'privilege accorded to the longitudinal succession of constituent events of life considered as history in comparison with the social space in which they are carried out' (Bourdieu 2000a, 303). The notion of trajectory therefore encourages us to consider the 'series of successively occupied positions by the same agent (or the same group) in a space which itself is constantly evolving and which is subject to incessant transformations' (303–4) rather than 'trying to understand a life as a unique and sufficient series of successive events (sufficient unto itself) and without ties other than the association to a "subject" whose constancy is probably just that of a proper name' (304). A career is not the strict analysis of a 'life history' either, to the important extent that it is not about considering a 'unique series' but rather about bringing out a collective order, as stated previously. However, I do attempt to understand successive events without ties other than the association to a diagnosis (in this case), while remaining perfectly aware that these events were selected, before the interview, through the encounter with the medical world. But this is only the first stage of objectivation. After having analysed the practical and temporal dimension of the process in question, I then situate this process within the social space. Even though these two approaches are not separate, it is necessary to distinguish them analytically before they can be combined. To take up a distinction made – critically – by Bourdieu in the same article I have just quoted, the aim is 'trying to make sense of a subway route' before 'taking into account the network structure, that is the matrix of objective relations between different stations' (Bourdieu 2000a, 304).[5] This metaphor of the 'subway route' is particularly relevant to the notion of career: a journey marked by sequences (between two stations) and turning points (at each station). Once you have got on the train, it is not necessarily easy to get off again but it is possible, particularly at those turning points, where you can stop the journey or change direction. From one sequence to the next, the social stage can change (there can be more or less people on the train, the people are not necessarily the same from one sequence to another, you can be sitting or standing, you can be criticized for being sat down at some times and not at others, etc.). So even though the term 'career' does not recreate the 'matrix of objective relations between different stations', it does offer an approach to a world that is logically smaller than the social space, namely the local space of interactions (not only face-to-face) which, to pursue the metaphor to the very end, does not only include the travellers on a particular train along with the individual but also the subway workers, the train driver, the advertising companies that produce the billboard posters on the walls of the station, etc. This second section of the book looks at this 'subway journey', and the 'network structure' will be considered afterwards, in the third section.

A 'deviant' career

Beyond its application to the field of work and occupations, the notion of career has proved its heuristic value in the study of deviance. However, this begs the question: can the career under discussion here be considered a 'deviant career'?

Two important principles of this approach – which constitute substantial shifts in perspective compared with previous theories[6] – are of interest in this regard: the 'neutral' point of view taken towards the object of study and the attention paid to labelling and the effect of reactions by the 'audience' of deviance.

The question of normality and abnormality

The simple fact of using the notion of career, when applied outside the professional field, in itself requires a certain form of neutrality: 'Such a career is not a thing that can be brilliant or disappointing; it can no more be a success than a failure' (Goffman 1961, 127). The notion of 'deviant career' exacerbates this requirement:

> We ought not to view [deviant behaviour] as something special, as depraved or in some magical way better than other kinds of behavior. We ought to see it simply as a kind of behavior some disapprove of and others value, studying the processes by which either or both perspectives are built up and maintained.
>
> (Becker 1963, 176)

A dual epistemological stance is therefore at work in this kind of interactionist approach to deviance. First, it entails setting aside the question of the distinction between what is normal and abnormal. From this point of view, it is less about saying that deviants 'are normal' than about studying them normally, applying a 'normal' sociological approach to the object being examined. Second, it entails reframing the question of normal and abnormal as an object of study by studying how deviance is labelled and above all the *effects* this has on the behaviour of those who are labelled that way (Becker 1963, 179). However, this distinction between normal and abnormal, understood as a social process of imputation, is not about addressing the essentialist question, which is never actually asked – it is not *because* deviants are labelled as 'abnormal' that they *are* in fact normal.

Howard Becker and Erving Goffman both took this approach although, as we shall see, the latter explicitly distanced himself from theories in terms of deviance. Indeed, both *Asylums* (Goffman 1961) and *Stigma* (Goffman 1963) aim to show that mental patients, on the one hand, and people who are stigmatized, on the other, have normal motivations and strategies, in the specific sense that these motivations and strategies require the same analysis that would be conducted with normal people. Similarly, Howard Becker's analysis includes studying the actions and skills of both 'moral entrepreneurs' and marijuana users. From this point of view, when Howard Becker describes 'deviant' behaviour, he does not do so in terms of what is normal and abnormal but in terms of behaviour that 'some disapprove of and others value'. In the present study, I set aside the question of normality and abnormality as an essentialist issue and instead construct the question of normality and deviance as an object of study, a locus for struggles, building out from the particular case constituted by a mental pathology. In this fundamental way, the career that I describe is a deviant career.

Reinstating principles of variation

In order to provide the best account possible of my object of study, I had to take on board the various criticisms levied by different interactionist trends against the notion of deviance. These constitute a series of suggestions or shifts allowing the analysis to be further refined and making the notion even more effective.

The approach to deviance advocated by Howard Becker leads to special focus on the variations involved in the labelling process:

> Deviance must be considered from the angle of a transaction between an individual and a social group . . . . The boundary between what is deviant and what isn't is impossible to fix once and for all, because it depends not only on the existence of a norm at a given time in a given group, but also upon the variable conditions in which it is effectively applied.
>
> (Queiroz and Ziolkowski 1994, 100)

As for the criticisms levied by both Erving Goffman and Anselm Strauss against the notion of deviance and its use, they emphasize identifying other principles of variation. In *Stigma*, Goffman makes no bones about expressing the view that for sociologists the value of the term deviance is far more institutional than intellectual:

> It is remarkable that those who live around the social sciences have so quickly become comfortable in using the term 'deviant', as if those to whom the term is applied have enough in common so that significant things can be said about them as a whole. Just as there are iatrogenic disorders caused by the work that physicians do (which then gives them more work to do), so there are categories of persons who are created by students of society, and then studied by them.
>
> (Goffman 1963, 167 n.1)

For Erving Goffman, the different ways in which norms are transgressed are too different to be grouped together in one general study of deviance and doing so would run the risk of slipping into substantialization. Moreover, he suggests that 'normal' and 'stigmatized' are not essences but the two sides of the same reality: 'The most fortunate of normals is likely to have his half-hidden failing, and for every little failing there is a social occasion when it will loom large . . .' (Goffman 1963, 152). I referred just now to 'setting aside' the question of normality and abnormality as an essentialist question and it is in this sense that Erving Goffman criticizes applying a particular approach across the board. In the following quotation, he taxes the deviant approach with essentializing and framing the deviant group as a single homogeneous category: 'Therefore the occasionally precarious and the constantly precarious form a single continuum, their situation in life *analysable by the same framework'* (Goffman 1963, 152, emphasis added). According to him, using stigma as an analytical approach allows the same analytical framework to be applied to very different situations, whereas using deviance as an analytical approach implies applying a single, homogenizing framework to very different situations that are presented as being similar. Although I will not enter into this debate here, it does draw attention to how important it is to take into account a whole continuum of ways in which information is managed; something which, in labelling theories, is sometimes treated only from the point of view of an alternative between secret deviance and an imposed label which then redefines the whole identity of the deviant in all his or her social interactions. In chapter six, I look at different ways in which information is managed and different forms of stigma; the different situations in which the individual is discredited but also discreditable. In doing so, I draw on the dynamic introduced by the notion of stigma within labelling theory making it possible to consider both a temporal continuum and the variety of problems raised by stigma in different social arenas.

While Goffman draws attention to the variations between 'deviants' themselves, which are masked by the too-general term 'deviance', Strauss levies a similar criticism (in terms of how deviance analyses forget certain variations), but this time at the level of how norms are produced and imposed. He calls for the struggles and conflicts inherent to defining norms and labels to be taken into account:

> The careers of patients within the hospital may be studied in terms of deviance. But we add a qualifying note: The usual sociological conception of deviance is too simple. It assumes a relatively homogeneous institution, with deviant acts in terms of a relatively firm core of norms and standards—and therefore with control mechanisms to handle deviants and deviant acts. We suspect that few large organizations have such homogeneous standards; certainly the hospitals we studied do not. No single set of values dominates either the whole institution or any part of it . . . . The imputation and handling of deviance often lead to a contest, unfolded through various strategies designed both to make the imputation stick and to gain support for appropriate courses of action . . . . Implicit in this position is that the defining of deviancy is a continual, never-ending process . . . . If I summarize where these cases have taken us, I would say this: each vividly illustrates the contest over what the proper definition of a given class of actions is to be.
>
> (Strauss 1967, 265–8)

Anselm Strauss illustrates this position through a comparative study of four cases: LSD, opium, debates about the rights of suspects being questioned by police and polygamy among Mormons. In all four cases, he shows both the debates and redefinitions surrounding what is normal and what is 'legal', as well the importance of the 'social visibility' of acts and the work conducted by various groups to obtain this visibility when it comes to the definition and imputation of deviance. It looks very much as if in this text Strauss is criticizing labelling theories for being too quick to think that, due to their position, 'moral entrepreneurs' have all power, and consensual power, over definitions of what is normal and abnormal.

In the present study, as we will see, the interviewees were all questioned at a moment when their anorexia had strong 'social visibility'; however, the imputation of deviance did not take place at the same time for all of them and in all social arenas. Having a psychiatrist in the family, for example, was a factor that tended to strengthen this social visibility; moreover, a particular weight could be labelled as deviant by the medical sphere and the family, but not by the peer group. Without questioning the very different legitimacy of these two groups, this discrepancy nonetheless requires us to take on board – in line with Goffman's criticism above – the variations that labelling theories sometimes flatten out in their haste to determine the effects of this labelling.

A specific deviant career

I have therefore attempted to include these different principles of variation in my approach to the anorexic career as a deviant career, albeit a very specific kind of deviant career.

First, it is only when viewed retrospectively that entering the career coincides with entering deviance. As we will see, where deviance in the anorexic deviant career is concerned, 'it all starts with a diet' (although this assertion will also be qualified to some extent). The first phase would not be a deviant phase if it were not continued and then reframed at the end of the journey as being the beginning of anorexia. From this point of view, the career outlined here does not begin by transgression but rather by submission to a norm, through socially encouraged, legitimate actions, which are not subject to disapproval. This raises the question of what later becomes deviant (that is to say, generates a reaction of social disapproval) in this specific case. It is not just actions that are labelled as deviant (not eating enough or making oneself vomit) but also, from a certain point onwards, the transgression of 'normal weight' that comes with being thin. And this does not result from having engaged in that career at a given time but from having maintained a commitment to that career. Even actions labelled as deviant are in fact the subject of struggles in definition and dependent on the social arenas in which they take place: normal behaviour at the school canteen ('all the girls pick at their plates') is no longer normal during dinner at home; normal behaviour during dinner at home (not eating a lot) is no longer normal once there has been too much weight loss or once the diagnosis of anorexia has been evoked. And yet the point at which weight becomes a transgression is, in itself, variable and can depend on local family norms of weight (we will see this with Véronique, who mentions that her thinness went unnoticed in her family where 'all the women are like matchsticks'), local 'professional' norms (Emilie was a dancer and her thinness was only noticed by her parents) and the interviewee's own local weight norms (Mathilde recounted that it was a long time before anyone worried because she had always been a 'thin little girl'). This explains the importance of the diagnosis: it is from that point onwards that the 'audience' considers that there is a case of deviance.

Before it became a sociological issue, identifying when deviance began was also a question that the interviewees and those around them had asked themselves. The transgression of norms did not begin at the beginning, as it were. Retrospectively, through the work done in the hospital reframing experiences, the narrative of anorexia as deviance comes to include what I will describe here as the first phase in the career (chapter four). This is very much a retrospective perspective, though: chronologically, these social reactions and this labelling only occur much later, during the phase that I describe as the third phase in the career (chapter six).

The deviant career described here is also very particular insofar as the deviant group is only present at the end of the anorexic career, during the hospitalization phase, where the hospital establishes a group of anorexics. For Howard Becker, before the person enters a real deviant subculture, the deviant group is one of the most important mechanisms for passing from one phase to the next, particularly given that it is the locus for learning. These two features are in fact linked: there are no magazines, books or television programmes that explain to novices 'how to smoke' the way Howard Becker's initiates do (except perhaps Becker's book itself!). The deviant group is the main social medium through which an individual can learn (the relevant techniques, how to perceive the effects and how to develop a taste for these effects). These things cannot develop without that learning process and Becker shows how important it is for moving from one phase to the next. However, it is much easier – and this is an understatement – to find similar information about 'how to lose weight'. There is no need for a deviant group, insofar as the deviant subculture overlaps considerably with a normal subculture or even culture – which brings us back to the question of when deviance begins: in the case of anorexia, there is no need to learn about deviance from a deviant group, it can be learnt from 'moral entrepreneurs'. The deviant career discussed here therefore has the peculiar feature of being mainly composed by normal actions, which are socially approved: going on a diet, watching what you eat, exercising but also, as we will see later, working hard at school. It is not so much the acts that are deviant as the career itself.

The effect of retrospectively labelling the initial phases as deviant obviously raises the more general question of the necessarily retrospective dimension to any career narrative. Erving Goffman notes this 'ticklish point' in his analysis of the career of a mental patient:

> if the patient wants to make sense out of his stay in the hospital . . . then he, too, will have reason to believe some of this psychiatric work-up of his past. Here is a very ticklish point for the sociology of careers. An important aspect of every career is the view the person constructs when he looks backward over his progress; in a sense, however, the whole of the prepatient career derives from this reconstruction.
>
> (Goffman 1961, 145)

The author highlights the 'peculiarly retroactive character' of this phenomenon (Goffman 1961, 145). It could also be referred to as a 'retrospective illusion', something that appears as a particular case of the 'biographical illusion' critiqued by Pierre Bourdieu. But the sociology of careers has developed its own tools to address this question. 'One cannot evade the question of the social mechanisms which favor or permit the ordinary experience of life as a unity and a totality' (Bourdieu 2000a, 301): not only does the sociology of careers not shy away from this question, conducting a critical analysis of the mechanisms and institutions which contribute to constructing this retrospective point of view, it also makes it into an object of study in and of itself. Studying a career also means studying how it has successively been reconstructed, how the present weighs on narratives of the past, not in terms of a limitation to the analysis but rather as a separate subject of analysis. Richard Ekins's stance towards the transsexual career illustrates how the 'obstacle' of the retrospective perspective can be overcome and converted into a privileged locus for analysis:

> Symbolic interactionism has a clear standpoint on all this [the fact that life history material is the product of its occasion]. All meanings emerge from within particular presents. All pasts are reconstructed from the standpoint of each present (Mead, 1932). This is inevitable and cannot be avoided. Appropriately, therefore, I make a virtue of that necessity in this 'consolidating' chapter. I take three lives as illustrative of the three major modes of consolidating [male femaling] . . . . This chapter uses the material collected in the interviews to example the informants' constructions of their pasts from the standpoint of the particular present of the interview.
>
> (Ekins 1997, 130–1)

As I outline the anorexic career, I will attempt to show how the moment of the interview (in the sense of a social moment, more broadly the 'situation' of the interviewees at the moment of the interview, particularly when this situation is that they are hospitalized) has to be framed as an object of study in order to work on that career. I already began this endeavour in chapter two and will develop in further in chapter seven (when I look at the phase of the career that corresponds to when the interviews took place). But I will also show that analysing this career does not just mean analysing its successive reconstructions. First, because through all the practices narrated, the things confided and the anecdotes recounted, something emerged other than an official version of events, that was officially constructed and imposed; second, because the point of view of the present does not always erase the point of view of the past, the two sometimes overlap instead, as we will see in chapter five regarding the taste for thinness or in chapter seven, when the interviewees give a new – and in fact opposite – meaning to the notion of 'taking themselves in hand'.

Following this logic of taking into account the effects of the present on narratives of the past, I have chosen, in this second section, to refer to the girls I interviewed in their capacity as anorexics as 'interviewees'. This places emphasis on the interview process and serves as a reminder that the main material of this second section is composed of these interviews, conducted at a given moment with given individuals. My aim was also, however, to avoid two other possible formulations. I did not want to use the expression 'anorexics' which would have the effect of generalizing the interviewees' words to a 'class of people', whereas the material was collated in a situated manner. Moreover, this generalization would also have had the effect of naturalizing a specific label. However, I did not want to completely erase this label either, given that I also wanted to bring to light its formative effects. In this regard, the most deconstructionist social science studies seem excessively idealistic. Julie Hepworth, for example, talks about 'young women' and 'women', criticizing other feminist works for using the category 'anorexics', thereby reproducing psychiatric domination and medical hegemony (Hepworth 1999, ch. 3). However, a sociological approach to anorexia could not ignore the fact that a diagnosis exists and is imposed, with very real effects in the way it is constructed. From this point of view, looking to avoid both naturalization and excessive idealism, the expression 'girls interviewed as anorexics' seemed an appropriate choice.

Notes

1 'Hughes does not limit the use of the notion of career to the field of work, once again he expands the comparison by referring to careers within religious, political and philanthropic organizations, to the careers of women in the family and to the careers of people being treated in medical institutions' (Chapoulie 2001, 238–9).

2 'Rather than "stages," it is probably more appropriate to talk about "moments" in order to insist on the way things overlap chronologically and the interactions between different times in the cycle' (Queiroz and Ziolkowski 1994, 105–6). I will use the term 'phases' to insist on this overlap because my interviewees used the term 'moment' a lot and the different phases that can be identified on the basis of their interviews do not necessarily coincide with their definitions of 'moments'.

3 It really is a question of *constructing* phases even when the interview begins with a chronological presentation of experiences and the interviewee's speech seems to be chronologically organized. In a methodological postscript, Diane Vaughan (1986) refers to the coding and categorizing necessary to recreate the chronological order of different phases on the basis of interviews. In the case of the interviews conducted in the hospital, the 'narrative of cases of anorexia' serves as a form of – also chronological – organization as we shall see. However, its strength rarely goes beyond the first moments and first pages of the interviews. In addition to my work objectivating this medical model of the case, I also had to conduct coding work similar to that described by Diane Vaughan.

4 On this point, see, for example, Passeron (1991, 204): the notion of career makes it possible for a 'both interpretative and explanatory description to grasp the inextricably subjective and objective meanings that a series of actions takes on (for the sociologist but also from the retrospective viewpoint of the subject) as a *career*' and for us to 'understand both the inextricably constraining and unwanted (objectivized) aspect and the personally experienced (subjectivized) aspect to a biography'.

5 For a critical analysis of the subway metaphor and a comparison of the career and trajectory schemas, see Passeron (1991, ch. 8).

6 On the shift from the notion of social disorganization to the notion of deviance in the Chicago School, see Chapoulie 2001 (ch. 7 and particularly 278–89).

4 'Beginning'

Taking themselves in hand

According to Richard Ekins, in his study of the career of cross-dressers and sex-changers – inspired by the works and methodology of Barney Glaser and Anselm Strauss – anyone observing children will see games involving the feminization of the male body, such as dressing up (Ekins 1997). When the people who play these games later forget about them, the games are not 'beginnings'. When, however, this 'male femaling' persists, these initial moments take on huge retrospective importance (62). This underscores the extent to which the very notion of 'beginning' presupposes a retrospective stance and how important interviews are as a way of approaching careers, trajectories or any individual process that takes place over time.[1] However, taking a retrospective stance does not mean arbitrarily constructing a beginning that was not experienced as a significant moment at the time. For a beginning to be reconstructed, it has to be defined on the basis of a break in continuity at the very least – an outside event, a change in practices, etc. In the case of the anorexia career, this discontinuity is not easy to pinpoint. In this sense, just realizing that there *is* a beginning is a key issue in itself. In my study, the question was whether the interviewees identified a beginning to their anorexia and, if they did, what that beginning was.[2]

Beginnings and questions

The instruction given during the hospital interviews, asking about the interviewees' 'experience', implicitly encouraged them to outline this experience in a chronological format (at first, at least) and this is exactly how they understood it. As they did so they were able to draw on the self-presentations they had to give in clinical interviews, particularly in pre-admission interviews, which sometimes aim to determine the date or period at which the first signs of anorexia appeared. The interview situation therefore strongly encouraged a 'beginning-based' narrative.

Different narratives of beginnings

The most frequent narrative mode I encountered in the interviews involved determining a clear and precise beginning. Excerpts from the first minutes of the interviews testify to this, with references to a given period (the beginning of Year 11,[3] the summer holidays) or month ('It was in February two years ago' [Christine, C]. 'Well it started in September, the anorexia nervosa' [Anne, H]). However, determining a clearly identified, dated and situated beginning was not the only narrative mode used. There were also three other forms of narrative that seemed to exclude the possibility of identifying a unique point in time, a break in continuity, when things 'began'. First, in the interview with Nadège, she eluded my questions about 'when it began' on several occasions: 'It came about progressively [pauses] . . . . It happened fairly progressively [pauses] . . . . I couldn't say when it started' [Nadège, H].

Second, certain interviewees recounted their story from a psychoanalytical point of view, with anorexia 'always already' there and the triggering of 'symptoms' viewed as an almost arbitrary moment with its truth to be found in their childhood past: 'Yeah, the beginning, actually what I found out retrospectively is that I had infantile anorexia, when I was little' [Sabine, N]. 'Well actually I think I've always had a little problem with food' [Anne, C]. Finally, in other interviews, several different 'beginnings' were described, arising at different dates and in different situations:

> Well, for me, at first, I was kind of, I'd say overweight . . . And that, well, it started like that, but, well, until then it wasn't pathological, and, honestly, I'd never managed to lose weight . . . . But then it wasn't [pauses] yet, well, not really, I'd say, not pathological yet. That happened a little bit later [pauses]. Something like half a year later, actually.
>
> [Priscille, C]

> It had vaguely started after the summer holidays before Year 10, but until Easter it wasn't [pauses] There was nothing alarming. Then, I'd say it was just a little gentle diet. But it all went downhill after the Easter holidays . . . . That's when I really started to go on a diet.
>
> [Mathilde, H]

V: 'Actually, it started . . . in 1981 [Véronique was 18 at that time]. Before, I wanted to lose weight, but at that point in time I behaved extremely morbidly. And it lasted [pauses], yes, I said [earlier in the interview] that it started in 1979 [pauses] I'd really situate the shift from diet [pauses] to illness at that point in time.'

MD: 'So do you mean that from 1979 to 1981, it was a diet?'

V: 'It was a strict diet. But it became unhealthy after 1981.'

[Véronique, N]

Beginning

A question of definition

What these quotations show is that the question of the beginning is perhaps less about when 'it' happened than about how 'it' is defined: what exactly is it that 'begins'? When the interviewees hesitated in determining when it began or referred to several beginnings, this was less because they had difficulty remembering dates or found it hard to define a break in continuity within their continuous experience and more because they had difficulty defining the beginning. In all the interviews, something was defined as beginning at a particular point in time. But the interviewees' hesitations beg the question: 'What exactly is it that begins'? Is a diet the beginning of anorexia? What should be made of experiences that were not experienced as deviant at the time, were not stigmatized, were not defined as pathological and may well even have been approved? Should they be included in a narrative about 'experience with anorexia'? Retrospectively, is a 'strict diet' or a 'little gentle diet' the beginning of anorexia or not?

The hesitations and variations between interviews therefore related less to any difficulty with saying 'when' it began than to the question of how to define that beginning. In all the interviews, a 'point in time' was mentioned that was sufficiently out of step with a more uniform past to warrant being called a beginning. This remained true in the interviews that referred anorexia back to an always already of infanthood and was even true in the interview with Nadège, who refused to specify a date for the beginning of her anorexia but nonetheless spoke of a point in time ('at the beginning') when she had started 'wanting to watch' what she ate. In this case, the issue was neither chronology nor memory, but the refusal to define this point in time as the 'beginning of anorexia' and to retrospectively label it as pathological. As discussed in chapter three, the question of whether or not they were engaging in deviant behaviour was raised by the interviewees' behaviour far before it became a sociological issue. In fact, the interview instruction required the interviewees to distinguish 'normal' from 'pathological' themselves, perhaps with the help of medical discourse, which also explains these difficulties and hesitations. But once again, although determining the beginning appeared to be a question of definition, this did not mean that the first point in time was purely arbitrary. Nor did it mean that it was produced by the interview situation, by the fact the interviewees were used to presenting their cases by beginning with the first clinical signs or by their internalization of the medical definition of anorexia. Nadège, who I interviewed at the very beginning of her first hospital stay, refused to talk about the beginning of her anorexia, despite the fact that the medical examination of her case gave a specific date (October 1996) for the first clinical signs. A possible interpretation would be that, unlike the other patients I interviewed in the hospital, who were further along their hospital trajectory, she had not yet 'learnt' this date or internalized the retrospective pathologization of her initial behaviour. However, as underlined above, she did mention a 'start', a beginning, that seemed relevant to her, independently of any medical definition. Moreover, even in cases when anorexia was mentioned as being always already there, the interviewees nonetheless identified a specific beginning much later than infanthood. Finally, sometimes an extremely precise beginning was identified, even in the interview I conducted with Annabelle, who had never followed medical treatment, never described her case before and never learnt to talk about it in a medical context:

> Actually I think it started with the first mark I got [in *Prépa* – post-secondary programme preparing students to sit the competitive entrance exams for prestigious higher education establishments] . . . and it began bit by bit. But actually what really triggered it was that I went on a diet, at the beginning.
>
> [Annabelle, N]

In all the interviews, at one point in time something happened 'at the start' and retrospectively 'began'. This beginning could be defined as the first phrase of the anorexic career.

The beginning

A diet?

From the medical and psychological point of view, there is a consensus. The thing that begins is anorexia and anorexia begins with a diet: 'The beginning is usually insidious and apparently ordinary; the teenage girl feels fat and decides to go on a diet' (Chabrol 1991, 8); 'It all begins in what is often an ordinary and insidious fashion: the teenage girl finds herself too plump and, like so many others at her age, decides to go on a diet to lose weight' (Apfeldorfer 1995, 34); 'Most often, it all begins by wanting to "go on a diet", sometimes seemingly justified due to [the adolescent] being slightly overweight' (Alvin 1996, 5).

This theory of 'beginning with a diet' is so consensual that it has become self-evident and is considered a feature of the pathology itself. For example, during the review meeting in ward I at clinic C, the head of the ward began his summary about an anorexic admission with the following words:

HEAD OF WARD: 'She's a young 18-year-old girl, who has presented with problems of anorexia for 2–3 years. . . . Of course, this all began with' [Three nurses beat him to it and say in unison:] 'A diet!'

HEAD OF WARD: 'Yes, a diet.'

FOURTH NURSE: 'Classic, classic.'

[FJ]

The interviewees who defined the beginning as a diet also sometimes underlined how typical this was, from a medical point of view:

> Well, for me, it began around a year ago, last summer, like everyone, I began wanting to go on a diet to lose a few kilos . . . . Anyway, it's the same process for everyone I think, it always begins with a little diet.
>
> [Julie, H]

For doctors, the self-evident nature of the diet as the beginning sometimes even made them question the words of patients stating they did not want to go on a diet. For example, in the presentation of a clinical case of anorexia in clinic C, the intern outlining the case emphasized: 'The patient said she never had a conscious desire to go on a diet at the start'. The grammatical form of the sentence (with the indirect speech underlined by the words 'the patient said') is a common way of marking distance from patients' words.[4] From the medical perspective, a diet has to be present at the beginning of anorexia. At the same time, it is more than simply a diet insofar as it is the beginning of anorexia: to take up the medical term cited above, it should be seen as the 'insidious' sign of the pathology.

In the rare sociological studies that focus on the anorexic career, the point of view adopted is different but not radically so. These works do not call into the question the idea of the diet as a self-evident way of entering the anorexic career. Nonja Peters refers to the first phase as 'The diet phase, initiated in accordance with sociocultural ideals' (1995, 50), while Penelope McLorg and Diane Taub talk about 'conforming behavior [where] dieting figures prominently' (1994, 252). Unlike psychological or medical approaches, sociologists do not describe this diet as insidious – it is not considered as containing the seeds of anorexia. In these texts, this initial point in time is only considered on the basis of contextual data: it is less a question of examining this first phase in itself and more a question of linking it to the 'slimness norm' 'in our culture' (252): 'The context in which anorexia nervosa emerges is the focus of the diet phase' (Peters 1995, 52). It would be difficult to be any clearer in replacing analysis of the first phase with an abstract outline of how cultural norms of slimness are imposed. In these texts, the self-evident and ordinary nature of the diet, defined as the beginning, obstructs any specific analysis of how people enter the anorexic career based on interviews (rather than forced upon them). The authors do identify, within the career logic, the 'normal' – as opposed to 'deviant' – way of entering the first phase (which is in fact common to a whole social group that will not go on to pursue this career). However, they also allow themselves to be driven by this normality and, instead of analysing their interviews in detail, they seem to dilute their analysis of this initial phase with the social context they describe. It could reasonably be suggested that it is the normal and non-deviant nature of this first phase, unlike other deviant careers, that explains how little it is analysed. The interviewees' perspective is not really analysed because it not considered necessary for understanding what is happening, given that this first phase conforms to norms rather than transgressing them. It is also true that such analysis is made difficult by the relative absence of sociological studies on dieting as a social practice – as opposed to nutrition as an institution for governing bodies or as the manifestation of the objectification of the female body and of male domination.

In defining this first phase, I therefore did not begin with the certainty that the beginning was necessarily a diet. Instead, I built out from the interviews themselves, asking the question: 'How do the interviewees define the "start" of their "experience with anorexia"?' All the interviewees did identify an initial point in time, which is a result in itself. However, the nature of these points in time varied substantially and their extremely visible common features – accentuated by the psychiatric point of view – should not mean these differences are forgotten.

Three ways of beginning

The interviewees did always talk about a diet when they defined the beginning. However, on closer examination, there were careers that started with a diet, others that did not immediately start with a diet and some which did not *only* start with a diet. My analysis of the interviews revealed three different ways of beginning, by which I mean three different ways in which the interviewees themselves defined this beginning. As we shall see, these three ways were three different ways in which these girls began to take themselves in hand, which can be seen as constituting the first phase of the anorexic career.

Beginning with a diet

The beginning was sometimes defined as a diet, that is to say a practice aimed at changing physical appearance by losing weight. The initial weight loss was the result of strategies deployed with that objective: 'I began wanting to go on a diet to lose a few kilos'[5] [Julie, H].

This type of beginning most often had a very marked public nature. Three types of social roles and external actors contributed more specifically to the public definition of this diet and to shaping how it took place. These were people in a position to prescribe a diet, people who encouraged the interviewees to go on a diet and people who joined them and went on a diet at the same time. Analysis of my interviews brought to light the existence of various 'roles' that could be played by various different people.

The people *prescribing* diets were professionals. They could be doctors, nutritionists or sports coaches, prescribing a diet spontaneously or at the interviewee's request – and the latter had sometimes been encouraged to ask for this prescription. They were people who did not belong to the family group or to those close to the interviewee and who were in a position to give legitimate professional views about the interviewee's body:

> I did classical dance at the Conservatory, and, erm, our teacher often said to us that we had to lose some weight so, even though she didn't say it to me, you always feel a bit as if it's aimed at you when that happens.
>
> [Isabelle, C]

> So I started to go on a diet, on my own at first and then the mother of a friend of mine said 'you should go and see an acupuncturist, etc.' [pauses] . . . . So I saw that nutritionist through my friend, who . . . put me on a diet with all that 'you have to eat this', 'you have to eat that'.
>
> [Sabine, N]

More surprisingly, sometimes these 'prescribers' were professionals whose position was less obviously legitimate than that of a doctor with a normal weight curve, for example Anne's violin teacher:

ANNE: 'And there was my violin teacher too, she was all skin and bone, and once, when I was playing the violin, and there was another girl listening to my class, she referred to my size, you know [trails off].'

MD: 'Your height?'

A: 'No, my weight [pauses]. She said I was a strapping girl and that, well [trails off].'

[Anne, C]

However, the teacher nonetheless had sufficient legitimacy for Anne to remember the violin classroom as the place where she decided to lose weight:

> I was in the violin classroom, I was working on my own, and there was a big mirror, like that, so I saw myself full-length, and I was wearing jeans, so they were figure-hugging, you know, and I said 'What on earth are those pillars, you know!?', when I saw my legs, I said to myself 'You've got to be kidding', you know, and then I [pauses] I couldn't stand it, you know.
>
> [Anne, C]

As for the people who *encouraged* dieting, they did not intervene on the basis of any professional position; instead, they belonged to the family group, to the people close to the interviewees or to their peer group. When someone in the family encouraged dieting, it was usually the mother, both as the person socially designated as responsible for the nutrition and bodies of her family[6] and as a woman herself, also subject to dietary and bodily norms.[7]

> My mum is someone who is pretty [pauses] attentive to physical appearance, so she thought it was good that I should lose a bit of weight.
>
> [Annabelle, N]

> My mum has always more or less been careful about her weight, careful not to put too much weight on, not to eat too much fat [pauses] So from time to time, we'd go on a little diet, just like that . . . . A bit before the summer, my mum, if she saw she wasn't ok with the few kilos she'd put on, she would decide to be careful [pauses]. Once, she'd seen a dietician who had drawn up some menus . . . . So we tended to follow that, from time to time.
>
> [Julie, H]

The girls interviewed as anorexics were frequently vocal in their rejection of the medical and psychological theory of the 'pathogenic mother'. This therefore meant that references to the social role played by their mothers in the early stages of their diet were few and far between, to avoid giving any traction to this view. Conversely, the interviews carried out in the school, where this theory was not present, did discuss their mothers' dietary and body concerns, both in terms of their own bodies and of the bodies of other family members, especially their daughters:

J: 'Well, for me, where, I dunno, food and stuff's concerned, for me, it's a bit odd [pauses] Because, well [pauses] my mum wants me to be slim and everything, so she stops me from eating a bit. Well, she doesn't stop me from eating but she pays loads of attention to what I eat, she wants [trails off]. That's why, you know, so there you go [trails off] . . . .'

MD: 'And so how does that happen, for example?'

J: 'Well, like, during a dinner . . . so I'm eating and everything and, like, if my meal was already pretty rich, my mum goes "No, stop, you know, that's enough" and she goes, say that I go and get a yoghurt, she goes, "No, no, have a satsuma instead", things like that you know . . . . Because, actually, she had problems with her weight and everything. So, in the end, well, now she doesn't want that to happen to me. And then, on top of that, my mum, she thinks that, anyway, in society it's obvious that it's better to be physically [pauses] good-looking [pauses] well it helps in [pauses], anyway, in life, always, that's why. . . . I pretty much agree with her, that's how it is . . . [but] my brother, she buys him brownies and stuff, Nutella, ... I mean, a girl [pauses] Right, you know, she's the little doll, you want to shape her . . . . There are days when she'll be like "Oh dear", well, it's more the way she looks at me, the way she is, not so much the words, it's like this, you know, like this [she imitates a disapproving sideways glance].'

[Juliette, S]

Juliette considered the control her mother exercised over her food and her body to be justified. In the interview, she recognized and outlined her mother's legitimacy on three separate counts: as a woman who was herself particularly subject to body norms and who wanted to spare her daughter the same stigma – 'because she had problems with her weight'; as someone representing the norm linking women's legitimate bodies with 'social success' – 'And then on top of that, my mum, she thinks that, anyway, in society it's obvious that it's better to be physically [pauses] good-looking [pauses] well it helps in [pauses], anyway, in life, always, that's why'; and, finally, as a mother who could, or perhaps should, 'shape' her daughter. On all three scores, Juliette's mother was therefore seen as legitimate in her social role encouraging dieting. Anne, a friend of Juliette's whom I also interviewed at the school, emphasized how illegitimate she considered this role, but, in the end, concluded that her friend's situation was not that unusual:

A: 'Oh well you must've had loads of stuff with Juliette and eating habits! . . . You didn't get the whole lock on the fridge thing? . . . Ahhhhh! There's a lock [pauses] there isn't an actual lock, but her mum, well, it's like it's there . . . . If I wasn't allowed to touch the fridge at home [pauses] there'd be war! . . .'

MD: 'And you've never had that?'

A: 'Actually yeah, yeah [pauses]. My mum at one point, she'd be like "right, that's enough, you've eaten enough".'

[Anne, S]

More generally, my analysis of the corpus of interviews conducted in the school highlighted the importance of the mother's social role in controlling family nutrition, while also suggesting that this role was subject to both inter- and intra-family variation. The limited and secondary nature of the investigation conducted through interviews at the school means that while my results do suggest several possible hypotheses, these would need to be confirmed by a full-scale investigation. Cautiously, though, it seems as if the inter-family variations surrounding the mother's role were structured around class differences. What came to light was an initial form of variation separating, on the one hand, the encouragement to 'eat properly' or even to 'eat more' in Soizic's family (the only interviewee in the corpus from a working-class background)[8] from, on the other hand, the encouragement to 'eat better' or even to 'eat less', in the other interviewees' families. A second type of variation concerned the intra-familial variability in how the mother's role of dietary warden was applied across the family – girls seemed to be targeted first and foremost, justified more by directly physical and aesthetic considerations than by dietary concerns; to a lesser extent, husbands and partners were then targeted, on the basis of health concerns; and finally, but more rarely, sons were sometimes also concerned.[9]

More often than not, among family and those close to the interviewees, it was therefore the mother who encouraged the diet. However, this was not systematically the case. Sometimes, a boyfriend played this role instead:

> I'd had a bit of a disappointment in love and that person had criticized my physical appearance . . . . He'd said that my bum had got bigger.
>
> [Emilie, C]

> I had a boyfriend, who one day said: 'It'd be good if you went on a diet'. Well, actually, no, I complained all the time, 'I'm fed up, I want to lose weight', so that same guy, he said 'you're great like you are' and after about 6 months he said 'well, right, yeah ok it'd probably be good if you did go on a diet' . . . . Actually, I remember it really really well, it was almost the day we went back to school, the boyfriend . . . who said 'you should go on a diet', it was the day before we went back to school, I remember it really well, it was at his house and I said to him 'I thought you didn't care?'
>
> [Sabine, N]

Finally, encouragement sometimes came from the peer group, female friends in particular, who sometimes served as a generalized encouraging force, due to the recurrent nature of conversations about weight and the importance of watching it. According to the American anthropologist Mimi Nichter (2000), 'fat talk' is an important feature in schoolgirl subculture. This sort of talk was presented in the interviews as being both characteristic and burdensome:

Everyone, everybody talks about weight, you have to realize that. When you go out in the evening, there's not a single moment when someone [pauses] There's not one evening where we don't talk about that.

[Sophie, S]

All my friends: 'I want to go on a diet'.

[Sidonie, H]

However, the stances taken towards this talk differed from one interviewee to another. The norm conveyed by the peer group was sometimes discredited through the use of irony, for example in the case of Anne, one of the interviewees from the school corpus:

MD: 'But is that [weight] a topic of conversation among friends?'

ANNE: 'Well, I don't know, when I talk about it, it's mainly [pauses] mainly ironic. Because when I talk about it with friends, it's because one of them has brought up the subject, "Ohhhhhhh I'm too fat" [ironic tone] when she's a size 4 or 6.'

[Anne, S][10]

But this doesn't prevent weight norms from being conveyed by the peer group, or some of its members, particularly through precise and repeated monitoring of weight:

MD: 'And is that an [pauses] important topic of conversation, weight and all that, between friends?'

JULIETTE: 'It depends on the friends, there are friends [pauses] Yeah, but still, honestly, the one who's a model and everything, so like, well she knows that I have loads of problems with that, at home and everything, so like to piss me off, she goes "Yeah I've lost 5 kilos, blah blah blah" and I'm kinda choking on them, you know, those 5 kilos! . . . Like, my friends I go on holiday with, sometimes on holiday, it just comes up [pauses] it's natural and everything, like "How much do you weigh?" "Well, I weigh 52". "Oh well me, I weigh 54". "Yeah I put on 2 kilos recently", you know. And like "Right, so you weigh how much?".'

[Juliette, S]

Because on top of it in my class, it's been the same class since year 7. . . apart from one [girl in the class] who's really tall and pretty heavy, they're all really really tiny and because it was THE topic of conversation, "How much do you weigh?", thingummy-jig, well, obviously they weighed less, they weighed 35 and I weighed 45.

[Anne, H]

Finally, while the people encouraging the diet could be the reason for that diet, a particular kind of 'encourager' intervened directly during the diet itself to publicly approve its results:

> At first, from 64 to 57 [kilos], I was happy to lose weight and one of my sisters said 'Oh look, you've lost your little tummy', really great, in Year 10 I had this little belly and [pauses] at 57 I didn't have my little belly anymore and it seemed good to me.
>
> [Anne, C]

> Well, now, I've just lost weight, she [her mother] goes 'Oh right, well how much do you weigh now?', she asks me [pauses] because she's all happy to see that I've lost weight.
>
> [Juliette, S]

The role played by these different kinds of encouragement was all the more important because often it came from people with whom the various interviewees were in constant contact, unlike the 'prescribers' with whom they usually had occasional and clearly defined contact in a professional context. The encouragement to go on a diet therefore took place continuously, through just being present in the family or friendship group. When some of these people joined in with the diet too, this reinforced the continuity and proximity of the imposed norm.

In all cases, the people who joined in were women, most often members of the interviewees' family ('It was the summer, like May or June, my mum and my sister and I had been on a diet, it was like "3 days–3 kilos"' [Sidonie, H]) or friends ('I began [the diet] with a friend' [Louise, H]). Sometimes the individual joining in was the person who first suggested the diet; sometimes the interviewee asked her to join in:

> [My sister] had been on this diet at the same time as me . . . I said to [my sister] 'Why don't we do it together? It'll be better and everything' and so she said 'Yeah, yeah' and she went to see the doctor that I went to see.
>
> [Sabine, N]

> Well at first, actually it was my sister who had started going on a diet [pauses] and, well, I started a diet as well . . . . Actually, my sister had been to see a nutritionist so I followed it like her.
>
> [Christine, C]

By participating in the activity, the people accompanying the interviewees lent it legitimacy. But they also served as a living reminder of that activity, sometimes even as an outside monitor ensuring that it continued properly. The argument used by the different interviewees in favour of going on a diet 'with others' referred precisely to how fellow participants monitor each other. Sophie discussed this both in terms of the purely food-related aspect to the diet and the physical activity that went with it:

> Last time it was my mum, she went 'Right, well, that's it I'm going on a diet' and my sister and I looked at each other and we went 'Yeah, we're going to join in too, eh?' So actually we decided then . . . we're going to do it together all three of us and if with three of us we don't manage! . . . . And after, when one of us is like 'Boohoo, I can't do it' then we'll take her by the arm, and go 'Come on, let's go, let's get back to it'. For example, here [in the park where the interview took place] we came running so we'd go round once and my mum would say 'I can't any more' so I'd go 'come on, let's get back to it' and I'd take her by the arm [pauses] Afterwards, the second time round, it was me, I was like 'Oh, I'm fed up', my sister was like 'Come on!!!', so after my mum went round the little loop in the middle, [and] a little loop with my mum, a bigger one. Like that, it was [trails off] Actually we really motivated each other! . . . Now when we go on a diet it's all three of us, my mum, my sister and me. It's always all three of us on a diet at the same time. That way, actually, we support each other, we say 'Yeah, we can do it, we can do it'.
>
> [Sophie, S]

The people prescribing, encouraging and joining in were therefore all responsible for passing on dietary and bodily norms, and were also all involved in controlling or monitoring the interviewees' practices. These three kinds of role reveal the public nature of dieting as an activity as well as its normative nature, situated in different specific interactions. They define the situated space of the interactions that mean that the person on a diet is 'done' by others. In studies on how a legitimate body and dietary and bodily norms are imposed, social science research gives substantial value to various elements including: institutional and structural pressure by magazines and advertising (Travaillot 1998); the medical establishment and insurance industry's charts for normal and average weight, as institutions for governing bodies (Brumberg 1989, ch. 9); the diet food industry with its vested economic interests in the social practice of dieting (Hesse-Biber 1996, particularly 31–43); and finally the 'unconscious collusion' of all these activities in an endeavour of symbolic domination (Bourdieu and Delsaut 1975, 35). However, it is important not to underestimate the role played by the people prescribing, encouraging and accompanying conduct how these bodily and dietary norms are imposed upon a given individual in a given set of circumstances. As Howard Becker underlines, 'we cannot account for rule enforcement by invoking some abstract group that is ever vigilant; we cannot say that "society" is harmed by every infraction' (Becker 1963, 121–2). Because 'specific rules are applied to specific people in specific circumstances, we must look to see who it is that has made it his business to see that application and enforcement of the rules takes place' (134). In this sense, the different roles identified above can be seen as cogs in the wheel imposing norms – a role that can also be played by Becker's 'moral entrepreneurs'.[11] This group includes the people joining the dieter, who reinforce the legitimacy of the dieters' action and can also play a 'policing' role, acting as external monitors ensuring that dietary prescriptions are followed correctly. The entrepreneurs of the diet (the interviewees) did not begin that diet in a relational void, shaped only by general social injunctions to watch their weight or to lose weight. On the contrary, the moral entrepreneurs of bodily or dietary norms were just as responsible for defining the situation. They did so, in particular, by drawing up specific norms based on general values – particularly in the case of those prescribing the diet – and by then imposing these specific norms on a specific individual in specific circumstances.

However, these actors involved in the beginning do differ from the moral entrepreneurs studied by Becker in one important way. For Becker, the role that entrepreneurs play in a career is linked to their power to label deviance. However, the deviant learns the techniques of deviance through initiators, other members of the deviant group. To put it briefly, moral entrepreneurs impose norms by labelling, while members of the deviant group initiate new deviants to their practices. One of the specificities of the anorexic career is the way in which the boundaries between the two are blurred: learning is not distinct from labelling and moral entrepreneurs both teach behaviour and impose norms. In the case at hand, the entrepreneurs were sometimes the ones who taught the interviewee how to go on a diet and how to lose weight; they sometimes also helped her stick to that diet by joining in with her. This combination of roles can be explained, as suggested in chapter three, by the fact that the practices engaged in during the first phase are not deviant practices but normal practices or, more specifically, practices regulated by norms.

This feature of the anorexic career is also obvious when we look at how the interviewees actually learnt the techniques they implemented during this first phase. Three sources of learning can be identified, which overlap with some of the roles identified above among the external actors involved in the beginning: professionals, laypersons and 'literature'.

First, sometimes the professionals prescribing the diet, in the case of GPs and dieticians, also provided a method at the same time, offering techniques for losing weight. When a medical prescriber was involved, the interviewees followed his or her prescriptions, for example in Sabine's case [N]. Sabine stuck to the lists of food allowed and forbidden by the doctor she had seen and took the thyroid extracts he had prescribed. Similarly, Christine followed the diet prescribed for her sister by a nutritionist ('It was just a little holiday diet, you know. I mean there was a bit of everything, bread, red meat, fish, everything you know' [Christine, C]), and Julie drew inspiration from the menus a dietician had given her mother:

> Avoid eating too much fat . . . [eat] mainly vegetables . . . . At first, I started at the canteen [pauses]. I often chose vegetables if I had the choice between vegetables and starchy foods . . . . At the start, it was the quantities, I reduced everything a bit.
>
> [Julie, H]

The 'laypersons' involved in encouraging or joining the dieters were sometimes also sources of information as underlined, regretfully, by the nurse at the school where I conducted the secondary school interviews. She implicitly contrasted their advice with the 'good' diets prescribed by doctors or the balanced diet corresponding to medical recommendations:[12]

> And there was one this summer, too, who went on a diet, completely crazy as well, a cabbage-based diet, for breakfast as well! . . . When they go on diets, they go on diets like cabbage soup, three days of meat, four days of pineapple, I'm just saying any old thing . . . . Often it's 'my friend said this' or 'my mum did it when she was young' or 'I've got a cousin who lost weight doing that'.
>
> [School nurse, S]

Indeed, the peer group was another potential source of information or at least a way of finding out about what information was available:

> It's with this friend that I met in Year 8 and who I went on this diet with in Year 9, it's with her that I started to know that you eat 'calories', that you have to lose calories, because before I didn't think about that *at all*, I didn't know that by running you'd lose more than [trails off] It just didn't occur to me. And it's with that friend that I started reading dieting magazines [pauses], that we started being interested in all that.
>
> [Louise, H]

Finally, a third source for learning techniques involved all the 'means of communication' that allow access to a given technique:[13] all the normative literature about nutrition, such as the diets in women's magazines or literature providing nutritional advice. Women's magazines and their articles on diets were mentioned very often by the interviewees, as well as books or guides providing calories counts for different foods:

P: 'Oh God yes, I could say how many calories there were in a tomato depending on its weight, oh yes, for that [trails off].'

MD: 'And was that something, things you knew before or [trails off]?'

P: 'Things I learnt, yes, in books [pauses]. Not [by going to see] doctors or things like that, but myself, on the lists, looking at the calories.'

[Priscille, C]

In fact, the dissemination of norms and techniques is so present and widespread in the case of nutrition and dieting that, quite often, they are learnt without any particular source being identifiable. Dietary knowledge is presented as common, the things everyone knows you have to do to lose weight.

The interviewees' first definition of the beginning therefore described a diet, a particular set of eating practices aimed at changing physical appearance through weight loss; practices that were both collective and regulated by norms, as we have seen. When the interviewees talked about this diet, some of them referred to the medical theories that see it as the first stage of anorexia. But when they said they went on a diet 'like everyone', they were not necessarily referring to these medical theories by pathologizing the diet after the event and by 'like everyone' they did not necessarily mean 'like all anorexics'. 'Like everyone' could also be understood as the exact opposite of a pathological reading, as an attempt to normalize something that is pathologized in other contexts. Comparing the interviews with the non-anorexics in the school corpus with those conducted in the hospital setting shows that, actually, 'like everyone' could also refer to all women (in the family or the peer group) who go on a diet. When the girls interviewed as anorexics used this expression, it may well have been to underline that there was nothing exceptional about what happened at this initial point in time; nothing that was particularly specific to them, except, as we will see, the fact that retrospectively it could be seen as a beginning. However, it is also important to note that the expression 'like everyone' does tend to hide the fact that not all the interviewees defined a diet as being the beginning of their experience with anorexia.

Not beginning with a diet (at first)

Some of the interviewees defined the beginning as an initial period of weight loss that did not result from a diet. In these cases, the first few sentences of the interviews did not mention 'I started by going on a diet', as identified above, but instead 'I started losing weight':

> Well, I was in Year 10 . . . and I weighed 39 kilos or something like that, and after 6 months I weighed myself, I don't know why, and I saw that I'd lost 5 kilos.
>
> [Camille, C]

> I started losing weight . . . it began like that . . . . At the start, I didn't realize I was losing weight, and didn't want to go on a diet at first.
>
> [Priscille, C]

More specifically, sometimes they had gone on diets 'before' or wanted to lose weight, but they did not link this weight loss to those endeavours; they presented it as an initial fact that triggered what came after, rather than as the result of an initial strategy. They did sometimes, however, link this weight loss to a specific occasion that resulted in them not eating or losing weight; in other words, an external, contingent event that marked the beginning, whether this was a negative event ('It was after I'd been hospitalized, I had my wisdom teeth taken out and I couldn't [pauses] couldn't eat, only fruit purees and things like that' [Sophie, C]) or a positive one ('Well, I'd met someone and well, you know [pauses] at the start, you live on love alone' [Priscille, C]).

The 'diet' and 'weight loss' models were not exclusive alternatives, however. In the second model, there was always a point in time – during this first phase – when the initial weight loss was then re-enrolled within a diet or within a desire to lose weight (triggered by that initial weight loss):

> [Following the wisdom teeth operation] *I must have lost 1 or 2 kilos and I said to myself, 'what if I carried on [pauses] like that?'* And in fact I fixed a beginning of [pauses] I don't know how tall I was, maybe 1 metre 60, something like that, and I'd said to myself, 'well I'll carry on until 40 kilos, I'll lose until [I weigh] 40 kilos'.
>
> [Sophie, C, my emphasis]

> [Following the living on love alone] And I think it was a bit like that that it began, you know [pauses]. *Because I started to lose weight, and I started to like it* . . . . At the start, I didn't realize I was losing weight, and I didn't want to go on a diet at first [pauses] *But afterwards, I did* [trails off].
>
> [Priscille, C, my emphasis]

This model wasn't specific to the girls interviewed as anorexics, however. Anne, one of the interviewees from the school corpus, also mentioned an initial time of weight loss that she later converted into a diet:

> This summer, I went to Africa for five weeks, I ate nothing! My father lives in Zaire, so I went to see him there for five weeks . . . . As I was ill regularly [pauses] I didn't eat when I was ill . . . . I lost around 5 kilos [pauses]. Yeah, not bad for the diet! . . . Weight-wise, it was a good thing . . . . *And afterwards I carried on losing weight* . . . . Well, obviously I was happy afterwards! Of course when you're ill, you don't care, it's horrid. But it's true that afterwards you think 'Ahhhh! Wow, I've lost 5 kilos [pauses] That's not bad!' [pauses] It's true that afterwards I was pleased.
>
> [Anne, S, my emphasis]

In this case, there was therefore an initial period of weight loss presented as unplanned but then taken up and pursued as a diet. This can therefore be seen as a sequential career model in which concrete 'motivations' do not precede the person entering the career but are born from their own dynamic and in which, to paraphrase Howard Becker, rather than motivation leading to behaviour, it is the other way round; in time behaviour produces motivation (Becker 1963, 42).

It is not so much the nature of these two models of beginnings that differs as their chronology. In the first case, the interviewees entered into the career almost immediately, while, in the second, they entered it much less actively, but then went on to pursue it in the same way. However, when the diet began later, it did have one specific feature setting it apart: in most cases, it was a secret or at least a solitary diet. In the interviews in my corpus, while all solitary diets did not necessarily follow on from an initial period of weight loss, all the diets that did follow on from an initial period of weight loss were solitary and had no public definition: no one prescribed the diet or joined in with it and written sources were the interviewees' main sources of dietary learning.

Not just beginning with a diet

Finally, a third model for beginning also emerged from my analysis of the interviews: a multi-faceted engagement that included a diet but also extended beyond it. The diet was sometimes part of a much broader set of bodily practices, related to sports or clothing, for example. In these cases, at the same time as they began the diet, the interviewees also started playing a sport or increasing their physical activities, either spending more time on them or diversifying them. They sometimes also actively changed their clothing style or more generally their appearance through a change in hair style or a new or different kind of make-up:

> [Before] I didn't pay much attention to my appearance, how people dressed . . . . [But then] I paid attention, I wanted to wear make-up, to wear jewellery, to wear different things . . . . I dyed my hair a copper colour.
>
> [Priscille, C]

> Bam! I started running to the shops, Etam, thingy, all that. Looking in magazines, wanting to dress much better, to [pauses] become fashionable.
>
> [Sophie, C]

> I bought lots of clothes, I wanted to change my style a bit.
>
> [Louise, H]

> So then, as I said to you, you know, I wore very short skirts, I spent hours getting dressed, hours doing my hair, hours putting on make-up.
>
> [Christine, C]

In certain cases – those outlined above – these various practices took place at the same time. But looking back over certain interviews that described the beginning as a diet, it becomes clear that this diversification sometimes happened over time, alongside the diet:

> I wanted to dress up more, to wear skirts and all that, so I bought myself clothes.
>
> [Julie, H]

> Actually, I didn't just want to lose weight, at the end [of the diet, that is to say of the 'beginning'] I also want to build up my muscles. Like 'right so first I'll also be good at sport'.
>
> [Anne, H]

Sometimes, the various actions in which the interviewees engaged at the beginning therefore also corresponded to a progressive and process-oriented variation, which took place over a long period during the first phase of the career.

Just as the diet introduced a certain break in the continuity of previous eating habits, these various physical practices also testified to a desire to transform physical appearance, beyond the question of weight. But what seems more surprising is that the interviewees' practices regarding school work also changed. The social definition of the diet sometimes included physical exercise as well as dietary restriction, and sometimes also comprised remodelling their physical appearance more generally, through clothes, make-up or hairstyles. However, the interviews showed that school was another sphere of commitment during this first phase of the career: the interviewees engaged a process of self-transformation that extended beyond physical appearance and the body.

The changes in school work practices sometimes began with an increase in the time devoted to it:

> Before I was average, you know, I mean it was ok but [pauses] there was homework that I didn't hand in. . . . . So then I really threw myself into my studies.
>
> [Christine, C]

> It was the second term [of Year 11], to know which branch we'd end up in. And I wanted to go into 'S' in Year 12 [science branch, requiring higher marks than the others], I said to myself 'right come on, I'll show them [pauses] I'm going to work' . . . I wanted to be even better than I already was . . . I was good before, in Year 11, . . . but I don't know, I just had to be brilliant you know . . . I started working loads.
>
> [Louise, H]

> I was even more into my work than usual.
>
> [Mathilde, H]

Some of the material collected during my investigation offered a 'real-time' approach to these school work practices rather than simply a retrospective perspective. The school files of the interviewees in clinic C also included their reports from when they were in Year 10 or Year 9. The teachers' comments and the overall summary on the reports corresponding to the period of the beginning indicate the teachers' perception of this transformation in school work. For the interviewees who mentioned in their interview that their school practices changed at the beginning and whose school files were available, the teachers' comments at that time confirmed the break in continuity generated by their heightened commitment to school work. On Priscille's report from her second term of Year 12, the following comments can be seen:

> 'Shows lots of sensitivity and interest in the class. Should continue her methodological efforts' (French); 'Good. You have applied yourself a lot and made good progress' (History-Geography); 'Serious and consistent efforts' (English); 'Has made substantial progress' (Spanish); 'A bit better' (Maths); 'Has worked regularly and this has been beneficial' (Physics); 'Better overall' (Biology); 'Progress in almost all subjects. There is still a lot of work to do in maths, but have faith, you're on the right track' (overall summary).

This break in the school trajectory was even clearer and more institutionalized in the case of Christine [C], Yasmine [C] and Sophie [C]. In many schools in France, students can be given three levels of 'distinction' on their report cards – *encouragements*, recognizing hard work; *compliments,* complimenting good results; and *félicitations,* congratulating excellent results. In this case, all three girls went from '*Encouragements*' to '*Félicitations*' in the overall summary for the term they defined as corresponding to the 'beginning'. The recurrent terms found in these reports also testified to a new form of commitment to school work and to its efficiency, with constant mentions of 'effort/progress' and, more specifically for Sophie, the words 'determined', 'motivated', 'very thorough work' and 'perseverance'.

During this initial phase, the interviewees therefore did not only work on their bodies and the weighing scales were not the only measure of the results of their endeavour. For the third model, rather than just a diet, it would be more accurate to talk about an organized set of practices that included a diet. This is not just because the physical endeavour happened alongside the school endeavour, temporally speaking, but also because the interviewees sometimes explicitly linked the two, for example when Véronique referred to a self-transformation that was both related to her body (no longer being 'fat and ugly') and to her school work (no longer being 'a dunce').

> [The 'beginning'] corresponded to my *bac[caulauréat],* equivalent qualification to A' Levels, after which I'd put on lots of weight. . . . I was fat and ugly, you know . . . . And so I went to uni and there I decided that enough was enough. It was marked by [pauses] not 'professional' but [pauses] intellectual stages, if you like . . . . I'd been a dunce until Year 11, in Year 11 it improved a bit, well I passed my *bac* first time round, and then I came into my own, as it were, at uni. In the first year, I got good grades and in the second year, I was top of my year.
>
> [Véronique, N]

In this context, the diet makes sense within a variety of broader practices and reducing the first phase simply to the diet itself fails to account for the links between the various fields involved in this multi-faceted engagement. This was evidenced most clearly in Yasmine's account of the beginning of her 'experience with anorexia':

> So, I said to myself, 'right, you'd probably better start building up your muscles, etc.' but as I've always been lazy, like, really lazy, [I just said] 'right, well, just lose your big bum and it won't show that you haven't got any muscles!' . . . . But there wasn't just that, there was also [school work] . . . . Even the subjects I used to hate, I threw myself into them completely, saying to myself 'there's nothing that can stand in my way' . . . . In the end, I threw myself completely into all of it [pauses]. Even sports, which I hated before, I've been rubbish at sports since I was little. So I 'made an effort' and everything . . . . And also, I started reading [pauses]. Quite a lot of books, etc. I wanted to build up some solid cultural knowledge. . . . . Because actually, before, I used to read but [pauses] whatever I wanted, it was pretty much about the books I fell for, but then I wanted to [she emphasizes the following words] 'BUILD UP' my cultural knowledge, give myself some solid cultural knowledge . . . I dressed a lot more chic and stylish etc. Often it was black jeans, a tight t-shirt or vest top, nice and low-cut, or a little top and black jacket, formal shoes. It was really as classic as it gets [pauses]. Hair nicely done, make-up.
>
> [Yasmine, C]

In this case, the diet was only one component of a wider endeavour marking the beginning of the anorexic career: a both diverse and coherent set of practices, which were first and foremost characterized by the determination with which they were conducted. It was not just that certain practices emerged or were transformed, they were deliberately implemented or transformed in a determined fashion. Yasmine wanted to 'build up' a set of things by 'really throwing [herself] into it': a particular body, a style of clothing, a level of education that she chose rather than endured and some 'solid cultural knowledge'. She talked about 'taking herself in hand':

> It began a bit like that, a bit, like, [pauses] "I'm taking myself in hand", it was really [pauses] "I'm going to take myself in hand" . . . . And so bit by bit, I started to take myself in hand.
>
> [Yasmine, C]

Annabelle used almost exactly the same expression, talking about 'taking herself back in hand', referring to the fact that she did this after a period during which she had let herself go:

> Because there was the whole side of things to *prépa*, because I didn't do anything anymore, well, I didn't work on my homework, I copied it off other students, after a while, I started to react, saying to myself 'Right, that's not OK, now, you're not doing anything anymore, you've got to find yourself again, you know, the energy of the good old days when you worked, and you've got to learn things, to get moving', and at the same time, it corresponded pretty much to the beginning of the anorexia. Where there's also the whole, you know, 'taking yourself in hand physically' side of things.
>
> [Annabelle, N]

The term 'taking oneself in hand' seems particularly appropriate and relevant for describing what happens at the beginning of the anorexic career. This term, which emerged from the interviews themselves, proves useful as a descriptive and objectivating category offering a way of grasping the cohesive meaning of the three different modes of beginning discussed above.

Taking themselves in hand

In the career of relationship break-ups described by Diane Vaughan, 'uncoupling begins with a secret' (Vaughan 1986, 11). Here, we could say that the anorexic career began with the interviewees taking themselves in hand, creating a break in continuity with the past. The nature and status of this endeavour therefore warrant detailed analysis.

Breaking with the past – a question of practices

At first, this discontinuity sometimes appeared as a change in certain habits: changes in eating habits (through dieting), practices related to looking after the body (through physical exercise, changing 'style') and practices related to school and culture. From this point of view, this initial phase of commitment to the anorexia career marked a break with how things were 'before' in terms of habits and practices in these different areas. The main characteristic of this change was that it was deliberate and chosen, although this should not overshadow the extent to which these practices were regulated by norms. In all the interviews I conducted in the hospital, the interviewees presented the changes in their eating habits as something they decided at a given point in time, either at the start of the beginning in the first and third models outlined above, or in the latter stages of the beginning in the second model. On several occasions, Louise [H] used the expression 'Right, come on!', addressed to herself, to refer to the kind of stance she took during the beginning. This can be linked to Sophie's 'Bam! I started . . . wanting to dress much better' [Sophie, C] to Véronique's 'enough was enough' [regarding being 'fat' and 'ugly'] [Véronique, N] and to Annabelle's 'I started to react' [Annabelle, N], as well as to the recurrent use of 'I wanted' and 'I decided' in the excerpts quoted above. The break in continuity with previous habits relating to food, clothes, the body and school was therefore not incidental but the result of a deliberate choice. It was explicitly about self-transformation, about 'building up' someone different, to take up Yasmine's expression, whether on a physical level (through dieting, changing style or sport), on an educational level or on a cultural level.

The girls I interviewed as anorexics did not just 'decide' to break with the past, they managed to do so effectively – they all lost weight during this initial phase. When they were available, their school reports also testified to the efficiency of their increased commitment to their work. The term 'taking yourself in hand' seems an appropriate way of referring to this temporally situated, determined and efficient engagement in the anorexic career. Taking yourself in hand combines the meaning of two different expressions: 'taking yourself by the hand' (that is, forcing yourself to do something, training yourself to do something) and 'taking [something] in hand', taking it on board, dealing with it. Taking yourself in hand therefore means forcing yourself to take yourself on board. The taking in hand described here could be defined as implementing a coherent set of actions breaking with previous habits, putting self-transformation into practice. This definition applies both to the simple diet and to the broader forms through which the interviewees took themselves in hand, as identified above.

The three models of beginning presented above therefore appear as three different modes on which the interviewees engaged in the same process of taking themselves in hand, with variations of two different orders. The first kind of variation was chronological, contrasting the two different temporal frameworks at play. In the first and third models, the girls' decision to take themselves in hand was at the origin of the beginning, whereas, in the second (which began with an initial period of weight loss), they made this decision later by actively re-appropriating this weight loss. The second kind of variation related to the different extended forms through which they took themselves in hand, including food, their bodies, school and culture. This second type of variation also had a temporal dimension as these different efforts sometimes took place on different timescales. These differences therefore delineated the different spaces and timeframes in which one identical process played out as the interviewees all took themselves in hand.

Entering and leaving the first phase

In order to continue examining how the interviewees took themselves in hand, it is important to position their endeavour within a broader range of possibilities. The corpus of interviews conducted in the school offers this comparative possibility.

As stated above, all the interviewees in the school corpus 'talked' about diets. This was also true for the only boy I interviewed, who discussed it in relation to his sisters. However, the omnipresence of this *discourse* about dieting did not necessarily translate into the same omnipresence of dieting *practices*.[14] Dieting as a way of taking oneself in hand should be differentiated from a certain number of other situations that the school interviews revealed. The content of the school corpus offers a way of situating the diet as a beginning within a broader spectrum of ways of 'not beginning'. As we shall see, 'not beginning' can also mean 'leaving' the initial phase, which is not then retrospectively framed as a beginning.

Examining the interviews conducted in the school revealed a cartography of relationships to dieting norms that I can only briefly touch upon here. The strong dieting norm at work seemed to produce three types of stances deviating from the norm and its implementation. First, dieting was sometimes discredited as something contemptible because it places physical appearance at the top of a list of priorities:

> That, personally, I can't be doing with girls like that, it's superficial you know. 'Yeah, blah blah blah, I'm too fat, I've put on 2 grams, oh my God, it's a disaster and all that' . . . . It's the tall blondes with long hair [pauses]. It's the superficial girls who are only interested in their looks, you know . . . . That's why I'm not very careful, you know [pauses]. But it's true, I should be more careful.
>
> [Caroline, S]

At the same time, in this excerpt we can see that while Caroline discredited the norm, there was nonetheless still a form of submission in her words ('It's true, I should be more careful'). This brings us to a second way in which the interviewees in the school corpus sometimes deviated from the norm – not because they refused to give it any credit, but simply because they were unable to stick to it. This was the case for Elodie and Juliette:

> I often say to myself, 'I'm going to go on a diet', but to console myself about the diet I haven't been on yet, I have an ice cream [pauses]. Except I never go on the diet [pauses]. So [trails off].
>
> [Elodie, S]

J: 'Honestly, diet-y things, if it's natural, I can do it, but when it's like "restricting", I so can't do it.'

MD: 'And what's the difference for you? Restricting is [trails off]?'

J: 'I don't know, it's like [pauses]. At the moment, I'm managing to cut down without it being hard for me, you know. And, like, it's restricting when it's just too hard. Like, I go past something, it makes my mouth water and I'm like "I want it I want it I want it". But, like, I really like my food, it's that too, I like my food too much.'

[Juliette, S]

In these cases, it was precisely the taking themselves in hand part of dieting that the girls defined as impossible. They did not take themselves in hand because there was no break in continuity, no 'before' and 'after' in terms of their practices, as evidenced by the way Elodie's remark combined different moments in time: 'to console myself about the diet I haven't been on yet'. As for Juliette, it was the self-restraint required to take herself in hand that made it impossible, the things she referred to as 'restricting', that went against what was 'natural' for her.

Finally, a third stance emerged that consisted in 'being careful [about what they ate]', which also contrasts with dieting as a way of taking yourself in hand. In this case, it was not self-restraint that was rejected or considered impossible, but instead the 'discontinuous' nature of the diet. Being careful was presented as a continuous process, with no specific beginning. And although there were small moments when things were taken in hand ('Right, I'll have an apple', in the example below), these remained one-off and not at all imperative:

MD: 'And what about you, you were saying, you've been on diets too?'

S: 'No, I've never been on a diet [pauses]. I'm careful, but I've never been on a diet.'

MD: 'And when you're careful, what do you actually do?'

S: 'Let's say that I'll try and eat less things on the side [pauses]. Because, often, when I get home, if there happens to be a chocolate bar or little chocolate-y thing around, I'll tend to have it, you know. But, right, for example, if I'm being careful, instead, I'll say to myself "Right, I'll have an apple, or a fruit". But, other than that [pauses] avoiding too much sauce, but, . . . when I really want something and it'll make me happy, well, I just have it and there you go.'

[Soizic, S]

These three stances (dieting seen as illegitimate, dieting seen as impossible and choosing to be careful, framed as a flexible and continuous constraint as opposed to dieting) are three different positions that all contrast with taking yourself in hand. By contrast, they therefore highlight the specific nature of the diets to which the previous interviewees managed to 'stick'. In the case of the diets defined as beginnings, marking the start of the anorexic career, the protagonists always 'stuck' to them. This contrasted with previous periods when the same interviewees had 'wanted to lose weight' but without any results or when they had been on diets but had not stuck to them as strictly or had not seen the same results. The beginning diets also contrasted with the attempts of the individuals joining in with them:

> I was proud of having *stuck to it*, it surprised them [her mother and her sister].
>
> [Sidonie, H, my emphasis]

> If she [her sister who was on a diet with her] wanted to eat cake once in a while, she ate some [whereas I didn't].
>
> [Sabine, N]

> Like everyone I started to want to go on a diet to lose a few kilos [pauses]. *I saw that I managed to do it.*
>
> [Julie, H, my emphasis]

> Before, I'd drawn up a little list, I remember, 'never have a second portion, only have one piece of cheese, only have a small finger-sized piece of bread for my afternoon snack' [pauses] but I know that I didn't *stick to it* at the time, so it must have been before the autumn half-term [defined as the time of the beginning].
>
> [Anne, H, my emphasis]

When a diet was described as being 'stuck to', this implied that it involved the interviewee taking herself in hand. She followed the rules and the results were efficient, meaning that her endeavour was successful enough to mark a significant break with the past and be defined as a specific beginning ('I didn't stick to it at the time, so it must have been before the autumn half-term').

However, within the school corpus, some interviewees also recounted periods when they took themselves in hand. Géraldine, who had already been on a diet, even used that very term to refer to how she reacted to a situation in the past:

S: [There are times when] 'you look in the mirror and [trails off].'
G: '"You're fat!"'
S: 'Yeah! [laughter] . . . . It's more the times when you look in the mirror and [pauses] yuck . . . . For example, that can be when at school, in terms of marks, things aren't great [trails off].'
MD: [to Géraldine] 'Would you say that too?'
G: 'Yeah, when you've got lots of work and you can't cope, you know.'
S: 'You feel overwhelmed by it all [pauses] . . . . It's when everything's going wrong.'
G: 'It's just everything, you know. And maybe too, I don't know, there are times when you want everything to go wrong. I don't know, maybe it also lets you *take yourself back in hand* when you tell yourself that.'

[Géraldine and Soizic, S, my emphasis]

As for Sophie, she also used the expression 'Right, come on!' when she spoke about taking herself in hand with her mother and her sister. In the excerpt in question, below, the practical and actual implementation of this endeavour was once again characterized by its break in continuity ('really doing' it as opposed to 'not really doing' it):

> Well, this time we decided, we were like 'Yeah it's stupid you know, we start [a diet and doing sport] we never stop, well, we never stop completely, we never do it completely'. So this time we were like, 'Right, come on! This year, sports, when the year starts in September, we're going to get to it, all three of us, to try and go to the gym, stuff like that'.
>
> [Sophie, S]

The corpus of interviews conducted at the school therefore included cases of diets in which the interviewees took themselves in hand. However, these endeavours were limited in two important ways. First, they were restricted to the sphere of food and the body. Even in Géraldine's case, when she decided to take herself in hand in the face of a situation where 'everything' – at school and in terms of her body – 'was going wrong', her endeavour did not affect areas other than her body. Or at any rate, the interviewees at the school did not mention this at all (these interviews were, of course, framed as an investigation on 'eating habits', which may have predetermined the topics of the interview to some extent). Moreover, these cases when the school interviewees took themselves in hand were presented as being always already limited in terms of timeframe or in terms of achieving a specific predetermined objective. There was always a beginning and an end. Mona [S], for example, said she 'decides' to go on a diet every year before the summer holidays: she fixes a start date, the amount of weight to lose and stops once she has reached that weight. When Sophie took herself in hand, with her mother and her sister, the same principle applied: 'We fix a weight. My sister, it's 52 [kilos], me, it's 50 and my mum [pauses] most of the time it's 55. . . . I said to myself "I'll stop at that weight" [pauses] and at that weight I stopped' [Sophie, S].

Moreover, when this endeavour clashed with other aims, such as 'sticking to' school work, they put a stop to it:

> For the mock *brevet* exams [the *brevet* is a qualification taken at age 15, a little like the GCSEs], all that, every time I came out [of the exams] I felt dizzy, I fainted . . . . So I ate more, because I had to stick it out, ... So, I'll eat so that I can, for example, in class, because I know that, before, I used to faint, to be able to keep up at school. . . . . When I know I have to do something important [at school] I have to eat [pauses]. I know I have to stick it out. . . . [For the *brevet*] I revised kind of at the last minute, but it was the days I revised that I started eating [pauses]. When I said to myself 'Yeah I absolutely have to do that' . . . . I know that I wouldn't stick it out [a diet during a heavy school period], because I've already tried: I faint!
>
> [Sophie, S]

Not all the school students I interviewed entered this first phase of the career. And of those who did, some of them then 'left' it, essentially just by no longer taking themselves in hand, either by not sticking to the diet or by stopping it altogether. From this point of view, leaving the career during or at the end of this initial phase was 'easy'. Continuing the endeavour was what the interviewees presented as difficult, particularly in the school corpus, because it required substantial effort. The body's momentum, its hysteresis as it were (in other words, the dynamics and internal strength of the 'dispositions' it has previously incorporated, in Bourdieu's sense of the term), pushes the person to stop. Specific work was therefore necessary to counter this and allow certain interviewees to continue taking themselves in hand.

This first phase of the anorexic career – which the interviews referred to using the noun 'beginning' or the verb 'begin' – always entailed the same commitment to taking themselves in hand, although this varied from one case to the next in terms of chronology or the domains involved. The practices of bodily transformation that they put in place cannot simply be reduced to techniques for weight loss: they included dieting and sports activities but also changes in clothing styles, haircuts and make-up. They sometimes also engaged in similar work on other fronts, through new ways of investing in school work or accumulating cultural knowledge, with a view to achieving excellence in these fields. The desire to 'build up cultural knowledge' or achieve a certain level at school mirrored the desire to build up a particular body. This endeavour to change previous practices and habits required them to really *work at self-transformation* in a variety of practical areas that the girls interviewed as anorexics then pursued in the following phase.

In terms of other deviant careers, one of the main specificities of this first phase is that the activity in question is not subject to social disapproval – quite the contrary – and is only labelled deviant after the event. The girls interviewed as anorexics and some of the students interviewed in the school corpus shared common practices. The only difference was that the majority of the latter left this first phase at one point or another and it did not go on to become part of a career for them. It is only during the next phases of the anorexic career that this career became deviant, in the sense that it was labelled as such. It was the fact that the interviewees 'continued', that they maintained their commitment to taking themselves in hand, that became deviant.

Notes

1 Interview investigations were the basis of the fieldwork in Howard Becker's analysis of the career of the marijuana smoker (1963, ch. 3), Diane Vaughan's analysis of the career of relationship breakups (1986), David Karp's analysis of the career of anti-depressant use (1993), and Richard Ekins's analysis of the career of male femaling in cross-dressers and sex-changers, as well as the two texts that have focused on the anorexic career: McLorg and Taub (1987, 1994) and Peters (1995).

2 A reminder of the indexing used for the interviews: the letter following the first name of the interviewee indicates the corpus from which the excerpt is taken (H for Hospital H, C for Clinic C, N for the interviews through personal network sampling, S for the 'non-anorexic' school girls in School S, sometimes also referred to as the 'School corpus').

3 UK school years are used throughout. Students are 15–16 years old in Year 11, 14–15 in Year 10, 13–14 in Year 9 and so on.

4 On the use of indirect speech as a mode of expression for medical scepticism regarding patients' discourse, see Barrett (1996, 132).

5 Metric measurements are provided throughout, in keeping with the usage both in the original French context and, increasingly, in the clinical context in the UK: 1 kg is approximately 2.2 lb.

6 The historical and social construction of this maternal role ensuring and managing the nutrition and bodies of family members has already been discussed in the first chapter.

7 For a summary about how dietary and bodily norms focus on the female body, see Schur (1984, particularly 66–81). Edwin Schur draws attention to the fact that, because women are particularly subject to norms in this regard, they are therefore particularly likely to be designated as deviant.

8 In other families, this role seemed to be played by grandparents.

9 In this sense, the twentieth century was less the locus for a shift in the maternal role from preventing malnutrition to preventing weight gain or obesity, as Joan Jacobs Brumberg (1989) suggests, than it was the locus for a new combination of these roles in a system of intra-familial variations in how they are applied.

10 UK dress sizes are used throughout the book. A UK size 4 is a French size 34/US size 2; a UK size 6 is a French size 36/US size 4; and so on.

11 'Two related species [of moral entrepreneurs] – rule creators and rule enforcers – will occupy our attention' (Becker 1963, 147). Eliot Freidson suggests that the term 'moral entrepreneur' could be used to designate any member of the medical profession given that 'There is . . . an irreducible moral judgment in the designation of illness as such, a judgment the character of which is frequently overlooked because of the virtually universal consensus that exists about the undesirability of much of what is labeled illness' (1988, 252).

12 In her analysis of early childhood, Séverine Gojard highlights and distinguishes two modes on which rules about feeding infants are disseminated: a 'scholarly' mode characterized by 'recourse to legitimate institutions such as the pediatrician or infant care manuals, and which is encountered most often among upper class women' and a 'family mode' characterized by inter-generational transmission' which is mainly frequent among working-class women' (Gojard 2000). It could be suggested that this same distinction is present in the dissemination of dieting techniques, with the second mode functioning through both 'family' and 'friends', and that the nurse's criticism reflects this opposition.

13 'Deviant motivations have a social character even when most of the activity is carried on in a private, secret, and solitary fashion. In such cases, various media of communication may take the place of face-to-face interaction in inducting the individual into the culture' (Becker 1963, 31).

14 This is the argument defended by Mimi Nichter (2000).

5 'Carrying on' I

Maintaining the commitment

The first phase is short – a few weeks – and results in the loss of a few kilos; however, the second and third phases of the career last much longer – several months, for example – and lead to much more substantial weight loss. When the interviewees referred to this moment in their trajectory, they talked about 'carrying on', sometimes in a repetitive fashion ('I carried on, carried on, carried on'). However, analysis of my interview corpus shows that the period during which they 'carried on' in fact spanned not one but two phases. These overlapped to some extent but could nonetheless be distinguished from one another. In the first of the two (the second phase in the anorexic career), the question of whether to carry on or whether to stop was an issue for the interviewees themselves. In the second of the two (the third phase in the anorexic career), the situation was increasingly defined by external actors instead, who framed it in terms of the interviewees 'not stopping'. The initial weight loss – which originally generated positive reactions – continued throughout these two phases. By the second phase, though, it had gradually reached the stage where a 'circuit of career agents' had formed taking certain interviewees 'from civil to patient status' (Goffman 1961, 142). In this sense, the boundaries between the two phases were not strictly demarcated: these two definitions of the situation progressively entered into competition during the second phase of the anorexic career, before the external definition was established and the 'circuit of agents' led to diagnosis and hospitalization. This chapter will look at the first of these two periods of carrying on from the point of view of the interviewees – as 'the commission of a given act', to use Becker's terms. In chapter six, I will go on to look at the reactions that act generates and the effects these have on the interviewees – in other words, the 'definition of that act as deviant'[1].

The second phase of the anorexic career consisted in the interviewees continuing to take themselves in hand, as described in the previous chapter. Whether they found this easy ('It fascinated me to lose weight so easily [pauses]. And to see I could control what I ate' [Christine, C]) or hard ('It's not as easy as that, when you've got an appetite, to go on a diet, it's not easy' [Anne, H]), its efficiency was a condition of possibility for them maintaining their commitment. Their success was what allowed them to carry on and enter the second phase of the anorexic career, unlike those who left the career at the end of the first phase as we saw earlier.

'Carrying on' was defined above all in terms of the diet. The interviewees were able to maintain their commitment because it had been efficient, because it could be used retrospectively as a test of possibility: 'It's like, by going on the diet, I realized . . . that I didn't need to eat as much as I thought' [Sabine, N].

The interviewees also defined 'carrying on' in contrast with how others stopped, particularly those who had originally joined in with them:

> Among my friends . . . everyone was on a diet [pauses]. Except, well, they held out two weeks and it was over.
>
> [Louise, H]

> [Christine began by going on a diet with her sister] Well, for her, it was just a little summer diet, so she lost the 2, 3 kilos she needed to lose and she stopped. And, well, I carried on, carried on, carried on, carried on.
>
> [Christine, C]

As we can see, the interviewees talked about this moment in their trajectory with very brief, and sometimes repetitive, mentions of carrying on. Talking about the second phase in these terms could give the impression that it was nothing more than an extension of the first phase over a longer period of time, which then led directly to hospitalization because of the resulting weight loss. Although I will use the interviewees' definition of 'carrying on' here, it is also important not to completely accept its seemingly self-evident nature. In this respect, it is useful to look to Howard Becker's analysis of the career of the marijuana smoker, which also takes distance from smokers' definitions of the type 'I started smoking and then I carried on' or 'I smoked more and more'. In order to break with this self-evident and continuity-based version of events, Becker's analysis brings in all the other elements that might be overlooked at first; in other words, the necessary conditions for this progressive commitment to the career. In his view, the notion of learning is key and informs the conditions of possibility, which are threefold (learning techniques, learning to perceive the effects and learning to enjoy the effects),[2] because the career is composed of activities that are new for the person engaging in them and because learning does not occur in the open but requires initiation within a deviant group. However, the techniques for 'losing weight properly' are not necessarily learnt during this second phase. They may well have been learnt before and, in some cases, simply put into action at this point. In the case of anorexia, 'learning' is therefore quite specific. In this chapter, I will try to distinguish between what the interviewees had already learnt in the past and what was new for them, in terms of techniques but also in terms of their perception and enjoyment of effects. This approach is useful in three particular ways. First, it makes it possible to identify the elements in the interviews that belong to the second phase of the career, even though the interviewees often mentioned them at other points in the interview (not just when they briefly referred to carrying on). Second, it highlights the work that the interviewees did to enable them to continue taking themselves in hand, despite the fact it was also passed over in the interviews. And finally, it means we can go on to look at the effects of this work and of the learning process involved, in order to unpack how the girls acquired the necessary 'dispositions' for carrying on.

Working on techniques

Analysis of this phase, during which the interviewees continued and intensified their endeavour to take themselves in hand, highlights just how much maintaining this commitment required considered and determined *work*:

> It's not 'I had a shock and I stopped eating because I was disgusted' [pauses] I thought about it so much, I saw the magazines, I saw the difference in weight and everything . . . the models weighed like 20 kilos less than their height . . . . I started counting calories.
>
> [Sidonie, H]

> Now I'm pretty impressed by the willpower it required! Because I've tried to stop smoking [pauses] and I don't have the same willpower that I had when it came to stopping eating! [laughs].
>
> [Véronique, N]

First of all, this work related to techniques. Most of the weight-loss techniques used in this second phase were those used in the diet that came before. However, during this second phase, they were increasingly used in an intensified and rationalized manner.

Rationalizing techniques

The interviewees adjusted their use of techniques according to their aims in such a constant and measured way that it could definitely be described as a 'rationalization' of the practices they used to take themselves in hand. The techniques in question were mainly drawn from nutritional science and similar to those used in the first phase. However, they also searched for specific information in order to increase the stock of available techniques. Progressively, they increased their knowledge in this domain, learning how many calories different foods contained, identifying which foods were 'fattening', classifying foods as 'starches', 'fat', etc. They then used this knowledge in two ways: first, to monitor their daily calorie intake and second, to choose foods according to their type. In both cases, this knowledge guided their consumption. Calorie counting was sometimes used both as a criterion for a specific food choice and as a way of controlling daily food intake:

> For example, when I ate an apple, I'd say 'Should I eat an apple or a pear?', I'd look in the book, which has the least calories, and, well, the one with the least calories.
>
> [Emilie, C]

> I had the table of calories and everything, it all interested me [pauses]. It was just the calories that interested me actually, I never read the stuff about the value of foods, what they provided, whether they provided calcium, iron, I couldn't care less. But it was also because I liked eating, and I wanted to know how far I could go [pauses] I spent entire days doing the maths, 'this morning I had a cracker, that's 20 calories' and each time I started the maths again.
>
> [Véronique, N]

> I counted, I counted [calories], I weighed [food], I had these little kitchen scales.
>
> [Sabine, N].

These calculations, along with all the figures mentioned in the interviews, show the importance of the reflexive nature of the girls' work. Constantly counting and measuring things contrasts with the 'natural inclination' described by one of the school corpus interviewees (quoted at the end of the previous chapter) as the reason why it was impossible for her to go on a diet. Isabelle, whom I interviewed just after her arrival in clinic C, described this constantly reflexive stance in the present tense and differentiated it from 'spontaneity', reflecting once again an opposition between letting herself go and working on her practices:

> But if I'm hungry in the middle of the day, like now, I won't let myself eat anything, well, I don't know [pauses]. You see, like now, look, you see? I brought fruit back, but I'm saying to myself 'no it's not time yet, wait till this evening, blah blah blah' . . . . I'll eat them, but maybe in the morning, I'll spread them out a lot, I won't just do what I feel like [pauses]. If I feel like a pear, I won't eat it until, it'll be really thought out before. Whereas it should be spontaneous, you know [pauses]. It's thought out, 'cos it's counted: 'Yes, but then that'll be more'. But it's only a pear.
>
> [Isabelle, C]

Certain techniques did not change radically from the first phase to the second (counting calories or weighing food can be part of a diet) but they were implemented more systematically. However, other techniques were more specific to this phase, such as using comparison with others as a technique for dietary restriction:

> I'd look at other people's plates, and I always had to eat less than other people.
>
> [Emilie, C]

> [In the canteen] I always looked at what my friend was eating, and every time I'd eat less than her, I'd eat half [of what she'd eat]. And because she was quite fussy, she already didn't eat very much, so, as for me, it was [trails off].
>
> [Anne, H]

In terms of food choices, in the first phase, dietary restriction was sometimes only quantitative – reducing portions or meals – but in this phase, the increase in nutritional knowledge made it possible to select food according to those principles:

> And after [the beginning], well, I plunged myself into books [about nutrition]. So then I realized that white meat was less fattening than red meat [pauses]. So bam! I cut out red meat. It's the first thing I cut out. Then I cut out starchy food. And then after I only ate vegetables.
>
> [Christine, C].

> So really quickly you know that you have to cut out sugar and fat, well, you think that you have to cut out sugar and fat. Then you cut out meat, because it's fatty, then you even cut out yoghurts, even the fat-free ones because you tell yourself that they're probably fattening anyway [pauses] And then, yes, lettuce. It's about the only thing where you don't see what you could cut out . . . . I know there were things I did eat. When it was strawberry season, I'd eat lots of strawberries [pauses] I lived off strawberries. Off fat-free yoghurts and Granny Smith apples, that's it.
>
> [Annabelle, N]

> Bit by bit, I ate my starter, and three bits of meat, and two vegetables, hardly anything. And then bit by bit, I cut back, cut back . . . . And I cut back even more, I didn't finish my plate . . . . At first it was the quantities, I cut back on everything, but then I actually stopped eating starchy foods, bread, cheese [pauses] I removed things bit by bit, you know.
>
> [Julie, H]

All three excerpts reveal the progressive and cumulative nature of dietary restriction. The interviewees constantly reiterated the fact they were taking themselves in hand – Christine's 'bam! I cut out red meat' is noteworthy – and each time, restriction and control was intensified, with every dietary restriction put in place making the next one possible. Several of the interviewees presented as a biological fact that it was 'not possible' to go directly from 'eating normally' to 'almost completely stopping eating'. The work at stake in maintaining the commitment was therefore about training both body and willpower in this progressive restriction.

Sorting and selecting food intake on the basis of calorie content was not the only mode of dietary restriction in play. Sometimes, only the overall calorie content was monitored and restriction entailed a compromise between very precise calorie counting, on the one hand, and carrying on eating high-calorie, fatty or sweet foods, on the other:

> I preferred to go without a meal to be able to eat a square of chocolate in the middle of the afternoon.
>
> [Véronique, N]

Y: 'In general, I said to myself 'right, if I cut out two hard-boiled eggs I can have an ice-cream'

MD: 'And did you do that?'

Y: 'Yeah, I could eat [almost] nothing for two days, but get really stuck into an ice-cream'.

[Yasmine, C]

> I'd eat fat-free fromage blanc, with no sugar and [pauses] at the same time, I'd eat pound cake with it [pauses] . . . . Because I told myself that the fat-free compensated for the sugar [of the pound cake].
>
> [Emilie, C]

'Counting' calories, 'weighing' food, 'choosing' food according to nutritional criteria and 'reducing' meals all point towards a rationalization of food intake. We can see a dual endeavour taking shape here: the interviewees worked at obtaining information about techniques and then worked at putting the latter into practice. In some cases, the weight loss was even made scientific, for example in the experiments Yasmine conducted:

Y: 'During the time I was really very anorexic, when I managed my weight loss really well, etc. I mean, I was in S [the science branch], I did all the stuff about the metabolism, etc. I studied the books, I really bust a gut, I even learnt it all like that [snaps her fingers], after reading the slightest thing I could reel off incredible stuff. And I was able to manage my weight loss, you know, scientifically [pauses] unstoppable. . . . And in Year 12, of S, I was doing 'experimental science' and I used myself as a guinea pig [ironic tone] it was great. I ended up with 19 [out of 20] . . . .'

MD: 'And what do you mean when you say you used yourself as a guinea pig?'

Y: 'About breathing etc. blood pressure, blood, all that, nutritional content, the effects [pauses], hypoglycaemia, hyperglycaemia [pauses]. You should've seen me, managing everything perfectly'.

[Yasmine, C]

The interviewees' endeavour to maintain their commitment also involved the other areas in which they took themselves in hand. Alongside the rationalization of dietary restriction, they pursued their work on their bodies through physical exercise:

> I'd gone back [to swimming] and I went all the time, all the time, all the time, I swam, I swam [pauses] It really became [pauses] The way of losing [weight], you know.
>
> [Christine, C]

> Every time that I'd eat 'a' chip in the week, it was a disaster, I absolutely had to do some sport. And at the weekend, I did a lot: gym, tennis or swimming [pauses] everything I could.
>
> [Louise, H]

> Abs morning and night, morning and night [pauses]. In general I'd do twenty minutes in the morning, twenty minutes at night.
>
> [Sophie, C]

The commitment to school work and cultural knowledge was also maintained by continued, sometimes intensified, practices. The interviewees' heightened and systematic investment in school work was analogous to the work they were doing on their bodies:

> I mean, spending six hours doing maths stuff, it didn't bother me, on the contrary . . . [and then I wanted] to be able to come out with a quotation every time, there you go, so that you couldn't talk to me about an author without me being able to talk about him or her . . . . I got stuck into classics, every time someone mentioned a name, etc., after I'd go to the library and I'd take out three books by the same author, I really went all out.
>
> [Yasmine, C]

> The subjects I was less interested in, I didn't want to set them aside anymore.
>
> [Isabelle, C]

> I've always been a perfectionist, I like doing things well [pauses]. But then it really intensified [pauses]. If I didn't know the lesson by heart, it was a disaster.
>
> [Mathilde, H]

> There was the *bac[calauréat]* and everything was planned, you know [pauses]. The times, the [trails off] . . . . If a history chapter wasn't finished at five o'clock when I'd planned to finish it at five o'clock, even at five past I'd become [trails off] . . . . If at five o'clock it wasn't done, I'd be angry with myself . . . . I read a lot. I couldn't stand not learning, I couldn't stand not being able to say 'there was that, at least, in my week, at least there was that novel'.
>
> [Christine, C]

The girls therefore implemented new techniques for excellence at school: exhaustive learning techniques in the case of Yasmine or Isabelle, stricter evaluation techniques in Mathilde's case and time-planning techniques in Christine's case. Their school reports once again offered a trace of their teachers' perceptions of this work. Looking at the comments between the moment of change identified in the previous chapter (the beginning of their heightened investment at school) and the interruption caused by their hospitalization, it is striking how recurrently they were encouraged to work at maintaining their commitment: 'Carry on' [Biology], 'Carry on!' [Maths], 'Promising work' [French], 'Must carry on' [Biology], 'Conscientious attitude and progress to be continued' [Maths], for Christine [C];

'Carry on' [MFL], 'Carry on' [Physics], 'You should carry on like this' [PE], for Yasmine [C]; 'Carry on!' [History–Geography], 'Constant progress. Carry on' [Physics], 'Carry on' [Biology], 'Carry on!' [overall comment], for Sophie [C]. Of course, these sorts of comments are standard categories used by teachers to recognize and value students' work and should not be considered as specific to the interviewees' school reports, much less as encouragement of the pathology on the teachers' part. Nonetheless, they testify to the fact that the girls did maintain their commitment on the school front. They also indicate that school practices 'appear' deviant much later than eating habits, insofar as – and we will see this in the next chapter – people started sounding alarm bells about the girls' eating habits or weight while their commitment to taking their school work in hand was still meeting with widespread social approval.

This second phase can be described as a veritable *rationalization* and *radicalization* of the interviewees' endeavour to take themselves in hand. This translated into constant vigilance over many aspects of their lives. Their day-to-day existence became governed by the 'rhythm' of the work involved, right down to the smallest detail:

> I organized my life around meals, everything I was going to eat, not eat . . . [and] my studies, my studies, my studies, it was my only centre of interest . . . . It was my rhythm, I was the one determining my life.
>
> [Christine, C]

Nothing was out of bounds for this rationalization and every activity could be reinterpreted and used in that framework:

> I did everything to lose weight: I never took the lift anymore, whenever someone needed something from a street round the corner I'd go and get it straightaway; there's the whole 'you have to burn off energy' side to it too.
>
> [Annabelle, N]

A: 'Well, I wouldn't go back to six hours of sport every day!'
MD: 'Because that's what you did?'
A: 'Not six, but four. Cycling [pauses] I went to school by bike, that was already 2 kilometres, I never sat on the saddle of the bike, I was always out of the saddle [pauses] Tennis, handball [pauses] and above all going down staircases [pauses] I don't know, I must have done like 50 kilometres of stairs . . . . I'd go to tennis, I'd go downstairs, bam!, I'd go up all the stairs, my house has two floors, I'd say to my brother 'I'm leaving for tennis', I'd go back down them all, I'd say to my sister, 'I'm going to tennis', I'd go back down them all, I'd get changed, I'd go back down them all, I'd get my racket, I'd go back down them all 'I'd get my jumper, I'd go and get my keys, I'd go and do my hair [pauses] And off I'd go! Just to go to tennis, instead of climbing 12 steps I'd do 804!'

[Anne, H][3]

To pursue a sporting metaphor suggested by Yasmine, one might say that after the 'sprint' of the first phase comes the 'endurance' race:

> In Year 12, when I was anorexic, it was the only time I got the average mark in PE! Before I always got around 8 or 9 [out of 20], and everything, then I ended up with 14s and 15s. Anyway, an anorexic [trails off] [at school, in PE] they had us do endurance [pauses] [with a smiley voice, as if speaking to her PE teacher] 'No problem! I'll do "endurance", are you kidding me??? Endurance is no problem for me!'.
>
> [Yasmine, C]

The term 'endurance' – used by Yasmine in a way that implied it extended beyond the realm of sports – reflects both success in maintaining the commitment in the long term and the efforts necessary to achieve that. The commitment was maintained but also endured. Certain strategies were also sometimes used to make that endurance race physically possible and to enrol its continuation into a bodily dynamic.

Building habits

'I don't remember regulating my life this much when I was little' [Isabelle, C]. The term Isabelle used was very apt as it was definitely 'regulation' that allowed practices to be rationalized in this way: precise, determined and constant regulation, in which counting and measuring were paramount. This regulation was established 'progressively', 'bit by bit' throughout the second phase. Rationalization offered the interviewees a way of carrying on their initial endeavour to take themselves in hand, in an 'unstoppable' manner, but it also allowed them to form habits which made it easier, less costly, for them to maintain this commitment. This phase was not just about losing weight, it was also about working to develop tools – in this case, habits – that made it possible to continue the efforts from the first phase over a longer timeframe.

Certain techniques were aimed at making it easier to deal with the work involved in the short term, for example drinking water or tea to 'trick' hunger: 'Sometimes, but not now, before, well my tummy still rumbled sometimes and all that [pauses] "Well, listen, it doesn't matter, you drink a bit of water and it'll pass", you know' [Isabelle, C]. Another set of techniques aimed to make it possible to pursue this work in the long term, with progressive rationalization taking place. By the end of the second phase, certain practices were possible – physically as well as mentally – that were not possible at the beginning, and the interviewees' aim was often getting used to these practices:

> At one time, what I did was I ate for my afternoon snack, I really ate lots for my afternoon snack [pauses] I drank milk, I ate biscuits, and that way I wasn't hungry in the evening . . . . And then it [the afternoon snack] wasn't once a day, it was every other day or every three days . . . . [Some food], I'd eat lots

> of it until I was sick of it [pauses]. That way I was sure I'd be sick [of that food] [pauses] 'That way, at least I won't eat any of that anymore'. So that's how I ended up liking less and less stuff, because I made myself sick of it . . . that way it made me feel sick and I didn't like it anymore . . . . I deliberately wanted to make myself feel sick, so I wouldn't eat anymore, to lose my appetite, I made sure I'd be sick of something.
>
> [Nadège, H]

> You realize that you can get used to eating whatever you want . . . . I liked sweet stuff, but I managed to convince myself that I was sick of it [pauses] I managed to say to myself: 'OK, this is ridiculous, don't eat it anymore, it makes you feel sick, it'll make you ill'. There's maybe a kind of pleasure in telling yourself that in the end you can get used to anything.
>
> [Annabelle, N]

In these two excerpts, the interviewees' aim was to deliberately make themselves sick of foods they had excluded from their intake as part of their dietary rationalization. In other words, they wanted to write the rules and reflexes of the diet into their very bodies, in a determined and deliberate fashion. In the same way, Anne [H] talked about 'getting a taste for' sports ('I started to do lots and lots of sport, and so I got a taste for certain sports that I didn't know'). The interviewees worked at getting a taste for things, learning to enjoy them, and, conversely, at finding ways to become sick of other things, to no longer enjoy them. In both cases, this contributed to them maintaining their commitment, as an active tool rather than a simple fact. This work on what to enjoy/not enjoy is a specific example of a broader endeavour to form specific habits; not the occasional habits of the first stage of the career, but new habits to thoroughly replace old ones. These efforts were part of a habit-forging rationalization aimed at making future efforts easier and therefore making it possible to maintain the commitment. In this sense, the techniques involved corresponded to a rationalization of daily life in the present, but are also to a commitment to the future.

Technical tests

This work on techniques was also apparent in the experimentation and tests involved. Certain techniques were explored and adopted, while others did not result in habits being forged and were therefore abandoned. For example, regarding mealtimes, most of the interviewees insisted on the fact that they continued to stick to the 'three meals a day' model in both structure and timing, even if they drastically reduced their meal content. For some other interviewees, however, skipping a meal was something they tested and then adopted given that it did not cause any immediate adverse consequences. Sometimes this test was accidental, for example when Anne discovered by chance that she could manage without breakfast: [During the beginning, Anne never skipped meals] 'And then, two mornings, I woke up at 8am, so I didn't have time for breakfast and I realized that I was fine, so I might as well skip the meal because I managed fine!' [Anne, H].

Here we can see a process at work that Howard Becker identified in the career of the marijuana smoker. Sometimes the latter discovered by chance, and to his great surprise, that it was possible to successfully do something complicated while high:

> One or more occurrences of this kind allow the user to conclude that he can remain a secret deviant, that his caution has been excessive and based on a false premise. If he desires to use the drug regularly he is no longer deterred by this fear [that nonusers will realize what state he is in].
>
> (Becker 1963, 71)

However the fear in question can extend far beyond just the fear of being discovered: Anne's 'I realized that I was fine' showed that, in this case, repeated experience alleviated the fear of not being alright if she skipped a meal. This was not so much about saving face and keeping deviant behaviour secret as it was about having discovered a new possible weight loss technique at little cost to herself.

Sometimes, however, new techniques were added to the available stock through proper experimentation. Techniques that had been tested were then deliberately transformed into habits:

> [Sidonie had got used to skipping lunch while on holiday, with the help of the particularly generous breakfasts provided by the holiday resort] But of course it was the holidays and here you can't do the same thing [pauses]. Breakfast is cornflakes, you can't do the same thing as at the resort [pauses]. And so then I tried with just cornflakes and I saw that I managed to hold out.
>
> [Sidonie, H]

> Nothing happened if I didn't eat a yoghurt, so why eat a yoghurt? . . . That happened with the things I ate regularly.
>
> [Christine, C]

Techniques were tested and certain habits then adopted, or even written into the body itself. However, these tests sometimes had negative outcomes. In these cases, the practice was not adopted and did not become a habit. Examples abound, involving practices with varying degrees of legitimacy – ranging from sports activities to making themselves vomit:

> I mean, before, I did quite a lot of sport [pauses] and then, as soon as I started losing weight, I started fainting from the very beginning, you know, automatically, and feeling really weak, and I didn't do anything, quite the opposite, I made as little effort as possible. I didn't do any sport at all anymore.
>
> [Julie, H]

> Like I said, I didn't do any emetics stuff [pauses]. At one time, I took diuretics and laxatives, well, I tried, but well it lasted like two weeks, but it was so disgusting I stopped [pauses] but I did it, I did it. Because being sick, I found that horrible and everything . . . . But so it didn't last. I tried, I tried. I also tried to make myself be sick once, I tried and I gave up, you know.
>
> [Sabine, N].

> But I've never made myself be sick [pauses]. I have tried, you know? It's true, but I never managed.
>
> [Christine, C]

This aspect of the work on techniques reveals two factors that affect the modes used to maintain the commitment: first, whether or not a particular activity is tested and second, whether or not the test succeeds and the practice can be made into a habit or not. The interviewees' work testing techniques and transforming what they did or did not enjoy shows that the resulting habits were not simply the result of the activity itself but the product of a veritable endeavour.

Measuring work

When techniques were put into practice, as described above, this often went hand in hand with specific work relating to measuring their results. These techniques for evaluating the body were based on four tools for objectivating self-perception: weighing scales, full-length mirrors, clothes and dress sizes, and comparison with others. The interviewees used these tools to measure the effects of the work they were doing to take themselves in hand, but also to enable or facilitate the possibility of continuing this work.

Rationalization of measurement

The extent of this measuring work reflected the extent of their work putting the techniques into practice: constant efforts to lose weight were matched by constant measures of their success. Both weighing scales and dress sizes were put to use in evaluating weight loss in numerical terms. In both cases, a continuously decreasing number was observed and judged:

> I was happy when I bought new clothes, 'Ah I fit in a size 10, ah in a size 8'.
>
> [Julie, H]

> I weighed myself all the time, all the time, all the time. I saw the scales going down, going down, going down, I was really happy.
>
> [Sabine, N]

Clothes could also be used for evaluation purposes, through comparisons with older clothes:

> Given that I was losing weight, in the evening I couldn't wait to get dressed the next day because I knew my trousers were going to be loose.
>
> [Julie, H]

> In terms of my old clothes, I absolutely had to keep my clothes to check where I was at, you know.
>
> [Anne, C]

At first sight, a full-length mirror might seem less likely to be used in a rational and numerical manner, but specific techniques were sometimes used to objectivate self-perception:

> I looked at myself in the mirror a lot [pauses]. I looked like this, from behind, and I pulled my legs together, and looked here at the gap between my two thighs [pauses]. And the bigger the gap, the happier I was.
>
> [Emilie, C][4]

> [When she would go down the stairs all the time]. And on top of it, the stairs are stairs like this and there, there's a mirror [pauses] And when you go down, you can see your calves in the mirror [pauses]. I spent my time looking at myself there.
>
> [Anne, H]

Different tools were also sometimes combined to achieve a more precise or accurate measurement:

> Because there's muscle mass and fat mass, so obviously the mirror was to see the difference between the two and the weight was to see if I'd lost any [pauses] and the mirror to see if I had lost some, where I'd lost it.
>
> [Yasmine, C]

This systematic self-observation and self-evaluation was also sometimes accomplished through comparisons with others: 'I was always looking at other people's calves, all the time. If someone was talking to me, I'd be looking at their calves [pauses], the teacher's calves, anyone's calves [pauses] . . . . Because I thought mine were fat [Anne, H]'.

Comparison with others was sometimes quantitative, for example when it came to comparing dress sizes:

> Last year, once, my friends and I started talking about the sizes of our jeans, and I couldn't stand the fact that my jeans were bigger than some of the other girls [pauses]. And they were, I was swimming in them but they were still bigger than the other girls.
>
> [Mathilde, H]

Where this last point is concerned, comparison with the school corpus is salient as it shows the specific work entailed in maintaining the commitment to the anorexic career. The non-anorexic schoolgirls interviewed also talked about comparing themselves with others, but in an envious, wishful mode – 'if only I were like that' – with resignation – 'but that's just how it is'.

MD: 'And when you say [pauses] [that there are times when you feel fat]. What were the times when you felt fat?'

S: 'Particularly with people who were slimmer than me. In the street, it was an obsession. I looked at girls' thighs and said to myself 'Oh my God, if only I were like that . . . . And of course when you see girls go by in the corridors and of course they're wearing something tight, miniskirts and [pauses] to find an ounce of fat, you've got to look hard! But that's just how it is, I mean, that's how they are [pauses] and we're just the way we are'.

[Sophie, S]

From this point of view, it could be said the work done to maintain the commitment transformed envy into comparison and resignation into action:

N: 'I always found someone thinner than me . . . . When I weighed 58 kilos [pauses]. At 55 kilos I said to myself, 'Let's say 52, 53' and then when [pauses] 'Well, alright, let's say 50' [pauses]. Always less, and I always saw someone thinner than me, so I always wanted to be thin, I always found myself fat compared to someone. And so I constantly wanted to lose weight, lose weight.'

MD: 'And when you walked in the street, did you look at people?'

N: 'Yes, that's it, I looked at people, I looked at how they were, "Oh my God, he or she's thinner than me, that's not OK" [pauses]. So, after, I carried on, I had to be as thin as that, and all the time.'

MD: 'And what about your friends, was it the same?'

N: 'I had a friend, she was quite thin, and at the beginning I said to myself "Oh my God, it's not OK, I'm too fat, I have to be thinner", I'd based it on her a bit. And then, . . . I think I weighed less than her, so I couldn't base it on her anymore [pauses]. So I based it on people I saw in the street. I started with someone, I think it must have been her, and, after, anyway, it didn't matter anymore. It was always "thinner" [pauses]. At first someone I knew and then, after, it was really just general [pauses] people in the street, people at school, people on TV [pauses] anywhere.'

[Nadège, H]

The interviewees' systematic and repeated use of these various measuring tools was therefore part of a broader endeavour aimed at taking themselves in hand in a systematic, radical and rational way.

Use of measurement techniques

Measurement techniques were also a way for the interviewees to implement their initial endeavour to take themselves in hand over the longer term and to make it possible, desirable and effective to maintain that commitment. The particular use they made of these techniques shows that it was just as much about maintaining the endeavour as about measuring its results. As we can see in the excerpt from the interview with Nadège quoted above, in order to be able to carry on, measurement tools had to be used in a very specific manner, as an active tool of encouragement. The weight on the scales, comparisons with others and dress sizes were all potential encouragements to keep going as opposed to final targets: the intended weight could always be lowered ('Well, alright, let's say 50') and a different standard could be chosen if the friend originally used as a yardstick could no longer fulfil that role ('I weighed less than her so I couldn't base it on her anymore'). The commitment could only be maintained if these measurement tools were used in a particular way and if they actively placed the person in a situation in which they could continue endlessly.

Using these tools in this way implied de-objectivating them: dress sizes or the mirror, for example, could be emptied of their apparently objective content. This content was then replaced with a personal definition that contributing to allowing them to carry on 'working' at their commitment:

> I said to myself, 'Oh it must be a big size 6, that's why' [it fits me]. 'They make big sizes because they want to make out women are slim, so when they wear size 6 it's actually size 12 . . . . If they say size 6 when actually it's size 12, all the customers will think they're slim, they'll like the shop, so they'll come back.
>
> [Louise, H]

> I remember having bought a size 8 skirt in Agnès b. and I made a scene with the salesgirl in Agnès b. saying 'it's not a real size 8'.
>
> [Sabine, N]

Here we can see a further demonstration of this specific use of measurement tools in the chronology of their use: when a given tool indicated a potential end, when it could no longer be used to encourage maintaining the commitment, it was set aside. The power of clothes as a measure, for example, had a shorter time-span than weighing scales – in other words, it could not be completely de-objectivated:

> They [clothes] were all baggy on me after a while [pauses] There was only the number on the scales left to really tell me [trails off].
>
> [Yasmine, C]

> Clothes, that didn't last the whole time . . . . After it was really the scales, you know [pauses] Every morning, I got up, I weighed myself [trails off].
>
> [Julie, H]

Although the interviewees did not specifically learn to use these evaluation tools during this phase of the career, and sometimes used them regularly before, this particular use only appeared at this point and revealed how they were working to maintain the commitment. They also worked on evaluation tools to make sure they did not indicate any minimum target weight. Evaluation techniques could therefore also serve as techniques of encouragement – partly by having no intrinsic final limit, partly by allowing or encouraging further weight loss. Identical use was made of evaluation tools in the other areas concerned by the interviewees' endeavour. School marks, as a quantitative judgment of the work completed to take themselves in hand at school, can also be seen in the same light:

> Eighteen out of twenty was never enough. It always had to be more, more, more [pauses]. Well, at first, I took those [students] who were better than me, in the class, and, even when I was top of the class, 'It's still possible to do better' [pauses]. It has to be possible to do better, it's the others who are rubbish . . . . And the fact that my teachers said it was OK, all that [pauses]. It wasn't nearly enough anymore, you know.
>
> [Christine, C]

If we compare this excerpt with the interview with Nadège [H] above, we can see similarities between the way Christine compared her body to other girls and Nadège compared her marks to those of her classmates. In both cases, first the comparison with others served as a situated encouragement (to be thinner, to be better),; then this aim was implemented (through dietary restriction, through school work); and finally, the initial target was reworked so that having achieved it did not mean no longer pursuing the commitment ('It was always "thinner"', 'It has to be possible to do better').

During the previous phase, we saw how tools for measuring the body – for example, dress size or the notion of a normal weight – were sometimes important components in the system that conveyed the requirements of a legitimate body. However, these tools can also be put to different uses – including, but not limited to, those chosen by the interviewees here. Framing them purely in terms of the constraints they impose fails to account for the ways in which they can be used and the other stances they can enable. In this regard, the lack of existing research on this topic is regrettable.

Enjoying the effects

Dietary restriction has several effects: it leads to weight loss but it also creates physical sensations (an empty stomach, for example) and a particular state at a given time (being thin). In the case of the marijuana smoker's career analysed by Becker, the activity was new and users only learnt to enjoy its effects during the different phases of the career. Where the anorexic career is concerned, however, the interviewees had already experienced, and perhaps even enjoyed, some of the effects of dietary restriction. This was particularly the case where becoming thinner was concerned. This had sometimes already led to satisfaction during the initial phase or during previous diets and continued to produce the same satisfaction, as evidenced in the interview excerpts above. However, enjoying the physical sensations of dietary restriction and enjoying thinness as a state were more specific to this second phase.

Enjoying the physical sensations

Earlier, we looked at how the interviewees worked on their tastes regarding food, learning to make themselves sick of certain kinds of food and to like others. They also worked at learning to enjoy the physical sensation of dietary restriction. They developed a taste for these feelings (having an empty stomach, feeling hungry, feeling faint)[5] and learnt to construe the effects of satiation (having a full stomach, feeling full) as unpleasant:

> For some time, when I'd lost weight, I was really [pauses] it was like I was euphoric.
>
> [Julie, H].

> There was a kind of state that felt really nice when I didn't eat. Both that thing where you're going against yourself, against what you want, you feel really strong, and everything. And there's also that thing where you're completely high when you don't eat, I don't know if [trails off] . . . . One way or another, you feel like you're high, like totally. And I found that really great.
>
> [Sabine, N].

> Because you know I was really pleased not to eat. It made me, kind of euphoric, you know, ... But I was, I don't know, you kind of feel [pauses] euphoric, happy, when you don't eat, you feel [pauses] good. Honestly, it's as if you were on drugs. Once you've started not eating much, you can't stop. At first it's really hard because your stomach hurts, but at the end, because you've had lots of willpower, all that willpower to not eat, your stomach doesn't hurt anymore, it only hurts when you've eaten a bit too much, and you feel good . . . honestly, you feel really good.
>
> [Louise, H].

This comparison with drug use (either explicitly or by talking about being 'high') came up in several interviews and may well have its origin in medical discourse, in which certain theories draw parallels between eating habits and drug use in terms of 'dependency' or 'addictive behaviour'. However, if we consider this recurrent metaphor to be more than simply an echo of a medical comparison, we have to look at the interpretation processes necessary to enable this view, revealed by Alfred Lindesmith in 1947 in his sociology of addiction. Lindesmith sought in particular to understand how certain opium users became addicts while others – for example, patients treated with morphine – did not. In his view, the main explanation lay in the fact that the former linked the withdrawal symptoms they experienced to the lack of opium, through a cultural and social process of interpretation:

> It has been shown that the opiate habit rests fundamentally upon the effects which follow when the drug is removed rather than upon the positive effects which its presence in the body produces. Addiction occurs only when opiates are used to alleviate withdrawal distress, after this distress has been properly understood or interpreted . . . . If the individual fails to conceive of his distress as withdrawal distress brought about by the absence of opiates he can not become addicted, but if he does, addiction is quickly and permanently established through further use of the drug.
>
> (Lindesmith 1947, 165)

Viewed from this perspective, the metaphor of drug use can be seen as a sign that, for the interviewees, two processes of interpretation were at work during this second phase: they linked the positive effects they experienced to the fact they were not eating and interpreted the negative effects ('your stomach . . . only hurts when you've eaten a bit too much') as resulting from having failed to abstain from food. The interviewees therefore worked on their enjoyment of the effects, at the very least on an interpretative level. However, analysis of the interviews would seem to suggest that this work was not only interpretative in nature. When the interviewees referred to satisfaction, for example in the excerpts cited above, they did not present it as purely physical. It was a question of learning to like the sensations in order to be able to maintain the commitment: for Louise, the 'euphoria' was linked to the 'willpower to not eat' while Sabine linked it to the fact she felt 'strong' and had gone 'against what [she] want[ed]'. From this point of view, one might suggest that they worked on the things they enjoyed and disliked in the same way that they worked on their tastes in terms of food. Their use of willpower in this second phase also consisted in actively interpreting the effects of dietary restriction as positive and the effects of letting themselves go as negative, or even as a source of physical pain – yet another component of the work entailed in maintaining their commitment.

Enjoying being thin

In addition to learning to enjoy the physical sensations of dietary restriction, the interviewees also learnt to enjoy being thin, which was a further condition for maintaining the commitment. In the context of an approach setting aside the essentializing distinction between what is normal and what is pathological, I will not look at the causes for their continued commitment ('Why do anorexics carry on?') but rather at the definitions of the situation ('How do the interviewees define the situation in such a way that it becomes desirable for them to carry on and that they actually do so?'). Of course, these definitions of the situation are retrospective, construed by patients who have been led to internalize the notion that their desire to carry on losing weight is pathological. These definitions are therefore a form of justification after the fact, responding to the presupposition that wanting to carry on losing weight in this way was not normal. At the same time, precisely because they are justifying themselves, they also outline how they defined the situation as normal 'at the time' and reveal the rationales underpinning their desire to carry on. Insofar as the issue is justifying behaviour, this requires showing that it 'seemed like a good idea at that time', to take up Howard Becker's expression regarding the analysis of deviant careers (1998, 25).

When the interviewees mentioned the satisfaction they derived from dietary restriction, as described above, this constituted an initial definition of a situation that made it desirable for them carry on and led to them doing so. However, a second type of situation also emerged, this time related to the aims they ascribed to maintaining their commitment. As long as they had not achieved their self-determined aims, there was no reason to stop:

> I still thought I was too fat [pauses] I thought I still had thighs, still had a tummy.
>
> [Priscille, C]

> Because in my mind, in my mind I wasn't thin, in my mind, I'd see myself in the mirror and I'd say 'Ah but I still have to lose more'.
>
> [Emilie, C]

> Anyway when I looked at myself in the mirror, I was always too fat [pauses], no, that's not it, it was more 'I'm not thin enough' . . . . It was, 'I think I'm fine the way I am, but I don't want to be more', I want to stay like that [pauses] I'm fine or only just [pauses] I need a little less.
>
> [Mathilde, H]

My intention here is not to determine whether this perception was accurate or not, or whether it is normal or pathological to consider that you still have 'thighs' and 'a tummy' when considerably beneath the 'normal weight for your height'; the issue instead is how the interviewees defined the situation ('I still thought I was too fat', 'in my mind I wasn't thin', 'I'm not thin enough') in such a way that it was desirable for them to carry on and that they actually did so.

Sometimes they defined their desire to carry on as a way of ensuring that, having achieved their aim, they remained that way:

> When I'd got to like 43 [kilos], I didn't particularly want to lose weight, but I was scared of putting it on [pauses] I don't particularly want to lose weight, but I'm scared, you know.
>
> [Sidonie, H]

> And then you want to have some leeway, some leeway, some leeway.
>
> [Véronique, N]

Retrospectively, the interviewees therefore defined two kinds of situations: on the one hand, a situation in which they saw themselves as suitably thin but wanted to stay that way – which therefore implied using techniques to maintain their commitment; on the other hand, a situation in which they did not consider themselves to be thin enough and wanted to change that. First of all, in both cases there was a taste for being thin, whether it concerned a future or current state. But above all, in both cases, they defined themselves as the only ones able to say whether or not they were thin. They defined a situation in which they were the only legitimate agents capable of defining their own bodies:

> Actually, I carried on losing weight, but what bothered me was that [pauses] people could see I was losing weight, you know. And I still wasn't satisfied.
>
> [Anne, C]

> People would say to me 'You're thin, you're not eating' but, well, it either made me happy or I couldn't care less . . . . I didn't see myself as thin enough.
>
> [Nadège, H]

> Everyone told me I was thin but I didn't think I was thin . . . . At the beginning of the anorexia, I didn't see myself as thin, and in the middle I didn't either.
>
> [Louise, H]

Sometimes they even sought to impose this descriptive category, applied to themselves, upon others:

> Honestly, there's nothing worse than 'Ah you look good' . . . . I can't stand it when people say that. Or 'Wow you're super skinny'. 'Super skinny' isn't enough. I was 'thin' two days ago, I was pleased.
>
> [Sidonie, H]

> In anorexia, it's really [pauses] a box: I want to be there; I want to be very thin, like a skeleton, I want to be like that . . . . I want people to like me like that.
>
> [Christine, C]

The way these girls enjoyed being thin can also be interpreted as a desire to control how they were labelled publicly. Being thin gave them satisfaction, but so did being described as thin. By continuing to lose weight, the interviewees ensured that after a certain point it was no longer possible for the public label to differ from how they themselves categorized their bodies. This sort of process of self-definition can be compared with the use of measuring tools analysed above: in both situations, the tools and the people producing social labels can only define what the interviewees have decided they will define. However, as we will see in the following chapter, progressively and with increasing force, this desire to control self-definition eventually clashes with increasingly established external definitions of both the interviewee and the situation. In other words, they are confronted with the medical diagnosis and trying to retain control over self-definition slowly fails in the face of the external stigmatizing definition of being 'anorexic'.

Work over time/the work of time

One of the main characteristics of the work done to maintain the commitment, described above, is that it took place over time. During this second phase, the person's work over time also became the work of time on that person. When the interviewees used this work in a deliberate and determined fashion to establish a 'mode of living', it led to long-lasting changes in habits and even to 'dispositions' being embodied (in Bourdieu's sense of the term, as we will see later).

Work over time – establishing a mode of living

In analysing the first phase, I tried to show that we were dealing with the interviewees' global endeavour to take themselves in hand rather than simply with a diet, despite the words they used to describe it. Where the second phase was concerned, however, they never described it as a diet. And yet, in a sense, the word 'diet' could be an appropriate choice of terminology if it were employed in its older, now obsolete, meaning – not simply to refer to a mode of eating but also a 'mode of living'.[6] In this sense, during this second phase of the anorexic career, the way the girls took themselves in hand became a mode of living; they worked deliberately, continuously and on all fronts to keep taking themselves in hand.

First, this mode of living implied substantial work on time management:

I: 'All day, it's, ridiculous, but I'll be thinking "What have I eaten?" "What am I going to eat" "What blah blah" [pauses]. And I think about it all the time, I've always got something on my mind, about food, or a timetable, I always have to fill it [pauses]. And [pauses].'

MD: 'You mean you always have to fill your timetable?'

I: 'It's always, like, the evening before when I'm going to bed, if I don't know exactly what I'm going to do the next day, a really tightly organised programme and everything, I can't sleep, right? I have to know, you see, what time I'm going to do something, you see. . . . Right down to the tiniest detail . . . . If I feel a bit tired, I won't lie down on my bed to [pauses] rest a bit, you know [pauses] I'll finish the day, right to the end, having done everything I wanted to do.'

[Isabelle, C]

Moreover, as we have seen, this work on time itself is also characterized by the fact that a certain number of techniques aim specifically at maintaining the commitment: developing new habits, working on tastes to make it possible and less costly to carry on in this way. Working at maintaining the commitment means working over time and counting on – and organizing – the effects of time itself on the individual. In this sense, the practical stance described in the interviews differed quite substantially from comments like 'let's hope it lasts' found in the school corpus of non-anorexic teenagers:

J: [Juliette had lost some weight at the time of the interview] 'So I was careful, I lost it really easily . . . .'

MD: 'And so do you feel like you're on a roll, do you want to carry on losing [weight]?'

J: 'Yes, I hope so, you know [pauses]. Let's hope it lasts! . . . And I didn't really make much effort, and it's been two days, well, like a week [pauses]. I haven't lost 10 kilos in a week or anything! Like, it starts with 1 or 2 kilos and you say to yourself "Yeah, let's hope it lasts" you know.'

[Juliette, S]

As we saw earlier regarding comparison with others, this model of 'desire' contrasts with the model of 'action' implemented by the girls interviewed as anorexics and the 'let's hope it lasts' contrasts with the practical work in which the latter engaged to maintain their commitment; not 'let's hope it lasts' but 'it will last'! The interviewees' endeavour to take themselves in hand described in the first phase saw them working to break with old habits; in this second phase, it entailed them working on maintaining their commitment by establishing a mode of living. They described the deliberate and determined way in which they did this through references to 'being in control' and 'controlling' things, notions that originate in medical and psychological discourse, as Camille underscored:

C: 'It's a lot of control . . . .'

MD: 'And why do you see it in terms of "control"?'

C: 'Because I [pauses] I'm in complete control of myself, well, I say to myself, even if I want to have fun and everything, I say to myself "No! Not now. One thing at a time, next weekend you can have fun" . . . .'

MD: 'And when you talk about controlling yourself and being in control, are these things that were there at the beginning of the anorexia, or before, or that came later?'

C: 'Actually [pauses] I used that word because they always say that "there's lots of control with anorexics".'

[Camille, C]

All the work maintaining the commitment would not be possible without a practical stance involving being in control. But the perspective adopted here differed in several respects from the medical or psychological meanings of these terms. First, this self-restraint was not an end in itself but rather the stance adopted within the work in question; it was not a 'feature of the pathology' but an essential condition of possibility for maintaining the commitment. In the absence of self-restraint, people will leave the career just like people left the first phase of the career. Moreover, here self-restraint was considered as a strategy with specific aims.

These kinds of practices were not seen as expressing an irrepressible desire for control, which just happened to be applied to certain areas. On the contrary, it was specifically the different areas in which the interviewees had decided to take themselves in hand that were controlled and monitored. In this case, self-restraint was work in and of itself.

At the same time, the interviewees talked about 'a moment' when they no longer had to work on this 'control', but when it 'worked upon them' as it were, when 'control' became 'natural'.

> Well, after a while it wasn't about losing weight anymore, I couldn't control it much anymore.
>
> [Annabelle, N]

> Let's say that I never realized I was controlling myself, because actually [pauses] that's all I was doing! For me nothing was natural, well, *control was what was natural for me* [pauses] . . . . I controlled myself for everything, I don't know what I'd be if I didn't control myself.
>
> [Camille, C]

> So it had really become [pauses] but I almost didn't realize it [pauses]. *It had almost become natural.*
>
> [Christine, C]

During the first phase and an initial period of the second phase, we saw that the interviewees sometimes contrasted the self-restraint required to take themselves in hand with what was 'natural' or 'spontaneous' for them. During the second part of this second phase, this opposition disappeared and control became second nature. Based on this shift from the feeling of being in control to the feeling of being controlled by a form of control that has become natural, it would be reasonable to suggest that the mode of living adopted led to dispositions being embodied. As we have seen above, some of the techniques they used had the specific aim of establishing long-lasting and embodied habits. In fact, it seems that all the work involved in the mode of living adopted could have this effect. To some extent, self-restraint became invisible beneath the very dispositions it aimed to create.

Incorporating dispositions

The work of time

Becker uses the term 'dispositions' very briefly in *Outsiders* to refer to a capacity, but also a desire, to act in a certain way that is perceived as pleasurable following a learning process.[7] However, this disposition is not embodied nor is it long-lasting – it can be revoked at any point in the future. In order to account for the interviews conducted in this study, and the categories used by the interviewees themselves, this conception of dispositions has to be completed with Pierre Bourdieu's theorization of the same concept.[8] First, because in the case at hand, we have a coherent set of dispositions that extend the interviewees' work on their food, their bodies but also their school work, whereas Becker was referring to a very local form of disposition. Second, because the habits described by the interviewees show how dietary rules became written into their very bodies ('You barely feel [the food] actually, you feel the calorie [pauses]. A lot less now, for me. But I know that before it was [pauses] I absolutely did not choose what I ate, I chose its composition' [Camille, H]). Finally, because the long-lasting nature of these dispositions appears when the people want or have to leave them behind, as we will see later when it comes to leaving the career or being taken in hand by the medical institution (chapter seven).

The long-lasting and embodied nature of these dispositions was also illustrated by the way the interviewees described the 'loss of control' that followed their initial 'control'. They often used the expression 'I can't help it', characteristic of acquired dispositions:

> There are two moments, the one when [pauses] you control everything, and the one when, in the end, you don't control anything because *you just can't help it.*
>
> [Emilie, C]

> I wrote lots of letters [pauses] for example to my parents, my sister and everything, telling them 'Ok now it's over, I'm going to do everything I can to pull through and everything, I promise' [pauses] And then when it was time for a meal *I just couldn't help it* . . . . And after, I'd say to myself 'why did you do that?' you're rubbish, why didn't you finish that meal [pauses] You like it, why didn't you have any?'
>
> [Julie, H]

The dispositions that had been embodied were apparent in the fact that they resisted any calls to 'stop' that appeared in the following stages of the career. The interviewees sometimes described the strength of these dispositions with the expression 'that was it, I was off', referring to the moment when the second nature took over:

> Before I was incapable of saying to myself 'Now I'm going to put some [weight] back on, it wasn't possible, from the moment at which I started to lose [pauses]. *That was it, I was off,* you know.
>
> [Camille, C]

> I was already in my thing, and you know, *that was it, I was off*.
>
> [Camille, C]

As for Véronique, she talked about something that had become 'engrained':

V: 'After that, it was engrained . . . .'

MD: 'And when you say it was "engrained", did that also mean that a big part of it was about habits?'

V: 'Yes, completely. And one day, I remember really clearly having realized that I'd only eaten a grapefruit all day, I realized that at six in the evening [pauses]. And I said to myself, "Well that's incredible, I hadn't even realized".'

[Véronique, N]

The interviewees also talked about their stomachs having 'shrunk' and about 'anorexic reflexes'. These expressions testified to how they categorized these dispositions as both embodied and long-lasting, just like no longer 'managing' to eat:

> At first, it's true it was to lose weight, I won't deny it, but at the end it wasn't to lose weight at all anymore, it was really [pauses] because I had a problem with food, I couldn't manage to eat.
>
> [Louise, H]

> But it wasn't only to lose weight. It was also, well, I suppose your stomach gets used to it, and after a while, you can't swallow things.
>
> [Annabelle, N]

This takes us beyond how the interviewees worked on and over time and shows how time itself also worked on the interviewees, writing long-lasting dispositions into their bodies; first at their behest, then on an involuntary mode. One final example can be seen in the way some people left the anorexic career at the end of this second phase:

Leaving the career

The way some of the interviewees left the anorexic career reinforces this idea of long-lasting embodied dispositions. Those who left the career in the first phase simply stopped (the diet, taking themselves in hand, etc.) often instantaneously and with no effort, as seen in the previous chapter (efforts were needed *not* to stop). Those who left during the second phase, however, had to work at losing the habits they had built up, which took much more time:

> There was a period of, re-feeding, I don't know how to put it. I *got used* to eating again.
>
> [Annabelle, N]

MD: 'And when you started eating again?'

S: 'Well it was completely disorganized, it was really [pauses] really really weird, it was by phases [pauses]. I could easily stop eating for two weeks, really with *reflexes* like that.

[Sabine, N]

MD: 'And did you start eating again just like that?'

V: 'No, not just like that, very slowly [pauses] Very slowly, it took me three years [pauses] to eat really properly again, from time to time I'd still have half a tomato, half a carrot [laughs]. And then, bit by bit, *I forgot.*'

[Véronique, N]

This slower, harder way of leaving the career, that required the body's memory to 'forget', implicitly reveals the embodied and long-lasting nature of the acquired dispositions. When the interviewees first took themselves in hand, it was still possible to simply stop. However, the work they then pursued to maintain their commitment to this endeavour produced dispositions that transformed leaving the career into an active process. The interviewees had to work at self-conversion again, slowly, with difficulty, countering everything they had accomplished in the first two phases. This effort implicitly highlights the incorporation of new ('anorexic') dispositions during the second phase. During this second phase, their bodily momentum, which had previously pushed them towards *stopping* in the first phase, now directed them towards carrying on. Of course, my intention in using the term 'dispositions' is not to take part in the medical debate surrounding biological and psychological factors in anorexia, nor to suggest that the stomach really does 'shrink'. Simply, analysis of the interviews does highlight a register of language reflecting the notion of writing things into the body, both voluntarily and involuntarily – something that is well reflected by the term 'dispositions'.

The interviewees often mentioned this second phase very briefly, reiterating the idea of carrying on as if it were simply the continuation of the previous inclination, without providing any details about it, without explicitly discussing new practices, and leaving the intense work it required in the shadows. The second phase continued the self-transformation they began working on in the first; it was the phase in which a mode of living was highly rationalized and extended to various practical areas. The interviewees pursued their commitment to the career by making the techniques of the first phase more systematic and more radical, applied across the board of the various areas involved in their endeavour to take themselves in hand. New techniques wrote the aims in question into their bodies' very habits, making sure they could be achieved and allowing the commitment to continue (e.g. through working on what they enjoyed/did not enjoy). The anorexic dispositions that they eventually incorporated constituted an internal driving force, propelling them towards maintaining their commitment. In parallel, systematic work designed to measure the results of their efforts evaluated and reinforced these efforts.

Where this second phase is concerned, two 'internal' sources emerged as having allowed the interviewees to maintain their commitment to the anorexic career: first, the work in which they engaged across the board (the commitment was maintained by actively working to maintain it) and second, the dispositions that resulted from this work and then took over from it. These dispositions were not pre-existing, unconscious dispositions. On the contrary, they were explicitly sought by the interviewees, who eventually acquired them through their work during this phase of the anorexic career. The next phase brings to light a third source underpinning the girls' continued commitment, external this time: chapter six will therefore now turn to labelling and its effects on the interviewees' activity.

Notes

1 'What the theory did, as Albert Cohen . . . has pointed out, was to create a four-cell property space by combining two dichotomous variables, the commission or non-commission of a given act and the definition of that act as deviant or not' (Becker 1963, 180).

2 'In summary, an individual will be able to use marijuana for pleasure only when he goes through a process of learning to conceive of it as an object which can be used in this way. No one becomes a user without (1) learning to smoke the drug in a way which will produce real effects; (2) learning to recognize the effects and connect them with drug use (learning, in other words, to get high); and (3) learning to enjoy the sensations he perceives' (Becker 1963, 58).

3 This use of the stairs as a locus for physical exercise and a calorie-burning technique, which came up regularly in the interviews, may well be the result of the recurrent advice given by women's magazines to women wanting to be slim ('don't take the lift anymore', 'always take the stairs'), although it is not possible to know whether this was definitely the 'media of communication' – to take up Howard Becker's term – at play in learning this technique.

4 In this kind of measuring work, we can see another technique taken from women's magazines, which sometimes suggest the 'three gap rule' as a way of judging the aesthetic perfection of one's legs, referring to the gaps that should appear when standing in front of a mirror above the ankles, between the calves and between the thighs. More generally, in this context, the female body could be said to be fragmented: 'strengthen your arm muscles', 'the waistline of your dreams', 'buns of steel', 'perfect legs for the summer' and so on.

5 This positive interpretation of sensations that could be defined as painful can be compared with a process observed by Sylvia Faure in the case of learning to dance when 'aching painfully [is] frequently perceived as a sign of having worked hard and a lot' (Faure 2000, 80). Faure refers to this process as 'accepting physical suffering'. In this case, the stance adopted was more than simply 'accepting' it, though; it was the result of the interviewees working specifically on how they interpreted sensations.

6 'In Greek medicine, diet (diaita or "mode of living") referred to the general conduct and organization of life, including form of dress, behaviour and attitudes' (Turner 1996, 76).

7 '[The user] develops a disposition or motivation to use marihuana which was not and could not have been present when he began use, for it involves and depends on conceptions of the drug which could only grow out of the kind of actual experience detailed above. On completion of this process he is willing and able to use marihuana for pleasure. He has learned, in short, to answer "Yes" to the question: "Is it fun?"' (Becker 1963, 58).

8 See for example Bourdieu (1990, chs 3–5) and (2000b, 138–72). Bernard Lahire pursues empirical sociological analysis insisting in particular on the importance of time and repetition in how they are embodied: 'A disposition . . . can only be constituted over time, that is to say through the *repetition of relatively similar experiences* . . . . One does not contract a disposition through a sudden and miraculous conversion and dispositions are not all equal in terms of how precocious, how long-lasting, how systematic and how intense their incorporation is' (Lahire 2002b, 20).

6 'Carrying on' II

Maintaining the commitment despite alerts and monitoring

In the last chapter, we saw that the interviewees used the same term – 'carrying on' – to talk about a period that, in their view, extended from the original diet to when they were hospitalized. We also saw that analysing this period distinguished two separate phases that sometimes overlapped to some extent. During the second phase of the anorexic career, discussed in the previous chapter, the definition of the situation changed progressively. 'Carrying on' was increasingly defined as a way of 'not stopping' despite the requests and demands of external actors:[1]

> At the beginning, my mum said to me 'Right, well, that's very good, if you've lost a bit of weight, if you're better like that, good for you, but now you have to stop' and then bit by bit she started saying 'Right, now, you really have to stop' and, [pauses] I didn't stop and that's when it started, they started to worry.
>
> [Julie, H]

The thing that then 'started', to take up Julie's term, was that maintaining the commitment was labelled deviant. This chapter examines this particular phase, which in fact sometimes began during the previous phase – either at the start or later on – and then continued. The potential overlap between the different phases underscores the importance (mentioned in chapter three) of talking about 'phases' rather than 'stages', which would suggest much stricter chronological divisions. As mentioned before, the focus in this chapter will be less the 'commission of a given act' and more the 'definition of that act as deviant'. Different trends in interactionist sociology of mental illness have looked at this question in detail. To borrow Philip Manning's rather pithy formulation, this perspective is defined by the fact that the DSM (the diagnostic manual discussed in chapter two) is 'a list of things not to be found doing in public' (Manning 1992, 101). The third phase of the anorexic career is the phase in which this is discovered, with all the resulting effects.

In his analysis of the pre-patient phase in the moral career of the mental patient, Erving Goffman gives particular emphasis to the 'circuit of agents – and agencies – that participate fatefully in his passage from civilian to patient status', stating 'Here is an instance of that increasingly important class of social system whose elements are agents and agencies which are brought into systemic connection through having to take up and send on the same persons' (Goffman 1961, 135–6).[2] This 'circuit of agents' includes several roles: the '*next of relation*', who is the 'the last to doubt his sanity and the first to have done everything to save him from the fate which, it transpires, he has been approaching'; the '*complainant*', the 'person who retrospectively appears to have started the person on his way to the hospital', usually acting in his or her 'lay capacity as a citizen, an employer, a neighbor, or a kinsman'; and the '*mediator*', a category that includes 'police, clergy, general medical practitioners, office psychiatrists, personnel in public clinics, lawyers, social service workers, schoolteachers, and so on' (136). These are roles not people and Goffman underlines that, for example, the person who plays the role of next of relation can also play the role of complainant; in our case, we will see that the same person can also play both the role of next of relation and that of professional mediator.

As well as identifying the active roles played in this circuit, Goffman also focuses on the consequences of its implementation on the 'feelings of the patient' (1961, 137), the reasons why the patient 'may feel that an alienative coalition has been formed against him' (138) and how, for the patient, the circuit of agents becomes a 'circuit of significant figures [that] can function as a kind of betrayal funnel' (140). In the sequential model put forward by the author, a few fixed spots remain, which may actually be blind spots. First, the label 'mental patient' seems to be present from the outset and present on the same mode and with the same content from one end to the other of the circuit of agents. In short, this label is not viewed as having a history. Moreover, while the patient does have 'feelings' (feeling publicly 'betrayed' (139), 'conned' (140), being 'progressively more at odds' with the administrative facts of the situation, and so on), he or she acts very little, whereas the circuit of agents acts almost inexorably upon him or her. Of course, for Goffman, this is precisely the effect of the circuit of agents – it removes any possibility of resistance – and he shows the mechanisms through which this occurs. However, resistance is perhaps not the only mode of action that should be taken into account.

Goffman's perspective might well be summarized by saying that he views the pre-patient phase as quick – the label does not have time to change, the patient does not have time to react – and inexorably directed towards hospitalization – the pre-patient is only ever described as a future mental patient.[3] This model no doubt results both from Goffman's field – the American psychiatric hospital in the 1950s – and from the perspective he adopted in *Asylums.* In the case of my study, though, the third phase of the anorexic career takes place over a much longer timeframe, with hospitalization defined by the circuit of agents as a 'last resort'. Over this long timeframe, the labels ascribed to the deviant person have their own history, as do the effects of these labels on the person. Given the fieldwork conducted in this study – I did not interview parents or doctors involved in the circuit of agents – I will be placing emphasis on the second aspect, although the interviews did still allow me to identify certain aspects of the history of the labels themselves as well. In order to account for what happens in this third phase of the anorexic career, compared with Goffman's pre-patient career model I will also add the questions of stigma – that is to say, the control and management of information on the part of the stigmatized person – and of labelling – that is to say, an identity that is ascribed with specific effects, particularly in terms of the reactions to which it gives rise.

The circuit of agents and labels

In a way, the circuit of agents is reminiscent of the circuit organized in the initial phase of the anorexic career, with the people prescribing, encouraging and joining in with the diet. In both cases, the circuit includes both laypersons and professionals, and in fact the same type of laypersons and professionals. In both cases, the roles composing the circuit aim to impose or convey a norm. More specifically, the same people sometimes play a role in both circuits. Finally, in both cases, highlighting the existence of that circuit answers the question '*How* did we end up "here"?' – whether here was on a diet or in hospital.[4] However, the norms conveyed by these circuits were of course polar opposites: the first circuit encouraged dieting while the second imposed an end to weight loss.

Giving the alert

The third phase begins with an 'alert' and the first role in this circuit of agents is that of the person who gives that alert. The first 'alerter' is the first person to publicly indicate that 'something is not right'. Sometimes this initial alert immediately leads to a circuit of agents being created, but sometimes many alerts are given without any apparent effects at first. The role of alerter could be compared with that of Goffman's next of relation: 'His next-of-relation presses him into coming to "talk things over" with a medical practitioner, an office psychiatrist, or some other counselor' (Goffman 1961, 137). However, the term 'alerter' does require opening up the black box of what actually composes the role of next of relation on three different levels: it is important to look at *who* gives the alert, *what* leads that person to show public concern (or in other words, what first appears deviant) and *what label* is ascribed. In many cases in my fieldwork, the first alerter was indeed a close relative, a next of relation as Goffman puts it:

> That meant I started to lose weight, my mum realized because, well, I've never been very big, so you could tell really quickly, and, in December, I cut my hair, which made my face even thinner, and, at that point, she took me to see a GP.
>
> [Anne, H]

However, in other cases, a professional played this role, as being at school in France implies institutionalized medical visits at regular intervals:

> In Year 12, I had to be vaccinated for different things, that I did late, I can't remember what, and at school they called my parents, telling them that I'd lost 8 kilos in a year.
>
> [Yasmine, C]

> [Louise was a border at her school] There was the traditional weigh-in at the beginning of the year . . . in January, they weigh us, and it was in January that I'd started to lose weight [pauses] and since Year 10, it had been a year, I'd lost quite a lot. So they were worried . . . the doctor said to me 'Right, listen, this isn't good' and everything.
>
> [Louise, H]

The alerter therefore acted out of 'concern', because he or she was 'worried' about a situation that was out of the ordinary. But people faced with the same situation will not all necessarily become alerters. The retrospective point of view, recounting this moment from the point of view of the diagnosis that came after, led many interviewees to express surprise at the lack of social reaction to the situation or the late stage at which it occurred:

> But what's funny, it's that in my *Prépa* environment, the people around, well, my friends even, no one noticed. That has always [trails off]. Well, on the other hand, we didn't talk about that . . . But no one noticed that I was losing weight [pauses] abnormally . . . But I think that they didn't know about this problem [= they didn't know about anorexia as a diagnosis; earlier she said 'I think at the time anorexia wasn't what it's become now. We didn't really know what it was, we didn't think it was an illness'], they thought I wanted to lose weight . . . . I don't understand how not one of my friends pointed it out to me [pauses] or maybe they didn't realize . . . they said to themselves 'it's normal, it's the phase of the *concours* [competitive entrance exams for which the *Prépa* provide training].
>
> [Annabelle, N].

> But on top of it, actually, for about a year and a half, I did it without anyone noticing . . . . They just didn't pay attention [pauses] or they thought it was a diet . . . . For a really long time, my parents didn't realize. And then one day, it was in summer, so I had bare arms and suddenly my father realized what I'd become. And at that point, they were pretty scared I think, and so they really insisted that I should stop.
>
> [Véronique, N]

The existence and identity of these alerters raise two types of question. First, the visibility of the stigma that will be seen as deviant. According to Goffman, the 'visibility' of a stigma is:

> how well or how badly [it] is adapted to provide means of communicating that the individual possesses it. . . . Visibility, of course, is a crucial factor. . . . Actually, the more general term 'perceptibility' would be more accurate, and 'evidentness' more accurate still.
>
> (Goffman 1963, 64–5)

This 'evidentness' can be related to certain practices but also to the body and how thin it is. The question of visibility does not, however, only bring into play the attributes of the stigma itself – its inherent attributes, how 'adapted' it is to reveal itself – but also the social knowledge of the public that results in it being labelled as deviant, and more specifically, in this case, as anorexic. In this respect, it is useful to call on Strauss's notion of social visibility, mentioned previously in chapter three. While Goffman defines self-evidence at the level of the interaction and the stigma itself, Strauss calls upon the notion of a much broader form of social visibility created in part by public debate and the media.[5] Both types of visibility – the interactional self-evidence of the stigma and the social visibility of a form of deviance – are at stake in whether alerts are given, what definitions are involved and when this takes place.

As we can see in the two excerpts above, thinness was sometimes related to a 'normal' situation, for example 'the phase of the *concours*' or the result of a diet. It could therefore be visible without setting off a process in which it was interpreted in terms of mental pathology. Conversely, the alert could immediately lead to it being labelled in terms of anorexia if the role of alerter was played by a close relative who was also a professional likely to interpret the deviance as anorexia very quickly. Having such a professional in the family could therefore accelerate the speed with which the alert was given and lead to the behaviour being very rapidly understood as anorexia:

> My mum talked about it a lot to my cousin, who had studied medicine, and, well, my cousin said to her 'You know, you should be careful because she's got this, this and this, and the symptoms a bit' and my mum soon realized.
>
> [Julie, H]

When the alert was given, the audience's differing levels of acceptance also came into play. The same situation could be coded as both deviant and non-deviant, depending on the diverse norms conveyed by the alerters – objectively identical situations were not always seen as transgressing a norm. In particular, the peer group often tolerated a situation that others perceived as a transgression much sooner:

> But, for example, I never had any remarks from the others [pauses] my classmates. People didn't [pauses] apart from my parents, who said I was thin, that I was a skeleton, that something had to be done, but people in general, at school, didn't realize . . . . People just didn't catch on.
>
> [Emilie, C]

> When [my friends] see me, they say 'But you're normal, I don't see why you have to put on weight' [pauses]. When I'm told that, at the same time, it kind of backs me up in my idea that I look good like I am, and at the same time, I say to myself 'Yes, but wait, who am I supposed to listen to, my friends or the doctors?'
>
> [Isabelle, C]

In this case, it is necessary to bring into play both the social visibility of deviance *and* the diverse norms that exist from one group to the next, rather than just the visibility or the evident nature of the stigma itself. This brings us back to Strauss's critique of the notion of 'deviance' and the conflicting definitions that surround the transgression of norms; something perceived as deviant by some people will not be seen the same way by others. Obviously, this observation does not detract from the fact that certain people have greater legitimacy not only to define an act as deviant but also to follow up this charge with specific consequences. This was the case for the doctors and even the parents who took the interviewees to see a doctor when their peer group did not see anything deviant about how thin they were – the peers' view quite often had no influence whatsoever on the parents' perspective and decision.

All the people faced with the same situation therefore do not necessarily become alerters, or at least not at the same point in time. It is not possible to discuss the reasons for this discrepancy in detail here, but I will point to a few hypotheses related to the various forms of visibility that exist. First, local norms of thinness can play a role. Véronique, who underscored that her parents did not react for 'a year and a half' also mentioned that, in her family, the women (her mother and her two grandmothers) were all 'string beans', 'really really thin'. And it could also be suggested that these local norms of extreme thinness also existed among peer groups: when Julie was hospitalized, her friends told her 'you know, you've lost too much weight, *it's not even pretty anymore*', suggesting that for a long time they had approved of her weight loss. These norms of extreme thinness conveyed by the peer group were even stronger when the interviewee was a dancer or a gymnast, for example, in the cases of Isabelle and Emilie mentioned above. Moreover, social visibility also played a role in whether the charge of deviance was levied. Annabelle described a situation where the lack of social reaction could be related to the lack of social visibility of anorexia as a diagnosis. More generally, we could suggest, first, that the more people knew about the diagnosis, the more people were in a position to give the alert, and to do so earlier; and second, in this case, the people engaging in the deviant behaviour were the target demographic of the diagnosis being disseminated (that is to say, teenage girls) and that, in this sense, the same practices on the part of boys or older women would probably have led to fewer, or slower, alerts.

The person giving the alert reacts by publicly expressing concern and pointing to deviant behaviour. However, it is not always the same deviance that is identified. In the same way that, depending on the audience, someone will or will not give the alert, there are variations in what is seen as deviant by different alerters. Of course, as we saw in some of the interview excerpts above, thinness was the transgression that was most often noticed, whether in terms of a norm based on the person herself – the interviewee had 'lost too much weight' – or formulated in absolute terms – the interviewee was said to be 'a skeleton'. Sometimes, eating habits were noticed instead. The interviewee 'wasn't eating anymore', that is to say was not eating the way she used to – again, a norm based on the person – or was not eating enough – another absolute norm, in terms of what would be normal:

> When my mum realized that I'd lost a lot of weight, and that I was still on a diet etc., she sent me to see a psychiatrist, to see an endocrinologist.
>
> [Anne, C]

> She [her mother] had taken me to see a doctor for a sports certificate [standard document required to participate in most sporting activities in France], and she came with me and she said to the doctor, she totally insisted, I was there, 'Anne's not eating anymore, she's losing weight'.
>
> [Anne, H]

Fainting and falling, as signs of physical weakness, were sometimes also the reason behind the alerter's intervention:

> I went skiing, and I fell, because I was skiing, I wasn't eating, and I fell. So my sister picked me up, said 'Right, we have to do something', so I went to see a doctor, [pauses] a psychiatrist.
>
> [Christine, C]

> Around mid-July, I started to come over all faint, to not feel well in the morning [pauses]. So then we started to see some doctors.
>
> [Julie, H]

Finally, sometimes it was the girls' period stopping that led an alerter to act and resulting in calling on a professional:

> I'd lost a bit but it didn't show much. It was just that I didn't have my period anymore [pauses]. The first time [the first doctor she met with] I went to the [pauses] . . . the gynaecologist.
>
> [Sidonie, H].

> I saw a doctor after 7 months, because, [pauses] my parents were worried, [pauses] because, well, it's a bit crude, but I didn't have my period for 7 months.
>
> [Annabelle, N]

At this stage in the circuit, there were therefore variations in what was seen as deviant. In parallel, there also were variations in how these different types of deviance were labelled. Taking into account the history of these labels – rather than just considering one univocal and inevitable label leading to hospitalization – shows that conflicting definitions existed depending on when these labels were applied. The person giving the alert was someone who was worried about the situation, but initially there were sometimes conflicts about how relevant or legitimate this concern actually was: 'I was like "no no, I'm OK, I feel great and everything, I've never felt better"' [Yasmine, C]. Similarly, at the same stage, Louise brushed aside her mother's initial concerns, expressed in terms of anorexia: 'I said to my mum, when she said I was anorexic: "But Mum, they all weigh 20 kilos, anorexics [pauses] you're being ridiculous, you know, I weigh 40, come on!"' [Louise, H].

Conflicting definitions were sometimes also at play regarding not the legitimacy of the concern but how it should be interpreted and what measures should be taken. As Anne [C] underlined, her father and mother labelled her behaviour in terms of physical health (in front of her, at any rate), whereas her aunt suggested an interpretation in terms of anorexia:

> Actually, when my parents told me I had an appointment with the doctor, erm [pauses] they didn't say 'anorexic'. And, [pauses], they said that, well, my mum said that Dad thought that some young people had problems, digestive problems, etc. It wasn't eating habits, it was digestive . . . . [The first time the word anorexia was mentioned] I think it was [pauses] shortly after I'd looked after my cousins in the February half-term . . . . My aunt phoned my mum and said 'Look, listen, when Anne was with us, she was behaving like an anorexic, are you, I mean, do you know? You have to realize, etc.' Well, I think she said it roughly in those terms, erm [pauses], and [pauses] Mum told me that [pauses] she'd found it hard to accept, you know, she'd said 'But how, how do you know, and what makes you say that?'.
>
> [Anne, C]

Anne took her own stance within this definitional conflict, positioning herself on the side of a biological interpretation – in terms of digestive problems – that was less stigmatizing for her but above all that allowed her to remove the question of her own responsibility for her weight loss and therefore to carry on: 'So straightway there was the possibility of [pauses] Well, I saw the possibility of making them think I was ill, that I had no influence, well, that I had no control over my body, you know' [Anne, C].

There was a similar conflict in definition between Mathilde's parents, who believed there was a psychological problem, but that it was 'depression', and her sister who mentioned anorexia:

> My parents realized that I wasn't OK . . . but the person who first said the word, the word 'anorexia', was my sister, who didn't live at home anymore, and who said to my parents that it was getting ridiculous [pauses] every time

> she came to see me, around once a week, she had the impression I'd got thinner, that I was getting worse and worse, she was the first one who pushed me to see a doctor [pauses] . . . . She was the first one to talk to me about it, one day when she'd invited me round to hers and she said 'It's not OK, you're not OK' . . . she was the first one to talk to me about anorexia.
>
> [Mathilde, H]

Among the alerters, one therefore played the role of complainant and their concern translated into a medical appointment. As we have seen in the excerpts above, this labelling process eventually resulted in an encounter with a medical professional. The type of label ascribed and the issues of conflicting definitions, when they occur, have an influence on the kind of professional first encountered.

The circuit of professionals

The alert, or the successive alerts, created a circuit of 'mediators' to take up Goffman's term – 'the sequence of agents and agencies to which the pre-patient is referred and through which he is relayed and processed on his way to the hospital' (Goffman 1961, 136). These mediators had in common their status as professionals – GPs, specialists (paediatrician, endocrinologist, gynaecologist, psychiatrist) or psychologists; in the interviews, the exact status of the 'doctors' or 'therapists' seen was not always specified.

There were common features in this circuit from one interviewee to the next. When a GP was consulted, this happened at the beginning of the circuit. Conversely, a psychiatrist was usually consulted at the end of the circuit. The longest circuits involved almost all the professions cited above. Moreover, the interviewees did not necessarily move from one professional to the next exclusively – the GP or the endocrinologist, for example, was sometimes present throughout the medical trajectory. However, important variations also existed from one trajectory to the next, and a distinction can be drawn between two types of model.

The first type of trajectory began with a medical focus on physical health before then continuing in the field of mental health. Sidonie [H] first consulted a gynaecologist, who referred her to 'specialists, psychologists'. Isabelle [C] first 'went to see' an endocrinologist who 'referred her' to a psychiatrist. Camille [C] who 'still had a paediatrician [at the time]' went to see him, and it was only later that her parents took her to see specialists and 'specialists in anorexia'. The medical trajectory sometimes stopped at the stage of physical health professionals, for example in the case of Annabelle, who was never hospitalized. The conflicting definitions, opposing a GP on the one hand, and Annabelle and her parents on the other, led to her medical career ending at the stage of physical health. The result of this conflict shows that lay definitions won over medical ones in this case:

> But, well, I didn't see psychologists or [pauses] I saw people about circulation. After that [her period stopping and having nose bleeds], for the whole 'strengthening your veins' thing, and that's when I saw a doctor who said

> 'right, this is a psychological problem'. But I didn't want to hear it, and there was no follow up, because my parents weren't ready to accept that anyway.
>
> [Annabelle, N]

The second kind of medical trajectory began with mental health – either directly or via a GP who made a referral to a mental health specialist – and followed various circuits. For example, Yasmine [C] and Sophie [C] first saw a psychologist then a psychiatrist, while Christine [C] saw a psychiatrist from the outset. The kind of circuit of professionals depended to a large extent on how the situation was defined when the alert was given, and particularly which of the conflicting definitions at play before the first medical appointment eventually won out. When a precise label was not ascribed, the first professional encountered was a GP – or a paediatrician in Camille's case; when the 'problem' was defined in terms of the interviewee's periods stopping, she saw a gynaecologist first. If, however, the label was immediately linked to anorexia or the risk of anorexia, then a psychologist or psychiatrist was the first port of call. The definition of the situation therefore influenced the medical trajectories that followed, although other factors obviously had an effect. In Sophie's case, for example, the fact she had already seen a psychologist 'for something else' in her early teenage years made it easier to turn to the same psychologist when the alert was given, and, in other cases, prevalent lay knowledge about the diagnosis or the family's close links with the medical world had an impact.

While lay definitions of the situation at the time of the alert did influence the early stages of the medical trajectory, the latter eventually fell into step with professional definitions of the situation. These definitions brought the question of diagnosis into play, whether one was given or not. They also implied referral from one doctor to another, raising the question of how labels changed throughout this professional circuit. On this point, the information obtained in the kind of fieldwork I conducted can only provide a broad outline of this evolution. The first consultations sometimes did not give rise to any particular label: 'So then, we started seeing some doctors [pauses] they didn't say much, just that I should be careful, that I should eat several small meals if I didn't want to eat big ones' [Julie, H]. The diagnosis of anorexia sometimes appeared later, framed by the doctors as a 'risk'. The interviewees described gynaecologists or GPs who suggested that 'it might well be anorexia', that the interviewee was 'maybe anorexic' or that anorexia was a possibility ('he told us that I was running that risk by carrying on like that'; 'He didn't tell me I was anorexic, he told me that I could become anorexic if I carried on with this diet').

These kinds of medical formulations imply that conflicts about definitions were still possible at this stage. The label could still be discredited in the same light-hearted fashion identified earlier:

> And several times, we were told 'Yeah, maybe she's anorexic' and everything and I was like 'What are you on about, with your big science-y words and everything?!'
>
> [Camille, H]

Yeah, the gynaecologist, I'd lost a bit, she was like 'It might be anorexia' [pauses]. Of course my mum laughed, I laughed.

[Sidonie, H]

In the last excerpt, we can see that, at that stage, conflicts about definitions did not only exist between the patient and her initial doctors. However, as the circuit continued, it became harder to discredit the diagnosis and the interviewee found herself increasingly in opposition with all the other people concerned. Finally, the label transformed into a diagnosis of anorexia nervosa, given by a specialist (a psychiatrist or a 'double specialist' that is to say, a psychiatrist specializing in anorexia). Discrediting the label then meant resisting a medical diagnosis that had increasingly gained in legitimacy (as they went from GPs to specialists) and had become more widely accepted:

M: 'I had the impression that I was eating like a young girl of my age, or that, like most girls in my class, I was watching my waistline [pauses]. It was completely normal.'

MD: 'And did you tell them that, was it an argument you used?'

M: 'No [pauses]. The rare times I mentioned it, "no, you're just completely caught up in your anorexia" . . . . But I have to say, too, no matter how much they told me I was anorexic, I didn't believe it, I just thought it was a little bit of anorexia, you know. For me, it was just a slighter stricter diet than other people's.'

[Mathilde, H]

From this point onwards, the medical diagnosis of anorexia was established as the legitimate definition of the situation, sometimes for the interviewee herself too. However, this was not always because of the defining power wielded by legitimate agents such as medical professionals. The 'anorexic' label was sometimes publicly accepted before hospitalization for reasons that had nothing to do with the efficiency of medical labels. Sometimes, it was initially accepted as describing a 'personality type', which meant the pathological implications of the term were rejected and, with them, the resulting demands to stop maintaining the commitment:

I mean for me it had gone in [pauses] It had become [pauses] my personality . . . . That's just how it was, you know. For me it had become a personality type [pauses]. There were anorexics, and they weren't necessarily ill.

[Véronique, N]

Going further still, the label was sometimes accepted and even voluntarily brandished as a distinctive and incomprehensible 'banner', in other words a label that was neither particularly reductive nor particularly objectivating:

Y: 'I'd really found the perfect label [pauses]. The banner that no one else had [pauses] and I felt that it suited me pretty well.'

MD: 'But was it important to you, that no one else had that banner?'

Y: 'Yeah [pauses]. And also, I'd say, that no one understood it.'

[Yasmine, C]

Finally, the label was sometimes accepted as the lesser of two evils compared with a label that was considered more stigmatizing. This appeared very clearly in Anne's narrative of a conversation with a friend, in which she first refused the label 'anorexic' before eventually accepting it in order to escape being labelled 'bulimic':

A: 'There was another of my friends, . . . it had been [pauses] two or three years since I'd seen her when, in Year 12, one of my aunts went to find Léa and said to her "You know, Anne's having problems at the moment, you have to help her, etc." And, well, she told her, I think, that I was anorexic [pauses]. After that, I sent a letter to my aunt asking for an explanation, she said "I never said anorexic" etc., but, well, she must have explained the symptoms, there you go, that's it, you know. . . . And so she, she came with Léa, and I was a bit surprised, I was a bit embarrassed as well, because, you know, and, well, Léa and I went for a walk, and she asked me, we were sitting outside in a park, "Is everything OK with your parents, etc.", and I was like "Oh yeah, yeah", well, [pauses]. We really felt the time going by. And she said to me "[Your aunt] told me you were anorexic?" "What? No! Why did she say that?" well, etc., you know, it was [pauses] really really hard [pauses] And, well, after [pauses]. There was an important point too, for me, anorexic meant not eating at all. And that seemed [pauses] really healthy actually [pauses], whereas I ate, but I threw up after [pauses]. And she said to me "so are you bulimic or are you anorexic? I said "Well, I'm anorexic" . . . . And I found it hard to take, you know, and I said "No! I'm anorexic!".'

MD: 'But what was difficult to take? The fact she thought you were bulimic?'

A: 'Actually [pauses] being sick, I couldn't stand it [pauses] and [pauses] it was really dirty and unhealthy, whereas anorexic was more [pauses] I dunno, it's all, like, fragile bird, that's it, like, you know?'

[Anne, C]

The label was therefore sometimes accepted, if not exactly 'independently' of the medically imposed diagnosis, at least for reasons that did not purely relate to having internalized this label by submitting to legitimate medical discourse. Sometimes a different kind of conflict over definitions was at play, with the medical term accepted but given a different meaning – for Véronique, anorexia was not a pathology; for Yasmine, it did not diminish her as a person; and, for Anne, it was socially preferable to bulimia.

At the end of this circuit, in addition to the medical diagnosis, there was also the risk of hospitalization if the patient failed to put any weight back on. The label then shifted from 'anorexic' to 'anorexic at risk of hospitalization':

> My doctor told me 'We're absolutely going to have to hospitalize you otherwise you'll never pull through' . . . And well after I passed out again, I'd come over all faint, I went back to the doctor, the doctor took my blood pressure, checked my pulse, said 'This is ridiculous, something absolutely has to be done, if you don't put any weight back on, you're going to be hospitalized, hospital right away'.
>
> [Louise, H]

The interviews provide an indication (although one that cannot be explored any further here) that hospitalization was sometimes subject to internal debate between professionals in the circuit, with the parents also involved in some cases and even – much more rarely at this stage – the individual herself:

> And so the GP and my parents were thinking about hospitalization, my health wasn't great anymore, I was coming over all faint, I had low blood pressure, and I'd had a blood test and it wasn't great, I had hormones, everything was out of order, the doctor and my parents were thinking about hospitalization, but, well, the psychologist [actually a psychiatrist] absolutely wanted to carry on trying, he thought we could maybe manage without hospitalization, but, well, the GP ended up writing to him, sending him medical certificates, asking to see him about hospitalization, and he was saying 'We're going to wait a bit more', but, well, my parents weren't reassured and nor was the GP.
>
> [Nadège, H]

Examining the circuit of agents but also the history of the labels applied by this circuit brings to light two factors leading to variations between cases: conflicting definitions and different kinds of labels. Given that most of my interviews were conducted in a hospital setting, the time during which this circuit of agents was in play was often determined by when it finally resulted in hospitalization. However, this was not always necessarily the case. The interviews I conducted through personal network sampling involved people who had never been hospitalized and showed different endings after the circuit of agents had been established. In Annabelle's case, discussed above, the circuit was soon suspended and hospitalization was never mentioned. As for Sabine, she also mentioned one threat of hospitalization, which she presented as what triggered her work to stop maintaining her commitment, described at the end of the previous chapter:

> I went to see a psychiatrist, who said to me, I'll always remember this, 'Right, well, listen, either you come and see me twice a week, or I have you hospitalized'. . . . Put like that, I preferred to see him twice a week! I didn't want [pauses] and you know, I didn't want it to be visible either [pauses]. The thing

> was that I managed to maintain a kind of social façade [pauses]. I didn't want it to be seen as a symptom, I didn't want to be marginalized because of it.
>
> [Sabine, N]

As for Véronique, she mentioned several threats of hospitalization and the strategies she used to avoid it:

> In my family, they would only realize that I was really thin in the summer, in June, at exam time, well, May, June. So he [her uncle who was a doctor] always threatened me with hospitalization in May, at the time I was going to sit the exams I'd been working for like crazy the rest of the year! So it always became a huge drama. So, two years in a row, they threatened to have me hospitalized, and I dunno how I managed the third year, but they pretty much left me alone [pauses] . . . . Because every time they wanted to put me in hospital, I found ways to say 'No, don't worry, it'll be fine, and, anyway, tomorrow, I'll eat again' and so I'd found that way, which was 'Well, I'm going to go into analysis and then we'll see', well, 'I'm going to see a psychoanalyst', and that way it showed my good will, that I wanted to pull through.
>
> [Véronique, N]

A network of monitors

Just like the stage with the circuit of agents was not solely defined by its results, its members' roles cannot solely be defined in terms of the hospitalization in which it usually resulted. Throughout the circuit, these agents played a role both in terms of conveying norms and monitoring the interviewees: the members of the circuit were active and this activity was not restricted to identifying deviance and prescribing hospitalization.

Demands to stop

First of all, the circuit of agents presented as engaged in a normalizing endeavour reminiscent of what we saw in the first phase of the career. At this stage, people 'encouraged' the interviewees to eat more (rather than less), others 'prescribed' weight gain (rather than a diet) and some even 'joined in', by eating meals with them to try and incite greater food intake, both through their own practices and by watching over the girls. The members of the circuit requested or demanded that the interviewees stop maintaining their commitment. After a certain point, the interviewees' parents would constantly beseech them to eat more:

> Well, we went to Ecuador, and there, my parents were scared stiff, they had the worst holiday of their lives [pauses]. It was all 'I mustn't get a holiday tummy, I had to eat properly' and everything.
>
> [Camille, C]

> They [her parents] were constantly saying 'Eat, you're thin enough like that, eat'.
>
> [Annabelle, N]

> When I'd eat 'this' [gesture indicating a very small quantity] and say I'd finished my meal, my dad, well, he'd be annoyed . . . . 'Go and eat! . . . You're scaring me, you're hurting me'.
>
> [Christine, C]

The agents of the medical circuit relayed this same demand, while also checking the interviewees' weight and exhorting them to stop losing weight or to put weight back on:

> What happened is that I had an uncle, who was a doctor, and he [pauses] he played the role of [pauses] it was him who told me off, who shouted at me, and my parents didn't. They never shouted at me, we never argued about that subject, well, ok, a bit with my dad, they were extremely tolerant [pauses] and it was my uncle who, so I had to go and be weighed every week, that was him [pauses] the big inspector, you know.
>
> [Véronique, N]

Both laypersons and professionals used a certain number of strategies to try and bring the commitment to an end. The interviews offered an indication of some of these. The professionals' strategies were similar from one medical trajectory to another. Some were even routinized in the context of prevention or treatment of anorexia. The GP sometimes tried re-nutrition, not by putting pressure on the interviewee to eat, but by giving a medical prescription: 'At the start [my doctor] suggested that I eat [pauses] and take Renutryl . . . . they're these really high-calorie things, little disgusting tins, caramel, yuck [pauses] And I had to eat them between meals' [Louise, H]. Putting weight back on was sometimes framed as a condition for being able to continue doing various activities, physical ones for example:

> Well first my GP, because I rode horses, said to me, 'well at the moment, you're not all that well [pauses] if you don't put a bit more weight back on or if you don't stop losing weight I won't be able to give you your medical certificate'.
>
> [Nadège, H]

Later in the circuit, gaining weight was sometimes presented as the only way to avoid being hospitalized:

> My psychiatrist would say to me 'Right, if you don't put on 2 kilos, I'm having you committed'.
>
> [Yasmine, C]

> This psychiatrist told me that she'd see me every two weeks, and that if I didn't manage to put a bit of weight back on [pauses] [I'd be hospitalized]. She wanted to bang the drum a bit, actually, to scare me.
>
> [Christine, C]

Obviously, if hospitalization was considered at this point, it was because the weight loss had become very concerning and it seemed an essential last resort. At the same time, as these excerpts show, the threat of hospitalization – which sometimes preceded its application – was also a possible strategy for imposing the norm of weight gain.

Where parental strategies were concerned, some resulted from parents applying medical instructions or advice:

> My mum anyway . . . the GP had told her 'No special meals, the same meals as everyone else'.
>
> [Anne, H]

> The doctor had said to my parents that, anyway, whether I did or didn't eat, I had to be present during family meals.
>
> [Mathilde, H]

Other strategies for imposing this norm seemed to be more personal, devised over time, and showed the parents' increasing concern and uncertainty about what means to use. They also showed the very real experience built up bit by bit as difficult situations were repeated over and over. This can be seen in the way Anne's mother [H] ended up dealing with a 'tantrum' caused by the question of food intake:

> So my mum would dish out my food [during meals], there were tantrums and everything, because she'd give me too much, actually, she'd give me the same portion as my little sister who's seven [pauses], it wasn't huge, she's got a good appetite but it's never huge. And I remember one evening, she'd given me some pasta, and I was sure I had even more than my little brother [pauses] And so I said to my mum: 'You've given me more than my brother!' She switched the plates! And she was right, she switched the plates, and so I had to finish. My mum, my parents, definitely made me eat.
>
> [Anne, H]

As Anne underlined in her interview, these personal strategies could be very diverse: 'They tried everything [pauses] They shouted at me . . . . They tried being nice, understanding [pauses] . . . . My mum tried to make things I liked a bit more' [Anne, H]. Isabelle, who had just arrived in Clinic C when I interviewed her, talked a lot about these parental strategies, which were still recent for her. First, her parents began cooking higher-calorie food than before: '[My mum] was always cooking pasta, or rice, and everything . . . . And then even my dad, once, he made chips with chops of something or other' [Isabelle, C]. Moreover, her father tried to show how absurd refusing food was by comparing it with situations of famine:

> [Isabelle had refused to eat]. It was impossible then, that day, and he called me 'a spoiled brat' and he told me 'you just can't turn it down like that when there are kids dying of hunger blah blah blah' . . . . Again, once, there we were, during the last holidays, we were in the car, and we heard, it was a programme on the radio about the war, the crisis in Russia and the famine [pauses] So they were saying, the people who ate the soles of their shoes or wallpaper and everything [pauses]. And we were driving and my dad was like 'Hear that Isabelle?' 'Yeaaaah.' 'And what does it make you think?' I knew exactly what he wanted me to say, so I was like 'Well [pauses] it's horrible, really, it's horrible to live through that, it really is'. 'Yes, but [pauses] you, in particular?'
>
> [Isabelle, C]

Finally, he also tried to play on the normative aspect of public situations, as opposed to the family context, where deviance would come at a greater cost, counting on the fact Isabelle would rather save face and eat:

> It was a week or two ago, we had friends over, I'd agreed to eat with them even though I knew it would be a bit hard and everything, but I had a really good friend of mine sitting next to me, and then I was interrupted, we were moving on to the main course, the phone rang, half an hour you know, I came back, they'd already dished up my food, you know . . . . But they'd really dished it up, you know, like a really decent portion, I sat down, I started to [pauses] . . . . He was opposite me, on top of it, and he was watching me [pauses] . . . . This time, he'd done it [pauses] so that I'd have a decent portion.
>
> [Isabelle, C]

Monitoring

From medical professionals to laypersons

All these strategies were, to some extent, linked to the central strategy focused on monitoring, which went hand in hand with the circuit of agents being put in place. As the main stigma – the interviewee's thinness – became more visible, and as the information about her was progressively disseminated and the labels evolved, more and more people were likely to become aware, first, that something was wrong, and second, of the diagnosis that had been suggested and then given.

The agents of the first circuit in place (during the first phase of the career) also played a role monitoring the interviewees – for example, we saw that people joining in with the diet would check that the interviewee was sticking to it. However, during the third phase, this became much more radical and a veritable network of monitors was progressively put in place as the agents of the circuit became increasingly concerned about the girls. This network had two consequences. First, more and more people were likely to become part of the circuit watching over the interviewees' behaviour. Second, more and more kinds of behaviour were likely to be judged worrying and therefore monitored by these people.

The number of people who could realize or be informed that something was wrong progressively increased. The circuit of doctors, for example, constituted a network of professionals in charge of monitoring weight – using scales – and general state of health – using medical tests, checking blood pressure etc. Where family was concerned, the brothers and sisters who had been informed sometimes also played a monitoring role when the parents were absent: 'My brothers and sisters were there, and they forced me, you know [when her parents were not there, at lunchtime for example]: "Yes, you'll have some cheese". "No, I prefer a yoghurt". "No, no yoghurt".' [Anne, H].

Similarly, sometimes the peer group was also alerted and once they knew about the label, they also became involved in monitoring:

> [A friend] soon realized that I was losing weight. So she warned me, she told me to be careful, that I was too thin . . . . And then after, I went out with this boy . . . . So that was when I was ill, and he would tell me to 'be careful' too, well, he didn't know much about it, but, well, he'd been told a bit.
>
> [Julie, H]

> [My friends] thought I was becoming thinner and thinner [pauses]. For example, when I went to eat with my friends from summer camp, and, on top of it, when I was at summer camp, it was a riding camp, so, well, they didn't want me to go out riding in the morning if I hadn't eaten, so they'd say to me 'You have to eat, this isn't good' and everything.
>
> [Nadège, H]

Moving out in concentric circles, monitoring even extended to people who were not family, friends or medical professionals:

> I had a French teacher who came to see me one day and said 'Listen Sabine, are you having any problems?'
>
> [Sabine, N]

> At school, there were remarks, some teachers, in particular a French teacher, who I was fairly close to, who asked 'And did Mathilde eat this lunchtime?' in the middle of class.
>
> [Mathilde, H]

Eventually, more and more people were therefore in a position to monitor the interviewees. More and more actions were also watched over, with meals, of course, the key social stage:

> My mum had said to me 'You're going to come and eat here every lunchtime'.
>
> [Sidonie, H]

> [Louise was a border at school] So they were worried, and at first I had to eat in the infirmary.
>
> [Louise, H]

> When I'm with my family . . . my parents are watching me . . . . It feels like their eyes are glued to my plate.
>
> [Isabelle, C]

> [At Christmas] I didn't want any chocolates [pauses], the *bûche* [traditional Christmas dessert], I had the tiniest bit possible, my parents glaring.
>
> [Anne, H].

Progressively, other moments and social spaces became the locus for this monitoring: '[My parents] are *always on the alert* where I'm concerned' [Sidonie, H]. As the circuit of agents and labels was established, the symptoms of deviance increased. At the beginning of the circuit, eating habits and weight were the main elements being watched over. The information that parents obtained from doctors then resulted in their range of concerns about behaviour extending. They also had to check that interviewees did not weigh themselves outside the doctor's surgery, or not 'too much' at least: 'The doctors had [said] to my parents: 'above all, she mustn't weigh herself, only once a week, hide the scales' [Julie, H]. Physical exercise was also monitored:

> Every time I said 'Right, well, let's go play some tennis', 'Well, listen Louise, maybe we'll just rest this weekend, ok'.
>
> [Louise, H]

> [Anne was 'doing' the stairs] At the end, I thought I was on my own and there was my brother who was like 'Are you exercising Anne?' I was furious [pauses] I was like 'I've been caught!'
>
> [Anne, H]

Even school work, a socially valued activity among teenagers if ever there was one, was monitored once it had been reinterpreted through the medical lens of 'hyperactivity' ('feeding themselves with work'): 'They [her parents] told me, during the French exam for the *baccalauréat,* 'actually you should be careful, because you're just feeding yourself with work [pauses] you work, you work, you don't think about anything else, you should stop a bit' [Julie, H].

Mathilde [H] particularly emphasized this aspect of the label, explicitly referring to it in terms of labelling. In her view, practices which had no link with those she eventually accepted as pathological were also being judged in terms of the pathology. As Becker would put it, 'the deviant identification becomes the controlling one [and results in] treating a person as though he were generally rather than specifically deviant' (Becker 1963, 34). The fact that she enjoyed cooking was henceforth read as an obsession with food and the fact she worked hard was perceived as hyperactivity, whereas she had 'always' done these things in the past without them being interpreted in a negative manner:

M: 'I always used to cook [pauses] So then they put a stop to it, very clearly, I'm not to cook anymore. . . . . That annoyed me too, "You're not to cook anymore", I've always loved it, since I was a kid, I've always helped out . . . . They [her parents] are worried when I work [pauses] because they think I'm working too much.'

MD: 'Are they making the link?'

M: 'Yes, and they aren't the only ones [pauses] the link's been made here too [in the hospital] [pauses] . . . . Anyway, people have a warped view of things, because I'm "an anorexic". If I wasn't labelled anorexic, I'd be normal for them. Now that's just how it is . . . . But I've always found it absurd that they make the link with the fact I'm good at school, that I work a lot [pauses]. I've been good at school since I was tiny, in that case I've been anorexic since I was tiny. It annoys me when people say [that].'

[Mathilde, H]

Throughout the phase studied in this chapter, a network of monitors was established that progressively extended in two ways – first, in terms of the number of agents involved, second, in the domains of social life being watched over. More and more people were likely to be involved in monitoring practices and this was likely to affect more and more social spaces: in terms of labelling theory, this means that more and more types of behaviour were likely to be considered deviant. From the point of view of the interviewees, to which we will now turn, as this network of surveillance was established, the stigmas increased along with the problem of managing information. Indeed, during this third phase, they found themselves faced with an increasing number of interactions in which they had to manage this information and there was more and more information to manage.

Being able to maintain the commitment

In this third phase of the anorexic career, the issue of 'wanting' to maintain the commitment, which we saw in the second phase of the anorexic career, transformed into the question of 'being able' to maintain it, despite the alerts and monitoring at work. How was it possible to carry on given the network of monitors in place?

This situation transformed the 'discreet work' done in the previous stage – where deviant practices were simply kept discreet – into 'deceptive work' – where these practices were kept secret so that they could continue.

Monitoring

From discretion to deception

As the circuit of agents was progressively established, different labels evolved over time; similarly, from the point of view of the interviewees, different stigmas also evolved over time and they had to learn to manage these in their interactions.

As we have seen, chronologically, the first stigma that required management was 'not eating normally' and this mainly had to be managed with parents, who were the most likely to be concerned. The interviewees sometimes had to deal with this from a very early stage, during the very first phase in Anne's case, for example, as she hid the fact she was on a diet from her mother 'because she would have been against it' [Anne, C]. In most cases, however, the need to manage this information began later, with the second and third phases, as the interviewees' practices were progressively labelled deviant.

At the beginning, simple strategies of discretion sufficed to hide this deviance from their parents. The main strategy of discretion involved playing on different social spaces – those that could be monitored by parents and those that could not, such as the school canteen:

> I was a three-quarters border, so I ate at school [pauses]. So it went by unnoticed there.
>
> [Annabelle, N]

> I ate at the canteen at lunchtime . . . . In the canteen, it wasn't hard to cut back. And breakfast, my parents weren't there, so I managed [to cut back] very easily.
>
> [Anne, H]

> On top of it, at the canteen, it was easy for me not to eat much, given that my parents weren't there . . . . At lunchtime, I'd make sure I ate on my own, that way I ate as little as possible at lunch [pauses]. Sometimes, when I could, I'd make sure I could skip lunch [pauses]. And in the evening, on the other hand, my parents were there so I'd eat a little bit . . . . On top of it, I made the most of the fact it was the holidays, so I'd go to bed fairly late, I'd make the most of it to get up around midday, so automatically I'd skipped breakfast, and I'd go out in the evening [pauses] so obviously I wasn't there to eat, so whenever I was somewhere else, I wouldn't eat.
>
> [Julie, H]

Initially, this work to be discreet was based on compartmentalizing social spaces, with deviant practices reserved for the spaces to which parents had no access. It sometimes also entailed more active strategies playing on these different spaces, using the fact parents could not watch over some social spaces as a way of acting almost completely freely in the spaces they did watch over:

> And after I started only eating for the afternoon snack and almost not at all in the evening, and I said it was because I'd eaten lots in the canteen [pauses]. But actually, on the contrary, I hadn't eaten at the canteen.
>
> [Nadège, H]

> At the canteen . . . . I could pretty much do what I wanted [pauses]. Then in the evening, sometimes I'd tell my parents that I'd eaten a bit too much at lunchtime and everything.
>
> [Isabelle, C]

Finally, working to be discreet (and working discreetly) sometimes led to changes in deviant practices, with a view to ensuring greater discretion. Anne, for example, went from 'not eating much' to 'eating properly' and making herself sick, after her parents brought up the fact she was not eating enough:

> At first, I didn't eat much and my parents, when they saw that I'd lost a lot of weight, erm [pauses] they said that things weren't OK, etc. . . . And well after I ate pretty much properly but . . . I'd go to the toilet straight after to bring up my meal.
>
> [Anne, C]

This way of managing information corresponds to a situation of 'primary deviance', a transitional period of transgressing norms which has no effect on the identity assigned to the individual transgressing them, and working discreetly and to be discreet is precisely a way of ensuring the 'primary' nature of such deviance.[6] However, because the main stigmas – the body and its weight loss – became more visible here, the audience's progressive concern made this discretion harder and harder to ensure.

As we have seen, as the circuit of agents became established as a network of monitors, there were an increasing number of interactions in which information had to be managed and more and more information to manage in these interactions: not eating normally, of course, but also the physical thinness that the interviewees had conceal once it was a stigma, the weight loss they had to dissimulate once it was seen as deviant and physical exercise or even school work that they had to be hide once they were perceived as signs of deviance. Simple discretion was no longer enough, in that it became less and less possible, and the interviewees therefore replaced it with deception.

The distinction between 'discreet' and 'deceptive' work to some extent brings into play Goffman's distinction between individuals who are 'discredited' and 'discreditable' due to their stigma:

> The term stigma and its synonyms conceal a double perspective: does the stigmatized individual assume his differentness is known about already or is evident on the spot, or does he assume it is neither known about by those present nor immediately perceivable by them? In the first case one deals with the plight of the discredited, in the second with that of the discreditable.
>
> (Goffman 1963, 14).[7]

However, this should not be seen as a strict temporal sequence in which the interviewees went from being 'discreditable' to being 'discredited'. Once their weight was very low, they could, of course, potentially be discredited in all spaces and all situations. But the way the monitoring network extended progressively created a continuum of situations and they were discredited in some spaces but only potentially discreditable in others. The interviewees worked at being discreet in situations where they were discreditable (for example at the beginning of the third phase, or in spaces where no alert had been given) and worked at deceiving in situations where they had already been discredited and where simply being discreet was not enough to keep their deviant practices secret or to manage the interactions around the stigma. At this point, the interviewees' strategies no longer aimed to control information or manage tension (the main problems faced by the discreditable and discredited individual respectively, according to Goffman),[8] but also – and this was their main aim – to allow them to maintain their commitment. These strategies were therefore part and parcel of the overall work in which they engaged in order to carry on. However, it was no longer about them, as was the case in the second stage of the anorexic career; at this point, it was about other people, about the alerts given and the monitoring in place. They did not only manage information and tension in order to save face, they also did so in order to maintain their commitment to the career despite the fact people had sounded the alert and were now watching over them.

At this stage, three new kinds of strategies were used both to deal with the network of monitoring in place and to enable deviant practices to continue: the first, following on from efforts to be discreet, entailed lying; the second entailed pretending; the third entailed removing themselves from certain social spaces. These three strategies lay at the heart of the new work required by the new situation – work aimed at deceiving others, in order to avoid the conflicts and blame that framed all practices as demonstrations of the pathology and in order to be able to continue these practices despite being watched over.

Strategies of discretion, as we have seen, implied actively concealing deviant practices. Once the alert had been given, questions about these practices became more frequent and more precise, first and foremost focusing on whether the interviewees had eaten or not, and the interlocutors in question became increasingly suspicious. *Lying* often became a constant strategy – or one used '75 per cent of the time', to take up Anne's estimation [H]:

> I've never lied as much as I did at that time.
>
> [Sabine, N]

> I lied a lot.
>
> [Christine, C]

> I lied so much . . . I've never lied as much [in my life] . . . I made up so much stuff [pauses] that I was going to eat at people's houses, but I involved everyone [pauses] I said to myself 'I can trick them', 'I ate before, you can say I ate with you' and everything [pauses]. I took stuff and threw it away.
>
> [Sidonie, H]

> My mum, my parents definitely made me eat. Because they knew full well that I wasn't eating at the canteen [pauses] that I wasn't having an afternoon snack, that I wasn't having breakfast [pauses]. Even though they told me, when they left for work, they couldn't be there [pauses] and oh how I lied to them! What happened is that out of [pauses] 75 per cent of the time, I wouldn't eat anything and I'd tell them I'd eaten. The other 25 per cent, 15 per cent of the time I hadn't eaten and I'd tell them, I'd admit it, and 10 per cent of the time, I really had eaten.
>
> [Anne, H].

Information control through lying sometimes consisted in hiding the main stigma with another, a physical illness for example:[9]

> [When she invited people round] I'd prepare something separate for myself, and with loads of apologies [pauses]. Or when I was invited to people's houses, I'd find myself all these illness . . . I'd say to people, 'I've got hyperthryoidism' or 'I'm allergic to that', I was allergic to almost everything!
>
> [Sabine, N]

A second set of strategies could be described as 'pretending' or what Goffman calls 'passing'.[10] This kind of strategy is mainly used in contexts of monitoring, when the person has been discredited and is likely to be accomplishing deviant practices under the watchful eye of someone in the know. In this case, passing related to three types of deviant practices or stigmas: pretending to eat (in relation to the deviant practice 'not eating'), pretending to weigh more (in relation to the stigma of weight) and pretending to be less thin (in terms of the stigma of the body).

The interviewees used several strategies to pretend to eat. Playing on different social spaces provided a means of continuing the work of discretion engaged in previously:

> Actually I didn't go [to the canteen], I bought the [meal] tickets, because, well, I had to buy the tickets, to leave one or two lying around so she [her mother] would see that I had bought the tickets, but that was it, you know [pauses] After, I didn't go to the canteen . . . . Sometimes, I made myself go and read the menu to be able to tell my mum what they had in the canteen, what I actually 'hadn't' eaten.
>
> [Anne, C]

Moreover, the interviewees could also use various means to get rid of food during a momentary lapse in monitoring:

> So at first I had to eat in the infirmary, but that didn't work that well, you know, because there was this dog, so as soon as they turned their backs [pauses] it all went to the dog! . . . They thought that I was eating because I almost always finished my plate, but I didn't finish it, you know. Everything I had supposedly eaten, three-quarters of it had gone to the dog. There was a quarter left for me.
>
> [Louise, H]

> My mum had said to me 'You're going to come and eat here every lunchtime', I had napkins, she'd be working upstairs, I'd be eating downstairs because it was quieter, I put stuff in the napkins, then in my bag [pauses] there you go [pauses] I didn't eat anything . . . . Loads of times, we were watching TV, we were at the table, I'd take the steak I'd put it in the napkins, like that, no one was any the wiser.
>
> [Sidonie, H]

> So then, after, the threat of the hospital again, etc., and so to calm things down a bit I said that I was going to live with my grandmother, at the start of the next school year. So I went and lived with my grandmother, who I put through absolute hell! I'd go to the table with plastic bags in my pockets and as soon as she turned her back I'd put everything in the plastic bags and actually not eat anything.
>
> [Véronique, N]

The strategies used to pretend to eat sometimes also included strategies pretending to eat the same thing as everyone else, by cooking the family meal for example:

> And then, after a while, I started doing it [the cooking], I said to myself, 'Right, I'm going to cook them a meal and I'll make my little meal on the side'. And so I'd put loads of butter in theirs, well, I put butter in, and for me, I'd put a tiny bit of steak on the side, in the pan where there wasn't any butter.
>
> [Louise, H]

In some cases, however, these strategies were identified by those observing the meals – and this was increasingly the case as family and friends became more watchful:

> [At Christmas] I managed to skip breakfast, I don't know if they realized or not [pauses] I'd got up really late, and I said 'No I'm going to wait for my big brother' and when my big brother arrived, 'No, I've already eaten'. Well, I don't think they were fooled, they realized, but they didn't say anything.
>
> [Anne, H]

> I'd even go as far as throwing away half a yoghurt without my parents seeing, but, well, in the end they still saw, I mean, anyway, they're not blind.
>
> [Priscille, C]

MD: 'And did she [her grandmother] realize that?' [the fact Véronique was hiding food in plastic bags].

V: 'Of course! Well she didn't realize everything, but once or twice she realized'.

[Véronique, N]

Other strategies for passing related to weight, for example artificially increasing weight when submitting to the mandatory and monitored weigh-in: 'I used tricks when I went [to be weighed by her doctor], I'd drink 2 litres of water, I'd put heavy jewellery on to put on an extra hundred grams' [Véronique, N].

Finally, strategies for passing were also applied to the stigma of being thin, with all its resulting concerns and blame. In this case, the aim was to pretend to be less thin, through changes in clothing:

> I'd wear things that were really long, because my mum could see it, you know.
>
> [Sidonie, H]

> Bit by bit, it was the way other people looked at me, when I realized that people didn't find it pretty. . . . I could see that, but I didn't understand it . . . . So then I started, I'd just wear track suits with long [pauses] to there [pauses]. I didn't get dressed properly anymore, I didn't want to be blamed for anything, so I hid everything. . . . . And often, my friends would say 'That's enough now, Christine, no that's horrible you know, don't wear [pauses]'. I dunno, I had these skinny jeans, 'No, that's horrible, no you can't wear something like that, it's horrible, you can't go out like that'. Even if I didn't see it, I kind of suspected, I just had to look at the expression on their faces to realize that I had to put something baggier on you know.
>
> [Christine, C]

> I tried to [pauses] hide a bit in my clothes, well, because everyone told me I was thin, so I said to myself 'Right . . . I'm going to try and wear other clothes, to look a bit fatter, you know'. I bought less black clothes, I chose paler colours, with stripes like that, round them.
>
> [Louise, H]

A third type of strategy consisted in the interviewees removing themselves as far as possible from the spaces in which they were monitored. Initially, the canteen was a space free from (parental) monitoring, but as the network of monitors extended and began to include friends, they were progressively watched over there too; for that reason, they often avoided it:

> I'd pull back from certain friendships, certain groups of mates, so I wouldn't have to go with them to the canteen.
>
> [Anne, C]

> Quite the opposite, I'd avoid friends [pauses] . . . . In terms of friends, there were comments at school . . . . So I avoided meals with friends a bit.
>
> [Mathilde, H]

Isolation from a friendship group was sometimes also the effect of other strategies, for example in Christine's case, who talked about cardiac problems as a way of managing information linked to her anorexia:

> So, then I had a lighter timetable [at school] because I wasn't OK at all . . . . So then, well, I had to say that I had health problems, . . . a heart problem [i.e. cardiac] because once in class I'd come over all faint, so it's true, it was plausible, you know [pauses]. And so then it really widened the gap [between her and the others]. I was really isolated [pauses]. Well, I had no one with me, I was really all alone . . . . And I lost people, there were really people who distanced themselves from me, who didn't call me to go out anymore, I wasn't invited to their evenings out.
>
> [Christine, C]

The interviewees sometimes also removed themselves from other spaces, as they began to fear the stigma being discovered, for example the stigma related to their bodies:

> It was hard for me to go to the babysitting jobs I did, because I knew full well that children notice everything, and, well, once this little girl that I was looking after sat on my knees and [pauses] well she sat right against my pelvic bone and she said 'what's that?' and I said 'it's my keys' and I changed position . . . So I stopped looking after those children.
>
> [Anne, C]

While their deception was efficient on occasion ('I tried to trick pretty much everyone' [Christine, C]; 'I deceived a lot of people' [Anne, C]; 'I pretty much managed to fool [them]' [Julie, H]), it necessarily met its limits as their weight continued to lower, ruining these strategies and constituting both the criteria and the lever for hospitalization.

Consequences of labelling

Moreover, these same strategies, despite being devised in response to the monitoring of the interviewees' practices, were also perceived as deviant and became further evidence justifying hospitalization. Given that the girls were monitored but nonetheless wanted to carry on with deviant practices, they had to develop strategies of deception. These strategies were then interpreted as patent symptoms of the pathology or as symptoms of it worsening, as 'abnormal' behaviour: making themselves sick rather than eating, lying, tricking, excluding themselves from their friendship networks or other social spaces. In this way, the labelling process itself can have the effect of increasing practices considered deviant. Unlike the strategies used in the second phase to maintain the commitment, all the interviewees' strategies discussed in this chapter have in common that they were a reaction to the labelling that occurred. In analysing this deviant career, it is important to consider not only the actions of the interviewees but also those of the audience of their deviance, as this reveals the important effects that labelling has on practice:

> [Interactionist theories of deviance] wanted to enlarge the area taken into consideration in the study of deviant phenomena by including in it activities of others than the allegedly deviant actor. . . . one of the most important contributions of this approach has been to focus attention on the way labelling places the actor in circumstances which make it harder for him to continue the normal routines of everyday life and thus provoke him to 'abnormal' actions . . . . The degree to which labelling has such effects is, however, an empirical one, to be settled by research into specific cases rather than by theoretical fiat. . . . The difference in definition, in the label applied to the act, makes a difference in what everyone, audiences and actors alike, does subsequently.
>
> (Becker 1963, 179–80)

What distinguished the practices in the second phase in the career (chapter five) from those outlined here was the effect of the labelling itself. This does not, of course, mean suggesting that the labelling process alone can explain these deviant practices; it just means showing the concrete ways in which this process influenced them:

> To suggest that defining someone as deviant may under certain circumstances dispose him to a particular line of action is not the same as saying that

> mental hospitals always drive people crazy or that jails always turn people into habitual criminals.
>
> (Becker 1963, 180)

In addition to these 'lines of actions' that arose due to the interviewees' practices being monitored, the label also had other direct effects. Being watched over brought about new deviant practices, but being labelled 'anorexic' also had effects in terms of identity, both for the actors and the audience. We saw earlier how – and for what reasons – the interviewees accepted and/or reinterpreted the diagnosis: they sometimes became 'anorexic' for themselves too. Moreover, the fact they were considered anorexic by others sometimes reinforced their deviant practices: Why 'make an effort' to eat, for example, if all behaviour would be linked to the anorexic identity one way or another?

> When we invited friends of my parents round, I'd try to eat normally [pauses] . . . . But when I was with my parents and my sisters, on the other hand, I made no effort at all.
>
> [Louise, H]

> They didn't believe me anymore! And [pauses] I'd say to myself 'What's the point seeing as they don't believe me anyway! I'm not going to eat'. So it got worse [pauses] . . . But what didn't help, was that, for example, we'd have sausages, it was two sausages per person, and in the evening my mother: 'Right Anne, what have you eaten?' 'We had sausages.' 'I bet you only had one.' Whereas I'd had two. If only I could just have one! The same with fish fingers and stuff like that.
>
> [Anne, H]

The anorexic label became a 'master status trait' in Hughes and Becker's sense of the term, a status that prevails over all others, and from that point of view 'the deviant label . . . reorganizes the economy of statuses' (Queiroz and Ziolkowski 1994, 105).

> Because after a while, you become convinced, 'I'm just an anorexic'.
>
> [Yasmine, C]

> Everyone is different in the group [of friends at school] but what characterizes me, last year, it was work, and this year, it's work and anorexia [pauses]. It's kind of heavy as labels go, you know.
>
> [Mathilde, C]

The work of deception, in particular, is part of the context of 'secondary deviance' that became established during this phase in reaction to the labelling process: 'Secondary deviation . . . becomes a means of social defense, attack or adaptation to the overt and covert problems created by the societal reaction to primary deviance' (Lemert 1967, 17). Identity is redefined around the label that becomes both the master status of that identity and the principle of the behaviour reinforcing it.[11]

The third phase was therefore the phase in which the commitment to the anorexic career was maintained despite alerts being given, despite being watched over by friends and family and despite the results of this monitoring and of the labelling of practices as deviant. During this phase, a network of monitors was established. More and more people (family, friends, teachers, doctors, and so on) became likely to watch over the individuals' practices, across an increasing range of social spaces (practices such as food restriction but also physical exercise, measuring their bodies, school work – now interpreted as 'hyperactivity'–, and so on). At this stage, maintaining the commitment therefore required working in new ways, despite the deviant label and despite being monitored. First, this entailed 'working to be discreet' in order to make the practices defined as deviant less visible than others (for example by playing on different social spaces, with deviant practices reserved for the spaces to which parents did not have access, such as the school canteen). Second, this required 'working to deceive' in order to keep these practices secret (by lying, through various strategies for passing – entailing pretending to eat, to weigh more, to be less thin – and finally by removing themselves from spaces where they were being monitored). The career may have begun in and through the group but it increasingly continued in a solitary fashion.

The work done to maintain the commitment in the second phase (chapter five) and the work involved in this third phase (chapter six) are two logical and chronological phases of the same endeavour. In the second phase, this involved the girls working 'for themselves' in various ways, and in the third phase, it meant working 'against others', countering the alerts given and the monitoring in place. However, in both cases, it remained a necessary condition for maintaining the commitment and pursuing the anorexic career. The radical difference between the start of the second phase and the end of the third lies in how the situation was defined. First, the interviewees' attempts to apply their own definitional categories and their own labels failed once the situation changed and they became 'anorexics'. The desire to master public labels came up against this particular label and its progressive consensus among the audience. Moreover, maintaining the commitment was now solely defined as a way of 'not stopping' despite demands to do so, of not giving in to these increasingly widespread, insistent and legitimate requests (legitimate professionally, for example, where doctors were concerned). These external – and unanswered – pleas for them to stop give us (but also the interviewees) a sense of just how strong the dispositions they had acquired were (as described in the previous chapter). And, in the next phase, we will see that the hospital institution then specifically targeted these dispositions with a view to erasing them.

Notes

1 The difference between the second and third phases of the career is not only marked by this distinction between 'carrying on' and 'not stopping'. The particular use the interviewees made of tools of measurement, for example (as mentioned in the

previous chapter) also relate to not stopping. The specificity of this third phase compared with the previous one lies instead in the intervention and influence of external requests to stop.

2 Before outlining this circuit of agents, Goffman insists on the importance of 'career contingencies' in whether someone enters the hospital or not: 'one could say that mental patients distinctively suffer not from mental illness, but from contingencies' (Goffman 1961, 135). The adverb 'fatefully' should therefore not be understood in any absolute sense.

3 This argument has also been levied against the notion of 'total institution': 'For Goffman the total institution was primarily coercive, and the patient's "moral career" was fatefully determined by the hospital. . . . For [Strauss], the institutional order was not an external force that controlled passive individuals. Individuals, including patients, participated in determining this order' (Barrett 1996, 8–9).

4 Asking this question consists in 'seeing everything that happens as an instance of collective activity, as the result of many people and institutions acting together' (Becker 1998, 198).

5 It should be noted, however, that Goffman does refer to the 'decoding power' of the audience, although he considers this more a scientific 'ability' to see something that other cannot see than the result of public decoding: 'A physician who meets on the street a man with dull red discoloration of the cornea . . . is meeting someone who . . . is likely to be syphilitic. Others present, however, being medically blind, will see no evil. In general, then, the decoding capacity of the audience must be specified before one can speak of degree of visibility' (Goffman 1963, 67–8).

6 See Lemert (1951) and (1967).

7 It is worth noting that Diane Taub and Penelope McLorg also address this question with reference to Erving Goffman, asserting that: 'Anorexics, on the other hand, suffered both discreditable and discredited stigmas —the latter due to their emaciated appearance' (McLorg and Taub 1994, 257). However, for Goffman, it is not the stigmas themselves that are discredited or discreditable, but the individuals in situation, according to the social spaces and systems of interactions in which they find themselves, which entails a genuinely interactionist perspective rather than one that is partly naturalizing in nature.

8 'The issue [of the discreditable person] is not that of managing tension generated during social contacts [the case of the discredited person], but rather that of managing information about his failing. To display or not to display; to tell or not to tell; to let on or not to let on; to lie or not to lie; and in each case, to whom, how, when, and where. . . . [Stigma] always give[s] rise to the need for tension management (in regard to the discredited), and information control (in regard to the discreditable)' (Goffman 1963, 57, 164).

9 'Another strategy [of information control] is to present the signs of . . . stigmatized failing as signs of another attribute, one that is less significantly a stigma' (Goffman 1963, 117).

10 Goffman refers to 'passing' to describe all the techniques entailed in the 'management of undisclosed discrediting information about self' (1963, 58). In this case, these strategies for passing can be wielded by discredited individuals who nonetheless want to deceive an audience that 'knows' to escape their vigilance. Again, these strategies are not just about managing tensions or information but also about finding a way to maintain the commitment despite everything in place to stop them.

11 McLorg and Taub (1994, 256) analyse this 'role engulfment'.

7 'Being taken in hand'

Giving themselves over to the institution

Given that my interviews were mainly conducted in a hospital setting, the final phase of my analysis of the anorexic career concerns the moment when the interviewees were taken on board by the institution. This situation defines, and perhaps even determines, the point of view underpinning the entire narratives provided by these patients hospitalized for anorexia.[1] In this chapter, hospitalization will be broached as a single phase and the 'end' of the career, although it is important to note that hospital stays can be part of diverse and discontinuous medical trajectories and can vary depending on the therapeutic orientation of the wards. Special focus will be given to the points of resemblance and common processes that can be identified across the different hospitalizations my interviewees experienced and recounted. These will be approached from the point of view of 'successful hospitalization' – the medical category that institutional treatment aims to have the patients take on board.[2] I will not analyse hospitalization in and of itself, but rather as the final phase in the career and in terms of its relationship with the previous stages.

In this final phase, the interviewees were 'taken in hand' by the hospital; in other words, the institution worked on them as individuals in an endeavour to fight the dispositions they had acquired to maintain their commitment to the anorexic career. Ultimately, the hospital hoped to obtain the patients' cooperation in their own treatment, leading to a voluntary end to their endeavour. The aim was for the patients to manage to see themselves from the hospital's point of view and accept this perspective. This was seen as a necessary condition for achieving the treatment aims. In the particular case of treating anorexic patients, the hospital situation is often very similar to the 'total institution' analysed by Erving Goffman as: 'a place of residence and work where a large number of like-situated individuals, cut off from the wider society for an appreciable period of time, together lead an enclosed, formally administered round of life' (1961, xiii). Drawing this comparison should not, however, mean mechanically applying this term to the hospital institution as it currently stands – Goffman devised his concept in a specific historical and political context. Nonetheless, it is important to note that when anorexic patients are hospitalized, the main effect of the total institution as demonstrated by Goffman – the individual's loss of control over his or her acts and biography – can be considered a deliberate and openly defended part of the treatment, a veritable therapeutic aim in itself. In order to treat patients, it is considered necessary to have some hold over them, insofar as the 'control' that they exercise over their behaviour is defined as a feature of the pathology that has to be worked upon in treatment. This was clear in my interviews:

> No, well, you know, their thing [doctors] with anorexics, it's that [pauses] before, we established the constraints. Now, it's up to them to establish the constraints, to turn things around.
>
> [Yasmine, C]

> You don't control anything anymore [pauses] so it's true that that's kind of the point [pauses] my doctor said to me 'You mustn't be in control anymore, so you have to let yourself be carried by what you're told'.
>
> [Julie, H]

In their treatment, the interviewees were explicitly supposed to 'lose control' and self-constraints had to be replaced with external constraints, at least at first.

The institution's work on the individual translated into a break with the past that was symmetrical to the break in the first phase of the career when the interviewees 'took themselves in hand' and began operating a deliberate and determined change in their lives. In this final phase, they were 'taken in hand' and, instead, it was the hospital institution that worked on *them* to generate a new change in their biographies. The focus in this chapter will be on the effects this endeavour had on the patients, identified in terms of links with the previous phases of the career. Hospitalization aimed to create a break in continuity on three levels: first, in terms of discourse about the self/about identity; second, in terms of the 'reference group' created by grouping the anorexics together; third, in terms of the body and habits relating to food, sports and school work (by forcing the interviewees to stop maintaining their commitment and by working on the dispositions they had acquired in the previous phases of the career).

Questioning identity and finding answers

During the previous phases, we saw that one of the issues at stake when the interviewees took themselves in hand and worked at maintaining their commitment was a desire to be in control of public labels. The previous phase started to set in motion a reversal of this situation, insofar as the interviewees' identities were progressively and increasingly defined externally through the label of the diagnosis. The hospital phase pursued this reversal, both institutionalizing and radicalizing it: 'And then it started, the questions and the questioning [pauses]. Before, I was totally sure, radically sure, I didn't let myself question anything [pauses]. [Now] I have to ask myself questions, have to manage to ask them' [Yasmine, C]. The institution called the girls' identity into question in multiple ways, as the clinical consultations worked on a range of different questions.

Furthermore, the institution attempted to provide specific answers to these questions and to bring the patients to internalize the hospital's point of view, with a view to successfully achieving the therapeutic aim. The interviews I conducted were strongly marked by the new self-definitions elaborated by the patients during the hospital phase. Given that I conducted my interviews with patients in two different places and at different stages in their medical trajectories, this 'invisible' process of internalization can be understood in terms of two principles of variation that led to substantial differences: first, the therapeutic orientation of the medical point of view, and second, the degree to which that point of view was internalized depending on the patient. Moreover, the interviewees sometimes used the interview as a space in which to rehearse or test ways of demonstrating this internalization with a student in sociology (bearing in mind that they often saw me as a student in psychology who might potentially report back to the medical team on their progress). For this reason, the interviews sometimes demonstrated (in the sense, 'revealed') the situation at a given stage in the hospital itinerary, but they also used them to demonstrate (in the active sense) that they had internalized the medical point of view. Based on various indicators, three stages can be identified in this internalization.[3]

First, the patients had to recognize that they were anorexic, rather than being in 'denial' – something doctors consider a symptom of the pathology. From this point of view, the hospital continued and institutionalized the process imposing a particular identity that had already begun with the circuit of agents. However, it was sometimes more successful:

> [Before the hospital] I couldn't quite manage to tell myself I was anorexic yet.
>
> [Louise, H]

> Before, even if my GP said it to me [that I was anorexic] I didn't want to believe it. Now, when I think about it, I am, because when I see how I behaved and everything [pauses]. Because, you know, we have four hours' rest every day, so there's time to think.
>
> [Anne, H]

> [During her second hospitalization] I'd realized that I was, that I am anorexic.
>
> [Mathilde, H]

For the doctors, internalizing this fact – much like breaking with habits of control – had a therapeutic aim. First, this recognition represented the first stage towards recovery and second, 'denial' was considered one of the symptoms that had to be countered: 'Once you say you're anorexic, you're already a little bit less anorexic' [Anne, H]. The therapeutic work done by the hospital therefore implied imposing the diagnosis, particularly when negotiating the need for hospitalization and treatment:

> [Solange, a new anorexic admission to ward I in clinic C, asks for an interview with the intern following her case because she wants to leave the ward] 'I've got digestive problems with this thing in my oesophagus and with food' . . . . The intern lets her speak then says firmly 'But you still have a problem with anorexia, don't you?'.
>
> [FJ]

When I negotiated my interviews, I presented my investigation as focusing on anorexia. I therefore also contributed to imposing the diagnosis to some extent, as it was the basis on which I asked particular patients to speak to me. At hospital H, all the patients indicated to me by the doctors accepted this presentation, except Nadège: although I reassured her that I was completely external to the hospital, she agreed to the interview with some reluctance, as if it were yet another thing she 'had' to do there. At the time, she was at the beginning of her first hospitalization. As we saw in the analysis of the first phase, she refused on several occasions to specify the 'beginning of her anorexia'. This wasn't because she couldn't remember or be specific enough, but rather because she refused to recount her experience in terms of the medical diagnosis. Moreover, hers was the only interview in my corpus which did not include expressions such as 'like all anorexics', 'when you're anorexic' or 'as an anorexic' and she was also the only person I interviewed at that particular stage of the hospital trajectory. The first component of internalizing the medical point of view – accepting the diagnosis – was therefore absent from this interview.

Internalizing the medical perspective also meant recognizing that the diagnosis implied a 'pathology' (in the previous chapter, for example, Véronique accepted the diagnosis but rejected its pathological nature) and that, rather than simply a term used to describe particular practices or behaviour, anorexia was in fact a 'real illness' [Mathilde, H]. The interviewees explicitly ascribed this realization to the effects of the medical 'work' done: 'And when I started talking with psychologists, things like that, I started realizing that I was [pauses] ill' [Emilie, C]. Accepting this part of the medical point of view also meant reinterpreting past itineraries. Practices and representations from the previous phases were revised in light of the medical point of view: '[Before the hospital] I didn't realize that I wasn't well: for me, it was normal and that was just how it was' [Camille, C]; 'It's going through a psychiatric hospital that makes you realize that it's not normal' [Christine, C].

At this stage, all the practices from the previous phases were reinterpreted as symptoms of a pathology: physical exercise and school work were redefined as 'hyperactivity' or as obvious features of the pathology; eating habits were redefined as 'obsessions' or signs of a pathological desire for control: the weight reached in the pre-hospital phase was redefined as abnormal, and so on. The fact that the interviewees had taken this point of view on board meant that, in many ways, our interviews were the narrative of a pathology, of how things progressively 'got worse' or 'deteriorated', until the person progressively 'fell' or 'sunk into' the illness.

Finally, the patients were supposed to both take on board hospital definitions of recovery or progress and display a practical stance of cooperation towards the institution's aims. 'Wanting to get better' or equivalent expressions ('being determined to get better', 'hoping to get better' and so on) were used to designate a break within the hospital trajectory, the point at which the interviewee agreed to espouse the institution's therapeutic aims: 'Now, my aim is to get better' [Yasmine, C]. This stance was increasingly contrasted with previous times when the patient did not, or did not really, want to 'get better':

> [During the first hospitalizations] I wasn't really determined to get better anyway . . . I didn't really want to get better . . . . [Regarding the current hospitalization] Given that I was determined to get better anyway, I was ready to listen to what I was told.
>
> [Julie, H]

> You've got to be able to be treated [pauses]. And now, with hindsight, I realize that the first time I just wasn't able, well, there was still a lot of pretending [pauses] 'Yeah yeah, it'll be fine, yeah, I understand that, I understand that', and actually not at all, not at all.
>
> [Christine, C]

'Wanting to get better' therefore meant being 'determined' or 'able' to be 'taken in hand' (with the notion of being 'able' placing particular emphasis on acceptance as the result of a learning process). At this stage, the institution built up consent (or at the very least a declaration of consent), which was then used as the basis for action. The word 'ready' was often used to refer to this stage in the medical trajectory, both by the medical teams and the patients who had internalized their point of view:

> I really really wanted things to get better, and I'd decided to go [back] to hospital [pauses] I was ready to go back in a way . . . . I told him [the psychiatrist]: "I'm ready to go back there"
>
> [Sophie, C]

Being 'ready' meant the interviewees were ready to accept the hospital's point of view about them and, above all, ready to recognize the legitimacy of hospitalization. The term was used to refer both to a stage in the medical trajectory (the stage when they were 'ready') and to a practical disposition (being 'ready' to cooperate). This is illustrated, implicitly, through the following example of the opposite stance:

[Solange, the anorexic patient who was admitted onto ward I the day before – and had not signed her contract yet – asks for an interview with the intern]:

SOLANGE [to the intern]: 'I've decided to leave here, I can't stand it, I want to leave, I know that if I stay here I'll carry on losing weight . . . . I want to get better now and I know that if I stay here I won't manage to, I know it, it's like the other hospitalizations, I'll start losing losing losing [trails off].'

INTERN: 'And where exactly would you like to go to get better?'

SOLANGE: 'I'd like to go home, to rest, for a start, and I know I'll get better [pauses] I've had enough, I want to get better.'

[The intern sends her to see the head of ward, who sees her and then comes into the nurse's station]

HEAD OF WARD: 'The anorexic in all her glory! "I'll get better on my own, I don't need anyone, I'll get better on my own".'

[Shortly after, the NURSE who witnessed the interview adds for my benefit]: 'At first, with [another anorexic patient on the ward] it was the same thing, but when [the head of the ward] said to her "just try it for a week and we'll see", she listened [pauses] Here, there's no compromise possible, she wouldn't listen to anything at all . . . . [Later, in a disillusioned tone] She wasn't ready, you know.'

[FJ]

In this case, Solange tried to negotiate leaving the ward by expressing the fact she 'wanted to get better' and by providing what appeared to be the proof that she had internalized the medical point of view. At the same time, the argument she used – in order to get better she had to leave the clinic – was not acceptable to the medical team, for whom patients prove that they 'want to get better' by accepting rather than refusing hospitalization. From this point of view, and because she refused hospitalization, Solange showed on the contrary that she was 'right in the thick of it' – 'the anorexic in all her glory' – and that she was therefore 'not ready' 'to get better'.

Ultimately, 'wanting to get better' therefore meant patients accepting the hospital's work on them, along with the resulting changes, as the only road to recovery at this stage – that is to say, once hospitalization had been prescribed. Isabelle, who had just arrived in clinic C, accepted both the anorexic diagnosis and its pathological nature – 'I can totally see that my state isn't normal' – but took some distance from the third part of this medical point of view:

> For example, this morning she [her referent psychiatrist] weighed me, and after, I said to her, 'You know, I don't even know if we'll see each other next time [pauses] I'll have put some on you know' [pauses]. I don't want to put any on! Well, I want to put some on, I want to get better and everything, but actually, I want to get better without getting fatter, but the two go together, you know, and that [pauses] . . . I can totally see that my state isn't normal, and that that's not how you have to act, how someone normal would act, but, well, for me, it's something that's stuck, that's rooted in me, and it's really hard [pauses], for a start, just wanting to remove it you know . . . . If I finish [my plate] I say to myself 'Wow, you've changed, wow!'
>
> [Isabelle, C]

On the contrary, 'wanting to get better' meant patients accepting that they would be transformed in and by the hospital and cooperating in this transformation. As Isabelle put it, it meant 'for a start, wanting to remove' a way of thinking, of being, or 'managing to stand having to leave anorexia' [Yasmine, C]. Agreeing to this transformation, which ran counter to all the self-transformation the interviewees had worked to achieve in the previous phases of the career, was therefore a key issue in them managing to take on board the hospital perspective. Some of them feared this transformation by the institution in and of itself, as the possible and dreaded result of the hospital's work on the individual; they feared that all the dispositions they had built up in the previous phases would be erased. The following example, regarding school work, illustrates this concern:

> [Following the hospital's endeavour to change her relationship to school work] But I'm always scared that I'll start enjoying doing nothing and become a bad student.
>
> [Mathilde, H]

> I also say to myself, do I have to force myself to become a bad student when I don't like that?
>
> [Isabelle, C]

'Wanting to get better' meant displaying a practical stance of cooperation with the transformations at work and this was the same in both the institutions in which I conducted fieldwork.

However, in my field investigation, definitions of 'getting better' did vary according to the institution and therefore in the interviews I conducted in each. 'Getting better' sometimes referred to putting on weight and to stopping behaviour labelled as a feature of the pathology. When discussing leaving anorexia, the interviewees in hospital H referred mostly to certain kinds of behaviour coming to an end. This reflected the importance placed on behaviour in that particular hospital context:

> Two weeks ago, I wouldn't have said this, but now [pauses] I really feel like I'm in recovery. I've had weekends, authorized visits outside, and I can see that the behaviour I had with food [I don't have it anymore].
>
> [Anne, H]

> Now, I don't want to go back ['to' anorexia] at all [pauses] Now I feel really well, when I eat I feel even better.
>
> [Louise, H]

Conversely, where the interviews conducted in clinic C were concerned, definitions of 'getting better' placed greater emphasis on the efficiency of 'working on the self' and on positions in terms of 'moving forward'. The medical teams in clinic C defined their treatment not so much in terms of anorexic behaviour as in terms of 'working with the patient'. It was about making the patient 'move forward' by making her 'hear' what she was then supposed to say (to herself):

> So my reasoning was crazy, but I couldn't manage to find a different way of reasoning, I didn't listen to anyone else [pauses] And that's precisely where I feel like I've moved forward a little bit, you know, because I listen to others. Because I try and listen . . . . I say to myself 'Hear that Christine, hear the fact that [trails off] try not to listen to yourself, you know'.
>
> [Christine, C]

The interviewees didn't use these terms to evaluate their weight, for example, but rather their attitudes towards the 'work' they were doing 'with the [medical] team' and 'on themselves'. For this reason, they defined leaving anorexia in terms of the progress they made towards understanding the subconscious and personal causes of their anorexia. The 'work done with the patient' ultimately had to translate into the patient 'working on herself':

> So it's afterwards, when I came to [ward I in clinic C] that I did all the work, that I discovered psychology [pauses] that I started to change [pauses] my state of mind. . . . . [I started to realize] that in order to get better, you have to work on yourself.
>
> [Emilie, C]

To take up Allan Young's terms about 'talking' in psychoanalytically oriented psychiatry, 'working on the self' is both a 'therapeutic modality' and 'evidence of a patient's progress' (1995, 185). From this point of view, questioning identity has to mean both seeking and finding answers to these questions. The following excerpt from an interview with Sophie is in many ways the ideal-type of this process:[4]

> Psychologically, emotionally, I completely cracked, I couldn't stop crying, at every interview, I really wasn't OK at all, and, well, one day, when I was with my psychiatrist, I started to just outpour again, crying and all that, and I don't exactly remember what I said, but there were things that just came to me like that, bam! I started to let it all out, quite a lot of family problems, and I was saying to him, because he wasn't talking at all, I was saying 'Your silence, it's a bit like what I sometimes have at home, you're not supposed to say anything, you have to hide everything, and I can't stand it, it drives me up the wall'. And from that point onwards, I don't know, I started to follow a thread, about my relationship with my parents, mainly my mother, and [pauses]. From that point onwards, a lot of things just came, one after another, and I really started *working on that* [pauses] and bit by bit, there were lots of things that became clear for me . . . . It was mainly to do with [my mother] that *I moved forward, I worked* with the psychiatrist . . . . After I was hospitalized the first time and after lots of [pauses] memories resurfaced

> to do with my family problems and all that, it's true, you know, that everything mainly focused on that afterwards, right? And well, right, it's true that you find *answers* that you can't find anywhere else, right? . . . Really, the first hospitalization was a revelation, in terms of my, well, psychological, problems, and all that.
>
> [Sophie, C, my emphasis]

These 'answers' constituted a form of 'self-discovery' and Sophie was so convinced of their relevance that she also wanted to convince me of it (as evidenced by her repeated 'right?' above). A further illustration of this notion of self-discovery can be seen in the following excerpt:

> Today [pauses] I'm not at all the same Emilie that I was before I was ill, that I was when I was ill, I don't recognise myself at all, and, it even feels like, I'm discovering myself, the real me [pauses] and [pauses] it feels so good! . . . That's [pauses] what manages to make me *move forward* now; I've found something within myself [pauses] and so it's, now, *that's where I'm at* . . . . It really made me think about myself a lot, I kind of realized who I was [pauses] I've really changed [pauses] changed, you know. And it's true that having worked on myself, having been ill, all that, you see others differently, you know . . . . Actually, that's what my recovery is, it's discovering myself.
>
> [Emilie, C, about to leave the clinic, my emphasis]

In my interviews in hospital H, there were no mentions of working on the self and the image of a line of progress towards self-discovery was not present. There were only two exceptions to this: the interview with Mathilde – who was being treated by a psychologist who worked using free association – and the interview with Anne, who, as mentioned previously, was also seeing a psychoanalytically oriented psychotherapist in parallel.

The difference in therapeutic orientations between the two corpora was also illustrated by the models with which actual or potential recovery were described. In the interviews conducted at hospital H, a model emerged in which the illness was seen as a 'hiatus', a mistake, something 'silly' or 'stupid', and in which non-specialist echoes of cognitive behavioural theory could be heard. From this perspective, recovery consisted in returning to the previous identity:

> Now I'm pleased because now that I can see this with a bit of distance, I think 'it's true, anorexia, it's ooooh [pauses] it's silly to do that, well, I've learnt my lesson and now I'll try not to do it anymore. I've been there and I know it's really stupid.
>
> [Louise, H]

> It's as if, for the past year, it wasn't really me anymore, that's why when I talk about it with my friends now, I say to them 'But you'll see when I get back, I'll be someone else, someone like I was before, it's not the Julie you

> knew when I was ill anymore', I've completely changed. It's as if I had a bit of a hiatus.
>
> [Julie, H]

Conversely, the psychoanalytical version of the process of 'leaving anorexia', as identified in the interviews conducted in clinic C, did not frame it as returning to a previous identity but rather as reaching a new identity, produced by work done 'on the self'. From this point of view, anorexia was no longer temporarily straying from one's self and could be reframed as a painful but creative experience.

> But you know I wouldn't go back for anything . . . . Doing psychological work on yourself, not everyone does that, and you're maybe closer to people and you see different things too [pauses]. I've still got things to work on, right, that's why I still see a psychotherapist, but you cope with it too [pauses] You do ask yourself questions, right, you call things into question, you listen to others more, when you have problems, they'll maybe be less serious than someone who's already had them, it makes us better able to listen to others than other people.
>
> [Priscille, C]

> For a start, my dad never stops going on about how I've ruined my teenage years, the best years of my life, because I haven't made the most of it like other people, because I've ruined my life with it and everything, I said to him 'You know, it's something that's also helped me grow, even if it's negative, it helps me to understand lots of things and to work on myself in a way that a lot of people will do later, you know'.
>
> [Isabelle, C]

From this perspective, to some extent the work done on the self repositioned anorexia within the individual's biography as an important, painful moment, but one that was also paradoxically enriching. One of the local sources of this thinking can be found in the words of a teacher I interviewed at the clinic, speaking in his capacity as a psychoanalyst:

> There are two directives though . . . . On the one hand, I take a fairly paternal position, in which I state that there actually is something that means that [pauses] means you have to get out of the vicious cycle . . . . But, so, after, more at the end of the trajectory, I still try, at the end of the trajectory, to make them feel valued, by saying, actually, 'Right OK they've experienced [pauses] lots of things [pauses] and now it can actually be helpful to them [pauses] to have something [pauses] that people who haven't been through what they've been through will never have'. In other words, I give value to their anorexia.

These two models for consolidating the narrative (on the one hand, the hiatus, on the other, the opportunity for working on the self and for self-discovery) are very different ways of constructing the break with the past created by hospitalization and all the work done in that context. In the first model, in hospital H, this change heralds a return to the pre-anorexic identity. Recovery is framed as breaking with the anorexic phrase and continuing the previous identity. In the second case, in clinic C, the change introduces a third identity, as it were. This identity is different from the identity during the symptomatic phase but also different from the previous identity due to the work done on the self.

A deviant group constituted by the hospital

During the first phases of the career, we saw that one of the specific features of anorexia as a form of deviance was that no deviant group was involved in the learning process and that moral entrepreneurs and other individuals responsible for passing on norms played a very particular role in this regard, whether in terms of diet or bodies. In the final phase, this question set anorexia apart once again: the deviant group was finally composed but very late in the day compared to other types of deviance. Moreover, the group was composed and imposed by the hospital. It was organized in and by the institution, when the patients were admitted to psychiatric wards specializing in eating disorders or to child/teenage psychiatry wards. At first, at least, these groups were not chosen peer groups, they were obligatory groups, which, depending on the hospital context, could be either informal – the 'anorexics on the ward' – or institutionally formed – the collective patient treated in group therapy. Finally, a third specific feature was how the deviant group became both something used to maintain the commitment (the classic role played by the group in career analyses) and something used to break with that commitment. Being placed in a group affected patients in different ways, and they used this in different ways, depending on the type of hospitalization and on when this occurred in their hospital trajectory. Three functions and uses can be identified in this regard.

In Howard Becker's analysis, even before the stage of 'mov[ing] into a deviant group', this group is a locus for learning deviance. As we saw, during the first phase this function was often fulfilled by 'the audience', by 'normal people' rather than by a deviant group. During the hospital phase, however, the deviant group sometimes played this teaching role. The hospital, a space for treatment with the aim of breaking patients' commitment to the anorexic career, paradoxically became a space in which new techniques for maintaining that commitment appeared. The deviant group organized by the hospital was also a potential locus for learning new things (when this had not happened earlier), for example, how to count calories:

> Eating half a chip or half a cucumber, it was the same for me, I had no idea about calories, nothing . . . . [At the beginning] I had no idea [pauses] And it was in the hospital, it was in the dining room [pauses]. We arrived at the table

> and the [anorexic] girls were like 'Right, so this lunchtime, there's beetroot, 230 calories, there's a piece of lamb, 160 calories, and there's beans, but when they don't have any beans, they put potatoes, so then the potatoes that's more, so if I were you, I'd have half your bread roll not the whole thing' . . . . And so with all that I knew all the calories by heart and everything.
>
> [Camille, C]

New forms of self-measurement and new deceptive practices aimed at countering close surveillance were sometimes also discovered:

> In psychiatric hospitals, you meet [anorexics who say]: 'I can hold the whole of my thighs like this [in the circle between both hands], can you?'
>
> [Christine, C]

> [In the dining room at the hospital] The girls were scheming all over the place! Wiping off potatoes here, hiding steaks in their knickers there.
>
> [Camille, C]

The techniques learnt during the hospital phase were sometimes then used by the girls in order to maintain, or even radicalize, their commitment to the anorexic career once they left the hospital. This was the case for Mathilde, who went from rationalizing food intake in terms of quantity to rationalizing it in terms of calories after her first hospitalization:

M: 'Before, it was the quantity, what there was in the plate [pauses] Even though, when it was pasta, I'd already eat less than green beans, but it became more pronounced [pauses] because it seemed heavier on my stomach [pauses], whereas now, it's more about [pauses] anorexic [pauses] calculations.'

MD: 'Of calories?'

M: 'Yes.'

MD: 'And you said that that wasn't something you did before your first hospitalization?'

M: 'No, not at all [pauses] It was an idea that was a bit foreign to me [trails off].'

MD: 'And so how did you actually discover it?'

M: 'Before the first hospitalization, I'd look at food packaging a bit [pauses] the idea of calories [pauses] I'd say to myself, "If it's less", but I didn't know exactly what that corresponded to. I had no real idea, it's more here, during the first hospitalization, with the dieticians [pauses]. And in conversations between anorexics [pauses] who knew much more about it [pauses] it was more here that that came.'

[Mathilde, H]

As we can see in this example, while the deviant group was not the only locus for learning, changes in practices were nonetheless directly related to the diagnosis, and therefore the group, with the expression 'anorexic calculations'. It is perhaps regrettable that I immediately linked that expression with the idea of 'calculating calories' without letting the interviewee develop a bit further what she meant exactly in terms of both learning and group identity. The medical teams themselves criticized the 'anorexic corridors' that exist on specialist wards and the patients used terms such as 'us anorexics', something that group therapy sometimes institutionalized even more clearly and visibly.

Framing the diagnosis as a collective identity had several uses, for both doctors and patients. One might reasonably assume that it made it easier to impose the diagnosis. For example, the expression 'anorexic rituals' often used on the wards had the connotation not only of the pathological aspect to this behaviour but also of its collective dimension. Highlighting and showcasing the common nature of this behaviour, shared by a group of patients, sometimes encouraged the latter to internalize its pathological aspects:

> Here, during my hospitalization, well, it was already there during the first one, but much less, there were group therapy sessions with other anorexics, comparing with other stories, that were completely different but at the same time that had things in common, that's when I realized that it really was anorexia.
>
> [Mathilde, H]

> And then, after, when I saw so many patients . . . . I mean it's awful how much the broad outlines, which are alike, are actually completely similar . . . . Of course, those broad outlines, it's what they [the doctors] know best because they're the same for everyone, for all anorexics [pauses] Of course, they just have to jump in and have a go at us, they know full well that we all have those broad outlines.
>
> [Yasmine, C]

In the hospital, being placed in a group, whether an informal group or a group that engages in therapy together, could also serve as a way of demonstrating the pathology. In my interviews, this was marked by recurring expressions such as 'like all anorexics, I' and 'anorexics [do this or that and so do I]', indicating that recognizing the pathology involved demonstrating its common and collective character. What might seem paradoxical – the fact that behaviour is abnormal and pathological because it is shared with others – in fact conveys and establishes the medical point of view, because the group is brought together in a social sphere in which their very presence is a sign of pathology. This situation then gives rise to what Erving Goffman has called an 'affiliation cycle', in other words, a stigmatized individual's relationship to a group of similar individuals that can shift and change, going from a reactive 'shudder' to 'freemasonry' (Goffman 1963, 51). In my study, the patients being put in a group to internalize the pathological dimension of their behaviour tended to mainly give rise to 'shudders'. However, another way in which the patients used the group did come somewhat closer to a freemasonry of misfortune. Behaviour became normal for the same reason it was pathological – because it was shared:

> And, well, what's really striking, you know, for all this time, I said to myself, my reactions, it was completely abnormal what I was doing, that I was the only person like that, and as I talked to others, bit by bit, as I read things, I realized that it was the same.
>
> [Julie, H]

> I felt like I'd never pull through, that being alongside other anorexics wouldn't help at all [pauses] and actually [pauses] now, it's kind of broken the mould of the huge monster I was, because [trails off] . . . . So now, I've kind of come back down to earth a bit, I said to myself, 'Anne, you're not the only one like that, so it's over, you're not a monster'.
>
> [Anne, C]

> I really met people, who'd already relapsed, who'd already been through stuff [pauses] and with who, really, I mean, my best friends, they're people who are anorexic, you know [pauses]. Because really [pauses] I don't know, understanding, knowing that what you feel is legitimate [pauses] and knowing that our way of functioning, which seemed so crazy, and almost hateful [trails off].
>
> [Christine, C]

The last two effects of being put in a group reflected the different points of view according to which the group was envisaged. In the first instance, the point of view was that of 'normals' – the collective identity was seen as a shared stigma imposed upon the individual. In the second instance, the group was described and used from the point of view of the stigmatized individual, where the identity was therefore 'normal' – for 'an anorexic'.[5] It could also be argued that in-group and out-group alignments can be cyclical. This is evidenced in the following interview excerpt, where Anne explicitly mentioned the passing of time to explain why she no longer saw things from the point of view of the group:

> I had, I still have actually, a thing with other anorexics, what's it called, group therapy, with a psychotherapist, with the few anorexics here and some from a different ward [pauses]. At first I liked it, because it was reassuring to see I wasn't the only one reading cooking recipes, climbing up and down stairs, but now it doesn't interest me anymore, because we talk about anorexic habits and everything, and I don't have them anymore [pauses] I've even completely forgotten [pauses]. They talk about things I don't think about anymore and on the contrary it [pauses] I'm bored, you know. It's a bit out of synch for me now . . . . These are anorexics who've been here for two, three weeks, now I'm the only one who's been here for a while [pauses] It was the same, when I arrived, there were girls who'd been here longer and it must have been the

> same for them [pauses] I didn't understand why they didn't like it [pauses] and now [trails off].
>
> [Anne, H]

As Becker writes:

> When a person makes a definite move into an organized group—or when he realizes and accepts the fact that he has already done so—it has a powerful impact on his conception of himself. A drug addict once told me that the moment she felt she was really 'hooked' was when she realized she no longer had any friends who were not drug addicts.
>
> (Becker 1963, 38–9)

In the case in hand, this organized group was imposed by the institution and it sometimes even used it to impose the diagnosis and demonstrate the pathological nature of shared behaviour. In this sense, to some extent the process described by Becker served the treatment aims of the hospital by making the patients feel 'anorexic', which was the realization the institution hoped to achieve. Once the patients had been put in a group, however, rather than using it to help them break with past deviant practices, they sometimes put it to a different use. Indeed, the hospital can also be the locus for a 'deviant sub-culture', which 'solidifies a deviant identity' (Becker 1963, 39).[6] However, the fact that in this case the sub-culture only took shape in the hospital, under supervision and under the aegis of an established diagnosis, meant that it was a structurally dominated sub-culture that could not present itself in the form of the 'ideologies' Becker discusses – for example, the 'working philosophy' aimed at certain individuals labelled as deviant which 'explains to [them] why [they are] the way [they are], that other people have also been that way, and why it is all right for [them] to be that way' (39). In this case, it was the doctors who were in a position to provide this working philosophy, at least in terms of the first two aspects – explaining that others had also been like them and explaining why they were the way they were.[7]

From 'letting go' to 'taking themselves back in hand'

The hospital institution worked on the girls in a third way, directly affecting the practices through which they maintained their commitment as well as the resulting dispositions. This hold taken over the patients bodies, ensured both by the hospital situation and by a variety of treatment techniques ranging from pure constraint (the feeding tube) to what is known as 'contractual constraint' (the contract), set in motion a process that unfolded in three stages. This process depended on the patients' cooperation and they were 'worked on' by the hospital, which forced them to adopt a particular point of view on themselves. First, they had to 'let go' – in other words, stop doing all the work from the second and third phases aimed at maintaining their commitment and hiding the fact they were doing so. Then they had to agree to be 'taken in hand' – in other words, they had to give themselves over to the institution and agree to follow the guide of conduct provided by the institution to the letter, rather than following the dispositions they had acquired. Ultimately, the patients were supposed to be able to 'take themselves back in hand' – in other words, engage in an active endeavour fighting the dispositions they had acquired in the previous phases, defined as bad and pathological, and replacing them with new ones, defined as good and healthy. This therefore constituted a new commitment to taking themselves in hand, a perfect (and opposite) echo of their commitment during the first phase of the career.

Letting go

No longer maintaining the commitment

The hospital situation can be defined as having a real hold over the patient's body. The feeding tube represented the most extreme form of this hold, insofar as it worked directly on the patient's body:

> They put a tube in me because I came over all faint [pauses] in the street, you know. So that, that's the worst thing that happened to me [pauses]. So if it's not OK in the morning, if you haven't put enough on, they increase the dose of calories and there you go, you know.
>
> [Christine, C]

> They put the tube in me and [pauses] I had two weeks of the tube with [pauses] yeah, I had four flasks a day and bit by bit on top of the four flasks they made me eat [pauses]. I had breakfast and an afternoon snack, and then they got rid of two flasks and I had a meal, and all that meant it was huge force-feeding, I put on 3 kilos a week.
>
> [Camille, C]

More generally, the hospital situation itself aimed to put a stop to the work being done to maintain the commitment. To take a prime example, all the deceptive work in which the patients engaged previously became extremely difficult in the hospital context. In the hospital, the monitoring from the previous phase transformed into radical institutionalized surveillance. Previously, the interviewees' deception played on different social spaces – obviously, the single hospital space (patients are forbidden to leave the hospital, and even, in some hospitalizations or at certain moments of certain hospitalizations, to leave their rooms) meant that this possibility disappeared. Their deception also played on the blind spots of the monitoring in place, but with the strict surveillance that existed in the hospital, all actions were likely to be noticed. In short, their previous deception had played on the possibility of hiding certain practices and on the efficiency of lying about these practices but the hospital made all these practices completely visible and discredited all potential lies:

> They suspected me of everything, they cut off my water because they thought I wanted to throw up, they spied on me all the time . . . [in isolation, with the feeding tube]. The doctors would arrive, change the flask, speed the thing up a bit, and then leave and lock the door behind them [pauses]. They'd open up the little flap to check I wasn't doing anything stupid and that was it.
>
> [Camille, C, about a previous hospitalization]

> One thing that has always bugged me, it's that people always say [pauses] when I arrived here, my intern said to me 'Anyway, we work on the assumption not that you're lying to us but that we can't trust you [pauses] we'll believe the facts, but we won't believe what you tell us' [pauses]. I always hated that, even though it's necessary [pauses] because it worked against me [pauses], for a start, when I was hospitalized in the clinic, and I only found this out afterwards, there was a nurse who had told my doctor I'd been sick, because she thought she saw traces [pauses] and I hadn't been sick, I knew that [pauses] but I couldn't prove it, you know [pauses] and it upset me [pauses] and even here, they noticed I was urinating more than I was drinking [pauses] so straightaway they thought I was drinking on the side . . . . At the beginning, when I arrived, I had my bottle of water, and I had to drink it during the day, and I had to wee in a cup and that way they compared what went in and what came out [pauses]. Because I think there are some girls who put on weight but it's just water . . . . And that carried on for two, three weeks. And I said: 'But I don't drink on the side' 'Listen, there are this many litres and this many litres, it's mathematical' . . . . You really feel powerless because you don't know what to say [pauses] to prove it and everything.
>
> [Julie, H]

This hold over the patients' bodies made it possible for the hospital to force them to stop maintaining their commitment, on all fronts. Practices relating to food, physical exercise and school work or culture were all regulated, or even prohibited where exercise and school work were concerned. The eating habits imposed in this way aimed to generate weight gain:

> I was admitted to hospital in February [pauses] They kept me in for four and a half months . . . . They'd made me put a bit of weight back on . . . . And with everything they gave me to eat, I don't think I've ever eaten as much in my life . . . . When I left the hospital, I'd put weight on because they'd stuffed me so full that [trails off] . . . . We were stuffed, you know, I'd really never eaten that much, four meals a day, starchy food at lunch and dinner, bread [trails off].
>
> [Sidonie, H]

Physical activities were monitored – sport and exercise in particular, but in some cases any physical activity was watched over and forbidden: 'I remember once, I was drawing, I got shouted at "Yeah you don't realize it, now, you're sitting up to draw, you're burning calories, who gave you permission to sit up?" [rather than lying down in her hospital bed]' [Camille, C].

As for school work, it was also regulated and reduced, or sometimes even forbidden altogether:

> But I wasn't allowed to work in the hospital either . . . . In the hospital, actually, they always stopped me from working, they stop all anorexics from working for a long time, from being interested in anything, from going out, from learning things, from having books [pauses] It's all forbidden [pauses] . . . . Well, let's say that during the first part, during isolation, it's forbidden [pauses]. Well, it depends on the case, but I used to read a thousand pages per day, they said to me 'Right stop, you know, no more books'.
>
> [Camille, C]

> But it was hard this year, not doing anything [pauses]. Well, I went to some classes, for my own general knowledge and all that but, here, they say that I've done a lot, but, well, I really don't think it's all that much [pauses] . . . . Because I used to work all the time, because [pauses] I always had my nose in a book and all that . . . . So that's hard too, stopping, well, working, working, working all the time.
>
> [Christine, C]

> Here [in the hospital] as soon as I worked for more than an hour, it was all 'Stop right there!' and waves of panic and everything . . . . There was a time when it was kind of insane [pauses]. When you're in Year 12 you can't exactly miss out on three months of school like you could in Year 7 [pauses]. When I'd do my French homework, obviously I can't do it for 15 minutes here, 15 minutes there [pauses] I mean I was already trying to do it in two hours when it's supposed to be done in four [pauses] and it was all like 'Oh no no Mathilde, you've worked too much, you're not going to work anymore'. And there were other things, even if I took a bit of distance from it, there were times when I preferred to get into a book than go and do collages, you know, like, although this is a ward adapted for teenagers, and it offers loads of great stuff, they really make an effort, but my friends, when they've got free time, they don't sit around doing collages or drawings [pauses] I mean I've got over it, but it made me laugh [pauses]. The first month, I really had trouble with it, the first week, when they said to me 'Right come on Mathilde, there are some ladies here to do beads with you [to make bead necklaces]' [pauses]. I said to myself 'Where the hell am I?!' But, well, I realized that I did have to rest as well [pauses] But when I had to go back to class, thirty hours a week, and catch up [pauses], I didn't have time to make bead necklaces then! Not that I missed the bead necklaces.
>
> [Mathilde, H]

The final phase therefore initially consisted in putting a sudden stop to all the work done previously to maintain the commitment to the anorexic career. This was made possible by the hospital situation and, more specifically, by the fact it was difficult – or even impossible – for the interviewees to keeping doing the work they had still been doing during the third phase (despite being monitored). The explicit and treatment-oriented aim of the institution was to make the patient let go. The interviewees talked about this early stage in terms that reflected the radical difference between their current hospital situation and the work and dispositions of the earlier phases in the career ('letting go of the reins', 'vegetating' etc.). The 'momentum' they had acquired in the previous phases was very clearly brought to a sudden halt:

> I was completely lost in the hospital actually, I'd lost everything . . . . Everything I liked and everything [pauses], I wasn't allowed to do sports anymore, I wasn't allowed to read, I wasn't allowed to work [pauses]. Well, I was allowed to *vegetate* and that was just the complete opposite of my life for the last 15 years.
>
> [Camille, C]

> I felt like I couldn't [pauses] control myself anymore [pauses] so I was losing momentum, I was questioning everything [pauses]. I couldn't really understand why this was happening to me, how it was happening to me, why now [pauses]. Why I was *letting go of myself* suddenly like that.
>
> [Yasmine, C, my emphasis]

> And [pauses] I really feel like I'm *letting the reins go,* you know [pauses] not functioning the way I did before, and that's really painful for me [pauses]. Because [pauses] it feels like you're losing control, and that [pauses] I find that hard to accept, hard to take.
>
> [Christine, C, my emphasis]

The institution's work on the patient therefore countered, point-by-point, the work done by the interviewees during the previous phases of the career: the various areas involved in the endeavour to take themselves in hand were brought under control, the things they had learnt to enjoy were prohibited, the momentum they had built up was brought to an abrupt halt, their work on time was impeded by a strict, externally dictated timetable and the 'mode of living' they had chosen was replaced by a mode of living entirely determined by the institution. The institution's work to put a stop to the commitment intervened at the level of the interviewees' work to maintain that commitment.

Giving themselves over to the institution

When the hospital obtained the interviewees' cooperation, they adopted the institution's point of view on themselves. At this point, leaving behind the work they had done in the past became an aim for the patients too and, with a view to this, they transformed the institutional situation into a behavioural guide. By forcing its perspective on the patients, the hospital's aim was for the latter to internalize the legitimacy of the work that the institution did upon them and to agree to let themselves be taken in hand by that institution:

> I wanted to be controlled [pauses] and I went to hospital for that, you know, saying to myself 'I won't have any more choices to make, I won't have anything to do anymore' [pauses] I wanted to let myself [go] gently, like a cow grazing in her field.
>
> [Camille, C].

During this second stage, the interviewees accepted that they would be 'controlled' by the institution, they let it act upon them without putting up a fight – sometimes this was even what they wanted. The contract played an important role in how they gave themselves over to the institution. Almost all the interviewees in the hospital had, at some point or another in their trajectory, been hospitalized with a 'treatment contract'. This tool is an important issue in the 'treatment struggles' between different therapeutic orientations, but is used in wards that lay claim to very different approaches.[8] Usually, the treatment contract is a written document that establishes the conditions and modalities of the hospital stay (and for leaving the hospital). Sometimes, for example, it makes very explicit links between the targets to be met by patients (particularly in terms of weight) and the privileges (in the sense given to the term by American sociology of psychiatry) to which these give rise within the institution. The widespread use of the treatment contract can be linked with the increasingly prevalent norm of obtaining patients' 'consent'. In this case, it should also be understood, more specifically, as a key technique for making the patients give themselves over to the institution. Institutional writings (the contract, but also in some cases, the meal plans that were written out, for example) replaced past habits, like a written programme embodying a 'practical sense' in Bourdieu's understanding of the term.[9] It is as if, by providing an imperative guide for behaviour, the institutions were telling patients: 'In order to act – to know what to eat or what to do – don't follow the inclination of your anorexic dispositions, which are pathological, just let yourself be steered by what the institution tells you to do in the guide it provides (and imposes)'. In the interviews, the treatment contract situation was mainly defined as being about 'not asking any questions'. The contract seemed to serve as a substitute for practical logic:

> So I was hospitalized, for ten days, and I lost 8 kilos in ten days, so I was sent to the psychiatric ward, so I left [for a hospital], I stayed there four months so then, well, then, it was easy, it was a contract . . . : you eat, you put on weight, you can see your parents, and then you can have contact with others, so of course, you eat, you don't ask any questions, you eat.
>
> [Christine, C]

> And honestly, once you're in hospital, you know the rules, you know you have to eat your tray, you don't ask any questions anymore and there you go, you know . . . . [Now] they've asked me to weigh 39 [kilos], and that's it, you know, I don't question things anymore, I'm just 39.
>
> [Camille, C]

As well as being a time for questioning identity, as mentioned above, hospitalization was sometimes also a time during which the interviewees called themselves into question by precisely not 'questioning' what they did anymore. When hospitalization included nutritional consultations, the patients therefore followed the institutional guidelines:

MD: 'And how long have you been here?'

L: 'Five weeks. But [pauses] I saw psychologists, psychiatrists before coming here, and I'd understood that I absolutely had to put on weight but I just couldn't do it. It wasn't willpower that [trails off] but I didn't know what to eat, I didn't know where to begin [pauses]. So, well, I said to myself that hospitalization wouldn't be that bad, I'd see a nutritionist, she'd tell me what I had to eat.'

[Louise, H]

> It's true that they [the hospital nutritionist's prescriptions] reassured me a bit in the idea that [pauses] 'if a nutritionist suggests that as a meal plan, it's a balanced meal plan that'll make you put on the weight you need without it being too much' [pauses] I preferred to follow her advice rather than eating what I wanted, without following any advice . . . . So then we started with very small meals, mainly vegetables, not much seasoning and all that [pauses] And then, well, from week to week she brought it back up, so at first, the first weeks, it was quite hard, you know, the increase, it seemed like a lot, but, well, it seemed, it was in my head, you know, when there was a lot on my plate, I'd say to myself 'Wow there's a lot' and sometimes I said to myself 'You'll have to tell her to increase a bit more slowly', but actually, I managed it, so I didn't say anything. Then afterwards it was really quick, really quickly I reached such an amount [laughs] [pauses]. My weight increased . . . I was ready to obey them, you know.
>
> [Julie, H]

The obedience to which Julie referred consisted in giving herself over to the institution, to an imperative code of conduct, rather than following her own inclinations, redefined as pathological by the hospital point of view.

'Taking themselves back in hand' – reversing categories

In order for the patients to take themselves back in hand, they had to engage in new kinds of work. Indeed, the third stage in the process was no longer about the interviewees giving themselves over to the institution and allowing themselves to be acted upon and guided by that institution. Instead, they had to play an active role in the institution's endeavour by working on their own practices. This work was described as being particularly hard because it required going against all the previous habits that they had built up. For both hospital and, ultimately, patient, (anorexic) dispositions were framed as habits that had to be fought, 'bad habits' in Bernard Lahire's sense of the term:[10]

> It's harder to be OK than not to be [pauses] . . . . Not being OK is [pauses] a sort of pace that I know by heart, you know, ... It's easier to control . . . . That's what I'm trying to find again, bit by bit, trying to fill myself up, to [trails off]. But it's hard because I'm not used to it, in fact [pauses] for three years, it was about emptying myself, trying to get rid of everything.
>
> [Christine, C]

> In the end, for me, now, it's easier to lose [weight] than to put it on [pauses] Whereas before [the anorexia], it was more the opposite.
>
> [Priscille, C]

> And it's much easier to go back there [anorexia] than it is to carry on eating, to force yourself.
>
> [Camille, C]

> It's a big flood, a huge wave that carries us with it . . . . And of course, going against the flow of the river, it's [pauses] really hard, you know [pauses] Because going with the flow is so much easier.
>
> [Isabelle, C]

Refashioning habits therefore required working actively, not just abandoning previous practices. The interviewees all engaged in a new endeavour of self-transformation, fighting against the dispositions that had resulted from the previous phases in the career and working towards acquiring new dispositions. They forced themselves to go against dispositions that were, once again, presented as being truly embodied:

Y: Now I've gone back to cooking, from time to time, with my sister [pauses] . . . . Actually, the thing to do, the technique, it's not looking. You put [butter] in, [look] to the side, 'Yeah that'll do', and that's it. You cut off any kind of thinking afterwards, you know, you tie a knot in a nerve, I dunno!'

MD: 'The thinking nerve?!'

Y: 'Yeah [pauses]. That's it, really, you cut out a bit of your brain . . . . But sometimes it's hard when I'm on my own'.

[Yasmine, C]

> Well, I didn't eat chocolate or cheese for three years, and, honestly, [now] when I'm in the canteen, sometimes I do [pauses]. I hate it, but I say to myself, 'Yeah so you hate that, but don't be all proud, you'll manage to eat it' . . . . And yet I do eat [pauses] and that's the hardest because I say to myself 'force yourself to eat' and that's the hardest moment actually, and that's the moment that I had every day in hospital.
>
> [Camille, C]

In many ways, this new work was the mirror image of the work the girls engaged in during their initial endeavour to take themselves in hand – it marked a break with how things were 'before', it entailed deliberately refashioning practices and dispositions with determination and it involved working on the things that they did and did not enjoy. Its success or failure was measured in terms of how efficient the interviewees' self-addressed 'Right, OK!' and 'Right, come on' actually were, once again mirroring the first phase where these same expressions marked the beginning of their endeavour to take themselves in hand:

> It was [pauses] really hard, I couldn't manage to say to myself '*Right, come on*', I wanted to get better, but every time I was in front of my plate [trails off].
>
> [Louise, H]

> There are days when I say to myself 'Get your arse in gear!' . . . But now I'm completely capable during an evening out of saying, '*Right, OK!* . . . and I'll eat exactly what my mates eat [pauses]. And then it's really nice, and you can sense that that's where the progress is, in fact, but it's not enough yet, because now it's when I'm with other people: when I'm on my own, it doesn't work.
>
> [Camille, C]

> It's kind of saying '*Right come on*, let's put some butter Yasmine, let's put some butter' [laughs].
>
> [Yasmine, C]

A truly new endeavour emerged, characterized by similar practices and expressed in the same terms as the initial commitment. This new break with the past led to a complete reversal of the descriptive categories used during the first phase. When the interviewees first took themselves in hand, they worked to break with a previous period in which they had 'let themselves go'. During the last phase of the career, they framed their commitment and its effects as them having let themselves go into the illness:

> [You start with a diet] and then *you let yourself go.*
>
> [Julie, H, my emphasis]

> And then, well, one day [a friend of hers] put some weight back on and afterwards I just didn't stop losing weight [pauses] . . . I *let myself go* a bit.
>
> [Emilie, C, my emphasis]

Giving themselves over to the institution became a way for them to fight this tendency to *let themselves go* and to prevent themselves from continuing habits that had become natural:

> I mean, anorexia . . . it's like a daily temptation. It's like something you have to fight every single day and it's pretty [pauses]. It's hard [pauses]. Honestly, I'd rather [trails off] that's why I prefer being here. I mean, at least there are people to deal with it [pauses] to say when things aren't OK, when things [trails off]. At least I know that even if I *let myself go*, or if there are moments when I really flounder, there'll be people who'll see clearly and will say to me 'That's not OK'. Otherwise, I know that I just don't have that notion in my head yet [pauses]. And I also know that I'm fed up with dealing with it [pauses] but I can't, I dealt with my illness, I don't think I could deal with my recovery. So [pauses] it's better to have someone I can lean on . . . I know they don't do it all, right, but it's a start.
>
> [Yasmine, C]

The main focus of the endeavour to refashion practices and dispositions as described above was about the girls taking themselves back in hand to avoid them letting themselves go in a pathological way. Trajectories of hospitalization and relapses can be read as wavering between two sets of dispositions – hospital dispositions and anorexic dispositions – and between two forms of taking themselves in hand – the first defined as pathological (the initial commitment) and the second as breaking with, and leaving, anorexia (the second commitment). To continue the parallel between the two forms of commitment, the 'relapses' mentioned in the interviewees' narratives could be seen as ways of leaving the second commitment begun by hospitalization. There were striking similarities between these relapses and the way people left the anorexic career at the end of the first phase, when they stopped taking themselves in hand and returned to their previous dispositions. The following interview excerpt (commented between square brackets) illustrates this wavering movement between the two sets of dispositions and shows how the first and second commitments could overlap:

> And after, when I really started eating properly again it was [during an initial hospitalization on a paediatric ward] from then on that I said to myself 'Right, well, I'm coming to try and *find my way back again*', I really started to feed myself properly again [working against anorexic dispositions] . . . I mean, I ate everything, I ate all my trays, I left a crumb, saying to myself 'I've left a crumb on my tray', I looked at that little dot, I said to myself 'I'm going to try not to be too traumatized about it, well [pauses] [giving herself over to the institution – the trays, rather than the anorexic dispositions,

> indicate what is supposed to be eaten]. But other than that, perfect, my trays, every last corner! And, after, when I went [to a convalescent centre for teenagers], I carried on, I ate relatively well, we served ourselves there, and, well, it was pretty much OK, and, then, after, when it was the holidays, during the two months of the holidays, I *tried to hold out* myself [i.e. on her own], I don't think anything changed, but I still had certain eating habits . . . I couldn't *really let myself go* [definition of anorexic dispositions as a way of letting herself go into the illness]. But I still kept, *I copied,* I'd taken sheets, well, meal plans [from the clinic], because we saw a nutritionist, and I'd taken the meal plans she gave us, it was per week, and well, I tried *to base myself on that a bit*, because . . . on my own, like that, it was difficult [giving herself over to the institution rather than following anorexic dispositions]. And then, after, when I went home . . . I didn't eat starchy foods anymore, well, I started being careful again, about how much I ate and about what I ate, well, the type of food . . . I didn't feel like I could cope anymore and, for me, something had been set off, and, actually, I really started to relapse then ['relapse', the return of anorexic dispositions and of the initial endeavour to 'take herself in hand']. . . . [She was then hospitalized in the intensive care unit in clinic C]. So I started eating again . . . I tried to follow my little path . . . . And then, well, finally I came here [ward E] . . . . And in fact, then, from January onwards, I lost weight again, 2 kilos below, and I realized, I said to myself 'Right, that just isn't OK, you know what's going to happen to you', well, I knew that I could end up back in hospital or in intensive care, so I didn't want to, so I said to myself '*Right, OK, you've got to take this all back in hand'* and well I managed to put a kilo back on on my own . . . , I managed to *find my way back again* [new way of working on dispositions defined as 'taking things back in hand'].
>
> [Sophie, C]

In the interviews conducted at the hospital with the patients who, at the time of the interview, had had the longest hospital trajectory, the hospital point of view prevailed: anorexia was seen as letting themselves go into the illness and breaking with anorexic practices was framed as an endeavour to take themselves back in hand. As we saw in the earlier phases, the previous approach (in which anorexic practices themselves were presented as a way of taking themselves in hand) did not necessarily disappear completely beneath this new point of view. Both perspectives sometimes coexisted within the same interview where, only a few sentences apart, the interviewees presented entering the anorexic career as breaking with a previous period in which they let themselves go, and then presented a successful hospitalization as breaking with a period in which they let themselves go into the illness.

The career analysed here therefore plays out between one 'break with the past' and another, between one commitment and another, between 'taking oneself in hand' and 'taking oneself back in hand' (after having been taken in hand by someone else). Analysing the four phases in question has highlighted the consistent anorexic *work* at play. In the first phase, the interviewees committed to changing their habits in two main areas –their bodies and, in some cases, their school work and cultural knowledge. In the second phase, they maintained their commitment by working on tools to measure their progress, working to change the things they did or did not enjoy and working to create new dispositions. In the third phase, they pursued this commitment, despite alerts being given and monitoring being put in place, through specific work dedicated to discretion and deception. Finally, during the fourth phase, the institution's work on the individual translated into the patients' commitment to a new form of work, aimed at bringing their previous work to a halt and at deconstructing the resulting dispositions. The key process in play throughout was therefore *working towards self-transformation*, towards changing dispositions, towards changing the individuals themselves. The initial commitment and the ensuing work to maintain it translated into dispositions being embodied that eventually constituted a 'second nature'. The work then done by the hospital aimed to counter this. It did so through a collective endeavour on the individual (with or without the patients' cooperation) aimed at erasing these dispositions and replacing them with new ones.

The analytical framework provided by combining interactionist approaches in terms of deviance, stigma and labelling has offered a way of highlighting the dialectic at work between 'doing' (anorexic activity) and 'being done' (normative impositions). This dialectic can be seen in the recurrent features of the careers at hand and in their variations (for example, by analysing the school corpus interviews and the different possible ways of leaving the career). This framework has also made it possible to place equal emphasis on the activities the interviewees engaged in, the reactions to which they gave rise and the effects of these reactions. Certain specific features of the anorexic career make it particularly interesting in this regard. These include: the importance and visibility of a real engagement in and commitment to the career; the complex changes that occur in how the person is discredited, which show the links between stigma and a given system of interactions; and the initial absence of a deviant group, which is constructed at a much later stage in the medical framework and under hospital control. An even more specific feature lies in the fact that *maintaining* the commitment is what is labelled deviant rather than the commitment itself. Two criteria which have been the subject of substantial debate in the sociology of deviance[11] can be used to identify when someone enters deviance: when a norm is transgressed and when an act is designated as being deviant. From this dual perspective, engaging in the anorexic career does not mean entering deviance, quite the contrary in fact: social norms are obeyed and the act is designated as virtuous. The career does not begin by transgressing a norm and it is not the 'first time' the person commits an act labelled as 'deviant', unlike with cocaine use for example. In this context, the question of deviance is not posed in terms of 'committing' or 'not committing' a deviant act – it is by maintaining the commitment to the career that deviance emerges. Moreover, it is not just that charges of deviance concern excessive or extreme application of norms (whether regarding food or school work). What appears as deviant is that these norms are applied *for too long a period*, that the commitment is *extended* despite the emergence of requests to bring it to an end. 'Carrying on' is what appears deviant and what progressively transforms weight into the main transgression that triggers the labelling process (whether weight loss, or, after a certain threshold, simply weight itself).

This is therefore a very particular kind of deviance; one that is rooted in conformity and in conforming. It could reasonably be suggested that this final specificity to the anorexic career is linked to the specific social characteristics of the individuals engaged in this deviance – mainly female, from middle and upper social classes. Once again, this is a specific feature of the anorexic career: studies of deviance have often mainly focused on male and working-class forms of deviance.[12] The last section of this book will now address this specificity in more detail.

Notes

1 It is perhaps somewhat unorthodox to have a deviant career end in the hospital, as if the medical perspective had eventually 'caught up with' the sociological perspective. However, in addition to the methodological reasons for this choice, mentioned above, it is also worth remembering that hospitalization is a common phase in any anorexic career, that those who leave the career before this phase make it a possible but not a *necessary* stage in that career, and that analyses of mental health in terms of deviance give substantial importance to the effects of hospitalization.

2 In the final section of the book, we will look at the case of Camille, a 'difficult patient' who resisted the hospital institution.

3 This question can be linked to the question of medical criteria for recovery, which can be analysed through medical practices. Allan Young, for example, applied this approach to the case of post-traumatic stress disorder on an analytically oriented ward (Young 1995, 186).

4 In order to better understand the way in which this narrative constitutes an ideal type, comparison with Robert Barrett's analysis of psychodynamic categories can prove useful: 'Interview etiquette – making the patient feel comfortable, the sober attitude of concern, the open-ended question, the establishment of a "trusting alliance" – was primarily aimed at eliciting inner mental symptoms. . . . The adept clinician was said to "uncover", "bring out", or allow the patient to "open up", as in the expression "he opened up and out it all came"' (Barrett 1996, 44).

5 According to Goffman, in-group and out-group alignments are imposed upon the stigmatized individual. He or she is forced to recognize that his or her 'real' group is the group of stigmatized people (in-group alignment) but must also consider him or herself from the point of view of normals (out-group alignment) (1963, 137–48).

6 'Thus, the deviant who enters an organized and institutionalized deviant group is more likely than ever before to continue in his ways. He has learned, on the one hand, how to avoid trouble and, on the other hand, a rationale for continuing' (Becker 1963, 40).

7 The situation has evolved to some extent on this point, with the Internet, for example, being used to share such a working philosophy both in terms of normalization and placing value on certain behaviour, outside the medical framework.

8 See Darmon (2001, 80–90) for an analysis of these treatment struggles around the treatment contract (which is a pivotal tool in behavioural approaches, but has garnered strong criticism from the psychoanalytical standpoint, although it still sometimes used and reinterpreted in that framework).

9 On writing as breaking with 'the practical logic of performing practices', see Lahire (1998, 137–67).

10 'The "I can't help it" that characterizes dispositions (as propensities, inclinations) can take various forms — the individual shape of a *passion* (disposition + strong affinity), of a simple *routine* (disposition + absence of affinity or indifference) or even of a *bad habit* or a *terrible compulsion* (disposition + disgust, rejection, resistance towards this disposition)' (Lahire 2002b, 414). The hospital therefore aims to create a situation in which anorexic dispositions would be 'destroyed by a systematic endeavour of counter-socialization' (Lahire 1999b, 130).

11 On this point, see, for example, Becker (1963, ch. 10).

12 With the exception of studies focusing explicitly on female deviance (see Schur 1984 for a list – Schur also denounces the limited space given to their sociological analysis) or on 'white collar crime'.

Part III

The social space of the anorexic career

8 The social space of self-transformation

Having looked at anorexia as a career, this career can now be situated not only in time but also within a particular social space. Its social topology can be uncovered and pieced together: having analysed 'what they do', we can look at how this fits into a social space; having analysed their 'trajectory', we can look at the 'network structure' in which it takes place 'as just so many *investments* and *moves* in social space' (Bourdieu 2000a, 304). More precisely, and to pursue this travel metaphor, my analysis will focus on the kind of 'ticket' necessary for such a journey, in other words, the social conditions of possibility which are necessary, although not sufficient in and of themselves (in other words, 'What social characteristics make the anorexic activity described above *possible*?'). I will highlight these characteristics by linking the career with the specific features of the recruitment of anorexics both as they appear in my investigation and as they have been identified in the epidemiology[1] – anorexics are predominantly female, adolescent and from a middle- or upper-class background – with particular focus on the variables of class and gender.[2] Positioning the anorexia career within the social space does not mean analysing the anorexics' family socialization nor is my aim to identify, within a set of individuals sharing the same social characteristics, those more likely to engage in such a career. Rather, my intention is to analyse which features, within the combinations of social characteristics defining the recruitment of anorexics on a structural level, can act as conditions allowing that career to take place.

This chapter will therefore take all the work of self-transformation analysed in the first two phases of the career and reposition it within the social space (the following chapter will do the same for the hospital phase). As we have seen, the anorexic career is organized around a process of self-transformation, not only in terms of weight but also, depending on the person, in terms of physical appearance, school work and tastes regarding food and bodies. Positioning this work of self-transformation within the social space means re-enrolling the study participants' habits concerning food, sports or school work within the social spaces of tastes and practices (which is also a space of judgements about tastes and practices).[3] However, this also entails analysing (in the chemical sense of the term, by identifying its different components) the full set of dispositions and beliefs underpinning and guiding this work of self-transformation. This set forms what I will call an 'ethos of tension': tension as opposed to relaxation (tension as strain, as effort, as control), but also tension as stretching out towards something and, extending the meaning slightly further, striving towards something. In this case, striving towards excellence or perhaps even being socially 'exceptional'.

Anorexic work

Practices situated in the social space

Analysis of the anorexic career revealed that self-transformation affected two main areas – the body and school work. But how are the practices involved in 'building up a body' and 'building up cultural knowledge' positioned in the social space? Anorexics' sporting activities and school work (considered as 'hyperactivity') as well as their eating habits tend to be linked to their illness. They 'do' these things because they 'are' anorexic. The perspective taken in this chapter will be different. I will try to reposition these activities within the social space of bodies, judgements about bodies and differentiated relationships to bodies, and within the social space of school work, judgements about school work and differentiated relationships to school work. We will see that the practices that appeared in my analysis of the career are *socially situated* and that the work of self-transformation identified is also *socially oriented.*

Building up a body

The expression 'building up a body' reflects the social processes at work in the career much more than the technical references of the term 'losing weight'. In the anorexic career, a range of practices related to food, sports and looking after the body are used to work upon that body and they are not neutral in social terms. The food the girls chose and the work they did to change their tastes were, in fact, not just about restriction and they were not just techniques for weight loss: they were not distributed randomly across the space of food consumption. Although the most obvious and operational principle of selection was perhaps calorie content, preference also went to food corresponding to the tastes of the dominant classes according to Pierre Bourdieu's diagram of the food space (Bourdieu 1996a, 186): fish, fresh fruit and vegetables[4] (except bananas, a calorie-filled fruit that is also the 'only working-class fruit'; Grignon and Grignon 1980, 533) or yoghurt.[5] The food consumed by the participants tended towards the 'delicate', 'lean', 'light', 'refined', 'natural', 'healthy', 'raw' and 'grilled' (Bourdieu 1996a, 186): they often used these terms themselves to define their food choices. Conversely, the food they restricted and then removed from their diet corresponded to the food defining working-class tastes in the same diagram ('fatty', 'heavy' or 'nourishing' with *charcuterie* and bread) as well as the food corresponding to tastes among those with high economic capital but low cultural capital ('rich' and 'fatty', for example *pâtisseries*). For my participants, restricting food intake therefore did not only mean restricting the quantity of food consumed randomly across the social scale of food, but instead selecting certain kinds of food and certain properties (in terms of calories and social value) rather than others. The perception of the 'calorie content' of food was not simply limited to technical and nutritional aspects: 'Among foods reputedly fattening, [the middle and upper classes] more often [avoid] reputedly "common" foods, that is to say foods overconsumed by farmers and blue collar workers, which act as a foil and become scapegoats' (Grignon and Grignon 1999, 168).

This dimension appeared very clearly in the descriptions given by certain participants of the changes that appeared as the career progressed and as they worked on their tastes:

MD: 'Compared to before, though, have there been changes in what you eat, things you didn't used to eat?'

P: 'Yeah. There've been loads of changes [pauses]. I've got this new-found passion for seafood, for fish, whereas I didn't like all that before, I hated it.

[Priscille, C]

Emilie described a very real trajectory through the space of food consumption:

MD: 'And so, actually, if you had to trace a kind of history of your eating habits, how would that [pauses]? I don't know, how you ate before, how you started eating during [trails off]?'

E: 'Well, before [pauses] I went to McDonalds [pauses] I loved chips, I loved food with loads of sauce! . . . I could eat, oh, I dunno, something with loads of béchamel sauce, well, anything [pauses]. You could've made me swallow anything. Well, apart from the things I didn't like, oysters, stuff like that, but, I'd have eaten [trails off] well, for example, when I went to my dad's at four o'clock, I always made myself a sandwich, dry sausage–butter–gherkins . . . . [Now] I'll eat vegetables much more easily than starchy foods . . . I'm very into fish, actually [pauses] fish, there's no problem!'

MD: 'And you didn't like that before?'

E: 'Fish? No, fish wasn't really my thing [pauses] fish wasn't my thing. . . . But now, you won't get me to go into a McDonald's anymore . . . . But, for example, [now] I like going to restaurants, tasting things I've never tasted before . . . . For example, last time, we went to an Indian restaurant, and we ate [pauses] I didn't used to like it, I didn't like prawns, I didn't like things like that, and, this time, there were king prawns with coconut milk, something like that, and, well, I had that!'.

[Emilie, C]

This trajectory can be interpreted as the social elevation of Emilie's tastes, shifting from meals with lots of sauce and her dry sausage sandwich ('simmered', 'fatty', 'heavy', 'cheap', '*charcuterie*' and 'pork' in the diagram mentioned above) to fish and 'king prawns with coconut milk' ('refined', 'light', 'recherché' and 'exotic' in the same diagram). Something other than simple calorie reduction was therefore at work – there was a *social* transformation in food tastes, with a shift towards the dominant model. This change could be understood as simply reflecting her age: Emilie could just be shifting from teenage tastes conditioned by her age group to adult tastes in which her social class played a bigger role. However, this reading would fail to take into account the specific nature of this particular transformation and the extent to which it was the result of a deliberate and determined endeavour. In general, the participants worked hard to change their tastes and this resulted in them choosing different kinds of food. In this regard, Emilie's trajectory in terms of food can be compared with the changes in clothing styles quoted in chapter four, for example Yasmine, who started to dress a lot more 'chic and stylish'; or Louise, who stated that she 'tried to change [her] style . . . . Dresses or skirts, but no jeans, trousers but no more jeans, no more tracksuit bottoms, no more trainers [pauses] high-heeled shoes [pauses], fewer tee-shirts' [Louise, H]. Just like tastes in food, the participants' tastes in clothing and appearance were also fashioned towards the top of the social space, breaking with the practices associated with their age group (eating 'anything except oysters', wearing jeans, tracksuit bottoms and trainers).

As we saw in the second section of the book, they worked on their food tastes, changing what they did and did not like, learning to feel sick of certain types of food and to interpret the sensation of an 'empty stomach' as positive and of feeling full as negative. Further light can be shed on this in social terms:

> The sensations that follow ingesting a starchy and fatty meal seem to be framed very differently according to social class. The number of people who select and classify them as belonging to unhealthy sensations – feeling 'heavy', 'sick', 'nauseous', 'drowsy' and 'congested' – as opposed to the euphoric sensations of being satiated – feeling 'stuffed' or 'full', having 'got one's strength back' – increase regularly from the lower classes to the upper classes.
>
> (Boltanski 1971, 211)

With the work they did on their tastes, the participants therefore deliberately forged a principle for perceiving digestive and bodily sensations that tended to correspond to the perceptions of the upper classes.

During the career, both the modes of food consumption and the actual food consumed *oriented* the work done on the body towards dominant uses of that body. The importance of the 'form' (of the food consumed, of the meals eaten, of the body) rather than the 'substance' (of the food in question) takes on a particularly concrete meaning in the case of anorexic eating habits:

> In one case [working-class tastes] food is claimed as a material reality, a nourishing substance which sustains the body and gives strength . . . ; in the other, the priority given to form (the shape of the body, for example) and social form, formality, puts the pursuit of strength and substance in the background and identifies true freedom with the elective asceticism of a self-imposed rule.
>
> (Bourdieu 1996a, 197–9)

The drastic selection of food, as well as throwing food away or constantly leaving some on the plate (practices described by the participants), denote a constant stance of renouncing food which is the polar opposite of the eating habits Olivier Schwartz has described among working-class women: 'Many women who are advised to go on a "diet" refuse to do so, because food is a vested right, a victory over deprivation, and renouncing food is not well tolerated' (Schwartz 1990, 479). The participants' constant inclination towards 'self deprivation' draws a stark contrast between anorexic practices and working-class culture regarding food:

> [For the working classes] eating as well . . . as possible is an obligation, almost a duty; depriving oneself means directly leaving oneself open to a series of 'weaknesses' and 'sanctions', both physical and social . . . . Working-class language constantly offers reminders that it is necessary to eat in order to 'hold up', 'hold out' or 'keep your spirits up', that it is necessary to eat to avoid becoming part of the 'lumpenproletariat'.
>
> (Grignon and Grignon 1980, 548)

As well as relegating substance to the background, the participants also gave particular importance to the form of their meals. In most of the descriptions they gave, they did not change this form even though they reduced the content to next to nothing ('I didn't skip any meals, but they were tiny [in quantity], knife–fork–glass' [Yasmine, C]). They also tended to stick to mealtimes with great discipline, sometimes aestheticizing food, whether through its presentation or its exotic character:

> I started selecting [pauses] it had to be things that were pretty to look at, nothing that looked too rich, you know [pauses] . . . I ate things that weren't too rich, vegetables, lettuce [pauses] it felt like they were prettier.
>
> [Nadège, H]

> [In an exotic supermarket, shopping to prepare the 'Caribbean therapy meal' for a ward in clinic C]. I'm with Hélène, she talks a lot about the food we see, she tells me the names of the things I don't know, she explains that she's been to the Caribbean several times, she points out the brands of fruit juice she's seen there and that we should buy, she looks at the specific geographical origin of all the products.
>
> [FJ]

As for Véronique, food became more acceptable when she was in a 'fancy restaurant', with the form making the substance easier to swallow:

> I had an aunt and uncle who, when they saw me like that, tried to take me to some really fancy restaurants, because they knew me a bit [pauses] And I agreed to that, even though I didn't eat for three days before and three days after!
>
> [Véronique, N]

The 'denial of hunger' identified by doctors and psychologists can be reinterpreted in different terms here. After the efforts of the diet, the interviews seemed to describe what one might call a 'state of grace' in which hunger was either forgotten or overcome. There is not necessarily any need to make a distinction between 'real' loss of appetite and 'denial', given that, in both cases, the content itself is relegated to the background and, in both cases, an elitist stance is adopted, as we will see again later: 'to listen to them, you'd think the members of the upper classes are never hungry' (Boltanski 1984, 93). Situating these eating habits as class habits can shed particular light on the asceticism of dieting, which cannot simply be linked to gender and the abstinence that patriarchal control over the female body requires of women.[6] Analyses of anorexia that draw on social questions only ever highlight the links between female dieting practices and anorexia. And yet, as we can see here, a further link can be drawn, this time between anorexic eating habits and positions within the class structure – a question that, in my view, has been much neglected. In my study, this dimension affected both the methods used to work on eating habits – which aligned with the dispositions of the middle and upper classes – and the trajectory of the anorexic career itself – which used the deliberate and determined elevation of tastes to transition to a higher level in the social space of food consumption.

This endeavour to 'build up a body' can also be analysed in analogous terms where sports are concerned. Sporting activities cannot be reduced to their technical and utilitarian dimension any more than eating habits can (the girls did not 'burn' calories through just any kind of physical exercise). Engaging in a regular sporting activity is, in itself, a socially divisive practice: directors, managers, and the intellectual and intermediate professions are traditionally over-represented in the sports world in France. This has remained the case despite a certain diversification from the 1960s onwards, which left this social hierarchy intact albeit slightly less marked (Defrance 2000, 24–5).[7] Moreover, the kind of sports engaged in by the participants also corresponded to this social distribution towards the upper levels of the hierarchy (tennis, skiing, etc.), along with several fairly feminine sports, such as gymnastics and swimming.[8] Conversely, they made much less mention of collective, masculine, working-class sports and often stated they 'hated' them. This shows clearly that the purely technical aspect to physical exercise (doing sports to lose weight) is not enough to account for the work these girls did on their bodies. A certain sporting asceticism could be said to mirror the asceticism of their eating habits, as described in my analysis of the anorexic career and confirmed by a physical education teacher at the clinic's school:

> In general, they're über diligent students, [in the pool it's] lengths, lengths . . . distance, regularity 'the more I do, the better' . . . . They're very much looking for the detail that'll bring them perfection, they're not so much interested in the practice itself as in the technical side to it [pauses] Which means, of course, they want to achieve a good performance [pauses] . . . . In floor exercise in gymnastics they're like proper little automated dolls [pauses]. But, you know, at the same time, they meet the necessary aesthetic criteria for gym, nothing hanging out of place.

Just like food consumption, the spaces of class and gender can explain the kinds of sports practices the participants used to work on the body, as well as the kind of body they 'built up' with these activities. The work of self-transformation accomplished during the anorexic career and the body it produces therefore have to be considered at the intersection of these two aspects. To conclude with a few reflections about the body created in this way, it is important to note that corpulence is a more divisive question for women than for men. When looking at women who are managers or who work in the higher intellectual professions and women of comparable heights and ages who come from a working-class background, the weight difference is much more significant than it is between men from both social categories: 'For women, social categories are much more clearly reflected in body weight than for men' (Bodier 1995, 3–4).[9] The bodily changes that occur in the anorexic career are therefore also socially oriented towards excellence, which would be less the case for men. However, while the participants' aim may have been to achieve a dominant body – a form of excellence that is inextricably physical and social – the actual result was an 'anorexic' body. As the people around them began to say they were 'too' thin and the diagnosis was established, their physical endeavour was both condemned and punished, with a particularly strong loss of legitimacy. A similar process also took place in the cultural and school spheres, in which they also worked towards achieving excellence in their methods until the diagnosis delegitimized their endeavour.

Building up cultural knowledge

In terms of the body, the work of self-transformation the participants accomplished was clearly socially oriented towards excellence. As for the increase in their commitment to school work, it took various forms: more time spent working, very detailed timetabling of that work, a desire for exhaustive knowledge and a wish to excel across the board. In addition to school work, there was also a more broadly cultural issue at stake: it was not just a question of 'building up' an excellent level at school, it was also about 'building up solid cultural knowledge', that was both legitimate and irreproachable. The work the participants did in terms of school work and cultural knowledge was therefore also oriented towards the higher levels of the social space. Emilie, whose rise through the space of food preferences was analysed above, described a perfectly symmetrical trajectory in terms of her cultural activities, which took her from illegitimate 'superficial' activities to legitimate, cultivated ones:

> [Before the anorexia] I'd never have enjoyed going to visit something! It was, like, for me, I had to go shopping, I had to buy stuff, to feel good [pauses] . . . . Going to the Louvre museum, or going to see an exhibition of paintings bored the hell out of me [pauses] . . . . I was very [pauses] superficial . . . . I know that now there's a huge gap [between her and her friends from 'before'] [pauses] That [pauses] I don't see things the same way as my friends [pauses] . . . . [My friends from 'before'] don't really

> question anything [pauses] . . . . Museums aren't really their thing . . . . And with that, I'm completely out of sync with certain people [pauses] And yet, before, before, I was like them, but now I've changed . . . I've completely changed, you know.
>
> [Emilie, C]

In this excerpt, Emilie's references to her network of friends confirm that her self-transformation produced the same effects as secondary socialization. The 'gap' she described between herself and her 'friends from before' translated into the kind of changes in friendship groups that are characteristic of the changes resulting from secondary socialization according to Peter Berger and Hansfried Kellner (she no longer saw those friends, who had 'remained superficial').[10]

Practices related to school work and cultural knowledge can therefore be analysed as investments in capital, oriented towards excellence in both fields. Concerning school work more specifically, the aim was to achieve 'brilliance' as a category of excellence in terms of the relationship to cultural knowledge (Bourdieu and Passeron 1979: 24):

> I only had one thing in mind, that was . . . to be as brilliant as possible, intellectually.
>
> [Véronique, N]

> [Following her work to achieve solid cultural knowledge] I knew that I managed to amaze people sometimes [pauses] I mean, there were more surprised looks, and all that, in a positive way, than there were before. Before, I felt more like I was invisible, a bit insipid, you know.
>
> [Yasmine, C]

The work done in terms of school work and cultural knowledge was therefore also socially oriented, in an even more obvious fashion than the work done on the body. However, my fieldwork in the school next door to clinic C (which teaches the clinic's patients during their hospital stays) offers a way of further refining this analysis of the school work dimension. The interviews I conducted with the teachers in this school provide a more in-depth approach to the practices of their 'anorexic students', along with the judgements made about them. It quickly became clear, as I was constructing the field for my investigation, that the teachers identified certain types of behaviour towards school work as specific to anorexics. The latter were recognized as often achieving good results and always proving capable of substantial efforts, linked to their intense investment in school work. They were also often charged with more ambiguous qualities such as being 'too academic'[11] and 'conscientious'. Medical texts on anorexia often identify 'overinvestment in school work', but it is usually only mentioned briefly in relation to other forms of 'hyperactivity' with no particular emphasis placed on the school aspect. In clinic C, however, the institutional links between the school and the hospital led to far more developed views on this question and provided more substantial material than could have been collated elsewhere.

A fundamental ambiguity seemed to underpin the teachers' categorizations of the anorexics as students. Many of the teachers initially foregrounded and valued their excellence (for example, when I negotiated interviews or during the first few minutes of those interviews):

> They're all good students, the anorexics.
>
> [interview negotiation with Mrs M., FJ]

MD: 'But in your view, what kind of students are they?'
MRS Q., with a heartfelt cry: 'They're the kind of students you dream about in other schools!'.

[FJ]

> In the teacher's room, Mrs R. who had refused to give me an interview, comes up to me: 'Ah, I've just heard something for you, something typical! Mrs M., a physics teacher, just said to me that with one of the anorexics, she did the whole year's programme in three hours!'
>
> [FJ]

> With the anorexics, you can't really say that [the teacher's work is] gratifying because they're good students one way or another, in a way, whether we're there or not, if you gave them a book it'd almost be the same thing! . . . I can compare them with students I had in other schools . . . : a class of anorexics would be a class that always had excellent results . . . . I didn't think there'd be such brilliant students actually [the implication being 'here', that is to say in an establishment dedicated to patients hospitalized for various illnesses].
>
> [Interview with Mr E.]

However, the teachers' compliance with the medical point of view (their students were both hospitalized *and* enrolled in school as patients) meant they tended to then go back on this initial definition, emphasizing instead the pathological nature of the anorexics' 'overinvestment in school'. In doing so, they described in more detail the practices that constituted this investment among the participants, while also providing material highlighting the very particular categories of judgement they used. These categories were not about excellence nor about discrediting the students; they related rather to criticizing the girls for being 'overinvested' in school', 'too willing' or producing 'hyper-correct' work that was 'too academic'.

In the teachers' descriptions of the anorexics as students, what first emerged was the huge importance that the latter placed on school work. Mr E., for example, described them as 'girls who are well behaved and who really cling to their work', while Mrs W. underscored 'their expectations regarding school work' and the fact that 'work' was an ever-present 'duty' for them: 'they're really completely caught up in the idea that they have to work, that it's a duty to work'. The importance and the time devoted to school meant that even a simple change in where they worked was enough to make them feel they were doing less:

H: 'Well, she's a huge perfectionist [a student who is a patient on a ward I haven't visited], she did eight pieces of homework for me in two weeks and said to me "that's how I revise" . . .'
W: '[speaking to this student] "there's been an improvement" and she says to me "yes, yes, I stopped working, in philosophy, and it did me a lot of good, because I stopped wanting to revise, to learn things, etc."'
H: 'Yes, but you know what that means, for her, "to stop working"! It's not really [trails off].'
W: 'Yes, yes, of course, but to stop [pauses] producing things [pauses] over and over, you know [pauses] Well, for her, stopping means that rather than sitting down at a table to read, she reads the same thing, but on the train! So, working, but in a space she doesn't consider serious, that's what it means to stop working! [laughs]'
H: 'Or reading outside in the sunshine.'

[Mrs W.; Mrs H.]

The importance given to work and to investment in school work were presented as symptoms of the psychiatric illness, to the extent that, conversely, when the patients began recovering, their academic achievements slowed down:

> Well, [she laughs], sometimes, when they're better, they start [pauses] letting everything slide . . . . And then, the following year [pauses] it's the following year, in their university choices, it can go completely [pauses] off track, a bit, and, so they can end up not making any university choices, any academic choices, and yet being much better physically.
>
> [Mrs H.]

> Really, the thing that managed to surprise me, was that you start worrying less about their pathology when they start to go downhill, as it were, when their school work goes downhill [pauses] I mean that they stop controlling themselves and clinging on to this work, and they think more about other things [pauses] about leisure activities, they try and diversify their centres of interest a little bit.
>
> [Mr E.]

The 'surprise' of this young teacher, who had only recently joined the school, highlights the paradoxical side to the medical orders relayed by the establishment. For the teachers, one of the specific difficulties of their work was that, for medical reasons, they found themselves having to restrict their students' investment in school work and sometimes even having to forbid them from working or handing in homework. This paradoxical pedagogical role suggests that it was not only the *students'* disposition towards school work that was thwarted by the hospital's requirement for them to 'let go' (chapter seven), but also the teachers' professional dispositions, as they found themselves delegitimizing investment in school work because of the illness.

Moreover, these students' substantial efforts led them to request more and more work from their teachers:

> With the whole side to it that's a bit [pauses] anorexic, you know, 'give me things to do, make me work . . .'. In general, it's more, when they're anorexic, when they arrive here, with, I'd say, an anorexic past, medically speaking, generally, they're all 'give me some work, I have to know everything, I have to' etc.
>
> [Mr W.]

It was the students who asked to work or to work more rather than the teachers asking this of them. This apparently atypical situation – which appears to be a complete reversal of the usual school dynamic – encouraged the teachers to understand it purely in terms of the psychiatric illness. However, the extreme nature of this investment in school work could also be linked to the participants' gender and social status. As Jean-Pierre Terrail has underscored, an 'active appropriation of school' is most often seen among girls, along with 'a use of self that is particularly intense [in the school context], generated by historical circumstances in which school success was the only path towards individual emancipation' (Terrail 1992, 667–74).

The anorexic students in question fundamentally requested more work than their teachers provided, because their investment in school knew no bounds and no amount of work would ever be enough: 'They'd always be capable of taking in more . . . . Because they'll ask for more [individual tutorials], systematically, anyway [pauses] Individual tutorials, they'd have as many [as we could give them] anyway' [Mr E.] The students sometimes also refused the normal limitations to school work, for example at the end of the year (when students and teachers were supposed to slow down a little) or the holidays:

> Ah, she's an anorexic of the sort we see regularly, I mean, so demanding, completely demanding [pauses] I mean, she was here today, 30 June, to see if Mrs . . . the German teacher was going to teach her at 10.30 am [pauses] And I had her till Monday, I had her in maths . . . because the class is until 30 June, so we can't [pauses] we can't stop her, we can't not 'feed' her until 30 June [laughs] And so what did she say to me? Right, she's staying here in July, in the clinic in July, she misses studying, she's going to be bored [pauses] because, she says, she likes it, she likes learning, and maybe that's true, right? It's often true, but also because she needs to have her timetable, she needs to learn, to be fed [pauses] to be fed school work [pauses]. And so she's sorry classes are over! . . . She has a right to have her classes right until the end! [laughs] Yeah, yeah, that's how she is!
>
> [Mr W.][12]

Finally, the girls' unlimited investment in school also translated into them refusing to be taken in hand by the medical institution and refusing to 'let go' of their school work, as we saw in chapter seven. It was therefore up to the teachers to place boundaries on that school work, out of concern for their students' health and in keeping with medical instructions:

> Yes, in fact, it's more that we have to put boundaries on their work [pauses] That's something they find hard to accept [pauses] They don't understand why we give them less work, it's more that they'd like to always ask for more . . . until, health-wise, they give in [pauses] anyway [pauses] But they find it hard when we refuse to give them extra exercises, when we refuse to give them [pauses] classes, when we even ask them [pauses] not to come to class.
>
> [Mr E.]

Another specific feature of the anorexic students' school work concerned its form and outputs. According to the teachers, the girls' work emphasized perfect structure rather than intellectual content. This emphasis given to form was illustrated by the care they gave to their essay plans, which was judged as being excessive:

> The impression anorexics often give, well, so I'm thinking of these two girls [Christine and another anorexic student] is that there's also a kind of [pauses] disembodied [pauses] knowledge, you know? It's sort of like dead knowledge, where they're capable of doing a piece of homework, that's really polished, in formal terms, so well constructed, so well written, there's a good introduction, there's structure, there's a conclusion, so you'd almost say 'it's good', but the content is a bit, disembodied, a bit, empty.
>
> [Mr Q.]

> Well, so, now I've got examples, things that are interesting, so, last year . . . , I'd given a discussion topic . . . it was extraordinary, we actually talked about it in a meeting, it was one of the first pieces of homework, it was an essay plan, a plan, first part of the essay, second part of the essay, last part of the essay, perfect, and a catalogue! And there was this impression of [pauses] of an empty body of text, really, you know, it was staggering! You see [pauses] There was something [trails off] And [pauses] Well, Rabelais this, bam bam bam, well, you know [pauses] It wasn't lively, it had no substance [pauses] . . . . So, there's, in my opinion, there can be that temptation, or that risk, sometimes, in some of the work, yes, some of the work by anorexics.
>
> [Mrs O.]

The teachers also linked this close attention to form with so-called 'inflexible' modes of thinking, in other words, to an established medical category regarding anorexia – lack of flexibility – retranslated into the school sphere: 'It's the whole inflexible side to it, it's [pauses] all that concern for essay structure, the different parts and subparts' [Mrs H.]

The second characteristic of this attention to form related to the fact that this 'lack of flexibility' or excessive rigour and this concern with methodology was the result of the students' excessive submission to school instructions. In France, the essay plan is a fundamental feature of school teaching and the girls' concern with formal structure can therefore be seen as them applying things they had learnt in the past to the letter:

MD: 'And I was wondering, actually, about these issues, I imagine you sometimes teach [pauses] methodology classes, or essay-writing classes, or [trails off] And in those cases, how do they react to that, when the method is clearly defined?'

MRS H: 'Well, they apply it!'

MRS W: 'Ah they ask for it, they really ask for it! . . . But yes, in terms of this question of applying the method, directly, blindly, it's true that she was more [pauses] into that [pauses]. At the beginning of the year, it was obvious, she had her methodology sheet, her topic, and back and forth between the two, like that, there was no room for any personal thought [pauses] Not at all at all.'

[Mrs W.; Mrs H.]

> It was all structured around [formal logical links such as] 'on the one hand, on the other hand', 'then, finally, moreover' . . . I said to her 'Right, it might be interesting to change the expressions, the phrases, a bit etc.' She said [curt tone] 'Yes, well, that's how I was taught it'.
>
> [Mrs O.]

> She had this way of writing that was really [pauses], well, in maths, right? extremely academic, like 'I'm going to do this', 'I'm going to do that', you know, like in some maths exercises, when they're little, that's how we explain it.
>
> [Mrs M.]

Applying strict rules was therefore considered detrimental to 'imagination', 'intuition' and 'personal thinking'. All the teachers made a distinction between applying the rules strictly, mechanically and exclusively, and being capable of taking some distance from these rules through personal thinking. They criticized this school work for just mechanically applying a technique:

> But then that means it'll be a string of recipes, where the class will just be reduced to a series of recipes, things they learn [pauses], and that they force down themselves [pauses] So, of course, there are a few recipes, but, they have to know how to adapt, to mix things up, to [pauses] in a particular situation, maybe, to, well, go about things this way rather than that way. It's

> a cooking problem, you see? [he laughs] Some people cook by following the recipe to the letter, right? Without tasting what they're doing [pauses]. And, well, you see, in the recipe it says this, there's this proportion, there's this ingredient, right, you cook it for this long [pauses]. They do it all, they follow everything that it says, to the letter, and they don't even taste it! And they serve up the dish [pauses]. They've done what they were supposed to do [pauses] I don't call that cooking, you see?
>
> [Mr Q.]

The term 'recipe' uses yet another food-related metaphor to pathologize school behaviour, but it also summarizes the various observations quoted above by drawing an opposition between, on the one hand, following the institution's instructions, and, on the other, developing self-expression: '[Teachers] can praise "creative" dispositions ("originality", "inventions", etc.) and personal qualities to the detriment of knowledge and technical mastery (downgraded to the level of 'academic recipes') (Bourdieu 1996b, 26). This opposition between formal thinking and personal thinking fits into the teachers' broader critique of the overly 'academic' nature (the term was used explicitly) of both anorexics and their work. This category seemed to be an important one, which incorporated the categories mentioned previously: they worked 'too much', they were 'too invested' in school, they applied the 'rules of school work too much'. All these categories are based on the definition of a very particular relationship to school work, in which the anorexics' excessive behaviour was seen as revealing a lack of necessary distance taken from classroom learning that characterizes the (elitist) 'culture taught in school' (Bourdieu 1979, 24).

This opposition in teachers' categories between students who are too academic and students who are brilliant can also be enrolled in the social spaces of both class and gender. First, it draws a distinction between 'hard working' members of less fortunate categories and a state of scholarly 'grace' with which those in more dominant positions are endowed. However, this distinction is also linked to questions of gender:

> [primary school] teachers' expectations distinguish overall capabilities according to sex: boys are casual and boisterous but also have the capacity to understand principles; girls are willing and industrious, but reach their intellectual limitations much sooner [which equates to an] opposition between being academic and being brilliant.
>
> (Terrail 1992, 667)

The teachers' judgements analysed above allow us to better situate anorexic school practices within the social space more broadly, as corresponding to female, middle-class practices. However, as we have seen, the social backgrounds involved in my corpus were more diverse than that and extended in particular to the upper classes. It would therefore be more accurate to consider the delegitimization of anorexic work (its formal characteristics or the fact it is too academic) as a set of categories that *borrow some of the features* which are present in the way the elite ethos judges the petit-bourgeois ethos (as described by Pierre Bourdieu and Jean-Claude Passeron)[13] rather than as categories that *reveal the existence* of such an ethos and the concomitant class positions of anorexic students. However, these categories do clearly bring out an important dimension to the participants' endeavour in terms of cultural knowledge, which sets it apart from a dominant position in terms of school work. They 'built up' their cultural knowledge, deliberately and with determination, giving importance and visibility to their hard work. They also clearly and explicitly obtained this knowledge through concerted efforts, as we saw where their school work was concerned. This was also evidenced, for example, by the fact Camille [C], who came from a background with high cultural capital, nonetheless bought 'general knowledge books' (in certain contexts, *culture générale* is taught in France as a specific subject, with its own textbooks and manuals) so that she could actively learn 'general knowledge' as if it were not enough to simply count on it being instilled invisibly. Just like building up a body, 'building up' cultural knowledge therefore seemed to require following a method, being determined and working hard.

Bodies and cultural knowledge

A strong analogy can be drawn between how the participants worked on their bodies and how they worked on their cultural knowledge. In both cases, the activities in question corresponded to activities characteristic of women from the middle and upper classes. In both cases, the self-transformation in question was oriented towards the higher levels of the social space and was at once a constant endeavour and part of a determined and deliberately chosen stance. And in both cases, if we consider body and cultural knowledge as forms of capital, the 'investment' made was unlimited. When we looked at the measurement tools used for weight loss, in the second section of this book, we saw that there was no lower limit to this weight loss: similarly, there was no upper limit to the investment in school work and cultural knowledge. The expression 'a woman can never be too rich or too thin', which I quoted in my introduction, takes on particular meaning when linked to this endeavour to maximize investment in physical or 'bodily' capital and cultural capital (with the latter being a new way for women to be 'rich'). Finally, in both cases, once again, this transformation resulted in attaining a 'state of grace', in which hunger was forgotten and thinness and intellectual brilliance were achieved:

V: 'And so, it's very very strange, because, since, I think I find it much harder to express myself, whereas before [that is, during the anorexia] I remember not having any intellectual difficulties, having even been brilliant, so, I dunno, maybe I'm looking at that time through rose tinted specs, a bit [laughs]. But now, I don't feel that way at all, I'm sometimes a bit hung up about it, as if giving up anorexia had meant giving up something intellectual too [trails off].'

MD: 'As if the two things were [pauses].'
V: 'Linked, yes.'

[Véronique, N]

This interview excerpt suggests a certain practical interaction between the physical and the intellectual (which I have so far addressed separately) and that warrants closer analysis.

First, some of the participants themselves equated the two aspects in practical terms. They had a specific way of presenting physical and academic capital as being connected, for example in Véronique's words above. Her 'I felt like I was thin and brilliant during the anorexia' had its polar opposite in statements about feeling 'fat and rubbish' before the anorexia, for example in the cases of Sabine and Annabelle:

> [In her *Classe Prépa*] I wasn't happy at all! I wasn't happy, I thought I was really really rubbish, really really stupid, really really ugly . . . . In *Prépa*, the girls that you say are 'really good', they're also really cute, really thin.
>
> [Sabine, N]

A: 'It's enough just to get a bad mark, one or two bad marks, and you start saying "Right, I'm not clever enough, I can't manage this, and all that". And it more or less translates into you being disgusted with yourself, intellectually but also just you more generally . . . . So, in the end, you end up hating yourself, thinking you're awful, thinking you're too fat, and there you go [pauses]. You tell yourself everything's easier when you're thin.'
MD: 'Easier intellectually as well then?'
A: 'Or, you know, it's linked to clothes too, when you start feeling bad, you dress badly, you think you're ugly, you wear a skirt, you're too fat, so that looks bad. When you accept your marks a bit too quickly, when you really take them as being a negative statement about you, about your capabilities.'

[Annabelle, N]

During the anorexia, the participants sometimes even engaged in veritable transactions between their bodies and their school work, revealing forms of compensation and therefore of conjunction between the two areas:

MD: 'And yes, when you said that, the fact things were going better in terms of school work, did that have an effect on your eating habits?'
S: 'Oh yes!'
MD: 'Did you eat more?'
S: 'I maintained, it wasn't worse, I maintained.'
MD: 'And how do you explain that, how did you experience it, the fact that things were going better at school and that therefore you maintained?'

S: 'I was more confident, I had something to hold on to [pauses] . . . . Well, sometimes I still allowed myself something as a treat, I'd have a brioche or [trails off].'

MD: 'In general, when you allowed yourself a treat, was it to celebrate stuff? Or [trails off]?'

S: 'Well, at one point, at the beginning of my illness [the anorexia] it was like that, actually, when I got good marks.'

[Sophie, C]

C: '18 out of 20 didn't reassure me anymore . . . .'

MD: 'And when it did reassure you, at first, did it have any effect on your eating habits?'

C: 'Yeah [pauses] I allowed myself more stuff [pauses] "Oh I got 19, I could add a yoghurt" or [trails off] . . . . Because I was tired at night, I couldn't go back to reading [pauses]. So that [reading] was something I wrote off, I said to myself "OK, so I just can't do that". And it's the same, I compensated with something else: "I can't do this but [pauses]" it was like an equivalence, "but I'll lose more weight next week".'

[Christine, C]

The participants therefore established a practical equivalence between 'bodily capital' and 'cultural capital' (in Bourdieu's sense of the terms); between taking themselves in hand in terms of food and taking themselves in hand in terms of school. They drew links between 'being fat' and 'being rubbish', 'being brilliant' and 'being thin', being successful at school and being successful at losing weight, whether they conducted both endeavours in parallel or whether one compensated for the other, as described above.

These processes of practical equivalence also played a role when they left anorexia, as evidenced by the teachers' comments above about how anorexics would let go of school work as they began putting weight back on. Yasmine described this, comparing her present situation with how things were 'during' the anorexia, when her thinness implied ease and assurance in terms of school work:

> This year, I started Year 12 again, I did a term, and then I ended up here and I let it all go [pauses]. I mean, each time I felt as if I'd never manage it anyway, because it was, either I managed in terms of school work and I lost weight, or I carried on working [in the sense, psychological 'work on herself' towards 'recovery'] and I got better [from the anorexia]. I didn't have the strength to do both, maybe I didn't want to . . . . I'd say that the thinner I am, the better I work . . . . In general, the thinner I am, the more confident I am, and so I'm more likely to be articulate, to find things easy in class. It's all in my head, I mean, but [pauses] it's true that it helps. Being thin helps . . . . And I reached the end of the first term, and I kind of let it all go . . . . I couldn't face going to class anymore [pauses] I felt like [trails off]. Because for me, the whole thing

> was systematic, 'the more weight you put on, the more rubbish you are, you know'. So I found it hard to face class [pauses] to face the teachers.
>
> [Yasmine, C]

In this case, the different areas involved in Yasmine's endeavour to take herself in hand were not only juxtaposed, they were also interdependent – 'linked' to take up Véronique's expression. This situation corresponds to the beginning of the career, discussed in the second section of this book. However, this also raises the question of the increasing conflict between these different areas. After a while (the second and third phases of the career), the work they were doing on their physical appearance began to jeopardize the work they were doing to improve their cultural knowledge. This was due to physical exhaustion, not being able to follow classes at school and even hospitalization in some cases. How, then, can we explain the fact that the work on the body took priority and was continued to the detriment of school work? For what reasons and in what ways was cultural knowledge sacrificed in favour of the body?

The possible answers to this question reveal certain internal variations within my interview corpus. For some of the participants, the physical side of things seemed to be a priority from the outset. School work was sometimes not an issue at all or was only present in a secondary fashion. For these participants, whom we could very broadly group together under the label 'physical anorexics', a certain number of criteria seemed to form a system: the beginning of the anorexia was linked to a relationship breakup, for example, or at least to the existence of a 'relationship market' (given the age group, it is perhaps too early to talk about a 'matrimonial market') in which being slim is a hugely important form of capital.[14] These participants were or wanted to be models or dancers, and described a family background in which physical appearance played an important role in the values instilled, especially among women. This group stood apart from a second group, who could just as broadly be described as 'cultural anorexics'. For them, the beginning of the anorexia was linked to a more specifically academic situation (starting *lycée* – the last three years in French secondary education – or facing choices about future academic paths). They imagined themselves in careers where physical appearance did not have any explicit capital (doctors, researchers, etc.) and the sports they engaged in were less typically female (tennis, rather than dance or gymnastics). They described physical appearance as not having substantial value in their families.

While the interviews can be very broadly divided according to these two models, it is important not to forget that such a division is necessarily oversimplified. My aim in drawing this distinction is not to offer an operational typology that can be applied across the board – certain interviews seemed to fit more into a mixed model, combining both sets of characteristics – but rather to highlight two tendencies, in order to better examine this issue of practical equivalence between 'bodily capital' and 'cultural capital'.

Ultimately, by continuing to work on their bodies, the girls put in jeopardy the work they were doing in other areas and this question was framed differently in the two models. Among the physical anorexics, the issue was solely the body, for example in Julie's case:

MD: 'And when you were told you had to put weight on, that otherwise you'd be hospitalized, would no longer go to class?'

J: 'I said "Yes, I know, I have to put weight on", but I didn't really feel like I was putting myself in danger, for a start [pauses] and I was convinced, in my head, that the thinner I'd be, the prettier I'd be [pauses] that someone fat isn't beautiful, and if I was going to be too thin, it was better to be too thin than too fat'.

[Julie, H]

Being thin was defined as a specifically physical feature, which is not necessarily self-evident as we will see a little further on. Working on the body therefore made sense as a strategy for accruing aesthetic capital or professional capital, in the case of occupations in which 'bodily capital' was the main capital at stake:

MD: 'And so, in terms of dancing, I don't know, didn't you tell yourself, as you were losing weight, that you were actually putting that in jeopardy a bit?'

I: 'Not at all! Quite the opposite, I felt like it was pretty beneficial! . . . I thought it would make me lighter, that I'd jump better'.

[Isabelle, C]

Bodily capital had different stakes in the case of 'cultural anorexics'. One might reasonably suggest that it appeared as a 'total' capital, that could both include and incorporate cultural capital. To pursue this metaphor of economic capital, we could say that, in the first case, 'bodily capital' was beneficial on romantic and professional markets as both aesthetic and physical capital. However, in the second case, bodily capital became efficient as cultural capital on the academic market. Some of the interview excerpts quoted above can therefore be understood from this perspective: to take up Yasmine's words, 'being thin helps' when it comes to feeling a certain state of grace that is as cultural as is it physical. This also sheds further light on the mechanisms through which these forms of capital were equated, as identified above. There was no danger of cultural capital being jeopardized by maintaining the commitment to improving bodily capital, because the latter was understood as *incorporating* other forms of capital and particularly cultural capital. It could reasonably be suggested that bodily capital serving as a 'total' form of capital is a more specifically female trait and can be linked to gendered power relations. It could be interpreted as indicating an internalization of a form of domination operating through metonymy, in which the part (the body) stands in for the whole (person).

> Many of the judgments men make about women can be interpreted as psychological or relational judgments (describing a partner's kind of relationship to others) and also as judgments on physical aspects (referring to the person's physical and clothing style). . . . When women are judged, psychological and aesthetic aspects are not separated. Both converge to form a judgment

> about the person's presentation and apparent style . . . . As a symbolic object, women continue to be judged more for their *visible* qualities than men.
>
> (Bozon 1991, 109–10)

It would therefore seem that two different modes of gender domination were at work here. In the case of physical anorexics, a 'traditional' model of objectification of the female body can be identified (you have to 'be pretty').[15] In the case of the cultural anorexics, the model seems to be more insidious: you have to 'be brilliant' – in terms of school work in these cases – but, for a women, 'being brilliant' is inextricably linked with 'being slim', as if female forms of capital could only achieve social recognition once transposed into the physical sphere.

Not only did the different participants take themselves in hand in different areas, but bodily capital did not always have the same stakes for them. And the distribution of the participants across the categories of 'physical anorexics', 'cultural anorexics' and 'mixed models' was, to some extent, correlated with their social backgrounds even though these backgrounds were less diverse in my sample than in society more broadly. The cultural anorexics tended to come from slightly higher social backgrounds and the physical anorexics from lower social backgrounds, with those following the mixed model falling between the two. This would seem to suggest some social differentiation within the work of self-transformation described in the second section of this book. Depending on the participants' initial position within the social space, priority seems to have been given to different areas and the physical dimension seems to have been invested with different social stakes.

Bearing in mind that the three models distinguished above, as well as the evaluation of the participants' relative social origin, have more heuristic than illustrative value, a hypothesis can be put forward concerning bodily capital. First, its signification, as highlighted above, contrasts with the notion of body as a form of *strength,*[16] a resource requiring sustenance. It relates instead to the notion of the body as a socially efficient *form.* However, conceptions of the body's actual efficiency vary and this hypothesis, which accounts for the participants' practices and representations, may also have wider relevance. In certain fractions of the social space, bodily capital may well also serve as cultural capital. Variations in the degree of investment in bodily capital have been analysed in terms of *level* of investment (Bourdieu 1996a, 206). What I am suggesting here is that there are also variations in (1) *how* people invest in physical capital and (2) in the different markets on which it is considered to be profitable and which not only lend legitimacy to attempts to accrue it but also lend it meaning.

Anorexic tension

A socially situated ethos

As we have seen, a range of similarities emerged across the various practical domains involved in the physical side to the participants' endeavour. These similarities were also present between the physical sphere and the cultural and academic spheres, bringing to light a single ethos that was applied across the board. Before trying to position this 'ethos of tension' within the social space, it is important to first identify its various components: asceticism; control exercised over physical and social destiny; and control exercised over public labels. I will now look at each of these in detail.

Asceticism

The practices involved in the anorexic career – dietary restriction, rationalizing repetitive and organized physical activities, an extremely strict 'mode of living' and unlimited school work – come together to reveal an ascetic mode of governing both the body and social life. This discipline and ethics of effort and self-constraint, which emerged in the second section of the book, appeared once again when analysing how practices relating to the body and to school work fit into the social space. Anorexic ascetic practices reveal a constant or almost constant tension, transforming all number of practical areas and moments in life into an occasion to work on dispositions and on the self. This was illustrated *par excellence* by the descriptions the participants gave of how they left anorexia. They talked about learning to be satisfied during moments when they were not invested in anything and not drawn towards achieving or changing anything:

> I'd like to have [pauses] not experiences because, you know, I've had experiences, honestly, I think where that's concerned, I've had them, where experiences are concerned. But I'd like to live through things, not experiences that are enriching, but I'd just like to [pauses] enjoy just living. Even on a small level, well, when I say on a small level, not even on a small level . . . . Smoking a cigarette on a bridge on a Sunday night before coming back [to the clinic], well, there you go, that's enough, I'm happy for the week, it's all a symbol, but, there you go, I feel good . . . . And that's what I couldn't do when I was anorexic.
>
> [Yasmine, C]

> I was allowed to appreciate just feeling good, you know, listening to music, lying on a bed . . . . I learnt to appreciate those things, so, just little things, futile things, that I didn't pay attention to before, have become really precious moments . . . . [In the hospital, following the instruction to reduce her school work] I remember, I felt like I didn't exist, I was asked to 'do nothing': 'no, no, I don't know how to do nothing'. Then, bit by bit, I realized that it was possible to do nothing and to feel good.
>
> [Christine, C]

Asceticism is a trait that has often been noted in sociological or social science studies on anorexia.[17] In general, it is linked with religious meaning, for example the search for spiritual order or a 'quest for spirituality'[18] and, as mentioned in chapter one, this often leads to a parallel being drawn between the 'anorexic saints' and modern anorexics. However, as we saw regarding practices related to the body or school work, this asceticism in fact fits into the social space of both class and gender. This does not mean, though, that it can immediately be positioned as a feature of *one* particular social position. Sociological work conducted on different social classes has shown that ascetic dispositions cross social spaces, although they do seem to be concentrated in the middle classes or within upwardly mobile trajectories.[19] In order to understand the form of asceticism at work among the participants, it is necessarily to specify what exactly it was and highlight the features distinguishing it, in particular, from working-class forms of asceticism.

An ethos of control over physical and social identity

Gordon Tait takes a Foucauldian perspective and suggests framing anorexic ascetic practices as a system of self-creation:

> As with the ancient Greeks, the 'self' is not something to be discovered, it is something to be created. Consequently, practices such as ascetic fasting . . . are the very practices by which a 'self' is formed . . . . They [anorexics] too are shaping themselves, both ethically and physically, in certain ways and for certain ends.
>
> (Tait 1993, 205)

This analysis could perhaps be taken one step further by trying to account for the way, in the present study, asceticism was also a method of self-transformation. I will look more systematically at the question of the social conditions of possibility for anorexic transformation a little further on; at this stage, though, we can already point to the fact that anorexic practices testify to an ethos of control over physical and social destiny that is not socially neutral. It contrasts with what is traditionally designated as working-class 'fatalism'.[20] This belief in fate is first and foremost physical. Oliver Schwartz has shown how, for women from certain fractions of the working class, particularly those who do not work, the 'imaginary' surrounding physical transformation and aspirations towards a legitimate body go hand in hand with strong, socially enrolled limitations on the possibility of putting this into practice. 'Me? I eat' affirmed one of Olivier Schwartz's respondents following medical instructions to go on a diet; 'with me, diets never last very long' said another. As for Martine:

> Her words clearly showed that she had given over her body to the marks of subjection, that she found it difficult to protect it against degrading effects and even impossible to really want to, given all the frustration and further deprivation it would entail. Martine wavered between refusing her current body, wanting to give herself a different, more gratifying one, and failing successively in her attempts.
>
> (Schwartz 1990, 479–83)

As the anorexic career unfolds, it calls upon the very opposite ethos, based on control and on implementing a change in physical destiny. The relationship to the body is not the only issue at stake here. The anorexic ethos of tension calls more broadly on a world-view in which social destiny itself must be controlled:

C: 'That's what's hard, too, there are things I can't control, things I don't know, things that are just down to chance, things that are part of the whole "that's just the way it is" thing. I think that's the hardest thing to accept, the whole "that's just the way it is" thing . . . . I'm just not used to doing things in a simple way.'

MD: 'And that includes, you were saying, about chance?'

C: 'Yes, exactly [pauses], everything that can [pauses] come into your life, without you having asked for it [pauses] everything that I [trails off] It's the idea of control again, everything that isn't in my power.'

[Christine, C]

On a medical or psychological level, this aspect can be understood in terms of the pathology and the 'desire to be all-powerful' that it supposedly entails. However, this rejection of 'chance' – evidenced by excessive planning and rationalization as well as the work on time and the dispositions highlighted in the second section – can also be interpreted in a different way. It contrasts with the working-class 'taste for chance', as highlighted by Florence Weber: 'Hoggart has already identified the first [foundation of this]: the belief in luck, in surprise, with two corollaries: negating the notion of absolute predictability . . . ; preferring fatalistic explanations of the world, "that's how it is and it's not any other way", it's not up to us, we're just subject to "fate" – the underside of the inability to make plans, the uselessness of making decisions' (Weber 1989, 197). The expressions used by Hoggart to refer to this working-class belief in fate include 'what is to be will be' and 'y've got to tek life as it cums', leading him to suggest that the members of the working classes tend to 'remove the main elements of the situation to the realm of natural laws' (Hoggart 1957, 70). If we take this even further, the expression could be reversed for the anorexic ethos, with natural 'constraints' (biological, physical) seen as subject to the 'social law' of control over fate.

Moreover, the second 'foundation' that Weber analyses also has resonance with the anorexic ethos:

> Luck restores absolute equality between players . . . . [The lottery as a game of chance] perfectly fulfils the requirement for equality that I identified as present on social stages . . . . No one is *had* by anyone in a game of chance; the dice aren't loaded. In addition to the fact that they 'play for their lives again' every week, what manual workers appreciate in the lottery (for example) is the reversal of the social game in which they don't have a 'chance' and which they experience as a permanent fraud.
>
> (Weber 1989, 197)

From this point of view, the lottery is not an 'anorexic game' unlike board games as described by Camille [C]:

> [In hospital] I played Chinese chequers . . . . It was really complicated Chinese chequers, it was a different kind of game, well, so, they were games that, we went really fast, you know, the aim was to create a path really quickly so that your opponent couldn't see it and couldn't take it back, we became champions in Chinese chequers at [hospital J, a ward specializing in eating disorders]!
>
> [Camille, C]

If we consider games as defining a model of society and of the relationship to that society, Chinese chequers represents a model in which it is possible to 'create' a path. It also designates a relationship to the world (and we will come back to this later) in which this path is created against other people, in which it is very explicitly about 'getting one over' on other people, winning for yourself and winning against them: in games of strategy, rather than chance, in order to win, the loser has to be 'had'.

The importance and control of labels

The anorexic tension reveals an ethos of control over physical and social destiny which makes self-transformation *possible* and which adds a particular dimension to ascetic behaviour. A third component in this ethos makes it socially *desirable:* it also involves extreme attention paid to other people's judgements and to social labels. The desire for self-control in individual asceticism is matched by the desire to control other people's judgements, particularly where the results of the ascetic work in question are concerned. Insofar as other people's judgements are 'terrible', it becomes necessary to find the means to control them. In my fieldwork, this was a recurrent theme:

> I don't want anyone to really know me, precisely so that I don't [pauses] generate any judgements, any, whether they're positive or negative, I don't want [trails off] . . . . It's pretty terrible, I mean, how others look at you.
>
> [Yasmine, C]

> I think about others first, about what they might think, about how others look at me, rather than about what I really want, you know, ... There's always this permanent self-control over what people will say, what others will think . . . . Well, for me, it was always about the image I wanted to project to other people [pauses] So I did everything to have that image that I wanted to project.
>
> [Isabelle, C]

Anorexia and particularly being thin were presented by the participants as ways of acting on public labels by becoming 'irreproachable':

> I don't know why, but I'm fascinated by thinness . . . . I can't manage to find it ugly [pauses] Even when I'm told, when I'm told it's not pretty, but, I don't know, there's something [pauses] It's always that idea of being irreproachable, there's nothing to be criticized, nothing that sticks out, everything is [trails off].
>
> [Christine, C]

Paradoxically, the radical nature of thinness was sometimes presented not only as a way of being irreproachable but also as a way of countering any possibility of being judged by others. For the participants, it was a way of changing the rules of the labelling game by choosing and imposing a category themselves. This links back to a hypothesis I made in the second section of the book, regarding the interviewees' desire to impose a particular category of self-perception (that of being 'thin') and, by the same token, remove themselves from other people's judgements. Extreme thinness creates a body that lies outside of the norm, too distanced from usual standards to be judged by others: 'I always had such hang ups [pauses] and then, well, I don't know, anorexia, then, finally, I had a non-body, no hang ups, etc. . . . [A body] that was outside of the norm' [Yasmine, C].

Working on the body sometimes aimed to impose a social label and social evaluation rather than allowing these to be imposed by others.[21] Wanting to be 'thin' or to be 'very thin' could be seen as a way of imposing a body that could not be evaluated in any other way (whereas a girl who is 'slim' could always be considered 'too fat'). It was possible to show, or even 'exhibit' the 'extreme' body shaped by anorexic work because it could no longer give rise to any judgement other than the one Yasmine, for example, wanted to hear (in the same way as her 'solid cultural knowledge' was publicly beyond reproach):

> I was so [pauses] so thin, so like this [she clenches her fists], so hard inside, I was so hard towards myself, I was hard with others too but that was pretty hidden, but my body, I could really see that it shook people, when people saw me in the street, it would be, like that [mimes someone jumping in shock]. All that, that way of shocking others, I liked it [pauses]. A small, constant, attack . . . . I showed myself off, I exhibited my little bones.
>
> [Yasmine, C]

And yet, as we saw earlier in the second section, while this attempt to gain control over interactions and over the labelling game does reveal a particular feature of the anorexic ethos of tension, in practice it also came up again the diagnosis of anorexia which was imposed as a particularly powerful external definition.

Anorexic elitism

Becoming socially exceptional

The components of this ethos of tension examined above all relate to tension as strain, as control, and the constant efforts involved in ascetic behaviour, in regulating physical destiny and public labels. However, this ethos can also be described as an ethos of 'tension' because the work of transformation was not just about 'effort' but also about 'movement'; it was not just situated, it was also oriented. The final dimensions of the anorexic ethos bring into play the relationship to others and *relative* positions. They offer a final piece of the puzzle showing that this work of self-transformation was directed towards becoming socially exceptional. Further analysis of this ethos brings out its elitist and agonistic elements, illustrated in particular in the competitive side to behaviour surrounding food and school work.

When we looked at physical and cultural practices, we saw that the anorexic work of self-transformation was partly oriented towards social excellence. However, the elitist dimension to the anorexic ethos actually means we can talk more specifically about striving towards being socially exceptional. The 'extreme' anorexic body already gave us a sense of this and the following quotations can tell us a little more:

> I didn't want to follow the same path as everyone else.
>
> [Emilie, C]

> I stuck out, I wanted to stand out a bit . . . . I couldn't see myself blending in with the crowd, right?
>
> [Sophie, C]

> At the same time, I knew it, that I was thin. But for me, that wasn't enough. I knew that in other people's eyes, it wasn't pretty, but in my eyes, it was different and I liked cultivating that difference.
>
> [Véronique, N]

> It's pleasure, displeasure, but it's really strong, you feel like you're experiencing something no one else could ever experience . . . . You feel like you're superhuman, a bit, on the edge of the paranormal.
>
> [Yasmine, C]

The asceticism that the participants exercised over several domains therefore takes on new meaning in this regard. It can be understood as a way of acting on symbolic classifications and as a channel for producing a 'sacred being' in Durkheim's sense of the term; that is to say, a being *distanced* from the profane by the rigour of his or her practice:

> [Asceticism] in a sense is a means to an end . . . . Not confined to protecting the sacred beings from ordinary contact, it acts upon the worshipper himself and modifies his state positively. . . . Before he was an ordinary being . . . . After . . . he has approached the sacred through the very act of distancing himself from the profane. He has purified and sanctified himself by detaching himself from the low and trivial things that previously encumbered his nature.
>
> (Durkheim 1995, 313–14)

Durkheim clearly specifies that asceticism should not only be interpreted in terms of religious ends and underlines that this way of 'subduing [our] nature' in order to take 'a special place in the world', of 'overcom[ing] our instincts' in order to 'go up the down staircase of nature', is in fact 'an integral part of all human culture' (Durkheim 1995, 321). The asceticism at work in anorexic practices has distinctly secular aims. But considering it as nothing more than a simple aspect of 'human culture', as something socially undifferentiated, would fail to account for how the 'solution of continuity' between the sacred and the profane that asceticism aims to establish is socially situated within the space of symbolic classifications.

Fat people as a social repellent

The participants presented themselves as people who were taking themselves in hand and working on their bodies and linked this stance with explicit contempt for those who, in contrast, 'let themselves go' in terms of their eating habits and their bodies. Eating (and particularly eating voraciously or making food into a convivial event) was perceived as contemptibly 'vulgar':

V: 'I remember having felt really deep contempt for people who used food for [pauses] as something convivial . . . .'

MD: 'And in terms of this question of conviviality, the image you had of meals, was it a negative image?'

V: 'It was the image of people letting themselves go.'

[Véronique, N]

> Seeing my parents eating sometimes, it seemed almost obscene to me, you know [pauses]. I couldn't watch them eat anymore, it's [pauses] . . . . I don't know, it seemed pretty gargantuan, you know, well, my dad's not very discreet, anyway, when he eats . . . . There's something really voracious about it, you know, that I don't like, well, it's obvious [pauses] . . . . Knowing that other people . . . are [pauses] vulgar, as in, common, well, that their reactions, that their lives are vulgar.
>
> [Anne, C]

This relates once again to the choice between form and substance that we saw earlier concerning food consumption. This time, it was explicitly presented in relation – and in opposition – to people who did not choose the same form over substance. Similarly, coarse people were considered as having 'fat' bodies, while refined people had 'slender' bodies:[22]

> So I wanted to do that [go on a diet] because it's true that I found myself, a bit, fat, I wasn't obese . . . but, well, it was me, I didn't feel good about myself. . . . Because, on top of it, compared to my friends [trails off]. For a start, in my family, we're of a certain stature, you know, kind of muscular, with big bones, we're not slender people [pauses] I always felt much fatter than my friends so I didn't feel good, you know.
>
> [Julie, H]

Sticking to the diet and to food restriction became the cornerstone of having a 'strong character'; one that testified to social excellence in marked contrast with those who 'couldn't manage it':

> Fat people, obese people [pauses] They're people who weren't strong enough [pauses] in terms of character. Whereas I, well, I don't know if I have a strong character, but at a certain time, I did.
>
> [Yasmine, C]

[The intern on ward I told me about a clinical interview with Hélène] MD: 'So then she said her sister was on a diet?'

INTERN: 'Yes, because she had weight problems, she wasn't obese, right, but she had a tendency to put on weight, Hélène told me that, and she said 'but it's not ugly at all', whereas I think she must find it ugly! She also said 'she goes on diets, but she never sticks it out to the end'.

[FJ]

These kinds of representations are far from being specific to my participants. As Jean-Claude Kaufmann has underlined:

> Morphology itself is increasingly considered to be the result of work, indicative of skill, a sign of distinction: someone who is fat is not only fat but, on top of it, they are someone who is incapable of not being fat. 'Some people are podgy and don't even realize it. It's a question of education, you have to be aware of your body' (F174); 'There are people who have the willpower to work on their bodies and there are others who don't have that willpower, that's all. We've got to start telling it how it is! Without talking about plastic surgery, you can make a lot of things better, you just need the willpower' (H89). Willpower, but also the necessary cultural background and money: in the face of biological fate, the rich and the poor tend to be distributed across a scale of beauty.
>
> (Kaufmann 1998, 226)

The link between having a 'fat' body and being 'vulgar' was also present in the distance taken by the participants from 'fat women' or 'women with curves':

> Because we had this neighbour, she matured quite early, she had curves and everything . . . . And for me, that girl, I found her dirty, shameless [pauses] with all these relationships . . . . And I was all 'Yuck yuck yuck, I don't want to be like her, it's out of the question'. Yeah. And I think it bothered me.
>
> [Sophie, C]

> For me, curves, they make me [pauses] I don't like it, you know, when I go to the psychomotor therapist, yesterday, for example, so she, she massages me, and, after, we talk and everything, and I was saying to her, 'But you know, when you massage my bones and all that, when you touch me, when you make me really realize they're there, it should give me a shock and make me say "That's horrible and everything", but it almost feels good, I say to myself "Well, turns out, I prefer my body to be all hard, and to feel its structure, rather than having" [pauses]'. I'd rather have a body like that than be soft and curvy, you know.
>
> [Isabelle, C]

Isabelle presented her 'hard' and 'structured' body in a positive light, as the preferable form for the female body, and contrasted it with a 'soft and curvy' body – implicitly, a body that could always be considered a 'fat person's body'. This highlights the different social models of femininity that exist, which combine factors of class and gender. Once again, these patterns of perception call on the social space of bodies mentioned above (the social situation of body weight and judgements about body weight) as well as on the link between the physical and the cultural. The porous nature of the relationship between these two areas, already mentioned, was also clear in the participants' views of the 'worst possible' categories. 'Fat women' were 'stupid' and their 'vulgar' nature was inseparably physical and cultural:

> My mother has a sister who has eating problems, who's, very, who's a bit obese [pauses] and I've always known her like that, a bit plump, now she's obese, but at the time she was plump [laughs]. There were quite a lot of jibes at her [pauses] nothing nasty, right, but she wasn't the one we admired [pauses]. And, well, I think that must have played a role, too . . . . Because she was extremely childlike, she hadn't done well in her studies at all, she always had these awful romantic relationships, well, you know, But now that I think about it, I have this family that's really multilayered, well, there was one part of the family where there were three girls who were all [pauses] fat, vulgar [pauses] ugly, stupid [pauses] well, you know [laughs] and it was like, a set of things together. And it's true that, for me, physical appearance went along with intelligence, and the slimmer I was physically, the smarter I was intellectually . . . . But I think I'd heard my dad saying how . . . well, likening

> fat people to stupid people [pauses] or to people who aren't intelligent. I'm sure that [pauses] I heard that several times.
>
> [Véronique, N]

The same social contempt was sometimes shown towards people who did not work at school and people who did not work on their bodies:

> I thought I was better than everyone, whether it was in terms of my body, or in my mind [pauses] I was in this world of strong people, I was the best, the most beautiful, the one who was best . . . . I fascinated myself: having lost weight, I thought I'd become [trails off]. It's like I was telling you, I was better than everyone else, more beautiful than everyone, I knew everything better than everyone . . . . There was always this group in class who messed around and stuff . . . . At first, I envied them, I'd say to myself 'Oh wow, I'd so like to be able to not give a crap', then, bit by bit, I said to myself, 'Wait, no, I'm the one who's right, they're rubbish' and it comes back to what I was telling you at the beginning, you know. Oh yes, there was really a [trails off]. I was really scornful, you know, after, I'd really become [pauses] horrible . . . . After, with fat people, I had this whole scornful side. I told myself I was better than them because I wasn't fat.
>
> [Christine, C]

People who let themselves go in their school work and in their bodies became a repellent model. They represented the inability to make a continuous effort, with pairs of opposites working together (fat/thin, rubbish/brilliant, letting yourself go/ being in control and making an effort). Ultimately, these repellent representations were all linked by the idea of the 'fat' body as a body to which the person was subjected, a body that was abominably natural, while the thin body embodied an ethos of work and of determined and deliberate self-construction, a culture of the body as superior to its nature:

MD: 'And how did you look at people you found too fat?'

L: 'I didn't envy them . . . . They were how they were . . . . I said to myself "It's not their fault, they're fat, it's just nature" . . . . When I saw fat people: "It'd be good if they could lose weight, but if they can't [trails off]".'

[Louise, H]

> What actually bothered me a bit more, it was the whole femininity thing, mainly with women, but, well, with men too, I'd say to myself, it seemed they were letting themselves go, sometimes, I don't know, I found it [pauses]. We'll, the whole feminine thing in women like that, with curves and everything, I have trouble with that, right? . . . I tended to think, a little bit, that they were letting themselves go. Yes [pauses]. But after, well, when I went there [a convalescence centre], it was a centre, well, there were all sorts of pathologies, and there were obese people too [pauses] and I think I really [pauses]

> started to think differently too [pauses] that it could be linked to psychological problems, and I was really tolerant, really, and it was natural, you know, no more problems with that.
>
> [Sophie, C]

Above and beyond the differences between these two stances – with Louise affirming from the outset the natural destiny of the fat body and Sophie talking about how she first condemned people for letting themselves go, before in the end becoming 'tolerant' towards this embodiment of other people's natural destinies – they both converged on one key point: their arguably condescending stance, which represented an open form of social contempt for fat bodies; something 'natural' that, in Louise's view, should not be blamed on its poor powerless victims. At the same time, it was precisely the body's 'natural' bent that the participants worked hard to overcome, until they became thin. So although Louise and Sophie both ostensibly seemed to be saying 'it doesn't matter because it's something you are subjected to, it's natural, you can't do anything about it', this can be understood in somewhat different terms when linked to their own endeavour to counter nature. Some people cannot do anything about it, but others manage to triumph over fate and attain the 'sacred' through their asceticism.

Not being 'normal'

The anorexic elitism evidenced in my study went even further than this, though. It was not just about not being 'fat', it was about not being 'normal':

S: 'The worst that I've ever been was 1.63 metres and 54 kilos. That's the fattest and I don't think it was that huge [pauses]. Normal, you know.'
MD: 'And now?'
S: 'Now I'd like to be slim, you know, I'd like to lose weight, that's all.'
MD: 'But you said that 54 kilos, for your height [trails off].'
S: 'Ah, yes, but I don't weigh that now! Oh wow, if I did [trails off].'
MD: 'But, at the same time, you said it was 'normal'?'
S: 'Yes, but I don't want to be "normal"!'.

[Sidonie, H]

> In my head, I just couldn't tell myself that I'm wearing a size 10, you know [pauses]. I know that'll always be a bit of a mental block [pauses]. At the moment, I'm between an 8 and a 6, and my mum doesn't want me to buy size 6s because otherwise I'll stay like this forever, so, at a push, size 8, why not, but size 10, I just can't . . . . And yet my parents are always saying 'you've got loads of qualities' . . . . For me, that's nothing much, it's normal . . . . It doesn't seem to be anything more than anyone else [pauses]. By losing weight, actually, we have a certain amount of power over ourselves, and over others, because, in a way, we're different from them . . . we have less weight that them . . . . Because I always felt like I was different from everyone [pauses]

> I don't feel 'normal', you see . . . . Everyone says I'm thin [pauses] But at the same time, it makes me happy when I'm told I'm thin . . . . I wouldn't like it if people told me 'you're normal' or didn't talk about it.
>
> [Isabelle, C]

According to this reading, not being 'normal' meant having 'something more than other people'. It was not enough to be safe from physical and social lack of dignity; Isabelle also wanted to stand apart from non-distinctive 'normalcy'. During the interviews, this elitism also emerged in the participants' relationship to me as an interviewer and how they viewed what they seemed to consider my 'normal weight'. Sidonie referred to normal weight as being 'for hippos'; Louise explained things that I 'couldn't imagine' – presumably because I didn't have any physical marks indicating an ability to fast; Isabelle did not want to 'offend me', but nonetheless expressed contempt for the type of body that 'suited me' but would not suit her:

> MD: 'When you say, "I worked out the difference in weight", do you mean the "calculation of ideal body weight"?'
>
> S: 'Yeah, no, it's OK! I was always underneath, still, because you have to be a hippo [to be that weight]!
>
> [Sidonie, H]

> [When you don't eat much] you feel good, you just can't imagine, honestly you feel really good.
>
> [Louise, H]

> MD: 'And, so, the other girls at dance class, how did you see them? For example, I don't know, those who weren't as slim as you, did you find them too fat?'
>
> I: 'Well, there was a time [pauses] so [pauses] don't be offended, right?'
>
> MD: 'No, no!'
>
> I: 'There was a time when, for me, everyone was really, well, even, not fat people, right, not obese people and everything, but I mean, everyone who was normal, I envied them, and then at the same time, I'd say to myself, well, at the same time, I envy them, and, at the same time, I think "that suits them, but it wouldn't suit me", for example, it suits you, but it wouldn't suit me [pauses]. And, well, now, I don't know, for a little while now, now I'm there, I find everyone, erm, well, I wouldn't want to look like them, and that [pauses] actually, I'm happy looking like I look and this way, it's just me and that's it'.
>
> [Isabelle, C]

The participants' aim of setting themselves apart from normal people also led them to downplay the work they actually did during the different phases of the career, both at the time and when talking about it in the interviews. While their actual practices revealed the extent of the anorexic work in question, an important part of standing out from the crowd was also about managing to hide their efforts:

> I always tried to eat normally, to show that I ate normally . . . . Because I wanted to show that I was thin while still eating . . . . I wanted to project that image: I was thin, but I ate normally, or [even] I ate more than normal [pauses] but I wasn't thin because I didn't eat.
>
> [Louise, H]

The 'labour' of dietary restriction, physical exercise and the various other practices involved when the girls took themselves in hand were sometimes masked at the time or passed over in silence during the interviews. With hindsight, this was also illustrated by the substantial time it took me before I finally interpreted these practices in terms of 'work' in my investigation, before I finally questioned the conditions of possibility for this self-transformation (including its physical aspects) and before I actually saw the effort involved in the ascetic exercise. In chapter five, we saw the interviewees making euphemistic references to their continued work with the phrase 'I carried on losing weight'. This can be understood in a different light now – by downplaying their efforts, they were also setting themselves apart from others and 'naturalizing' the fact they were socially exceptional. Their various secretive strategies (discretion, deception) allowed them to pursue their commitment, of course, but they also contributed to defining the situation in terms of 'distinction'.

Competition and agon

Finally, the girls' stance was not just about not eating much, it was about eating less than other people ('At a pinch, when I ate, it was OK as long as everyone ate more than me [pauses] or, at a pinch, as much as me, but if someone ate less than me, that wasn't OK' [Anne, H]; it was not just about being thin but about being the thinnest (see, for example, the way Nadège compared her body with others, as discussed earlier in the book); it was not just about being good in class, it was about being the best:

I: 'Yeah, I always want more, in every area, it's not enough for me, I either have to get a better mark, or I have to [trails off].'
MD: 'And better compared to other people or better in terms of yourself?'
I: 'In terms of myself, above all, erm, well, no, for marks, it's compared to other people . . . . Because I'm always comparing myself to other people.'

[Isabelle, C]

> [Véronique was top of her year in university] And from that point onwards, I absolutely had to stay there, you know [pauses]. So that was my fear . . . . I just had that worry about going back down . . . . I never told anyone about it, but I had this fear of not being at the top anymore, and the idea that, well, a kind of paranoia, that people wanted to take my place [pauses] so, well, it goes really well with the anorexia, too, it's that need to be admired, adulated

> [pauses] well, I wasn't admired or adulated, but, at any rate, I had this feeling of huge success, at my own level.
>
> [Véronique, N]

My fieldwork in the clinic's school highlighted the extent to which these comparative practices testify to a more specifically agonistic dimension to the anorexic ethos of tension. As well as categorizing the anorexic students as too academic, the teachers also referred to their competitive ethos and practices. To varying degrees, the teachers all mentioned the anorexics' relationships to other students in terms of more or less theatrical and staged contempt for those who were not 'as quick' as them and they all framed this as a feature of anorexic students within a group:

> There are students who have questions, who ask themselves questions, things they haven't understood [pauses] whereas those girls, they've understood [pauses]. They've understood the class . . . . So they'll have this attitude, that's very, well, I'd say, very 'teacher-y', saying 'Yes, well, we're wasting time here, and they're annoying us, asking too many questions, we have to get back to the lesson, we're not going fast enough'.
>
> [Mr Q.]

> Charlotte puts a lot into my class. She's hard with her classmates who, in her view, disrupt the class . . . . She's exasperated with 'untimely' questions and 'her classmates' agitation', she goes outside for a few moments, so as not to explode.
>
> [teacher's notes]

Mr E., the young teacher who had only recently arrived in the school, was particularly struck by this type of attitude. Having mentioned it during the interview, he came back to it again at the end, emphasizing it as the element that seemed most specific to him:

E: '[At the beginning of the interview] But other than that, in terms of the group, the anorexics are pretty [peculiar] as well, because they . . . it seems to me like they find it hard to accept the rest of the group, in fact, it holds them up [pauses]. So as soon as you try to explain something to another student who has more difficulty understanding, straightaway, well, there you go, you've opened yourself up to [sighs] 'pfff', she huffs and puffs, she waits, she's finished her exercise, I have to give her another one ahead of time, and half an hour later, you correct the exercise she'd already finished . . . .'

[. . .]

E: '[At the end of the interview] Well, what was important, was perhaps the whole 'group' thing. It's pretty funny to watch [pauses]. With the impression, for them [the anorexics] that you're dragging around dead weight, people stopping us moving through the class or the topic as we should, that's something that struck me this year, actually.'

MD: 'And what kind of "dead weight"?'

E: 'They're [pauses] people who ask them questions that they think are completely ridiculous [pauses]. And it's not just that it seems ridiculous to them, but on top of it, that it holds up them up in their own progress [pauses] because we might fall behind a bit, because [pauses] that's what bothers them, the risk of falling behind because of people who don't understand things quickly enough.'

[Mr E.]

The anorexic students viewed their classmates as 'dead weight' 'slowing down' the class and as potential impediments to their investment in school work, but also as 'ridiculous' students whom they treated with obvious marks of contempt. They sometimes also supplemented this contempt with active strategies to discredit them by showing off their own skills:

> I mean, she'll say something in class, for example, after another student has said something, and she knows perfectly well that her point of view will, perhaps not necessarily invalidate what the other one said, but, well, that it's at least, well, on another level, you know. So, it's kind of 'let's raise the level of debate', right, so it all depends which student spoke before [pauses]. Sometimes, they're not too happy, right, I mean it's understandable, it's understandable [laughs]. And then she takes that tone of hers, she's all, What? What? But no one's fooled!
>
> [Mrs W.]

Striving towards being socially exceptional also contributed to concrete practices of comparison and competition. In analysing the anorexic career itself, we saw how comparison with other people's food consumption, bodies and school work served as tools for self-evaluation and therefore as techniques for maintaining the commitment. Eating less than others was a technique for eating less; being thinner than others was a technique of self-evaluation and self-motivation in weight loss; getting better marks at school was a technique encouraging greater investment in school work. But these practices can also be interpreted in terms of the agonistic dimension to the anorexic ethos of tension. Two lexical fields were strongly present in the interview corpus: the lexical field of 'fighting', 'competition', sometimes even 'war' and the lexical field of 'game' playing ('It's a game, for me, this illness, it's a game' [Isabelle, C]). These fields are clearly evocative of a culture of *agon* ('combat, fighting, competition, rivalry . . . culture of fighting in all aspects of life[:] Olympic games, tragedy competitions, war'; Baudelot and Establet 1992, 155), something that we saw earlier with Camille's game of Chinese chequers. This agonistic ethos operated through constant self-evaluation in terms of others and constant comparison with other people's capacities and productions.[23] It was about knowing exactly who they were because they knew exactly where they were positioned in relation to others, and about constantly working to improve that position:

> Before ['during' the anorexia] for me, the difference [between people] was 'How much am I compared to so and so?' You're either below, or, better, you're above. Whereas now, I'm different and that's all. And even, I weigh 4 kilos more than her, so what? I got five marks less in maths, so what? . . . [During the anorexia] you're always in a power relationship, it's simple. All the time [pauses] like that, saying [pauses] one way or another, there's the person who's the best and there's [pauses] the person who's not as good [pauses] and so obviously you have to fight to be the best. It's all about comparisons: 'I'm less than him but more than her'. It's all management, calculations.
>
> [Yasmine, C]

This excerpt reveals an extremely hierarchized and competitive vision of the social world, in which a social status is achieved and fiercely defended on the basis of cultural objects (the body, food consumption, marks at school) as these are taken as summarizing a person's social value in absolute terms.

The body as 'total capital'

This particular social topology was the backdrop for all the physical and cultural work accomplished by the girls I interviewed and it transformed their bodies into a 'total capital', a form of capital that could include other forms as we saw earlier. Its role among these participants can once again be interpreted in terms of their social characteristics.

First of all, historically speaking, the body itself has now become a determining marker of distinction and not just in terms of how clothes transform it:

> More subtly, clothes are no longer aimed at 'correcting' the body in cultural terms, but rather at enhancing its natural appearance. This highly cultural exaltation of the natural body assumes that the body itself becomes the medium for social distinction, instead of social symbols of wealth and authority. And, by the same token, it also becomes the main target of work aimed at cultural transfiguration.
>
> (Bourdieu and Delsaut 1975, 34)[24]

In terms of social class, representations according to which the body is a 'sign' and can therefore be used as a marker of distinction contrast with representations framing the body as 'strength'. In the former case, the body is no longer a resource used to 'hold out'; instead, it acts as a sign used for purposes of representation. Moreover, as mentioned previously, weight is a far more divisive marker for women than it is for men – height, rather than weight, is the main marker distinguishing male manual workers and managers. Given that it is possible to work on weight in a way that has no equivalent in terms of height (wearing heels does not actually change the body itself the way a diet can), the socially divisive factor for men cannot be altered, whereas for women this factor can be changed provided they work at it.[25] From this perspective, the female body may well be socially established as less 'finalized', less complete, than the male body. In other words, it constitutes a space of work in which the benefits of distinction can be derived both from working on that body (as opposed to letting oneself go) and from the physical results of that endeavour (the body that is built up). The importance of the body as a total capital therefore lies at the intersection of historical changes, social class and gender, thereby creating a socio-historical locus in which the 'distinctive' body can summarize all a person's social value.

The first phases of the anorexic career therefore fit into a social topology that can shed informative light on the practices the participants engaged in to take themselves in hand and on the aims of the self-transformation towards which they worked. However 'abnormal' and 'obsessive' these practices may seem, they are nonetheless practices that are characteristic of women from the middle and upper classes. Positioning the anorexic career with the social space also shows the particular way in which anorexic activity is aimed at 'becoming different'. First, it is about becoming different from oneself (compared with before) by systematically working towards transformation and elevation within symbolic classifications, both of which are oriented towards social excellence, particularly in terms of the body and school work. Second, it is about becoming different from others by using asceticism to establish a 'solution of continuity' between self and other that not only frames how other people let themselves go (in physical and cultural terms) as a social repellent but also frames working to change physical and social destiny as a sign of being exceptional.

Notes

1 See, for example, Ledoux (1994, 53), Flament (1995, 215–17) and McClelland and Crisp (2001, 150–6).

2 To give an indication of the social positions within my interview corpus, class membership ranged between the two 'extremes' that follow: [Anne, H]'s family was among the most well-endowed. Her father was a company director (who had completed extremely high-level competitive studies) whose father was the CEO of an automobile company. Her mother was an engineer (same high-level competitive studies completed as her father) whose father owned a shoe shop and whose mother was a cleaning lady. [Sidonie, H]'s family was among the least well off. Her father was a restaurant owner (who had obtained the *baccalauréat*) and the son of railway workers. Her mother helped her father in the restaurant (she had stayed in secondary education until the age of 17) and came from a family of sewers. As we can see, while the difference between the two families was significant at the level of the corpus, it was much smaller in terms of the broader social structure.

3 In this chapter, I will discuss things said 'about' the interviewees and my own in situ observations much more than I have done so far. In order to account for this shift in analytical framework, I will use the term 'participants' rather than 'interviewees', as a way of referring to them as 'study participants observed in their capacity as anorexics' (as opposed to 'people interviewed in their capacity as anorexics').

4 Today, fruit, green vegetables and fish are still 'not very present in the shopping baskets of poor households' (Herpin and Manon 1997, 118).

5 It is worth noting that the strong increase in yoghurt consumption has not reduced the differences in consumption between social categories, which have just shifted up a level (Grignon and Grignon 1999, 157).

6 For an analysis of women's dieting habits as internalizing the tools of a biopolitics of the female body, see, for example, Germov and Williams (1996).

7 This result can be seen for young people between the age of 12 and 17 – the higher their parents' level of education, the more frequently they play sports (Moreau et al. 2002, 2).

8 See Ministère des Sports et Institut National du Sport et de l'Education Physique (2002): 'Les femmes' (27–33), 'L'environnement social des pratiquants sportifs' (107–11) and 'Le niveau d'études des pratiquants par discipline' (table 40 in the appendix).

9 The average weight for comparable ages and heights is 56.9 kilos for women who fall into the category 'high-level managers and higher intellectual professions' and it then rises through the categories 'artisans, retailers, company directors' then 'intermediate professions', 'farmers' and finally 'employees', before reaching 62.5 kilos for women who are 'manual workers'.

10 On how friendship networks are recomposed as an effect of secondary socialization, see Berger and Kellner (1964).

11 The term used in French is '*scolaire*', which could literally be said to mean 'school-y'. 'Academic' is the closest possible translation, in that it has the name notion of rigorous and serious work corresponding to what is taught in formal education. In this chapter, the word 'academic' should be understood as a translation of the French term *scolaire*, referring specifically to the school context and to school work. It is not used with any of the common connotations related to higher education or to forms of knowledge contrasting with 'practical' or 'real-world' knowledge.

12 The use of food metaphors when talking about anorexics' behaviour regarding school work is noteworthy in this excerpt, as in others. The teachers often used such imagery, which can be read as reflecting a medical influence (psychologists, psychoanalysts and psychiatrists often use metaphors referring to food or the body, and the patients themselves sometimes used them in their interviews with me) but also as a technique for labelling deviance and for recalling the pathological nature of the behaviour they were describing.

13 'The reversal of the scale of values, which, by inverting the signs, transforms seriousness into the "spirit of seriousness" and the valuing of work into a trivial, laborious pedantry suspected of making up for a lack of talent, takes places as soon as the petit-bourgeois ethos is judged from the standpoint of the ethos of the "elite," that is measured against the dilettantism of the cultivated, well-born gentleman who knows without having struggled to acquire his knowledge and who, secure about his present and future, can afford detachment and risk virtuosity' (Bourdieu and Passeron 1979, 24).

14 If we look at what young men consider as the ideal female physique, according to their current social category, 'slimness' is preferred across all social classes, but the rate of this preference is lower among unqualified manual workers, artisans, farmers and public-sector employees. See Bozon (1991, 95–6).

15 On the importance of women's aesthetic 'excellence' on the matrimonial market in personal ads, see Singly (1984).

16 Olivier Schwartz talks about the working-class body as a 'great reservoir on which people draw to make it through daily life; they count on the strength it contains, not on its chances of being valued in visual terms' (Schwarz 1990, 477).

17 For example: Turner (1996), Garrett (1998), Peters (1995) and Tait (1993).

18 Particularly when this link between anorexia and spirituality is the central argument of the study, such as in Garrett (1998).

19 Olivier Schwartz refers to asceticism as a 'traditional workers' ethos', where 'deprivation is systematically accepted, the aim being to "make it"; a general mobilization

of strength in order to seize all work opportunities' (1990, 110–11). Pierre Bourdieu (1996a) refers to a working-class ascetic disposition that is 'often linked to the ambition of upward mobility' (390), to the 'aristocratic asceticism' of teachers, public-sector executives and members of the professions (286) and finally, in much more detail, to petit-bourgeois asceticism (331).

20 See, for example, Hoggart (1957, 70).

21 From this point of view, the anorexic work of self-transformation can be compared with the work analysed by Frédérique Matonti in a case that might seem very removed at first – the example of Hérault de Séchelles, a parliamentary aristocrat under the *Ancien Régime* and the French Revolution: 'When you want to exercise some measure of control over labels, and then manipulate them to serve your purpose — and this was definitely Hérault's concern — you have to work at self-construction . . . . By modelling the body and its preservation, you have to impose the meaning you want to produce yourself and thereby grasp the possibilities of power it affords. This logic is similar to the logic governing face-to-face relationships, when it is a question of playing the role you have chosen rather than the role others have ascribed to you' (Matonti 1998a, 38–45).

22 This is quite the opposite of the working-class high regard for the 'big, fat roundfaced . . . man' (Hoggart 1957, 108).

23 It should be noted that competitive practices perhaps reach their epitome within the group of anorexics themselves, as constituted by the hospital, because it is difficult to share the status of being 'exceptional'. For an analysis of this intra-group competition, see Darmon (2001, 364–72).

24 The fact that beauty care has taken priority over buying clothes (Herpin and Verger 2000, t. 1, 77) could be seen as a statistical translation of this.

25 For a literature review of work on the 'objective' and 'modifiable' nature of the female body (but only taking gendered aspects into account), see MacSween (1993, ch. 6): 'Second only to messages of female obligation to maximize physical attractiveness are promises of its attainability (Ferguson, 1983) . . . . Women's bodies are "on show"; they are obliged to produce their bodies as adequate and acceptable "spectacles", as objects external to their selves' (174).

9 The social space of the hospital

Having considered the first phases of the anorexic career in terms of their position within the social space, the same now remains to be done for the hospital phase. In examining this social space, I will focus on two main areas, leaving other aspects aside, particularly inter-patient variations regarding relationships to hospitalization. I will begin by looking at how the anorexic diagnosis and the opposition between anorexia and bulimia are situated in the social space. And I will then ask the same question about the resistance that certain patients put up to the medical point of view encouraging or forcing them to change and give up their commitment to the career.

The diagnosis in the social space

In the hospital, the 'social' did not simply bow out in face of the 'medical', as if the two spheres were mutually exclusive. First of all, the medical label of anorexia has signification in a far wider social space than simply the hospital. 'Social representations' of both the diagnosis and the people diagnosed testify to this. Descriptions of anorexic patients and their behaviour in my investigation often revealed social judgments indicating the patients' relatively high social position. This was sometimes explicitly the case, for example when the director of the school in the clinic defined the 'typical anorexic' as 'a real young lady from the olden days':

> [In the teachers' room, the head teacher at the clinic's school comes up to me]. Ah, I thought of you, because I saw an anorexic, a real typical anorexic! I asked her why she wanted to come here, so of course she didn't talk to me about the anorexia, that's for sure, but, well, she said to me she'd been hospitalized, and so she hadn't managed to finish her academic year properly, she's studying French literature, the second year of her university degree. . . . So then I asked her what she does apart from studying, if she's only interested in that, 'no, no, of course not, I've got loads of other interests', so what are they: 'well, the piano!' So the piano, she does competitions, exams etc.

And what else? 'Well, dance', it's the same, exercises, exams, competitions [pauses]. So dance, piano, studying [pauses] like a real young lady from the olden days! [ironic tone].

[FJ]

The many comments made about anorexics being intellectually competent patients can also be understood in the same way, particularly in terms of the dispositions presupposed by the fact they had 'worked on themselves' in order to learn a particular kind of discourse about the self.[1] Among many other interlocutors, one of the nurses told me: 'It's good that you chose anorexics to do interviews, because they're high functioning, they have some distance from themselves' [FJ]. Both the doctors' views and the nurses' handover notes often revealed this same reading of the patients' discursive competence and reflexive capacities. One patient was described as being 'good at repartee' because she was 'dynamic in conversation, pretty subtle and sharp', while, according to a nurse, another patient had 'underst[ood] everything about herself, about what [was] happening to her' and was capable of 'really sharp, really intelligent analysis' of the situation [FJ]. The professionals sometimes tried to take some distance from this skilful self-discourse, relating it to a social 'façade' that they contrasted with real psychological depth. However, they nonetheless noticed and valued these skills:

[Informal conversation with an intern] The anorexics on our wards, they respect the framework, they talk in interviews, it's true that sometimes I'm impressed by what they have to say, but at the same time, you have to know that it's just a façade, what they're presenting, it's just a façade, it's not [deep].

[FJ]

The terms used to describe this ability to 'work on the self' (usually categories of academic excellence) show that these skills are cultural and linked to social background. The following opposition drawn by the hospital team between two patients – one the daughter of a *lycée* head teacher (the anorexic patient) and the other from a working-class background – can also be understood in these terms:

[Review meeting] The head of the ward is talking about two patients, one of whom is anorexic, and who both adopt a 'parental role' towards their own parents: 'The parental role, it's a prestigious position, there's no reason to let it go. We managed to get out of it with [the anorexic patient] by getting her to understand the Oedipal fantasy underpinning it' [pauses]. Intern: 'That won't work with [the other patient]! He's not about to understand that, nor are his parents!' Head of the ward: 'No, you're right, he's not really there is he'.

[FJ]

The anorexic label therefore includes an assumption that the person has a certain set of social skills, which they probably do indeed possess. This distinctive nature of the anorexic diagnosis was also illustrated in descriptions given of anorexics as a special group. The tendency towards homogamy was identified, using other terms, by both the medical team and teachers: ('the anorexics group together', '[the anorexics on the ward] are always together', 'they sit next to each other in class'). Moreover, the recurrent expression 'us [anorexics]' that emerged in the interviews was sometimes not just used to refer to common clinical features, but instead to display affiliation with the group created in the hospital (as we saw in chapter seven). And this group was more than just a group of patients brought together by the same diagnosis, it was also perceived and presented as a group of excellence that the participants could be proud to belong to:

> At any rate, what I've seen, with all anorexics, it's that they are all . . . either excellent at school, or they find it easy to understand, or they're physically fairly pretty, or they have quite a lot of qualities, whether they're artistic or really good at maths, or literature [pauses], I mean, the anorexics in general, they [pauses] excel in quite a lot of fields. I mean, we've had quite a range, it wasn't just girls who were completely nutty or limited, I mean, even in interviews, or group therapy, when they managed to drop their whole immature side, there were really things where you'd say to yourself, they were really smart girls.
>
> [Yasmine, C]

This notion of shared characteristics was reinforced by the fact the participants talked not just about how they resembled each other but also about how they 'recognized' each other:

S: 'I've never talked about my problems to anyone, whether in my class or where I board [for school], well, next to me, there was a girl who apparently had the same problems as me, who, I dunno, we'd sensed it, or something, but, well, she came to find me, she said to me, "yeah, I think you have problems like mine", and I just denied it all, and she said "OK, well, you can do what you like, you can deny it, but I know it's true", I said to her, "you can think what you like, I don't care", etc. . . . . There are common character traits [among anorexics], of course there are. And we [pauses] we recognize each other, anyway . . . . Even the girls who, even that girl at boarding school, we'd never talked to each other before about [pauses] we just felt it, we followed our noses . . . .

MD: 'And with that girl at boarding school, . . . was it just physical [the way you recognized her]?'

S: 'Physical, no, she seemed just about OK then . . . . [It's] when I'm first in contact with someone, something in the way they are, I dunno, it's hard to give a typical picture, but it's, you feel it, it's [trails off], apart from those who are completely better, who don't have, anymore [trails off]. No, when they still have symptoms [you can feel it].'

[Sophie, C]

> It's true that, for example, in the street, among anorexics, we'll recognize each other . . . . If the anorexia has really set in, and the person hasn't really got better, you'll see it in their features, in the way they are, in [trails off] . . . . Well, with some, it's just obvious, when they're really thin, and then you say to yourself [pauses] but there are people who are naturally thin, but, the anorexics, you recognize them! . . . . For example, now, I [pauses] the girl who was admitted earlier, who's been anorexic . . . . When she arrived, you can't see it on her anymore, all that much, but [pauses] there was something that meant that when we talked, she didn't say it, but I understood, we both felt [trails off] . . . . It's pretty strange, it's true, you sense it, it's pretty strange, you know. But I know that it's everyone, well, girls like that, every time we talk about it, we say 'yes'. In the street, we'll walk past, we'll walk past a girl: we know it, we know it. [In the street], there was this girl, and I just looked at the girl and said [to her father]: 'like me'.
>
> [Emilie, C]

The 'culturally thin' (to coin an expression, in contrast with the 'naturally thin') therefore presented themselves as a group that shared a 'way of being' rather than just physical features. To some extent, this recognition is reminiscent of the social recognition that exists between members of the same social group.[2]

However, this distinctive element of the diagnosis played out mainly in a relative manner. The differences between anorexia and bulimia or, more practically, between anorexics and bulimics, appeared to be situated in an oriented social space in which each diagnosis lay at opposite ends of the spectrum. The medical and diagnostic opposition between the two was therefore also a social opposition. This was clear when the participants themselves distinguished anorexia from bulimia, defining the former as a 'gratifying' diagnosis and the latter as purely stigmatizing:

> Y: 'Anorexia, bulimia, generally [it's all or nothing]. I had a few bulimic crises, and it's really like "I won't eat anything for a week and then I'll have this bulimic crisis". I mean, like it's serious, like, it's awful, it's the kind of pathology you wouldn't wish on anybody. Oooooh [disgusted expression].'
>
> MD: 'More bulimia than anorexia? Or both?'
>
> Y: 'Well, anorexia, it's, it's bearable, because it's [pauses]. It's ridiculous to say this, but it's gratifying. You push past boundaries. Bulimia, it's the opposite, it all happens to you. You can't say "no" to yourself. I mean, it's really weakness. It's really all the body's weaknesses that are expressed, in the mind, you're incapable of saying no to this little thing that's in front of you.'
>
> [Yasmine, C]

On this point, it is worth recalling the interview with Anne [C], quoted in chapter six, in which she reported a discussion with a friend where she first refused the anorexic diagnosis before eventually accepting is as a preferable label to bulimia. She stated that she saw bulimia as being 'dirty and unhealthy', whereas anorexia was 'all, like, fragile bird, that's it'. A lot of the participants stated with a form of pride that they had 'never made themselves sick' – 'I can't stand that' [Isabelle, C] – or instead did not mention (or only mentioned briefly) any behaviour that might be considered a 'bulimic crisis' or 'anorexia with purging'. This social stigma surrounding bulimia may even derive from clinicians themselves, as Richard Gordon noted in the case of Hilde Bruch, even though he made no links with class categorizations:

> In contrast with the perception of incredible self-discipline, for which the anorexic is admired, bulimics therefore tend to be disdained and misunderstood. Negative attitudes towards bulimics are unfortunately shared by some clinicians. Among these was the otherwise impeccably objective Hilde Bruch, who lamented the passing of classical anorexia nervosa and the ascendency of bulimia [. She stated]: 'They make an exhibitionistic display of their lack of control or discipline, in contrast to the adherence to discipline of the true anorexics . . . . The modern bulimic is impressive by what looks like a deficit in the sense of responsibility . . . . Though relatively uninvolved, they expect to share in the prestige of anorexia nervosa. Some complain about the expense of their consumption and will take food without paying for it'.
>
> (Gordon 1990, 135)

'Prestige' is reserved for anorexic restraint, whereas the bulimic's lack of control is associated with basely material concerns (the financial cost of bulimia crises) or even with delinquency ('stealing' food).

Social categorizations clearly underpin the medical distinction between the two illnesses – the very same categorizations we saw in the previous chapter contrasting restraint and letting oneself go. In addition to the repellent categories of 'being fat' and 'being normal', the hospital space of the diagnosis added the third category of bulimia, potentially even more threatening given its proximity to anorexia as another form of 'eating disorder':

> [In the flash meeting on ward I] A nurse explains that an anorexic patient, who had first gone to a reading group, came back complaining of hypoglycaemia. She offered her a banana, 'something nourishing', but she asked for bread with jam. [Nurse]: 'Every time, she's worried about eating again, she asks me "Is this what it is to become bulimic?"'.
>
> [FJ]

In hospital, as well as the fear of becoming 'fat' or 'normal' after treatment, there was also the fear of 'falling into' bulimia. This expression used by the participants reflects the idea of falling from grace, of being demoted, degraded, through loss of social status. Sidonie [H], for example, explained that she could not go to school when she had a bulimic crisis, as if it were a form of social dishonour that prevented her from being seen by others. 'Falling' into bulimia meant 'falling from grace'. In the extract from Yasmine's interview, quoted above, bulimia was presented as the flip side of the coin compared with anorexia. Or, more specifically, the flip side of the coin in terms of anorexic work of self-transformation, in which it was possible to say 'no', in which the person was strong rather than weak. However, it is also the flip side in social terms: stigmatizing bulimia equates in many ways to stigmatizing an ethos with no restraint or self-control.

In fact, the diagnostic opposition between bulimia and anorexia could also be related to the symbolic differentiation drawn between the working classes, on the one hand, and the middle and upper classes, on the other, and indeed borrows many of its features. The fact that psychiatric illnesses are situated in the social space in this way is not just due to the patients. In my investigation, traces of this thinking could also be seen in the doctors' words, for example describing the typical family of an anorexic ('feminine', 'self-effacing' and 'intellectual' father, 'ambitious' mother, a family that 'doesn't show their feelings' or in which 'conflicts are not expressed' for example) and the typical family of a bulimic:

> [Head of ward I] 'So these families [of anorexics] are nothing like the families of bulimics who are, on the contrary, very conflictual, unstable, with no organization, no stability, lots of shouting, it's really the negative, there's a photo [the anorexic family] and its negative [the bulimic family]. In X's family interview, who was bulimic, they were tearing strips off each other, really yelling.'
>
> [FJ]

Finally, the interactions I observed between patients also situated this diagnostic opposition within its symbolic class dimension, although this did not necessarily mean that the social origin of the bulimic patients was lower than that of the anorexic patients. The example of the relationship between Hélène and Elise, two anorexic patients, and Nathalie, a bulimic patient, offers a good illustration of this:

> [Review meeting] One of the nurses tells us about one of the weekend meals, where Hélène, Elise and Nathalie were opposite each other in the self-service cafeteria: 'It was really hard to intercede, they were there, all three of them, and you should have seen how Hélène was looking at Nathalie who kept taking more helpings! With this horrified look, disgusted'.
>
> [FJ]

> [During a meal on the ward] The fruit juice is passed around, Hélène doesn't take any, she looks regularly at Nathalie's glass, which she fills to the brim, drinks in a second, and then fills up again. Nathalie asks Elise to keep the bottle near her and not pass it around. Elise does so with a sardonic smile.
>
> [FJ]

> [In an occupational therapy workshop, painting on silk] We can hear the music coming from Nathalie's room, who has left her door open. Elise and Hélène both say 'it's driving me mad', and in answer to the occupational therapist's

question 'does it happen a lot?' Hélène replies 'all the time'. At one point, Elise says 'it's really driving me mad'. Towards the end of the workshop, Nathalie calls her mother from the public phone box on the ward, she yells, she calls her mother a 'cow' and cries loudly. [Two patients] say that 'it puts a bit of downer on things', that 'it's hard when someone snaps', etc. Hélène doesn't say anything, carries on painting as if nothing were happening. Elise is openly scornful, she says to the occupational therapist: 'it's one thing to snap, but you don't have to make a show of yourself'.

[FJ]

[During the preparation of the Caribbean therapy meal, I go shopping with two nurses and Hélène and Nathalie. We left late and it is nearly lunchtime]. What strikes me is that I'm watching a sort of game of social ping pong between them, which focuses on food, but not only food [when the nurse describes the journey in the flash meeting later, she only mentions the interactions around food]. It's a game of ping pong because they exchange 'I like/I don't like's about a series of objects and attitudes that aren't insignificant. Nathalie starts a conversation about cars. She says that her dream is to have a big convertible. Hélène contradicts her in a very self-assured tone (although in physical terms, she's the weaker of the two) and tells her that it's ridiculous, that's it's not sensible, because it's just to show off, on top of it, it's really expensive, you can only use it three months a year, you need a more discreet car, more classic. . . . . Very soon, Nathalie says she's hungry; on top of it, she went swimming that morning. She talks about McDonalds and Quick [another fast food restaurant] with enthusiasm, giving details of the menus she'd choose and says 'I miss that, I miss that!!!' The nurse asks her how often she goes when she's not in the clinic, she says around twice a week. And then the nurse asks Hélène the same question, who explains that in the fairly bourgeois little town where she lives, there is no McDonalds, which Nathalie just can't believe because she lives in a *banlieue* [deprived suburb] where there are two. Hélène then specifies that she has already been, but that 'anyway, I only have the salads' . . . . Nathalie asks if she can smoke in the car, Hélène comments that she doesn't smoke, that no one in her family smokes and that she'd rather Nathalie didn't smoke in the car (which is forbidden, anyway). . . . . In the car, Nathalie's window is wide open. Hélène asks her to close it a bit, telling her it's too windy. Nathalie asks to turn the radio volume up, Hélène asks for it to be turned down . . . . In short, Hélène criticizes Nathalie explicitly or implicitly for eating things that are too fatty, smoking, putting music on too loud, wanting to drive too fast in a convertible that's too expensive, letting too much wind in the car! [During the shopping] Nathalie carries on saying she's hungry, that it's lunchtime etc. but the nurse discourages her from buying something to eat. Hélène looks over all the labels of the products, compares the prices, tells me about her trips to the countries from which all the different products on sale come. On the return journey, Nathalie carries on complaining that she's hungry. Hélène, who has limited her conversations with her from the start, acts a bit more sympathetically towards her (she puts her hand on her shoulder) and 'encourages' her, by the end, it's even condescending: 'Are you alright Nathalie? Are you holding up?'

[FJ]

A sort of symbolic clash took place in the car, which fits in with a number of social contrasts. Nathalie played the role of someone embodying a working-class deviant ethos (with no shame, letting herself go, excessive behaviour, etc.) while Hélène played the role of someone embodying the ascetic petit bourgeois ethos (restraint, sobriety, etc.). On the one hand, convertible cars, Big Macs, music blaring, air blasting through the windows and making a show of oneself; on the other, classic cars, salads, silence, a controlled flow of air and restraint. On the one hand, bulimia; on the other, anorexia.

'Resistance'

A socially situated stance

The social space of the hospital, which is the backdrop for the final phase of the anorexic career, can also be analysed by focusing on attitudes of resistance towards the medical institution.[3] The topic of anorexic patients' resistance to the hospital emerged quite early on in my investigation, particularly because it was a recurrent feature in the medical literature, which approaches it from the perspective of how 'difficult' such patients are to treat. Moreover, at the very beginning of my observation in clinic C, medical categories once again drew my attention to the issue of resistance and, more specifically, the negative reactions of the team on ward I when a new anorexic patient arrived:

NURSE [in the nurse's station]: 'Oh dear oh dear, how many will that be [anorexics on the ward]? Three, four?'

ANOTHER NURSE: 'Three.'

NURSE: 'I'm warning you, if we get a fourth, I'm quitting!'

[FJ]

INTERN: 'So what wrong with this patient? Oh dear oh dear, another anorexic; on top of it, she's mine, this one.'

[FJ]

More generally, dealing with anorexic patients on the ward was described as being 'difficult': the anorexics were said to be 'hard', 'strong' and 'manipulative', focused on being 'divisive' (term used to refer to the destructive effects – on team work and treatment – that can result from a patient attempting to divide the nursing team, or pit nurses and doctors against each other around her case). In short, they 'resisted'. Anorexic patients were therefore not just seen as difficult collectively, due to the 'emulation' and 'competition' resulting from being in a group, they were also seen as difficult individually. I observed several scenes that illustrated this.

When the new anorexic patient arrived, one of the interns had to write out her weight contract. In doing so, she copied a contract written by a doctor for another patient with great attention, changing the relevant weight levels, and asked for my help checking it over at the end, insisting several times that I had to 'read it all', that I must not 'forget anything'. She then explained the reasons why, which were not only linked to her own inexperience in the matter: 'With "them", you have to be really careful not to forget anything, because when you forget something, they come and say "yes, but you wrote this, blah blah blah"' [FJ]. Negotiations with these patients were presented by the intern as a real battle of wills. Similarly, another intern treating anorexic patients for the first time refused interactions with patients she thought would be difficult with her:

> [In the nurse's station] A nurse arrives who says to the intern that an anorexic patient is 'missing her scales' (she is insisting to be able to weigh herself, whereas weigh-ins are performed on a weekly basis) and that she's refusing to go to the self-service cafeteria, even if someone goes with her. She asks the intern to 'do something', the intern replies that if she doesn't want to go to the cafeteria, there isn't much they can do, and that she doesn't want to see her because the intern looking after her is [the other intern on the ward, who's not there that week] and that the patient in question can be very manipulative. As she [the intern] doesn't know her, she [the patient] could tell her anything she wanted to convince her to let her weigh herself, etc.
>
> [FJ]

Finally, on the same ward, a new patient leaving against medical advice, twenty-four hours after her admission, created quite a stir. Many informal and formal discussions took place and the issue of the difficulty of dealing with anorexic patients came up again. '[Nurse, discouraged tone] "they're not easy patients, you know"' [FJ]. This patient's discharge and her refusal of treatment were commented by the team as the typical attitude of an anorexic patient: 'the anorexic in all her glory' 'a real hard-core one, that girl!' [FJ].

All anorexic patients were potentially 'difficult patients', but a specific medical category – 'difficult anorexia' or 'difficult anorexics' – was used to distinguish the most difficult of these already complicated patients: 'It's a case of difficult anorexia, as we call it today, the term seems to be established now: they're difficult cases that really put us through the mill' [head of ward I, FJ]; 'the difficult anorexics are the ones that make it hard for us as a care team: they refuse treatment or appear to comply [but] with a worrying somatic state' [Intern in clinic C, FJ].

This definition is informed by two separate issues: on the one hand, the trouble that these patients can cause for the medical and care teams,[4] and, on the other, in terms of the patients, the refusal to be treated. More specifically, 'difficult' patients are in fact patients who put up resistance for an abnormally long length of time. An initial stage of resistance to the medical point of view and to treatment can be considered normal. Allan Young has underlined this in the case of psychodynamic treatment of post-traumatic stress: 'In practice, resistances are something positive [for doctors] . . . . Patients are expected to resist the ideas on which the model and treatment program are based, for this is the nature of their disorder' (Young 1995, 189–211). Similarly, the case of an anorexic patient who adapted to the ward 'too well' at first, who put weight back on 'too quickly', was not considered to be following the normal or desirable road to recovery. Instead, this was even seen as predicting future resistance:

> We'll have to see what she's like [an anorexic admission] in a week, because at first, anorexics, they're a good 'object', but after [ironic tone] the situation changes slightly.
>
> [Head of ward I, FJ]

> At first, she seemed to adapt too well to the ward, applying herself to being the 'perfect' patient. Progressively, things changed, she presented the usual picture of a typical anorexic patient, with voluntary food restriction . . . . Divisiveness, denial, attitudes of opposition and a desire for control or even manipulation.
>
> [Letter from ward I to ward E]

A stage of resistance is therefore part and parcel of the normal road to recovery. The 'difficult' anorexics are the ones who drag that stage out. From this point of view, the category of 'difficult anorexics' can be linked to the category of 'manipulative patients' that has long been studied in the sociology of psychiatry. For Anselm Strauss and his team, the term 'manipulator' designates the most difficult patients: 'Sociologically, a manipulator is someone from whom the personnel cannot escape: their own biographies become inextricably and distressingly enmeshed with his' (Strauss et al. 1964, 335). The term also serves to categorize a certain relationship to the medical institution. According to Robert Barrett, a manipulative patient is a patient who exhibits 'active and knowing resistance to professional power' (Barrett 1996, 162) while Anselm Strauss and his team also linked this category to the relationship to psychiatric power:

> We have already mentioned 'acting-out' as a technical term that masks moral judgments of patients who violate conventional behavior. Several other terms are also used to label disapproved behavior. If patients are not acting out, the chances are they are 'manipulating', 'testing limits', or 'provocative' . . . . The behavior the staff calls 'manipulative', 'provocative', or 'testing' is built into the institutional situation . . . . Since [the patient] has a great interest in molding his living arrangements, he is very likely to test and push and argue, seeking maximum results. The tendency of psychiatrist and staff is to interpret all such behavior as the product of individual psychodynamics. We believe it also reflects a more general tendency toward control.
>
> (Strauss et al. 1964, 291)

The definition of anorexic patients as particularly difficult raises the question of the particular form of resistance they put up within the hospital context. From the medical point of view, their opposition to the institution and its representatives is the manifestation of their pathology: they are in opposition, they are inflexible, they are manipulative. However, within a sociological framework, this resistance can be interpreted as a set of strategies made possible by a set of resources. A set of strategies, first and foremost, because this resistance appears very clearly as a set of means devised in order to achieve certain aims. When we looked at the hospital phase in the anorexic career, we saw the different stages of the hospital's work on the patient and the different areas it affected. The anorexic patient's resistance can also be described in relation to these different stages and areas: the patient puts up resistance to the point of view the hospital tries to impose on her – refusing to recognize that she is anorexic, refusing to recognize that it is a pathology, refusing to cooperate with treatment – and also puts up resistance to the changes in practices required by the hospital (in terms of food and school work, etc.) – refusing to 'let go', refusing to accept being 'taken on board', refusing to 'take herself in hand'; in other words, refusing to give herself over to the hospital. Moreover, analysing these strategies sheds light upon the specific resources on which the patients call in these cases, in turn shedding light on the specific features of resistance in anorexic patients, which make them so difficult for the medical and care teams. I will identify these strategies and resources by analysing one particular example, the case of Camille, whose constant and extreme 'stance of resistance' made these strategies and their social conditions of possibility extremely visible. In doing so, I will look once again to the social space of the hospital, considering this particular type of resistance as a particular type of relationship to medical authority and to the hospital hierarchy, as well as a stance that can be socially situated through the dispositions it reveals.

Camille

Verbal and practical resistance

The doctors were not the only ones who referred to the category of 'difficult patients'; sometimes the patients described themselves with the same term. Camille used it when she introduced herself to me. In the two interviews I conducted with her, she described her entire medical trajectory from that perspective. In her first interview, she also alluded to her decision to leave ward E in clinic C against medical advice – something she then went on to do. She contacted me again afterwards and I conducted a second interview with her at her home. Camille was 17 years old when we did our first interview. She had just spent a year on ward E in clinic C and had obtained her *baccalauréat* shortly before we spoke. Since she was 14, she had been hospitalized on psychiatric wards on several occasions, sometimes for extended periods (particularly in hospital J, on a ward specializing in anorexia) where she was diagnosed with and treated for 'anorexia nervosa'. She had two sisters who were students at university and a brother studying engineering. Her father had graduated from one of France's prestigious political science institutes and worked as a communications consultant, while her mother was a speech therapist. Camille was one of the participants from the highest social background, which was not insignificant when it came to the forms of resistance she put up against representatives of the medical establishment. She was also the patient who had spent the most time in hospital at the time of our interview, which was another factor that affected her modes of resistance.

Camille immediately framed these interviews as the narrative of a *medical* trajectory. Her interviews were the only ones in my corpus in which the instruction 'can you tell me about your experience with anorexia?' was interpreted almost exclusively as relating to the history of diagnosed anorexia and in which the hospital context was the central focus of the narrative and descriptions. These interviews therefore provided unique material for broaching the question of resistance through close-up details of interactions illustrating it at work. They were also unique because the participant herself framed resistance as a key component in her self-description. Throughout the interviews, she described herself, with a certain amount of pride, as being engaged in a constant battle with the medical institution:

> That meant that, either I managed to beat them, to fight, and everything and I won, because it was just fighting, all the time, everywhere, on every front. Sleeping, going to eat in the canteen, being allowed to leave my room, being allowed to go outside, it's all fighting.
>
> [Camille]

Two lexical fields ran through Camille's narrative – 'fighting' and the 'battle' against the medical establishment and its representatives, on the one hand, and 'playing a game', on the other (she was the patient quoted in the previous chapter about the game of Chinese Chequers). In both cases (war and games), the aim was to chalk up victories against opponents – the institutions, the doctors and the nurses. She did this in a number of ways: by managing to refuse treatment such as clinical interviews or medication; by managing to exempt herself from the hospital rules and 'framework'; by managing to keep up illicit practices (not eating, not putting on weight, doing school work when forbidden, etc.); by managing to leave the hospital with the doctors' permission (day release or holidays) even when they disagreed but without circumventing the institutional rules (a process designated by the administrative term 'leaving against medical advice'); and even by leaving without permission (running away) in an act of extreme defiance. This resistance towards the institution and the people working in it and representing it – which echoed the psychiatric categorization of anorexic patients as particularly 'difficult' – was the main topic of my interviews with Camille. The fact that she chose to present herself in those terms was, in itself, a form of resistance or challenge. During the interview conducted in the hospital, whenever she mentioned an anecdote illustrating her practices and stance of resistance, she systematically raised her voice, sometimes even shouting. For Camille, raising her voice during violent narratives was a way of asserting her resistance, which she knew was perceived by the doctors as a classic symptom of her pathology. She used her interview with a 'sociology student' who 'didn't belong to the clinic' to reverse this categorization and give value to her resistance within the interaction.

Strategies of resistance

Analysing Camille's interviews reveals the great variety of strategies of resistance that can be brought into play in this context. Among these strategies, the most radical was no doubt 'exit', to take up Albert Otto Hirschman's term (1970). There were two possible ways of 'exiting' the hospital – either by 'running away' or by leaving 'against medical advice'. Camille only ran away once and was keen to explain the context in which she resorted to this extreme strategy and to justify it. In comparison, being 'discharged against medical advice' – a medical and administrative category – was also viewed badly by the hospital, but Camille was able to talk about the times this happened more lightly:

> And I often left 'against medical advice', again, before the end of my contract . . . . And so I was completely depressed, I couldn't take it anymore, and we were supposed to be going on holiday, but I needed 2 kilos more to leave, and I said to my parents 'listen, it's ridiculous, anyway, the 2 kilos, they'll end up coming one day, when I eat all day without stopping, although that's maybe not the point either.' And so they signed a discharge, because obviously the doctors didn't want to let me leave before the weight.

From Camille's point of view, the main difference between these two 'exits', these two forms of deviance, lay in the fact that, in one case, her parents helped her in her resistance (she was a minor and they signed the discharge) and, in the other, she was alone in committing the act, which reinforced the radical nature of running away as an exit strategy. She gave a long account of that episode during the interview, providing details about the techniques she used to avoid being 'caught':

> I arrived in the *métro* [subway] wearing a small cardigan, it was Christmas . . . and I arrived near my house, in fact, I'd done the whole journey by *métro* because, by bus, it's direct, but I was so scared they'd catch me that I went straight down into the *métro* station, and I went right the way round the town that way, the police had already been alerted and everything, I arrived outside my house and I saw my mother downstairs, she was waiting for me, you know.

Although she did not exactly recount the experience with pride, she did provide sufficient details to give the impression that she drew some satisfaction from talking about such a patent act of resistance. Julie, another participant who had run away during her hospital career, recounted her experience in a similar way:

J: 'And even when I think about it again, the last time I ran away from a hospital, the few weeks after, just thinking about it, I found it [pauses] it impressed me, you know, even now, when I think about it, I feel like it's a story I read or a film I saw . . . . Now, for a start, I wouldn't be capable of it at all, I don't know how I was capable of doing that [pauses]. I left there, it was nightfall, pretty much, my sister was in [the town where Julie was hospitalized], of course I knew that, but I didn't know her address or anything, so I got on a bus, I asked.'

MD: 'And how had you managed to get out of the hospital?'

J: 'It was a hospital that was open, I mean visits were allowed every day, so there were doors that were constantly open, and I left there, the unit itself, and I walked, I walked, and it was a very big hospital, I walked and I ended up outside . . . . And so I called my sister and she came and got me from a place I knew, where I'd kind of ended up, she came and got me, and she was really surprised, because she hadn't sensed I might do that.'

[Julie, H, about a previous hospitalization]

In this case, Julie narrated the episode with an even clearer sense of pride in having discovered she was 'capable' of doing something like that, something 'impressive' that a character in a film or novel might do. Both examples show how being labelled as someone who 'resists' was desirable in itself; that this deviance – always justified by how hard the hospital situation was – could generate a sense of pride. Alongside the immediate aims of resistance – keeping control over self-definitions rather than accepting the viewpoint imposed by the hospital, continuing practices aimed at maintaining the commitment in a space in which they were forbidden – one might also reasonably suggest that the strategies of resistance implemented by the participants were also aimed at obtaining a desirable label, for themselves and for others: the label of being someone who 'resists' medical power. During the second interview, Camille recounted her last discharge from clinic C against medical advice with the same satisfaction and the same attention to detail:

> I'd already said several times [to the head of ward E], let's say that I started three months before I left, I'd said 'listen, I'm fed up of being here, anyway, if I get my *bac[calauréat],* it's clear, I'm leaving' . . . . And one day, after having got my *bac,* I said to him, 'well, we'll see about it in the family interview, because we have an interview next week', and so we're in the interview and everything, I said 'right, well, this is my last day, so I'll say goodbye', and he said 'no, not at all, leaving is something we plan together, you can leave in September if you want', I said 'so I'll leave for a month on holiday, and then you'll stop me having three months holiday, just so I can stay in the clinic and be depressed, you won't offer me anything, because you haven't offered me anything for the past year, and then you'll have me leave through the main doors rather than through the back door, as you put it!', he said 'yes, yes, because it changes everything, in substance and in form, it's not the

> same thing'. I said, 'right, OK, well, I don't give a crap about the form, I'm counting on the substance', and in fact, that's kind of how I left, slamming the door behind me.

Leaving the hospital in this way was therefore a form of resistance that operated by *exiting* the establishment. Other forms of resistance were also possible within the hospital walls, however. Among these, a certain number of strategies took up the 'deceptive work' conducted previously. These strategies had already been tried and tested, learnt and incorporated. More generally, retrospectively all the work involved in the participants continuing to maintain their commitment despite alerts and despite being monitored served as a form of training for the resistance to come. The hospital was just the last (albeit the most powerful) authority trying to force them to end their commitment. From this point of view, it could be suggested that resistance to hospital instructions falls under the same category as the resistance put up previously in the face of instructions from parents, friends and doctors. This resistance could also be productively related to the difficulties inherent in changing the incorporated dispositions acquired in the previous phases of the career. Moreover, the strength of the dynamic in place thanks to these previous phases also trained the participants in using and publicly displaying their willpower as a disposition. During my observation of ward I, I noticed the same recurrent gesture made by the nurses and doctors to underline what they had to say about how 'difficult' anorexic patients were:

> [In the nurse's station, a conversation between a nurse and the head of ward I]
>
> NURSE: 'And also, they resist.'
>
> HEAD OF WARD: 'Yes, they're [makes a gesture: clenches her fist, with her palm facing her, and raises and lowers her forearm with sharp movements], they're strong.'
>
> [FJ]

This gesture could be interpreted as indicating that the participants had strength from their 'training' – their training in strength, in refusal and in resistance, which was the result of a learning process that took place as the career progressed. Patients could therefore draw upon this strength to devise strategies of resistance to counter the transformations the hospital tried to accomplish. However, the hospital left much less room for manoeuvre than the network of monitors in place in the third phase of the career. For this reason, some of these strategies could perhaps be seen more like the 'secondary adjustments' that Erving Goffman describes in *Asylums:* 'practices that do not directly challenge staff but allow inmates to obtain forbidden satisfactions or to obtain permitted ones by forbidden means' (Goffman 1961, 54). In Camille's case, it was, in particular, a question of obtaining forbidden satisfactions (not eating, not putting on weight, doing school work when it was forbidden) by using forbidden means. These meant sometimes called on the 'solidarity' between patients that Goffman mentions regarding secondary adjustments:

> For three years, I didn't [have the right to] work . . . . When I had my BEPC [the first secondary school qualification in France, taken a year earlier than GCSEs], I hid books in my nightstand, so I'd quake in my boots, I'd listen behind the door, I found it hard to work. And I even asked to go into a shared room! Because I knew there was a girl working, and so I'd put my books in her pile, 'you'll say they're yours, right? You'll say they're yours!' and everything, and I worked all the time when she was there, and she hid me, and because, anyway, I did everything the opposite to what was prescribed!
>
> [Camille]

But, more often than not, Camille described solitary strategies of resistance to the changes required by the hospital:

> I'd go and get my tray myself, except the last day, they spared me that, because I found it a bit hard to get up. I'd look at the lid, I'd lift it, just to say 'It's disgusting', I'd close it again and I'd take the tray back. When I wanted to make them think I was eating, because they'd also bring me snacks, all that, I'd go to the loo and I'd flush it [pauses]. But it never touched my lips, you know. And when they gave them to me [medication], anyway, I took them in my hand and I chucked them in the bin.
>
> I knew to the very minute exactly what I was going to do the next day, and I knew exactly how I'd hide my bread, how I'd hide my meat, how I'd mask it all, throw it in the bin quickly [pauses] how I'd skip the two hours of rest [in other words, not spend them 'resting']. Anyway, everything was thought out in advance.

This first type of strategy was aimed at resisting the changes in practices required by the hospital situation. Other forms of resistance consisted in playing on the definition of that situation, by explicitly refusing the official designation of the hospital as a treatment facility and adopting instead a personal definition of a 'pick and mix' hospital:

> I dunno, I was there and I was saying to myself 'What am I doing in this clinic [clinic C] because I was OK [pauses] and now I'm not OK and everything' [pauses] but I just hadn't lived with my family for a year yet, you know, and that, that wouldn't have lasted either. So I said to myself, 'Right, it's simple, I'll just treat it as a hotel–restaurant and I'll go to class'. That's what I did all year.
>
> [Camille]

By using non-specialist vocabulary refuting the break between the outside social world and the hospital, and by positioning herself as the 'customer' using a service rather than as a patient, Camille reversed the official definition of the situation in two important ways. The highly deviant nature of this attitude was also illustrated by the fact it generated her only explicit request in our interviews for me to be 'discreet' as far as the medical team was concerned:

C: 'It was to say to myself "I don't have to stay an extra year in the clinic", well, the "hotel–restaurant–class", there you go.'
MD: 'The hotel–restaurant–class!' [laughs]
C: 'It would be best if they didn't hear that!'
MD: 'As I said, they won't!'

For Camille, the 'hotel–restaurant–class' even became a place to 'make the most of', in terms of the leisure activities it offered, thus emptying these of all therapeutic meaning. She took this attitude, for example, with the 'therapeutic trips' organized (in which groups of patients would visit a town for a few days or do an activity outside the walls of the clinic), which were defined as part of the treatment programme by the medical and nursing team:

> [Camille had announced to the doctor that she was going to leave the clinic]. And I went on a therapeutic trip in the meantime, before [pauses] well just after I told him [the head of ward E] that I was leaving and just before leaving, that way I made the most of it right until the end!

During her interview, Camille therefore called into question the primary definition of the hospital as a treatment space and completely reversed the legitimate definition of hospitalization. Similarly, appropriating the power to define the hospital situation in our interview was a way for her to reverse the rules of the power game – it is the doctors, not the patients, who are supposed to define the conditions of hospitalization and the necessary circumstances for 'good' hospitalization. In this case, Camille resisted by reversing, or overturning, the norm. This attitude was also at work in her prolific descriptions of her relationships with her doctors and was clearly the mainstay of her resistance to the institution. The 'secondary adjustments' described by Goffman – those which 'do not directly challenge staff' – were visibly less important for Camille than situations in which she entered into direct confrontation with her doctors.

Silence is no doubt the most extreme form of resistance that can be put up against a treatment that presents itself as a 'talking cure' and against doctors who use speech as their main tool (both wards Camille mentioned in particular were psychoanalytically oriented). Refusing to talk means preventing oral communication, as in any other interaction, but in this context, it means above all that the psychiatrist has nothing to work with and it therefore radically compromises therapy through clinical interview:

> And, well, they left me the same team and everything, and so it was people forced on me, and I didn't talk, you know. I had fun, in the end, during every interview, because they'd give me them more and more often, I had fun

> calculating how often I stayed the longest without speaking, and them too, I managed 20 minutes, that's my record [laughs].
>
> [Camille]

Camille presented this particularly strong form of opposition on the register of both playing a game and putting on a performance. Her silence was never framed as resulting from intimidation or a fear of talking, but rather as a strategy for resisting the clinical interview and a means of retaliation against both the team 'forced' upon her and the increasing number of interviews. Moreover, the fact she 'had fun' and established a 'record' also indicated a certain practical distance taken from the hospital point of view, translated by the social model of a game: 'the institution can become defined as one's opponent in a serious game, the object being to score against the hospital' (Goffman 1961, 313).

However, this strategy did also have the potential to fail. Questioning the legitimacy of both the doctor and the interview is a stance that can be turned against the patient: Why is she there, if she will not speak? Camille was aware of this, as evidenced by the fact that immediately after the excerpt quoted above she added: 'but of course, that wasn't very productive [laughs again]'. This remark could be interpreted as a sign that she had internalized the point of view of the hospital, according to which silence is not 'productive' in the case of 'talking therapy'. However, it can also be understood in a completely different light, if the laughter that followed is read as a form of distance. 'Talking' can in fact prove an even more efficient stance of resistance when it means taking control of the speech situation at hand.

The first talking strategy Camille used lay somewhere between strategies of silence and strategies of taking control over speech. She took extreme care in 'managing' her words, only saying things that were difficult for the doctor to use, things that were 'empty' from a psychiatric perspective. In a sense, this just came down to a different form of silence: 'Well, it's true that I didn't talk to him [the head of ward E], every time, it was about permission to leave for the weekend, for the holidays'. This strategy was, however, not very efficient insofar as the medical team is specifically trained in 'working' on such requests and in using apparently practical issues to begin a conversation about the patient's psyche.[5] It was therefore difficult for Camille, like the other patients, to maintain a purely practical definition of the interview.

Camille also used a second, more directly aggressive, strategy involving speech in the shape of the insults she addressed to doctors: 'And you there, in front of me [a doctor in hospital J], I don't want you anymore either, you're too much of a pain in the arse . . . To tell him [the head of ward E] that his nurses were shit and he was a right arsehole'. Camille raised her voice as she recounted these insults and visibly seemed to be enjoying reliving these moments of confrontation, rebellion and challenge during the interview, offering a theatrical representation of her different forms of deviance. However, these insults directed at her doctors were in fact fairly rare; as we will see, she usually reserved them for the nurses. With her doctors, she preferred to use another kind of speech. So far, the two 'talking' strategies we have looked at involved resisting 'from the outside': in the first case, by escaping psychiatric speech, in the second, by using deviant language to mark her opposition. With the third strategy I identified, Camille 'fought' directly on psychiatric ground, to take up her own expression. She tried to question the doctor's competence by contrasting her own personal experience with the necessarily external knowledge that doctors had about her. The doctor was considered incompetent in the sense that he or she was not 'living' his or her patient's 'life':[6]

> I couldn't take it anymore, I could feel that it [hospitalization] was harming me rather than helping me! And the doctors said 'No, no, it's because she doesn't want to go right to the end of it!' and everything [pauses]. And I could feel it, I was there 'D'you want to live my life as well?! I'm telling you, it's harmful!' And I fought like that.
>
> [Camille]

Self-knowledge, presented here as superior to medical knowledge, led Camille to declare that her doctors 'didn't understand anything', in the sense that she did not find their explanations satisfactory and did not believe that they sufficiently accounted for what she was feeling:

> I told [the head of ward E] . . . that he was a broken recorder . . . . Because I felt like he listens to what I say, but doesn't remember any of it, he records it onto a tape and on top of it, it's broken, you know [pauses]. He doesn't understand anything.

In this case, Camille questioned medical knowledge about herself in her capacity as patient. Her resistance was rooted in her own medical experience and she criticized psychiatry 'from the inside' in two important ways: first, she wielded her personal experience as a weapon against medical knowledge and second, she worked towards re-enrolling her experience as a legitimate point of view *within* the medical world.

One final kind of strategy took this one step further, by reversing psychiatric categories. This form of resistance consisted in taking the categories used by doctors to refer to patients and turning them back against them. The fact that Camille seemed to spend time talking about the doctors themselves during clinical interviews was, in itself, indicative of this role reversal – usually, the patient is the subject of the clinical interview. When, for example, she labelled her psychiatrist a 'paedophile' ('[I said to him] that I felt like I was in front of a paedophile'), in addition to the insult itself, there was also a clearly adopted position in which she turned his sexuality into the topic of conversation. More systematically, she quoted herself on several occasions saying to her doctors: 'You're not interesting anymore'. Here again, she was 'reversing' the psychiatric term that doctors or nurses use to talk about the patients (albeit sometimes with some discomfort): '[Anorexia] it's a very interesting pathology, well, I don't like saying that, because the pathology is never interesting for the person who suffers from it, but anorexia is very interesting' [nurse on training placement, on ward I in clinic C, FJ]. For the medical team, the term 'interesting' sometimes meant that the patient would be a 'good clinical case' but also sometimes that the patient 'listened properly' and 'heard' what she was told, that it was possible to 'work well' with her, that she was 'ready' to begin or continue a talking therapy. When Camille declared that the doctors were not (or no longer) 'interesting' she reversed the psychiatric categorization based on this second meaning of the term.

Finally, Camille's re-enactment of her criticisms of a doctor at hospital J also showed this same reversal of norms. She complained about his silence: 'You do not say anything, I feel like I'm in front of a corpse' and ordered the doctor to 'speak', despite the fact that, as we have seen, she gave herself the right to silence, in a complete reversal of the rules of the game. The following scene provides a perfect example; Camille resisted (physically and verbally) a 'big head' of psychiatry (to take up her description) who was a specialist in anorexia and made the most of the situation to criticize and undermine the credibility of the clinical interview and the technique of psychodrama:

> And on top of it, I don't know, you don't say anything anymore, you're not interesting anymore, you don't understand anything, and your stupid theatrical scenes [psychodrama], I'm fed up of playing Punch and Judy [pauses] and I got up to leave and he pinned me down, he caught my wrists and everything, and he kept me there, and I said to him 'Ah yeah, so that's what free speech is for you, well, you won't see me again', well, it lasted two months, he wrote me letters every week and everything, I didn't want to reply, but after a while, I said to myself 'Alright, OK, I'll made an appointment, we can have it out'. And I saw him . . . [Camille explained that she didn't want to continue therapy with him, he tried to convince her to make another appointment with him, she didn't do it and told him she would 'stay in touch']. I've not spoken to him since.

In addition to having reversed the definition of the situation ('you don't say anything anymore, you're not interesting anymore, you don't understand anything'), it was also Camille who brought both interactions to an end, as well as her treatment itself. Here again, she took upon herself something that is usually a medical prerogative in anorexic treatment. Given that interactions with doctors are the locus *par excellence* for imposing the medical approach upon the patient, they were also the ideal locus for Camille's resistance.

In presenting Camille's strategies of resistance, I deliberately looked at the case of doctors separately from that of the nursing staff, because there were substantial differences between the two. First, during her interviews with me, Camille recounted many more interactions with doctors than with nurses. Given that daily contact with nurses was much more frequent than with doctors, this might seem surprising. It seems to suggest that she reproduced the institutional hierarchy of the hospital by placing more importance on the doctors. Moreover, on ward E, relationships with nurses, whether formal or informal, could potentially involve more choice than where doctors were considered, at the patient's request. Resistance to nursing staff was therefore possible simply by avoiding interactions with them:

> We have to think with her about what the nursing staff represents for her and what they conjure up for her. She only looks for contact with the doctor. Rejects the paramedical team => why?
>
> [Ward E, nurses' handover notes, recounting the content of a clinical interview with the psychiatrist who is head of the ward].

> Will be seen in an interview by the doctor. Camille 'always talks to the organ grinder, not the monkey, like her (paternal) grandmother' (journalist [for a major French newspaper]).
>
> [Teachers' notes, notes taken during a review meeting; the quotation marks indicate Camille's reported speech in the meeting]

These strategies of distance operated according to a mode of (social) contempt that explicitly called on the institutional hierarchy (with the doctor the 'organ grinder' and the nurses his 'monkeys') and sometimes even meant refusing to consider the nurses as socially legitimate members of a network of interactions. The efficiency of this strategy was threefold. First, making explicit reference to hierarchical and institutional boundaries, Camille was able to target not only the nurses but also the doctors: when my investigation took place, there was a certain amount of conflict between the doctors and nurses on ward E and, in that context, it was not desirable for the doctors for a patient to put her finger so directly on these hierarchical divisions. Moreover, the 'resistant' nature of these strategies taking distance from the nursing staff was exacerbated by the fact that the nurse/patient relationship is, in itself, supposed to be defined by closer proximity than the doctor/patient relationship. By playing on distance, Camille therefore countered the psychiatric definition of that relationship. Finally, this kind of strategy also worked much like the reversal strategies discussed above: the doctors ask the nurses to 'keep their distance' from patients and not let themselves be caught up in a relationship that becomes 'too close'. By using distance in this way, Camille not only countered the psychiatric norm, she also reversed it to her own advantage.

Distance was not always, however, available as a strategy, for example on the specialist ward in hospital J. In its place, Camille therefore resorted to verbal and even physical violence:

> Oh yes, that too, every time you go back to the hospital, no matter how much I [trails off]. I had a nurse called Jacques, my main nurse, and in all my hospitalizations, I was like [she almost shouts]. 'Hey, fat bastard, get the hell out of my room', and he wouldn't move; 'Hey, fat pig, are you deaf or something?' And the poor bloke, he took some real punches to the stomach and everything, it was incredible! The first time I came out of isolation, I went straight to Décathlon [a sports equipment shop], I bought a punching ball, I drew his

face on it and everything! When I went back the second time, I said to them 'listen, alright, I'll come back, but without "Fat Pig", I don't want him'.

Camille did not report any speech directed to nurses that did not involve insults. Moreover, compared with the insults she used with the doctors, the insult quoted above was striking both in terms of how personal it was – as evidenced by the fact she went on to use it as an individual nickname ('Fat Pig') – and in terms of how it called upon the sort of social discrimination mentioned in the previous chapter, albeit in a much less euphemized form. In terms of the ethos described previously, the insult 'Fat Pig' cast complete social disgrace upon its target. Moreover, in her interviews, Camille never mentioned any physical violence towards her doctors, whether direct or indirect (e.g. the 'punching ball' that stood in for the nurse) and in the interaction quoted earlier, when she described herself as being 'pinned down' by a doctor, she did not respond in physical terms.

These varied forms of resistance reveal a keen understanding of the hospital 'game' and a form of respect for professional and hierarchical positions. It is also clear that Camille used different, very specific, resources depending on the situation at hand: with her doctors, she wielded speech as a weapon (calling on cultural resources) and with her nurses, she used self-assurance and social contempt (calling on symbolic resources), but also physical violence with her male nurse (calling on physical resources, but also symbolic resources with her 'Fat Pig' insult). In fact, Camille's resistance was always based on the type of capital underpinning the power relation in question and always involved reversing the specific tool of domination at hand: speech, and control over it, in the case of doctors, and physical strength, in the case of a male nurse. She did not present herself as being indiscriminately violent or aggressive, rather she demonstrated her ability to adapt the intensity and forms of her resistance depending on the situation.

Although Camille called on numerous and varied strategies, many of them fed into an attempt to overturn psychiatric norms. This was quite clearly an important component in the 'difficulties' she posed for the medical and care teams:

> Camille . . . will use any means to get what she wants . . . . Won't let go. *Very* manipulative.
>
> [Nurses' notes]

> She even managed to turn [a psychiatrist in hospital J], you know, his office was open to her at any time, to her personally!
>
> [Psychiatrist on ward E, FJ]

The psychiatrist's last remark was aimed at me, after Camille and her parents had declared that she was about to leave the hospital against medical advice. Mentioning how she had 'turned' a psychiatrist around, to the extent that he even changed the hospital 'framework' for her, was a way for this doctor to explain his own failure to make Camille stay. However, this remark also gave credence to Camille's own narrative about her power relations with the psychiatrist in hospital

J, which she presented as a personal victory. This therefore gave greater substance to the resistance she described, showing that it was clearly more than just a stance she adopted in our interviews.

The social conditions of possibility for resistance

However, the 'efficiency' of these strategies is perhaps not the most important issue to address. As Erving Goffman has underlined, in a slightly provocative fashion:

> But precisely what an individual 'gets out of' a practice is perhaps not the sociologist's first concern. From a sociological point of view, the initial question to be asked of a secondary adjustment is not what this practice brings to the practitioner but rather the character of the social relations that its acquisition and maintenance require. This constitutes a structural as opposed to a consummatory or social-psychological point of view.
>
> (Goffman 1961, 200–1)

Having given an idea of the strategies Camille used, it is now worth looking to the social conditions of possibility for these forms of resistance. In particular, it is important to ask what made them possible in relationships that, at first glance, seem so unequal both individually (nurse/patient, doctor/patient) and more generally (in terms of age, status and gender). First of all, Camille's relative control over her interactions with the representatives of the medical institution was grounded on her almost 'professional' experience of the situation. Camille had been hospitalized on many occasions ('I've done this eight times', she summarized at the beginning of the first interview, after recounting her first hospital stay and discharge against medical advice) and those hospitalizations had lasted for long periods of time; 'because, I was there for three years, you know [in hospital J], I know [pauses] all the people here and who've come from there, I know half of them! The nurses, I know them by heart, well, anyway [trails off]'. Moreover, the fact that these hospitalizations took place on at least three different wards no doubt gave her a more global vision of the way a psychiatric institution functions, above and beyond the specificities of each individual ward. This was evidenced in the interviews when she spoke about 'doctors' in general, using the adverb 'always' and insisting on the similarities from one ward to the next according to her observations.

This inductive knowledge of the hospital and the psychiatric point of view was also marked, for example, by her mastery of local categories; of the 'right' terms to use in order to get what she wanted. She used this knowledge in her strategies of resistance, but also to get hospitalized when that was her aim:

> Well, I'd ask to go there [to hospital] . . . and I'd speak to the doctors, tell them, what I was thinking, how I was, and the pressure on me in the family, because [pauses] it damages the whole family, the whole family is on edge

> and you say something wrong and it's all shouting, they snap, it's awful, and I'd say that I couldn't take it anymore, you know, because on top of it, I could feel that it all depended on me, that as soon as I felt better, it relieved the strain in the family [pauses] so of course, every time, they wouldn't even let me go home, they'd put me straight in a room [pauses] whereas before, they didn't have a bed! But once you've been to [hospital J], they get rid of someone and you take their place, because once they know you, it's a bit strange, actually [pauses]. The first time, I almost died and they didn't have a bed for me, and after that, I could always have waited a bit, but no, they never made me wait.

In this excerpt, Camille described explicitly and implicitly the means through which she obtained the doctors' consent, testifying to her mastery of certain psychiatric categories. Moreover, her use of the term 'obviously' indicated that she was perfectly aware of how efficient her words were. She told them exactly what they needed to hear in order to obtain the hospital admission she wanted immediately. Finally, the second part of this interview excerpt, in which she staged a certain naivety ('it's a bit strange actually') and made various accusatory allusions, again testified – albeit euphemistically – to her understanding of the codes and systems at work on the wards.

This kind of experience served as a resource for her resistance. She defined it as learning 'diplomacy', in other words, as acquiring a specific form of language aimed at obtaining what you want, while pretending to make concessions. This form of learning could be compared to professional socialization and is based on understanding and mastering the 'right categories' and the 'right' terms, just like a foreign language. In this case, Camille was perfectly aware of the efficiency of this language.

> I was very diplomatic because you learn to be diplomatic when you talk to psychiatrists! I said to him 'right, listen, it's very simple, for the moment, I don't have the strength to deal with a psychodrama like that', I didn't mean a word of it and everything! 'but when I'm better and everything, I'll take the necessary steps, I'll make an appointment'.

Camille's defensive 'diplomacy' sometimes also served her attacks, as she used her knowledge about certain theories to try and call the medical point of view into question:

> And, actually, it's the mother, above all, always, anorexia is always the mother's fault [pauses]. And it's such a pain. And I'd spend my time telling the doctors, 'every time, in the family interview, you start all that again, stop making my mum feel guilty, enough! It's not her fault, she doesn't understand why you keep on at her like that'. But they still carried on, you know. And here, it's pretty much the same.

In many ways, Camille therefore resembled the 'professional patients' studied by Robert Barrett:

> A patient stereotype that epitomized resistance to psychiatric authority was the 'professional patient'. Professional patients were characterized as 'manipulative' and 'controlling', as 'skilled', 'consummate' and 'resourceful' . . . Professional patients also accrued a detailed knowledge of the hospital staff. They were reputed to be familiar with the personalities of staff members and even the details of the roster. They knew the 'system'. . . . The danger represented by professional patients was that they wrested power from the staff, especially the power to define their illness and control their location within the hospital. . . . [For the staff] denigrating them . . . neutralized their power, redefined the distinction between staff and patient and reasserted professional power.
>
> (Barrett 1996, 162–3)

The value of linking professional patients with 'resistance' also lies in the fact that this link can shed particular light on the complex relationship between taking on board the medical point of view and resisting that point of view. As we have seen in the examples above, Camille's resistance was based on her knowledge of the psychiatric point of view, perhaps even on its internalization to some extent. Erving Goffman briefly refers to cases of 'intransigence' from this point of view, in which the patient: 'intentionally challenges the institution by flagrantly refusing to co-operate with staff. . . . Sustained rejection of a total institution often requires sustained orientation to its formal organization, and hence, paradoxically, a deep kind of involvement in the establishment' (Goffman 1961, 62).

'Involvement' is therefore, in part, a condition of possibility for resistance. Internalizing the psychiatric point of view and resisting it are not two opposite stances, but rather two sides of the same process: in Camille's words, it was about 'learning to be diplomatic' in order to be able to continue the 'fight'. This kind of resistance is not possible for a patient who has just arrived in the hospital. One might suggest, although I cannot verify this hypothesis here, that resistance also has its own history and its own career, in which there are not only different levels of resistance depending on the patient, but also different types and modes depending on the stage of the hospital trajectory in question.

Although Camille explicitly presented her knowledge of psychiatric 'diplomacy' as a resource in her resistance, she was less explicit when it came to a second kind of social condition of possibility for resistance: the resources offered, in this fight, by dispositions related to social class.

These emerged very clearly when she was faced with the nurses: 'Camille went to see [a nurse] twice at the outpatient clinic. She had an appointment with her at 1.15pm. She forgot! I told her off, she was almost arrogant' [nurses' notes]. In this regard, the expression Camille used to justify her refusal to interact with the nurses (mentioned earlier) is interesting – it is better to 'talk to the organ grinder, not the monkey'. It is also important that she attributed the expression to her grandmother, who was a 'journalist [for a major French newspaper]'. Camille therefore brought into the clinic context much broader social attitudes, which testify to a certain sense of control over the social world. The distance she took from the nurses, described above, was partly rooted in class contempt, which other participants in my corpus also demonstrated:

> [About the restrictions placed on school work on the ward]. Sometimes, I find it strange, and sometimes I even just can't really believe it [pauses]. I work, and when a nurse, or someone like that says to me, 'Julie, you're working too much, you should stop', I say to myself, 'What does he know, he doesn't know what it's like to sit your *baccalauréat*'.
>
> [Julie, H]

Camille's irony towards 'jobs that aren't very gratifying' was also noted in the nurses' notes: 'Even though professional avenues without the *bac* do exist, she [Camille] can't imagine having a job without the *bac*. She is ironic, citing jobs that she considers "menial"' [nurses' notes]. Similarly, when I pointed out to Camille at the end of our interview that 'in her family, there were lots of different occupations', she immediately interpreted my remark in terms of 'distinction' and replied: 'Yes, obviously, well, given what the people in my family do, I wouldn't want to be a postwoman'.

In the second sentence of the excerpt above, from the nurses' notes, the person writing clearly expressed distance from Camille's contempt, whether he or she felt targeted by Camille's words or, at the very least, because he or she condemned that attitude of social contempt. Camille's teachers were also critical of her class-related attitudes, particularly in terms of the elitism she displayed: 'Says that in the end she doesn't want to do an *LEA* (language degree) because certain subjects don't interest her. Only seems interested in the 'veneer' (being an interpreter, being a translator) but becomes disillusioned very quickly when confronted with the reality' [teachers' notes]. The first moments of my second interview with Camille offered a direct illustration of this elitism:

> She tells me that she does not want to be an interpreter anymore, because it's not interesting enough and it takes a long time before you gain recognition and make a name for yourself, and translating stupid texts about growing corn in the meantime is not very interesting.
>
> [FJ]

In our interview, the same stance was also visible, this time applied to the institution, in the terms she used to describe the hospital as a place not worthy of accommodating her. From the very first sentences of our interview, she placed herself in the position of the demanding customer, with a keen awareness of the aesthetic qualities of her living environment. As I began the recording, I placed the recorder on the bed where she had sat down and made a remark about the bed cover on which the recorder was resting: 'MD: "This bed cover's great!" C: "Yeah, I had it changed, they'd given me this shabby purple one, I had it changed".'

The adjective 'shabby' was recurrent in the interview, as well as the term 'grotty':

> After a while, I said to him [her psychiatrist in hospital J] 'I can't take this anymore, listen, it's already seriously depressing having to be in your [pauses] grotty building . . . .' [During the interview, the door opens (on its own?), she goes to shut it] The doors are a bit shabby.
>
> [Camille]

This offered a further illustration of Camille's way of defining the hospital as a 'hotel'; a hotel whose standards did not meet her requirements as a customer (as opposed to as a patient). The same categorization was also present in her repeated requests to 'change rooms' at the clinic, once again more reminiscent of a demanding client 'threatening to leave' (the 'hotel') if she did not get a better room. The nurses' notes testified to long-standing negotiations on that matter:

> 17.09. Notes: Not happy that we didn't let her change her room, which she thinks is too small.
>
> 10.22. Clinical interview: Camille is very provocative, aggressive towards [the doctor]. Talks about her room again, provocatively. 'Threatens' to leave if we don't change her room.
>
> 21.01. Family interview: Her mother falls in with her daughter's complaints and even asks if changing her room wouldn't be a solution given that she's surrounded by the two noisiest people . . . . The idea of changing Camille's room seems more appropriate now than before. Can change room.

It would seem that, in the end, it was the family interview that enabled Camille to get the room change she wanted – her mother's intervention was perhaps a factor (parental resources), although the fact a patient had left, freeing up a room that had been occupied until then, probably also helped. Ultimately, the two modes on which Camille expressed her social contempt (towards the nurses and towards the hospital environment) came together to create a 'system': if the clinic was nothing more than a 'hotel', then the nurses were just its employees from whom a certain distance should be kept, allowing for 'arrogance' when interactions were inevitable.

Where the doctors were concerned, however, Camille aimed for familiarity and social ease, afforded by the self-assurance inherent to sharing the same social background. Camille tried to use class solidarity to circumvent the local hierarchy establishing strict barriers between doctors and patients: '[Camille] wants to be doctor X's favourite girl [Head of ward E] [review meeting]'. Within the clinic, such a remark no doubt referred to a form of transfer or anorexic manipulation. However, it could also be understood as relating to her desire to play the card of social proximity against the distance imposed by respective roles in the hospital. Indeed, Camille described the hospital world as a universe in which social capital has an important role to play:

> So in the end, I saw Mr X [head of ward E, whom she deliberately did not describe using his professional title – NB: unlike in Britain, consultants are also addressed as 'Doctor' in France] and I said to myself, 'Yeah, he seems super nice and everything' [pauses] and he was saying to me 'Whenever you want, there'll be room', and often you wait a year or two to come here, and after three days I had the answer [pauses]. I said to myself 'This is a bit fishy' And after, I understood that there must have been a phone call between [her psychiatrist in hospital J, a specialist in anorexia] and X which must have speeded things up a bit [pauses]. And he [X] said to me 'whenever you want' and so 'Well, yes, right, I might as well have my holidays! I'll come in September'.

The head of ward E seemed 'super nice' to her at first and the expression suggests that her 'wanting to be his favourite girl' was part of the familiar relationship that she wanted to establish with the institution's representatives. Camille's social ease was reinforced by her conviction that she was not a patient 'like any other', that she was not one of the indeterminate 'you's' who had to wait for a reply, that she had connections (her psychiatrist in hospital J) which afforded her special treatment. Her negotiating power with the head of ward E was based on this same conviction, as was her request to 'come when she wanted' and 'have her holidays', as if the 'professional' patient could just decide to take holiday leave. In addition to her use of the clinic as a 'hotel–restaurant–class' (at least in discursive terms), this could all be compared with a model of private appropriation of public space, which is possible for certain dominant classes in certain spaces (see Pinçon and Pinçon-Charlot 1989, ch. 8). But we can also read it as a form of what Goffman, in *Asylums,* calls 'working the system': 'we have an extension and elaboration of existing sources of legitimate satisfactions, or the exploitation of a whole routine of official activity for private ends' (Goffman 1961, 210). Career and capital work in the same direction here, towards appropriating or reversing the institutional framework. A number of Camille's remarks in the interview testified to her reading of the hospital as a space in which social capital played a substantial role and in which she was not a patient like any other, given her substantial resources in that regard:

> Hospital J is super well known for anorexia, with Professor Y and all that . . . . [After several hospitalizations in hospital J, she went to clinic C]. And, well, in parallel, I saw Mr Y [her psychiatrist in hospital J], which Mr X [her psychiatrist in clinic C] here doesn't like at all, because I've always seen THE head of the ward and everything, and he feels like I'm being the little spoilt brat who'll only see the top dogs. So I saw him once a week and I got on super well with him because, on top of it, he knew my psychiatrist outside.

The last sentence shows how Camille presented an interaction with a therapeutic aim (from the point of view of the hospital), as something that was almost social ('I got on super well with him') and that was based on common social 'connections' ('he knew my psychiatrist outside'). Camille therefore took the usual practices and codes in use in the medical world (the follow-up of a patient from one doctor to another or the contact that is always supposed to exist between an outside therapist and the medical team of the ward where the patient is hospitalized) and revised them according to a more general vision of the benefits of social capital. This representation of the medical world was structured (Camille applied an interpretive perspective she had learned and that applied to the social world more broadly) and also went on to be structural in her resistance, insofar as this attitude had real effects in terms of the strategies she devised based on her belief that she 'wasn't a patient like any other'. The doctors' comments about her also showed that they perceived and interpreted this social familiarity:

> Camille seems to be trying to ask for help in a more genuine manner while at the same time maintaining a relationship that is full of mischief and manipulation.
>
> [Written by an intern]

> No, it's true, she's endearing.
>
> [Head of ward E, FJ]

The terms 'endearing' and 'mischief' both have positive connotations, even when used in conjunction with comments about Camille's 'opposition', 'manipulation' and 'lack of flexibility'. They should not, however, be interpreted as approval of Camille as a patient (being mischievous did not make her any less 'difficult') but rather as approval of her social personality: the doctors recognized in these strategies certain dispositions which they valued due to their own social positions. This would seem to imply that Camille had contrived to no longer be simply considered or described as a 'patient'. This hypothesis was confirmed by absence of any similar positive connotations in the nurses' judgements, which simply criticized the attitudes of a difficult patient whose social contempt they perceived quite clearly. In addition to their comments about her 'arrogance', the nurses also referred to her using the derogatory labels of 'spoilt child' or 'princess'. While they shared the doctors' categorization of Camille as a 'difficult' patient, they were less inclined than the latter to compensate with a positive evaluation of Camille as a 'person' – no doubt because the effects of her class-related characteristics would be more negative for them than for doctors.

Finally, Camille's conviction that she was not a patient 'like any other' was not just a factor in her relationships with doctors and nurses. Her elitist rationale, highlighted with the nurses, also targeted other patients. She did not perceive them as potential partners for interaction anymore than the nurses: '[In hospital] I played Scrabble, on my own, because the others . . . . I found them too rubbish'.

This attitude was clearly apparent in the ward notes, because it created problems for the medical and care teams:

> She keeps herself to herself and finds it difficult to accept the environment *by placing herself on the same level as the other patients* (asks for appointments with doctor Y outside the allotted times).
>
> [Written by the intern]

> Camille complains about the other patients: their conversations are mundane and uninteresting.
>
> [Nurses' notes]

While these comments clearly denounce her attitude, Camille sometimes managed to make acceptable the idea that she did not want to associate with just anyone:

> [In a review meeting, the case of a very violent patient is being discussed] The question is: 'Should we keep him on the ward or not?'. From the outset, the discussion turns to the idea of the patient leaving for a different ward, but the discussion is long . . . . At one point, a nurse uses the other patients' reaction as an argument: 'The other patients can't stand him. Camille told me she didn't like him and that she wouldn't go on the [therapeutic] trip if he was there'.
>
> [FJ]

This argument used by a nurse who wanted the patient in question to leave was not considered legitimate in the meeting (as it was not a 'good reason' in medical terms – something the head of the ward underlined). However, it was probably no coincidence that Camille's name was the one mentioned in this context.

Once again, Camille's 'refusal' of the 'hospital framework' can be explained by her refusal to place 'herself on the same level as the other patients'; in other words, by the fact she wanted her exceptional nature as a social person to be recognized; in the shape of privileges, for example, such as having the psychiatrist's office 'open to her at any time, to her personally'. Her resistance was based on setting herself apart from the other patients and the nurses alike. On this point, her strategies of resistance seem to fit in with the elitist ethos mentioned previously, through the way she did not want to be treated like 'the others' by the institution. Analysing Camille's case has brought to light some possible strategies of resistance as well as their social conditions of possibility. However, my fieldwork was not sufficiently broad to offer an exhaustive overview of this question of resistance or to provide complete contextualization of Camille's case within the corpus. She was clearly the participant who adopted the most open stance of resistance; however, there were not sufficient variations within my corpus to enable me to link them to different positions in the social space or different situations within the hospital trajectory. Nonetheless, it is worth noting that another patient on ward E, who had only just arrived when I conducted my second period of observations and whom I therefore did not interview, seemed to be engaged in the same kind of resistance to the medical institution. She also resembled Camille in terms of both her social position (she was the daughter of a university professor and a secondary-school head teacher) and her situation within the hospital trajectory (she had been hospitalized several times for long periods before arriving in clinic C):

> [Nurses' notes, written by different members of the nursing team]: Will be seen this afternoon by [the intern] due to the difficulties of the [nursing] team to build up a rapport with her. (13.10).
>
> Demanded her magnesium at lunchtime . . . . Answered that she was in a hurry and no one [among the nurses] was giving it to her: 'well, you know, here' she said, trailing off with a pretty contemptuous air. (12.11).
>
> Very cheerful, smiley. Jokes with us, but can't help herself from being caustic. (16.01).
>
> Account of the medical interview: she is not very talkative. Very insolent, provocative, manipulative. Refuses verbally to recount her past, to look at the beginning of the anorexia, gives the impression she couldn't care less. (21.09).
>
> Account of the medical interview: Still as manipulative and provocative. Turns [the psychiatrist]'s questions round very skilfully. Remains very distant from the other patients. (28.09)
>
> Account of the medical interview: She has started talking a bit, but refuses to delve further into the cause of her refusal to eat. (16.11).
>
> Account of the medical interview: Very peculiar interview. She didn't say anything. Not a word. (11.01)

Once again, we see silence and reversing norms used as strategies of resistance, along with distance taken from nursing staff and other patients alike. The same class contempt highlighted in Camille's case is also suggested in this case, with the 'insolence', 'caustic' remarks and 'contempt' addressed to the nurses. Once again, one might reasonably suggest that this particular kind of resistance requires specific resources.

We have seen that the social conditions of possibility for this kind of resistance can be divided into two kinds: first, knowledge of the hospital world acquired by almost professional socialization into the status of 'patient' (which continues the 'training' in resistance accomplished in the previous phases of the career); second, class dispositions brought to bear on the hospital context. These two kinds of resources combine to create a very particular kind of 'diplomacy', to use Camille's term, which is both about attack and defence, about resistance and integration. The term 'diplomacy' ('you learn to be diplomatic when you talk to psychiatrists') conjures up both kinds of resources. Being 'diplomatic' is a general skill used in various settings, but being a 'diplomat', using diplomatic language in the professional sense of the term, is also a key skill necessary for a specific occupation and learnt throughout that professional career. This career also often presupposes a certain social status, which provides a form of primary socialization through which some of these skills are learned before entering the profession itself later in life. Moreover, the exceptional status that Camille explicitly asserted throughout her interview linked these two aspects together: due to her longstanding hospitalizations, she was not a patient like any other; and, due to her social position, she was not a person like any other. Positioning the hospital phase within the social space and analysing the social conditions of possibility for resistance underscore the value of looking to social characteristics when accounting for the particular 'difficulty' that anorexic patients, or at least certain anorexic patients, pose for medical and care teams. The effects of the participants' career and the influence of their social characteristics combine to offer a practical account of anorexia, on this point in particular but also in much broader terms.

Notes

1 On the 'unequal social distribution of dispositions towards talking about the self', see Poliak (2002).
2 'As the bourgeois master the art of details that will set them apart and that, much like a ritual, will consecrate them, they "recognize each other" in the urban crowd' (Le Wita 1988, 76).
3 For a comparison of the different strategies of resistance put up against representatives of medical and educational institutions, as well as an analysis of the relationship between the rapport to each institution, see Darmon (2001, ch. 8).
4 In the wards in my study, the 'medical team' referred to the doctors on the ward, while the 'care team' referred to the nurses and health care assistants.
5 Baszanger uses the term 'boomerang effect' to talk about practices that aim to 'totally enclose . . . [the patient] in a universe separate from the physician's, for example when a doctor faced with a patient trying to change their treatment neutralizes the patient by framing that request as a symptom of the patient's depression' (Baszanger 1998b, 242–4).
6 This expression can be compared with those used by the patients observed by Allan Young: [a patient to a therapist:] 'You had to be in Vietnam to know what I'm [not] talking about' . . . . 'Who should know better what these things [events, experiences] mean, you or me? Hey, they happened to me, not you!' (1995, 189–221) and by Baszanger: [a patient to the doctor:] 'You're not the one who's hurting!' (1998b, 287).

10 Conclusion

In 1924, Marcel Mauss presented a paper to the French Society of Psychology about the relationships between psychology and sociology. He concluded his initial section by promising, in the name of sociologists, not to overstep onto the ground of psychology:

> But do not be afraid. We have an out-and-out respect for your frontiers, having a sense of justice, and it is enough that there be an element of individual consciousness, large or small, to legitimate the existence of an individual discipline devoted to it. Besides, we would not dream of denying it. Even when the mind of the individual is completely invaded by a collective representation or emotion, even when its activity is entirely devoted to a collective effort . . . even then, we accept, the individual is a source of action and of particular impressions. Even then his consciousness can and must be an object for your considerations and we ourselves are obliged to take this into account. For whatever the suggestive power of the collectivity, it always leaves the individual a sanctuary, his consciousness, which is yours.
>
> (Mauss 1979, 10)

However, respecting these disciplinary boundaries does not necessarily mean accepting that a certain domain of facts 'belongs' solely to the realm of psychology. Within Mauss's paper, a second, more belligerent stance overlay this first one. He gave psychologists the 'permission' to consider social facts and, by the same token, gave sociology a symmetrical right regarding psychology:

> The contribution of collective representations: ideas, concepts, categories, motives for traditional actions and practices, collective sentiments and fixed expressions of the emotions and sentiments, is so great, even in the individual consciousness – and we make a very energetic claim to study it – that at times we seem to want to reserve for ourselves all investigations in these higher strata of the individual consciousness. Higher sentiments, mostly social: reason, personality, will to choose or freedom, practical habits, mental habits and character, variations in these habits; all these we claim as part of our province, along with many other things.
>
> (Mauss 1979, 9–10)

By devising a sociological approach to anorexia, I hope to have shown that avoiding any 'sense of justice' (to take up and reverse Mauss's jibe) in fact made it possible for me to construct a different view of anorexia and that this different view brought out aspects of the condition that had previously gone unnoticed.

My approach focused on highlighting a central process in the anorexic career, namely the work of self-transformation it entailed, both in physical and cultural terms, which operated through methodical steps to change dispositions. This self-transformation began with the person engaging in an endeavour to take herself in hand and was then pursued across various practical domains. The dispositions resulting from these two first phases eventually created a 'second nature'. When the person was hospitalized, the institution worked to counter this second nature with more or less cooperation from the patient. Collective work was 'done' on the individual, in a second form of transformation. This aimed to erase these dispositions and replace them with new ones, first of all by the patient giving herself over to the practical guidelines issued by the institution. From this perspective, anorexia can be understood as a form of secondary socialization, but one that initially takes place in a solitary fashion. No institution was directly involved in the powerful and multi-faceted self-transformation that took place in the first phases of the career. However, by the end of the career, the hospital apparatus did come to play the traditional role of the institution. And in doing so, it underscored just how necessary the full weight of the institution was in order for the new transformation to be able to counter the initial one. The disciplinary institutions described by Michel Foucault, or the total institutions analysed by Erving Goffman, are apparatuses that organize ways of changing people, as my study of the hospital phase illustrated. But my analysis of the first phases of the career showed a deliberate, determined and individual mode of self-transformation. During the first phases, it seemed as if my study participants were being violently transformed by an institution. And yet this institution was patently absent, almost entirely pieced together on the basis of more or less broadly disseminated social norms and instructions.[1] It is perhaps in this sense that my sociological approach found a new way of broaching the 'a-normal' nature of anorexia: the participants were, in a sense, their own total institutions.

The fact that there was no 'institution' as such highlighted just how much 'work' was accomplished in the anorexic career – and indeed made it necessary to use the term 'work' to describe anorexic activity. From this point of view, anorexia constitutes an extreme case of work aimed at self-transformation. We could perhaps talk about a 'work of the self', so as to avoid referring to 'work on the self' which, although sometimes used in this sense in sociology, tends to designate the process of self 'discovery' (learning to understand yourself and to 'make do with' yourself) rather than self-transformation, as we saw when analysing the hospital phase.[2] However, this extreme case (both in terms of the methods used and the fact that the practices involved were labelled deviant) is also just one case among many others of work of the self. It simply makes this process – which is also at work in other situations – particularly visible and salient.[3] The deliberately determined way in which my study participants worked towards transformation should not, however, make us consider it as a 'life choice'. Of course, its methodical and planned nature, and its orientation within the social space of tastes and practices might give the impression it was 'making a necessity out of virtue'. It was, after all, about forging dispositions and attributes oriented towards excellence or even towards becoming socially exceptional. However, 'making a necessity out of virtue' is also a way of 'making a virtue out of necessity' as highlighted by the very situated social and structural conditions of possibility for this individual work of self-transformation. Analysing the social conditions of possibility for anorexic work outlined the socio-historical 'locus' where this work took place, at the intersection of the social variables (gender, class and age) that tend to define the recruitment of anorexics. First, we can note (along with sociologists of the body) that a set of representations and norms exist today that make bodily transformation both possible and desirable. Current representations of the malleability of the body, and particularly the female body, are part of a much deeper movement. Based on Anthony Giddens's theories about 'projects of the self', Chris Schilling has described the current importance of the 'body project' as a system of practices and representations related to the body's transformable nature. In this system, the body becomes something to be worked upon and the notion of its malleability and 'unfinished' nature is imposed:

> There is a tendency to see the body as an entity which is in the process of becoming; a *project* which should be worked at and accomplished as part of an *individual*'s self-identity. . . . its appearance, size, shape and even its contents, are potentially open to reconstruction in line with the designs of its owner. . . . In this context, bodies become malleable entities than can be shaped . . . by the vigilance and hard work of their owners.
>
> (Schilling 1993, 4–5)[4]

More specifically, three sets of social conditions of possibility seem to be at work in the case of anorexic work of the self. This 'unfinished' nature of the body, requiring more work in order to 'complete' it, is a norm particularly imposed upon women, as we have seen. Gender is therefore one of the social conditions of possibility for anorexic work of the self. The individual re-shaping of the female body is socially imposed as both possible and necessary, whether through the available techniques on offer or through the socially imposed legitimate body. Age seems to be a second condition of possibility. The idea of fate, or of the hope of bodily transformation, seems to be linked to age. It could be argued that today the teenage years, or even childhood, are construed as periods during which eating habits and bodies can and should be worked on (cf. anti-obesity campaigns). This establishes a norm, but also defines the possibility of reshaping one's body at those ages. Finally, where social background is concerned, situating the different phases of the career within the social space highlighted the links between anorexic work of the self (including the resistance sometimes put up against those trying to stop that work) and the dispositions of the middle and upper classes. These included: socially situated practices related to eating, the body and school work;

'bodily capital' as a 'total capital' that could potentially incorporate and demonstrate cultural capital; an ethos of control over both physical and social fate as well as public labels; and an elitism that was both physical and cultural.

I took the social background of the participants into account through an admittedly stark opposition drawn between the anorexic ethos and the working-class ethos. As we saw, though, this also corresponded to how the participants themselves envisaged the social world: through binary symbolic classifications, which overlapped in their different dimensions (for example, in terms of the body and school work). It is probable that further investigation could establish the 'social position' of anorexia with more accuracy. The intermediate position of the middle classes would be a promising avenue to explore in this regard. Situating anorexia in this middle ground could potentially offer a way of 'lodging' the characteristics of anorexic work of self-transformation 'between' (1) the presence of an ethos of physical and social malleability that makes that work possible (bottom-up differentiation) and (2) the absence of self-assurance or the search for social 'grace' that makes it desirable, as a social requirement for improvement (top-down differentiation). If this were the case, anorexia would fall under the same social positions as those that determine what people do about their ageing bodies and whether or not, for example, they decide to go to the gym or have plastic surgery[5] (those who choose to work on their body do so in contrast with others who do not, either because they have given up on it or because they are too self-assured for this to be necessary).[6] Another, perhaps even more tempting avenue to explore would involve linking anorexia with trajectories of upward social mobility. These trajectories correspond to another 'in-between' position that could perhaps play a role in the extreme asceticism of the career as well as the 'hypercorrection' of practices involved and the whole ethos of tension identified. Indeed, all these elements could potentially be linked to a feeling of illegitimacy in terms of social position. If the epidemiology were to demonstrate that anorexic recruitment depended on one of these two principles (belonging to the middle class, in the strictest sense of the term, or being engaged in a trajectory of upward social mobility), it would be easy to link this to the results presented in this book.

It is important, though, to avoid drawing too hasty or too direct correlations between anorexia and a given social position or trajectory. From this point of view, my method (looking at social conditions of possibility rather than building a directly causal model and looking at the broad and deliberately vague category of 'middle and upper classes') may have been too general, in one sense. However, it did present the advantage of avoiding any oversimplification of the issue that would have come with working on more detailed hypotheses about these questions. One way or another, it also avoided falling unquestioningly into the general view of 'pathogenic social mobility', which always runs the risk of making any upwardly mobile social trajectory into the matrix for necessarily 'suffering' individuals who would perhaps have done better to stay in their place. Moreover, some of the variations that emerged in my investigation, despite the small size of the corpus, already complicate any hypothesis put forward in terms of upward social mobility. Although a substantial proportion of the participants could be considered as engaged in upwardly mobile trajectories over two generations, a certain number of them also came from clearly 'established' upper-class families. For the latter, the work of self-transformation could be linked to a process of capitalization rather than accumulation. In terms of this investigation, at least, the similarities that exist between this 'work of inheritance'[7] and the work involved in climbing the social ladder make any strict distinction between trajectories of mobility and trajectories of reproduction less relevant.

Rather than addressing the question of the social production of anorexia, this sociological approach to anorexia therefore opened up the question of social modes of self-transformation. 'Embodiment', one of the trends in the sociology of the body, has provided the foundations for a theory of internalization and of bodily hysteresis. However, to a large extent, the notion of transformation has yet to be considered within this framework. The founding text in the sociology of embodiment – Mauss's paper on 'techniques of the body' – touches upon this question without actually raising it directly. The main issues addressed by his text are embodiment and the body's 'resistance' to change following this embodiment, as evidenced by the personal example the author provides about learning to swim: 'In my day, swimmers saw themselves as a kind of steamboat [swallowing water then spitting it out as they swam]. It was stupid, but in fact I still do this: I cannot get rid of my technique' (Mauss 1979, 99). And under what conditions might he do otherwise? What might enable him to transform this technique of the body? What kinds of individual exercises, how many instructors, how much time would it take? What methods would be necessary for him to engage in, and then stick to, this endeavour? These questions might seem anecdotal, perhaps even disrespectful given the far more serious problems raised by anorexia. However, in the case of anorexia and its treatment, these are precisely the questions at hand. And they concern the power that practice has to transform the individual, to do and undo the very things that individual has produced. By approaching anorexia as work of self-transformation, I chose to analyse this kind of process at the level of the practices it involved, while trying to reveal how three of the principles underpinning these practices intersect – the local dynamic of interactions, the internal dynamic of dispositions and the external dynamic of institutions. In many ways, the extreme case examined in this book has offered a demonstration of exactly how society 'creates' self-creation.

Notes

1 *A contrario* this indicates just how strong an institutional force is at work in the 'conversion' and 'inculcation' done by total institutions like the army (Pinto 1975) or Catholic secondary schools training priests (Suaud 1976) which, in this sense, is comparable to the work of the hospital in the last phase of the anorexic career.

2 In his class at the Collège de France on the morals of the Hellenistic and Roman period, Michel Foucault showed that these were based on 'a work of the self on the self, an elaboration of the self by the self, a progressive transformation of the self by the self for which one takes responsibility in a long labor of ascesis *(askesis)*' (Foucault 2005, 16). However, he contrasted this notion of 'work of the self on the self' with another conception of the way a subject can become free through the revelation of the truth of

his or her past, of whom he or she actually is and of what he or she actually desires. In his view, this second conception was characteristic of the 'techniques of the self' of Christian monasteries in the first centuries of our era and he saw psychoanalysis as one of its main contemporary heirs. In a very different context, we can see this same opposition between the 'work of the self on the self' and 'work on the self' as an enterprise of self-discovery.

3 In this regard, we can look to the sociological analysis of things as different as 'the making of a boxer' (Wacquant 1995), the 'work of self-construction' done by an aristocrat during the French Revolution (Matonti 1998b), the 'work on the self' done by the petit-bourgeois under the Third Republic in France (Memmi 1996) and the 'continuous project of self-improvement' in the case of a young man who had decided to change sex (Garfinkel 1984, ch. 5 and appendix). For a systematic comparison of these different types of self-transformation, see Darmon (2001), ch. 9.

4 On how the notion of a 'body that could potentially be endlessly transformed' was progressively established see also, for example, Vigarello (1993, 326).

5 For a summary of these issues, see Détrez (2002, 207): 'The members of the middle classes are the main target of this guilty conscience about the body, created by the gap between the emancipated image imposed on them and a reality that does not always live up to the ideal . . . . Moreover, it is worth noting the correlation, in this same social background, between, on the one hand, an ethics of effort, personal discipline and applying oneself on a daily basis in order to obtain the shape of this emancipated body and, on the other, behaviour towards school, characterized by belief and trust. Similarly, the "natural grace" of members of the more privileged classes . . . could be seen as corresponding to the ideology of being academically gifted'.

6 'Featherstone . . . suggests that while the working class tend to be more prepared to accept bodily decline as inevitable with age, the "new" middle classes find the ageing body a source of anxiety. Consequently, body maintenance techniques tend to be employed as a way to combat age and its associated characteristics. In contrast, the upper classes tend to have acquired orientations to their bodies which can overlay and disguise many of the effects of ageing, "wearing" their age unselfconsciously as a mark of status rather than decline' (Shilling 1993, 139–40) about M. Featherstone (1985).

7 François de Singly talks about the 'specific work of heirs, even if they conceal it by talking about donation' and about the 'heirs' work of appropriation in order to become an "heir"' (1996, 65, 66).

References

Agman, Gilles, Maurice Corcos and Philippe Jeammet. 1994. 'Troubles des conduites alimentaires'. In *Encyclopédie Médico-Chirurgicale*, 'Psychiatrie', 37–350-A-10. Paris: Editions Techniques.

Alvin, Patrick, ed. 1996. *Anorexies à l'Adolescence*. Vélizy: Doin.

American Psychiatric Association. 1987. *Diagnostic and Statistical Manual of Mental Disorders*, Third Edition Revised. Washington, DC: American Psychiatric Association.

—— 1994. *Diagnostic and Statistical Manual of Mental Disorders, Fourth Edition*. Washington, DC: American Psychiatric Association.

Apfeldorfer, Gérard. 1995. *Anorexie, Boulimie, Obésité*. Paris: Flammarion.

Banks, Caroline Giles. 1992. '"Culture" in culture-bound syndromes: the case of anorexia nervosa'. *Social Science and Medicine* 34(8): 867–84.

Barrett, Robert. 1996. *The Psychiatric Team and the Social Definition of Schizophrenia*. Cambridge: Cambridge University Press.

Baszanger, Isabelle. 1998a. 'The work sites of an American Interactionist: Anselm L. Strauss, 1917–1996'. Special Issue: legacies of research from Anselm Strauss'. *Symbolic Interaction* 21(4): 353–78.

—— (1995) 1998b. *Inventing Pain Medicine. From the Laboratory to the Clinic*. New Brunswick: Rutgers University Press.

Baudelot, Christian and Roger Establet. 1990. *Durkheim et le Suicide*, Third Edition. Paris: PUF (first published 1984).

—— 1992. *Allez les Filles!* Paris: Seuil.

Beaud, Stéphane and Florence Weber. 1997. *Guide de l'Enquête de Terrain*. Paris: La Découverte.

Becker, Howard. 1963. *Outsiders. Studies in the Sociology of Deviance*. New York: The Free Press.

—— 1998. *Tricks of the Trade. How to Think About Your Research While You're Doing It*. Chicago: The University of Chicago Press.

Bell, Rudolph. 1985. *Holy Anorexia*. Chicago: University of Chicago Press.

Berger, Peter. 1965. 'Towards a sociological understanding of psychoanalysis'. *Social Research* 32(1): 26–41.

Berger, Peter and Hansfried Kellner. 1964. 'Marriage and the construction of reality: an exercise in the microsociology of knowledge'. *Diogènes* 12(46): 1–24.

Bodier, Marceline. 1995. 'Le corps change, son image aussi'. *INSEE Première* 356: 1–4.

Boltanski, Luc. 1971. 'Les usages sociaux du corps'. *Annales ESC* 26(1): 205–33.

—— 1984. *Prime Éducation et Morale de Classe*, New Edition. Paris: Editions de l'EHESS (first published 1969).

Bourdieu, Pierre. (1980) 1990. *The Logic of Practice*. Cambridge: Polity Press.
—— (1979) 1996a. *Distinction. A Social Critique of the Judgment of Taste*. Translated by Richard Nice. Cambridge, MA: Harvard University Press.
—— (1989) 1996b. *The State Nobility. Elite Schools in the Field of Power*. Translated by Lauretta Clough. Stanford: Stanford University Press.
—— (1986) 2000a. 'The biographical illusion'. In *Identity: a Reader*, edited by Paul de Guy, Jessica Evans and Peter Redman, 299–305. London: Sage.
—— (1997) 2000b. *Pascalian Meditations*. Translated by Richard Nice. Cambridge: Polity Press.
Bourdieu, Pierre and Yvette Delsaut. 1975. 'Le couturier et sa griffe: contribution à une théorie de la magie'. *Actes de la Recherche en Sciences Sociales* 1: 7–36.
Bourdieu, Pierre and Jean-Claude Passeron. (1964) 1979. *The Inheritors. French Students and Their Relation to Culture*. Translated by Richard Nice. Chicago: University of Chicago Press.
Bozon, Michel. 1991. 'Apparence physique et choix du conjoint'. In *La nuptialité: évolution récente en France et dans les pays développés*, edited by Thérèse Hibert and Louis Roussel, 91–110. Paris: PUF-INED.
Brumberg, Joan Jacobs. 1982. 'Chlorotic girls, 1870–1920: a historical perspective on female adolescence'. *Child Development* 53: 1468–77.
—— 1989. *Fasting Girls. The History of Anorexia Nervosa*, Second Edition. Cambridge, MA: Harvard University Press (first published 1988).
Bynum, Caroline Walker. 1985. 'Fast, feast, and flesh: the religious significance of food to medieval women'. *Representations* 11: 1–25.
—— 1987. *Holy Feast and Holy Fast. The Religious Significance of Food to Medieval Women*. Berkeley: University of California Press.
Chabrol, Henri. 1991. *L'Anorexie et la Boulimie de l'Adolescente*. Paris: PUF.
Chapoulie, Jean-Michel. 2001. *La Tradition Sociologique de Chicago*. Paris: Seuil.
Chernin, Kim. 1985. *The Hungry Self. Women, Eating and Identity*. New York: Times Books.
Chevalier, Louis. (1958) 1973. *Laboring Classes and Dangerous Classes in Paris During the First Half of the Nineteenth Century*. Translated by Frank Jellinek. New York: Howard Fertig.
Corbin, Alain. (1978) 1996. *Women for Hire. Prostitution and Sexuality in France after 1850*. Translated by Alan Sheridan. Cambridge, MA: Harvard University Press.
Corcos, Maurice and Philippe Jeammet. 1993. 'Épidémiologie des troubles des conduites alimentaires: réflexions critiques'. *Confrontations Psychiatriques* 35: 311–26.
Darmon, Muriel. 2001. *Approche Sociologique de l'Anorexie: un travail de soi*. PhD diss., Université Paris V.
Defrance, Jacques. 2000. *Sociologie du Sport*, Third Edition. Paris: La Découverte (first published 1995).
Deleuze, Gilles and Claire Parnet. (1977) 1987. *Dialogues*. Translated by Hugh Tomlinson and Barbara Habberjam. New York: Columbia University Press.
Détrez, Christine. 2002. *La Construction Sociale du Corps*. Paris: Seuil.
Durkheim, Emile. (1912) 1995. *The Elementary Forms of Religious Life*. Translated by Kren E. Fields. New York: The Free Press.
—— (1897) 2005. *Suicide. A Study in Sociology*. Translated by John Spaulding and George Simpson. Taylor & Francis e-Library.
Ehrenberg, Alain. 1998. *La Fatigue d'Être Soi. Dépression et Société*. Paris: Odile Jacob.

Ehrenberg, Alain and Anne Lovell, eds. 2001. *La Maladie Mentale en Mutation. Psychiatrie et Société*. Paris: Odile Jacob.
Ekins, Richard. 1997. *Male Femaling. A Grounded Theory Approach to Cross-Dressing and Sex-Changing*. London: Routledge.
Faure, Sylvia. 2000. *Apprendre par Corps. Socio-anthropologie des Techniques de Danse*. Paris: La Dispute.
Featherstone, Mike. 1985. 'Leisure, symbolic power and the life course'. *The Sociological Review* 33(S1): 113–38.
Flament, Martine. 1995. 'Epidémiologie des troubles des conduites alimentaires'. In *L'Epidémiologie Psychiatrique*, edited by Frédéric Rouillon, Jean-Pierre Lépine and Jean-Louis Terra, 211–30. Paris: J.-P. Goureau.
Foucault, Michel. (1976) 1978. *History of Sexuality. Volume 1: An Introduction*. New York: Random House.
—— (2001) 2005. *The Hermeneutics of the Subject. Lectures at the College de France. 1981–1982*. Edited by Frédéric Gros under the direction of François Ewald and Allessandro Fontana; translated by Graham Burchell. New York: Palgrave Macmillan.
Fourgnaud, Agnès. 1998. 'Boulimie, anorexie, tout se joue à l'adolescence'. *Le Figaro*, 28 March: 54.
Frances, Allen and Ruth Ross. 1996. *DSM-IV Case Studies, a Clinical Guide to Differential Diagnosis*. Washington, DC: American Psychiatric Press.
Freidson, Eliot. 1988. *Profession of Medicine. A Study of the Sociology of Applied Knowledge, Second Edition*. Chicago: University of Chicago Press (first published 1970).
Garfinkel, Harold. 1984. *Studies in Ethnomethodology*. Cambridge: Polity Press in association with Blackwell (first published 1967).
Garrett, Catherine. 1998. *Beyond Anorexia. Narrative, Spirituality and Recovery*. Cambridge: Cambridge University Press.
Germov, John and Lauren Williams. 1996. 'The sexual division of dieting: women's voices'. *The Sociological Review* 44(4): 630–47.
Goffman, Erving. 1961. *Asylums. Essays on the Social Situation of Mental Patients and Other Inmates*. New York: Anchor Books.
—— 1963. *Stigma. Notes on the Management of Spoiled Identity*. London: Penguin Books.
Gojard, Séverine. 2000. 'L'alimentation dans la prime enfance. Diffusion et réception des normes de puériculture'. *Revue Française de Sociologie* 41(3): 475–512.
Goldstein, Jan. 1987. *Console and Classify: The French Psychiatric Profession in the Nineteenth Century*. Cambridge: Cambridge University Press.
Gordon, Richard. 1990. *Anorexia and Bulimia. Anatomy of a Social Epidemic*. Oxford: Blackwell.
Grignon, Claude and Christiane Grignon. 1980. 'Styles d'alimentation et goûts populaires'. *Revue Française de Sociologie* XXI(4): 531–69.
—— 1999. 'Long-term Trends in food consumption: a French portrait'. *Food and Foodways* 8(3): 151–74.
Guillemot, Anne and Michel Laxenaire. 1995. *Anorexie Mentale et Boulimie. Le Poids de la Culture*. Paris: Masson.
Hacking, Ian. 1998. *Mad Travelers. Reflections on the Reality of Transient Mental Illnesses*. Charlottesville: University Press of Virginia.
—— 1999. *The Social Construction of What?* Cambridge, MA: Harvard University Press.

Helfter, Caroline. 1998. 'Venir en aide aux jeunes anorexiques et leurs familles'. *Le Monde*, 2 April: 30.
Hepworth, Julie. 1999. *The Social Construction of Anorexia Nervosa*. London: Sage.
Herpin, Nicolas and Nicole Manon. 1997. 'Approvisionnement, menus et obésité dans les foyers les plus pauvres'. In Stéfan Lollivier and Daniel Verger, 'Pauvreté d'existence, monétaire ou subjective sont distinctes', *Economie et Statistique* 308–10, 117–18.
Herpin, Nicolas and Daniel Verger. 2000. *La Consommation des Français*. Paris: La Découverte.
Hesse-Biber, Sharlene. 1996. *Am I Thin Enough Yet? The Cult of Thinness and the Commercialization of Identity*. Oxford: Oxford University Press.
Hirschman, Albert Otto. 1970. *Exit, Voice, and Loyalty*. Cambridge, MA: Harvard University Press.
Hof, Sonja van't and Malcolm Nicolson. 1996. 'The rise and fall of a fact: the increase in anorexia nervosa'. *Sociology of Health and Illness* 18(5): 581–608.
Hoggart, Richard. 1957. *The Uses of Literacy. Aspects of Working-Class Life*. London: Chatto and Windus.
Hughes, Everett C. 1984. 'Cycles, turning points and careers'. In *The Sociological Eye. Selected Papers*, 124–31. New Brunswick and London: Transaction.
—— 1997. 'Careers'. *Qualitative Sociology* 20(3): 389–97.
Karp, David A. 1993. 'Taking anti-depressant medications: resistance, trial commitment, conversion, disenchantment'. *Qualitative Sociology* 16(4): 337–59.
Kaufmann, Jean-Claude. 1998. *Corps de Femmes, Regards d'Hommes. Sociologie des Seins Nus*. Paris: Nathan.
Kirk, Stuart A. and Herb Hutchins. 1992. *The Selling of DSM: the Rhetoric of Science in Psychiatry*. Hawthorne, NY: Aldine de Gruyter.
—— and Herb Hutchins 1997. *Making Us Crazy. DSM: The Psychiatric Bible and the Creation of Mental Disorders*. New York: The Free Press.
Knibiehler, Yvonne. (1991) 1998. 'Bodies and hearts'. In *A History of Women in the West. IV. Emerging Feminism from Revolution to World War*, edited by Geneviève Fraisse and Michèle Perrot. Cambridge, MA, and London: Belknap, 325–68.
Lahire, Bernard. 1998. *L'Homme Pluriel. Les Ressorts de l'Action*. Paris: Nathan.
—— 1999a. *L'Invention de l'"Illettrisme". Rhétorique Publique, Ethique et Stigmates*. Paris: La Découverte.
—— ed. 1999b. *Le Travail Sociologique de Pierre Bourdieu*. Paris: La Découverte.
—— ed. 2002a. *A Quoi Sert la Sociologie?* Paris: La Découverte.
—— 2002b. *Portraits Sociologiques. Dispositions et Variations Individuelles*. Paris: Nathan.
—— 2003. 'From the habitus to an individual heritage of dispositions. Towards a sociology at the level of the individual'. *Poetics, Journal of Empirical Research on Culture, the Media and the Arts* 31: 329–55.
Ledoux, Sylvie. 1994. 'Épidémiologie des troubles des conduites alimentaires'. In *Les Conduites Alimentaires*, edited by Bertrand Samuel-Lajeunesse and Christine Foulon, 49–72. Paris: Masson.
Lemert, Edwin M. 1951. *Social Pathology*. New York: McGraw-Hill.
—— 1967. *Human Deviance, Social Problems and Social Control*. Englewood Cliffs: Prentice-Hall.
Le Wita, Béatrix. 1988. *Ni Vue Ni Connue. Approche Ethnographique de la Culture Bourgeoise*. Paris: Editions de la MSH.
Lindesmith, Alfred R. 1947. *Opiate Addiction*. Bloomington: Principia Press.

Luhrmann, Tanya M. 2000. *Of Two Minds. The Growing Disorder in American Psychiatry*. New York: Alfred A. Knopf.

McClelland, Lisa and Arthur Crisp. 2001. 'Anorexia and social class'. *International Journal of Eating Disorders* 29(2): 150–6.

McLorg, Penelope A. and Diane E. Taub. 1987. 'Anorexia nervosa and bulimia: the development of deviant identities'. *Deviant Behavior* 8(2): 177–89.

McLorg, Penelope A. and Diane E. Taub. 1994. 'Anorexia nervosa and bulimia: the development of deviant identities'. In *Constructions of Deviance: Social Power, Context, and Interaction*, edited by Patricia A. Adler and Peter Adler, 249–61. New York: Wadsworth.

MacSween, Morag. 1993. *Anorexic Bodies. A Feminist and Sociological Perspective on Anorexia Nervosa*. London: Routledge.

Maître, Jacques. 1996. 'Les deux soeurs'. *Genèses* 24: 33–56.

—— 2000. *Anorexies Religieuses, Anorexie Mentale. Essai de Psychanalyse Sociohistorique. De Marie de l'Incarnation à Simone Weil*. Paris: Cerf.

Manning, Philip. 1992. *Erving Goffman and Modern Sociology*. Stanford: Stanford University Press.

Matonti, Frédérique. 1998a. *Hérault de Séchelles ou les Infortunes de la Beauté*. Paris: La Dispute.

—— 1998b. 'La beauté capitale'. *Sociétés & Représentations* 6: 309–32.

Mauss, Marcel. (1950) 1979. *Sociology and Psychology. Essays*. Translated by Ben Brewster. London: Routledge and Keagan Paul.

Memmi, Dominique. 1996. 'L'ascension sociale vue de l'intérieur: les postures de la conquête'. *Cahiers Internationaux de Sociologie* 43(100): 33–58.

—— 2003. *Faire Vivre et Laisser Mourir. Le Gouvernement Contemporain de la Naissance et de la Mort*. Paris: La Découverte.

Mennell, Stephen. 1985. *All Manners of Food: Eating and Taste in England and France from the Middle Ages to the Present*. Oxford: Blackwell.

—— 1996. 'Sociogenetic connections between food and timing'. *Food and Foodways: Explorations in the History and Culture of Human Nourishment* 6(3–4): 195–204.

Ministère des Sports et Institut National du Sport et de l'Education Physique. 2002. *Les Pratiques Sportives en France. Enquête 2000*. Paris: Ministère des Sports et Institut National du Sport et de l'Education Physique.

Moreau, Audray, Alexandra Pichault and Guy Truchot. 2002. 'Le sport chez les jeunes de 12 à 17 ans'. *Stat-info* 2–4 (October): 1–4.

Nichter, Mimi. 2000. *Fat Talk. What Girls and their Parents say about Dieting*. Cambridge, MA: Harvard University Press.

Orbach, Susie. 1986. *Hunger Strike. The Anorectic's Struggle as a Metaphor for our Age*. New York: Norton.

Passeron, Jean-Claude. 1991. *Le Raisonnement Sociologique. L'Espace Non-Poppérien du Raisonnement Naturel*. Paris: Nathan.

Perrot, Philippe. 1984. *Le Travail des Apparences. Le Corps Féminin, XVIIIe–XIXe Siècle*. Paris: Seuil.

Peters, Nonja. 1995. 'The ascetic anorexic'. *Social Analysis* 37: 44–66.

Pinçon, Michel and Monique Pinçon-Charlot. 1989. *Dans les Beaux Quartiers*. Paris: Seuil.

Pinto, Louis. 1975. L'armée, le contingent et les classes sociales'. *Actes de la Recherche en Sciences Sociales* 1(3): 18–40.

Poliak, Claude. F. 2002. 'Manières profanes de "parler de soi"'. *Genèses* 47: 4–20.

Queiroz Jean-Manuel de and Marek Ziolkowski. 1994. *L'Interactionnisme Symbolique*. Rennes: PUR.

Robertson, Matra. 1992. *Starving in the Silences. An Exploration of Anorexia Nervosa*. New York: New York University Press.

Rollet-Echalier, Catherine. 1990. *La Politique à l'Égard de la Petite Enfance Sous la IIIe République*. Paris: PUF-Ined.

Rosenberg, Charles E. and Janet Golden, eds. 1992. *Framing Disease: Studies in Cultural History*. New Brunswick: Rutgers University Press.

Shilling, Chris. 1993. *The Body and Social Theory*. London: Sage.

Schur, Edwin M. 1984. *Labeling Women Deviant. Gender, Stigma, and Social Control*. New York: McGraw-Hill.

Schwartz, Olivier. 1990. *Le Monde Privé des Ouvriers. Hommes et Femmes du Nord*. Paris: PUF.

Shorter, Edward. 1987. 'The first great increase in anorexia nervosa'. *Journal of Social History* 21: 69–96.

Showalter, Elaine. 1985. *The Female Malady. Women, Madness, and English Culture, 1830–1980*. New York: Pantheon Books.

Singly, François de. 1984. 'Les manœuvres de séduction: une analyse des annonces matrimoniales'. *Revue Française de Sociologie* XXV(1): 523–59.

—— 1996. 'Le travail de l'héritage'. *Revue Européenne des Sciences Sociales* XXXIV(103): 61–80.

—— 1997. 'Entretien'. *Synapse* 138: 14–23.

Strauss, Anselm. 1967. 'A sociological view of normality'. *Archives of General Psychiatry* 17(3): 265–70.

Strauss, Anselm, Leonard Schatzman, Rue Bucher, Dantua Ehrlich and Melvin Sabshin. 1964. *Psychiatric Ideologies and Institutions*. New York: The Free Press of Glencoe.

Suaud, Charles. 1976. 'Splendeur et misère d'un petit séminaire'. *Actes de la Recherche en Sciences Sociales* 2(4): 66–90.

Tait, Gordon. 1993. 'Anorexia nervosa: asceticism, differentiation, government'. *Australian and New Zealand Journal of Sociology* 29(2): 194–208.

Terrail, Jean-Pierre. 1992. 'Destins scolaires de sexe: une perspective historique et quelques arguments'. *Population* 3: 645–76.

Tomes, Nancy. 1990. 'Historical perspectives on women and mental illnesses'. In *Women, Health, and Medicine in America, a Historical Handbook*, edited by Rima D. Apple, 143–71. New Brunswick: Rutgers University Press.

Travaillot, Yves. 1998. *Sociologie des Pratiques d'Entretien du Corps. L'Évolution de l'Attention Portée au Corps depuis 1960*. Paris: PUF.

Turner, Bryan S. 1982. 'The government of the body: medical regimens and the rationalization of diet'. *British Journal of Sociology* 33(2): 254–69.

Turner, Bryan S. 1996. *The Body and Society. Explorations in Social Theory*. London: Sage.

Vandereycken, Walter and Ron Van Deth. 1994. *From Fasting Saints to Anorexic Girls. The History of Self-Starvation*. New York: New York University Press.

Vaughan, Diane. 1986. *Uncoupling. Turning Points in Intimate Relationships*. Oxford: Oxford University Press.

Veblen, Thorstein. 2007. *The Theory of the Leisure Class*. Oxford: Oxford University Press (first published 1899).

Vigarello, Georges. 1993. *Le Sain et le Malsain. Santé et Mieux-Être depuis le Moyen Âge*. Paris: Seuil.

Wacquant, Loïc. 1995. 'Pugs at work: bodily capital and bodily labour among professional boxers'. *Body and Society* 1(1): 65–93.
Weber, Florence. 1989. *Le Travail À-Côté*. Paris: Editions de l'EHESS-Inra.
Weissman, Elizabeth. 1998. 'Comment réagir face à une adolescente anorexique ou boulimique?' *Elle*, 15 June: 168.
Werner, Dorothée and Nathalie Dupuis. 1996. 'Top modèles: maigrir jusqu'où? La folie des femmes brindilles'. *Elle*, 11 November: 78–83.
Young, Allan. 1995. *The Harmony of Illusions. Inventing Post-traumatic Stress Disorder*. Princeton: Princeton University Press.

Index